CHAIN OF COMMAND

CHAIN OF COMMAND

THE ROAD FROM 9/11 TO ABU GHRAIB

SEYMOUR M. HERSH

HARPER
PERENNIAL

HARPER ⬤ PERENNIAL

Portions of this book were previously published, in somewhat different form, in *The New Yorker*.

A hardcover edition of this book was published in 2004 by Harper-Collins Publishers.

P.S.™ is a trademark of HarperCollins Publishers.

FIRST HARPER PERENNIAL EDITION PUBLISHED 2005.

Maps by Paul J. Pugliese

Library of Congress Cataloging-in-Publication Data is available upon request.

ISBN-10: 0-06-095537-6 (pbk.)
ISBN-13: 978-0-06-095537-3 (pbk.)

05 06 07 08 09 ❖/RRD 10 9 8 7 6 5 4 3 2 1

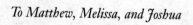

To Matthew, Melissa, and Joshua

Contents

INTRODUCTION

On November 14, 1969, the readers of an assortment of American newspapers encountered a story with such headlines as "Lieutenant Accused of Murdering 109 Civilians." It ran courtesy of the Dispatch News Service, a year-old marketing service for reporters working in Vietnam, and under the byline of a former wire-service reporter named Seymour M. Hersh. The opening paragraphs, written in a direct, laconic style, described how one morning the previous year soldiers of the Army's 11th Infantry Brigade went on a killing rampage in the Vietnamese hamlet of My Lai:

> Fort Benning, Ga., Nov. 13—Lt. William L. Calley Jr., 26 years old, is a mild-mannered, boyish-looking Vietnam combat veteran with the nickname "Rusty." The Army is completing an investigation of charges that he deliberately murdered at least 109 Vietnamese civilians in a search-and-destroy mission in March 1968 in a Viet Cong stronghold known as "Pinkville."
>
> Calley has formally been charged with six specifications of mass murder. Each specification cites a number of dead, adding up to the 109 total, and charges that Calley did "with premedita-

tion murder . . . Oriental human beings, whose names and sex are unknown, by shooting them with a rifle."

The Army calls it murder; Calley, his counsel and others associated with the incident describe it as a case of carrying out orders.

"Pinkville" has become a widely known code word among the military in a case that many officers and some Congressmen believe will become far more controversial than the recent murder charges against eight Green Berets.

As it turned out, soldiers of the 11th Brigade had killed five hundred or more civilians that morning—mainly women, children, and elderly men—in what had started out as a search for Vietcong soldiers. They shot some from helicopters, others from the ground and at point-blank range. There were rapes, torture, babies and young children shot. After hours of killing, the soldiers set fire to the hamlet and left behind a landscape of corpses.

Working on a tip from a lawyer and with a modest grant from the Fund for Investigative Journalism, Hersh arrived at the Army's base in Fort Benning and went from building to building looking for Calley, who was awaiting court-martial proceedings. Knocking on doors, and avoiding the pursuit of officers on the base, Hersh finally encountered "Rusty"—a former railroad switchman—and asked to talk to him. After they had talked for three or four hours, they went to a local grocery store, bought steaks, bourbon, and wine, and ate and talked some more at the apartment of Calley's girlfriend. Calley told Hersh that he was only following orders at My Lai, but he spoke freely about what had happened. A total of thirty-six newspapers ran the story, eventually causing a sensation, and sometimes disbelief, in the journalism world and beyond. When a Pentagon reporter from the *Washington Post* was charged with following up the My Lai stories, he called Hersh and said bitterly, "You son of a bitch, where do you get off writing a lie like that?"

The jealousy and bewilderment among his competitors was, perhaps, understandable. Hersh was thirty-two when he broke the story of My Lai and not at all well-known. He had plenty of connections in newspapers, but he was working freelance on My Lai. With the help of a friend, David Obst, he sent the story via Telex, collect, to dozens of newspapers. Although soldiers in the unit spoke to Hersh extensively and in the most horrifying terms, and Calley's own lawyer was willing to confirm the story, some of the big papers, including the *New York Times*, did not run it. "But I kept on writing," Hersh has said, "and by the third story I found this amazing fellow, Paul Meadlo, from a small town in Indiana, a farm kid, who had actually shot many of the Vietnamese kids—he'd shot maybe a hundred people. He just kept on shooting and shooting, and then the next day he had his leg blown off, and he told Calley, as they medevac-ed him, 'God has punished me and now he will punish you.'" After Hersh published that interview, CBS put Meadlo on the evening news and the story broke open. The next year, Hersh won the Pulitzer Prize, a rarity for a freelancer.

By the time Hersh was ready to write a book about the massacre, *My Lai 4*, he had interviewed dozens of participants and officials and discovered myriad macabre details, including how Colonel George S. Patton III—son of *the* Patton—sent out a Christmas card reading "Peace on Earth" with photographs of "dismembered Viet Cong soldiers stacked in a neat pile." In 1972, he published a long account of the government's secret investigation and coverup of the My Lai massacre in *The New Yorker*.

It is an open secret in journalistic circles that reporters, like detectives and sprinters, lose their legs. Eventually, they go to grass, they retire, they get desk jobs, they become columnists or, worse, editors. Sy Hersh is my colleague and friend, but I also know that his general regard for editors can best be reflected in what the late Shirley Povich, of the *Washington Post*, used to say of the breed: "An editor is a mouse training to be a rat." Hersh, who is in his mid-sixties, is a reporter and he always will be. If anything, he has even more energy now than he did in his thirties. And the results are plain: his work for *The New Yorker* during the Administration of George W. Bush, which is reflected in this book, represents an achievement, journalistic and even moral, as striking as his reports on My Lai.

Hersh's parents were immigrants from Lithuania and Poland who came to Chicago and eventually opened a dry-cleaning store on the South Side. His father, Isidore, died when Hersh and his twin brother were just seventeen. At the University of Chicago, Hersh majored in history, but he also spent a lot of time doing crossword puzzles, playing bridge, and hanging out. He spent less than a year at the law school there before he was kicked out for poor grades. His first job out of school was as a liquor-counter clerk at Walgreens at $1.50 an hour. This was not a wholly satisfying line of work. He got a job at the City News Bureau, where he began his distinguished career covering such stories as a fire in a manhole. After a stint in the Army—he was a public information officer at Fort Riley, Kansas—he worked for U.P.I., then for the A.P. as a Pentagon correspondent. He quit the A.P. in 1967 after his editors diluted and cut a story he had written investigating the government's development of biological and chemical weapons. After selling a version of the story to *The New Republic*, he spent a few months working as press secretary and speechwriter for Eugene McCarthy, and then he got serious again about his career as a reporter.

With his stories on My Lai, Hersh joined a tradition of muckrakers, including Upton Sinclair, Ida Tarbell, Lincoln Steffens, Rachel Carson, and I. F. Stone. Theodore Roosevelt had adapted the term from Bunyan's *Pilgrim's Progress*—the man "who was offered a celestial crown for his muckrake, but who would neither look up nor regard the crown he was offered, but continued to rake to himself the filth of the floor"—in order to criticize "reckless journalists," like David Graham Phillips, who were attacking some of his allies in the Senate for their fealty to corporate interests. After My Lai, Hersh applied his rake to a huge variety of fields of public endeavor and malfeasance. In his career, as a freelancer and as a staff writer for both the *New York Times* and, since 1998, *The New Yorker*, Hersh has cracked so many stories of major importance that his only conceivable rival is Bob Woodward, of the *Washington Post*.

During Watergate, when Woodward and Carl Bernstein were soundly beating the competition week after week, the editors of the *Times* tried to catch up by the only means possible—deploying Seymour Hersh. Although the *Washington Post*, in both legend and reality, remained ahead on the story until Nixon's resignation, Hersh scored numerous beats and was a constant prod to Woodward and Bernstein. The three reporters occasionally met for dinner during the most intense months of the scandal, trading jibes and gossip but always carefully avoiding giving away secrets and leads. In their book *All the President's Men*, Woodward and Bernstein write of Hersh showing up for those dinners in ancient sneakers, a frayed shirt, and "rumpled bleached khakis. He was unlike any reporter they had ever met. He did not hesitate to call Henry Kissinger a war criminal in public and was openly attracted and repelled by the power of the *New York Times*."

At the *Times*, Hersh broke a series of stories about the C.I.A.'s illegal spying on domestic "enemies," Henry Kissinger's surveillance of government employees, the U.S.-backed coup in Chile in 1973, and the secret bombing of Cambodia. Since the early 1990s, Hersh has been writing long investigative pieces for *The New Yorker*, including a prescient article in 1993 describing how Pakistan had built its nuclear program and one in 1999 on the decline of intelligence analysis in the National Security Agency. He has written eight books, including *Chain of Command*.

For many years, Hersh has worked in a spare office on Connecticut Avenue in Washington, a room and a half stacked with countless books and yellow legal pads with scrawled notes and telephone numbers. It is the office equivalent of a freshman dorm room, minus the pizza boxes. On one wall there is a typed memo from Lawrence Eagleburger and Robert McCloskey to Kissinger, their boss at the State Department, that is dated September 24, 1974. It reads, "We believe Seymour Hersh intends to publish further allegations on the CIA in Chile. He will *not* put an end to this campaign. You are his ultimate target." Later, Hersh would write a book, *The Price of Power*, which remains the definitive investigation of Kissinger's activities during the Nixon era.

On the morning of September 11th, just a couple of hours after hijacked airplanes had rammed into the World Trade towers, the Pentagon, and a field in Pennsylvania, Hersh and I talked. We agreed that he would have to follow this story no matter where it went and that he would likely have to publish more frequently, ranging into foreign and domestic intelligence communities, the military, the State Department, and the White House.

Since then, Hersh has written twenty-six stories for *The New Yorker*, nearly a hundred and ten thousand words—an astonishing output considering the intensity of the reporting that each piece has required, the number of leads he's looked into and discarded. The work he has done in that period, in both the magazine and as it is presented here, does not pretend to be an encyclopedic history of September 11th, the Bush Administration, or the wars in Afghanistan and Iraq. But his achievement since that morning has been remarkable: he has produced a body of inquiry that has shed light on, among other subjects, the intelligence failures leading up to September 11th; the corruption of the Saudi royal family; threats to the security of the Pakistani nuclear arsenal; the grievous shortcomings of the wars and postwar planning in Afghanistan and Iraq; the mishandling of the case against Zacarias Moussaoui; the Administration's attempts to promote dubious intelligence on an Iraqi nuclear program; the Pentagon's Office of Special Plans and how it "stovepiped" its intelligence and ideological arguments to the White House; and, finally, the torture scandal at Abu Ghraib.

*   *   *

Hersh cuts a singular figure in Washington. Even as a staff reporter for the *New York Times* or *The New Yorker* he has always been a kind of lone wolf, operating out ahead of the pack, sometimes seeing things well before others, often discovering details that become leads for other investigations. It's clear in hindsight that no reporter, not even one as energetic and fearless as Hersh, was able to get the absolute full story of the post–September 11th crises in real time. No one was able to expose in fact and in full, before the war, what the Administration's critics were rightly asserting as a matter of possibility or likelihood—that the White House's claims of an imminent threat were false or exaggerated, that weapons of mass destruction would not be found after the invasion. But Hersh did expose clear evidence that the Administration was playing a dangerous game with intelligence. Before the invasion of Iraq, he published a story laying out the implications of the forgery of documents "proving" that Iraq had made arrangements to purchase nuclear materials from Niger. Some of what he wrote is now part of the received wisdom—for example, that key information from Iraqi defectors was unreliable—so it is worth remembering that much of it was highly controversial when his stories were first published. In piece after piece, he showed how, by manipulating the process of intelligence analysis, the Bush Administration deceived itself as much it did the American people. He was able to do this because of his knowledge of how the intelligence community works and because he had developed, over the years, an extraordinary stable of knowledgeable, well-placed sources, who trust him.

A word about sources. Throughout this book you will encounter unnamed sources—officials, analysts, ambassadors, soldiers, and covert operatives—described by their jobs or their ranks, by their levels of expertise or their possible motivations, but not by their proper names. Readers are often frustrated by this, and understandably so. Far lesser reporters conceal names because it is easier to do or even gives the piece the shadowy sense of a big-time investigation. The problem is that in the areas in which Hersh reports, especially intelligence, it is

usually impossible to get officials to provide revelatory, even classified, information and, at the same time, announce themselves to the
world. They risk their jobs and, at times, prosecution. Also, contrary
to what seems to be a very popular belief, the editors do not read the
phrase "one high-ranking Army official said" and nod in immediate
and grave assent. Trust but verify, as one president used to say. In every
case, at *The New Yorker*, editors working on the piece ask the reporter
who the unnamed sources are, what their motivations might be, and
if they can be corroborated.

"I don't go around getting my stories from nice old lefties or the
Weathermen or the America-with-a-k boys," Hersh once said. "I
get them from good old-fashioned constitutionalists. I learned a
long time ago that you can't go around making judgments on the
basis of people's politics. The essential thing is: do they have integrity or not?"

Hersh's reports certainly did not delight the military and intelligence establishments, to say nothing of George W. Bush, but he is
not generally regarded as an outlaw either. High-ranking officers,
intelligence analysts, and other officials do not make it a habit to
talk to reporters they do not trust. Intelligence reporting is incredi-
bly difficult and, even for someone on Hersh's level, there are sometimes mistakes. In March 2003, a week into the invasion of Iraq,
Hersh, like some other reporters, wrote that the Army was in danger of being bogged down in its advance on Baghdad, that its supply
lines were overstretched and undersupplied; not long afterward, of
course, the advance accelerated, successfully, to Baghdad. And yet
that same report contained other points that much of the rest of the
press had not yet come to terms with: that there were not enough
troops to stabilize the country; that there was a breach between the
uniformed military and the Pentagon's civilian leadership; and that
Donald Rumsfeld's desire to "do the war on the cheap," as one
source put it, would lead to terrible problems in the months after
the fall of Saddam.

The fact is that—not to make a very tough-minded man seem sentimental—Hersh has enormous affection for the people who serve in the military. "The military is still one of the most idealistic societies we have," he once told an interviewer. "There are more people there who believe in the Norman Rockwell version of America, and they carry out those principles, and with enormous integrity. The thing that's interesting about them with me is that they really don't care about what my personal views are, whether I vote Democrat or Republican, or whether I like the war or don't like the war, or if I'm a hawk or a dove. Even during the Vietnam War, what they cared about was whether I would get the story right and tell it right, work hard enough to do it and protect them in the process. And then they'll talk. Then they'll tell you what they think."

It is asking too much that this process be appreciated by its objects. At one point last year, Hersh wrote a piece describing how Richard Perle, the chairman of the President's Defense Policy Board and one of the leaders of the neoconservative movement around the Pentagon, was also involved with business interests that could well profit from a war in Iraq. This was one of those stories in which Hersh broke the news and other reporters, at the *New York Times* and elsewhere, subsequently added to the picture, a process that ended with Perle resigning from the D.P.B. In what seemed like unhinged fury, Perle went on CNN, with Wolf Blitzer, prepared to throw muck at the muckraker.

"Look," Perle said, "Sy Hersh is the closest thing American journalism has to a terrorist, frankly." Perle assured the press that he would file a lawsuit against Hersh and the magazine. He never did.

———

On a Saturday morning last spring, Sy called me at home to say that he was in possession of a series of horrendous photographs—"ten times worse than you can possibly imagine"—along with an internal military report, conducted by Major General Antonio M. Taguba, which described, in detail, beatings, sexual humiliations, and other tortures that were being committed by Americans in Abu Ghraib prison outside Baghdad. This was the same prison where Saddam's Baathists killed countless political prisoners at twice-weekly hangings. I knew that he was looking into the possibility that Iraqis were being tortured—a few days earlier, he had abruptly cancelled a trip to the Middle East to meet with a source who said he had photographs and other material. Now he had the story. Hersh had also learned that the producers of *60 Minutes II*, the CBS magazine show, had obtained the photographs, though not the Taguba report, and had held off broadcasting them at the request of the Pentagon. We decided to ignore CBS and to publish immediately, assuming that we were confident of the story. (There were dangers, to be sure. One English tabloid, the *Daily Mirror*, later published phony pictures, an embarrassment that led to the editor's resignation.) On Wednesday evening, April 28th, Dan Rather went on the air with an excellent report on the photographs and with an Army spokesman's extensive expressions of regret; at the end of the report, Rather allowed that the network had delayed airing the report after an "appeal" from the chairman of the Joint Chiefs of Staff but that, "with other journalists"—meaning, as it turned out, only Hersh— "about to publish their versions of the story, the Defense Department agreed to cooperate in our report." Two days later, Hersh's story and a portfolio of the horrifying pictures from Abu Ghraib (including some that CBS hadn't shown) went up on our website, www.newyorker.com, and the story became the basis of what came to be known as the Abu Ghraib scandal. Every major paper in the country carried a long report that relied on Hersh's reporting, and many of those papers eventually carried articles on Hersh himself, pointing out the thirty-five-year arc from My Lai to Abu Ghraib.

Hersh published three stories in as many weeks—"Torture at Abu Ghraib," "Chain of Command," and "The Gray Zone"—and in each successive report it became clear that Abu Ghraib was not an "isolated incident" but, rather, a concerted attempt by the government and the military leadership to circumvent the Geneva Conventions in order to extract intelligence and quell the Iraqi insurgency. By now the Bush Administration had made a habit of casting doubt on Hersh's work in the most direct and strenuous terms. Woodward, in his book *Bush at War*, recounts the President's first meeting with the Pakistani leader, General Pervez Musharraf. At one point, Musharraf mentioned an article that Hersh had published in *The New Yorker* in which he said that the United States, with the help of the Israelis, had drawn up emergency contingency plans to seize Pakistan's nuclear weapons should Pakistan become dangerously unstable. "Seymour Hersh is a liar," Bush told Musharraf, according to Woodward. After Hersh's third piece on Abu Ghraib, the Pentagon spokesman Lawrence Di Rita felt free to use similarly crude terms. Hersh, he said, merely "threw a lot of crap against the wall and he expects someone to peel off what's real. It's a tapestry of nonsense."

In the following weeks, as it became increasingly clear that Hersh's reporting on Abu Ghraib, like his first report on My Lai, was, if anything, an achievement of understatement, Di Rita did not throw any more charges against the wall. Seymour Hersh's reporting has stood up over time and in the face of a President whose calumny has turned out to be a kind of endorsement.

David Remnick
New York City
August 2004

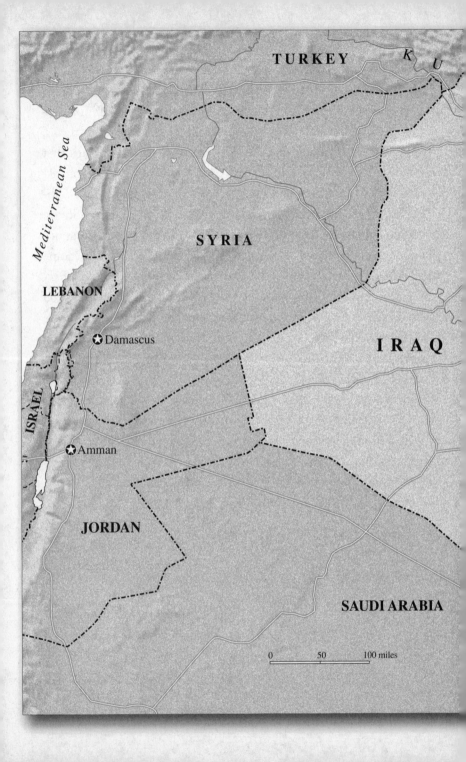

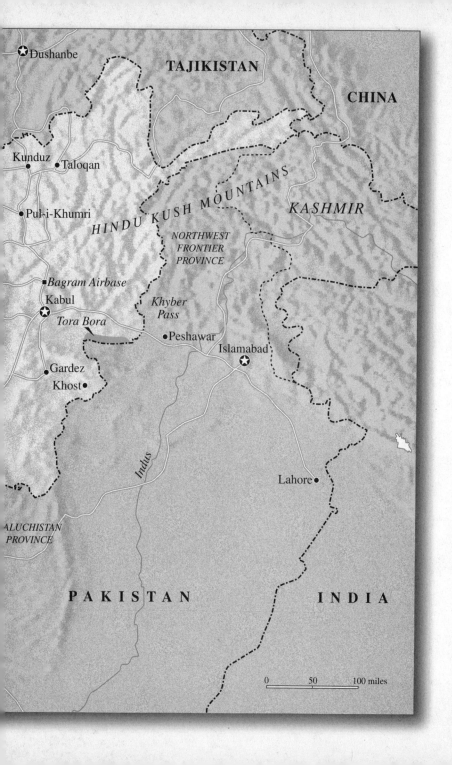

CHAIN OF COMMAND

I.

TORTURE AT ABU GHRAIB

1. A Guantánamo Problem

In the late summer of 2002, a Central Intelligence Agency analyst made a quiet visit to the detention center at the U.S. Naval Base at Guantánamo Bay, Cuba, where an estimated six hundred prisoners were being held, many, at first, in steel-mesh cages that provided little protection from the brutally hot sun. Most had been captured on the battlefield in Afghanistan during the campaign against the Taliban and Al Qaeda. The Bush Administration had determined, however, that they were not prisoners of war, but "enemy combatants," and that their stay at Guantánamo could be indefinite, as teams of C.I.A., F.B.I., and military interrogators sought to pry intelligence out of them. In a series of secret memorandums written earlier in the year, lawyers for the White House, the Pentagon, and the Justice Department had agreed that the prisoners had no rights under federal law or the Geneva Conventions. President Bush endorsed the finding, while declaring that the Al Qaeda and Taliban detainees were nevertheless to be treated in a manner consistent with the principles of the Geneva Conventions—as long as such treatment was also "consistent with military necessity."

Getting the interrogation process to work was essential. The war on terrorism would not be decided by manpower and weaponry, as in the Second World War, but by locating terrorists and learning when and where future attacks might come. "This is a war in which intelligence is everything," John Arquilla, a professor of Defense Analysis at the U.S. Naval Postgraduate School and a consultant to the Pentagon on terrorism, told me. "Winning or losing depends on it." And President Bush and his advisers still needed information about the September 11, 2001, hijackings: How were they planned? Who was involved? Was there a stay-behind operation inside the United States?

But the interrogations at Guantánamo were a bust. Very little useful intelligence had been gathered, while prisoners from around the world continued to flow into the base and the facility constantly expanded. The C.I.A. analyst had been sent there to find out what was going wrong. He was fluent in Arabic and familiar with the Islamic world. He was held in high respect within the agency and was capable of reporting directly, if he chose, to George Tenet, the C.I.A. director. The analyst did more than just visit and inspect. He interviewed at least thirty prisoners to find out who they were and how they ended up in Guantánamo. Some of his findings, he later confided to a former C.I.A. colleague, were devastating.

"He came back convinced that we were committing war crimes in Guantánamo," the colleague told me. "Based on his sample, more than half the people there didn't belong there. He found people lying in their own feces," including two captives, perhaps in their eighties, who were clearly suffering from dementia. "He thought what was going on was an outrage," the C.I.A. colleague added. There was no rational system for determining who was important and who was not. Prisoners, once captured and transported to Cuba, were in permanent legal limbo. The analyst told his colleague that one of the first prisoners he had interviewed was a boy who was asked if he "did jihad"— participated in a holy war against America. "The kid says 'I never did jihad. I'd have done it if I could, but I had no chance. I just got thrown into jail.'"

The analyst filed a report summarizing what he had seen and what he had learned from the prisoners. Two former Administration officials who read the highly classified document told me that its ultimate conclusion was grim. The wrong people were being questioned in the wrong way. "Organizations that operate inside a country without outside direction are hard to find, and we've got to figure out how to deal with them," one of the former officials, who worked in the White House, explained. But the message of the analyst's report was that "we were making things worse for the United States, in terms of terrorism." The random quizzing of random detainees made it more difficult to find and get useful information from those prisoners who had something of value to say. Equally troubling was the analyst's suggestion, the former White House official said, that "if we captured some people who weren't terrorists when we got them, they are now."

That fall the analyst's report rattled aimlessly around the upper reaches of the Bush Administration until it got into the hands of General John A. Gordon, the deputy national security adviser for combatting terrorism, who reported directly to Condoleezza Rice, the national security adviser and the President's confidante. Gordon, who had retired from the military as a four-star general in 2000, had been head of operations for the Air Force Space Command and had also served as a deputy director of the C.I.A. for three years. He was deeply troubled and distressed by the analyst's report, and by its implications for the treatment, in retaliation, of captured American soldiers. Gordon, according to a former Administration official, told colleagues that he thought "it was totally out of character with the American value system," and "that if the actions at Guantánamo ever became public, it'd be damaging to the President." The issue was not only direct torture, but the Administration's obligations under federal law and under the United Nations

Convention Against Torture, ratified by the United States in 1994, that barred torture as well as other "cruel, inhuman or degrading treatment or punishment." The C.I.A. analyst's report, in Gordon's view, provided clear evidence of degrading treatment. Things in Cuba were getting out of control.

At the time, of course, Americans were still traumatized by the September 11th attacks, and were angry. After John Walker Lindh, the twenty-year-old Californian who joined the Taliban, was captured in Afghanistan in December 2001, his American interrogators stripped him, gagged him, strapped him to a board, and exhibited him to the press and to any soldier who wished to see him. These apparent violations of international law met with few, if any, objections. Justice Department documents turned over to Lindh's attorneys revealed that the commanding officer at the base at Mazar-i-Sharif, where Lindh was being held, told his interrogator that "the Secretary of Defense's counsel had authorized him to 'take the gloves off' and ask whatever he wanted."

There was, inevitably, much debate inside the Administration about what was permissible and what was not. But the senior legal officers in the White House and the Justice Department seemed to be in virtual competition to determine who could produce the most tough-minded memorandum about the lack of prisoner rights. (Several of those documents were first made public by *Newsweek* in May 2004.) The most suggestive document, in terms of what was really going on inside military prisons and detention centers, was written in early August 2002 by Jay S. Bybee, head of the Justice Department's Office of Legal Counsel. In an apparent effort to undercut the legal significance of the United States' obligations under the Geneva Conventions and the federal anti-torture statute, Bybee's memorandum redefined torture. "Certain acts may be cruel, inhuman, or degrading, but still not produce pain and suffering of the requisite intensity to fall within [a legal] proscription against torture," Bybee wrote to Alberto R. Gonzales, the White House counsel. "We conclude that for an act to constitute torture . . . it must inflict pain that is difficult to endure. Physical pain amounting to torture must be equivalent in intensity to the pain accompanying serious physical injury, such as organ failure, impairment of bodily function, or even death." (Bush later nominated Bybee to be a federal judge, and he now sits on the U.S. Court of Appeals for the Ninth Circuit.)

"We face an enemy that targets innocent civilians," Gonzales would tell journalists two years later, at the height of the furor over the abuse of prisoners at Abu Ghraib prison, in Iraq. "We face an enemy that lies in the shadows, an enemy that doesn't sign treaties. They don't wear uniforms, an enemy that owes no allegiance to any country. They do not cherish life. An enemy that doesn't fight, attack or plan according to accepted laws of war, in particular [the] Geneva Conventions."

Gonzales added that Bush bore no responsibility for the wrongdoing. "The President has not authorized, ordered or directed in any way any activity that would transgress the standards of the torture conventions or the torture statute, or other applicable laws," Gonzales said. The President had "made no formal determination" invoking the Geneva Conventions before the March 2003 invasion of Iraq, he said, "because it was automatic that Geneva would apply" and it was assumed that the military commanders in the field would ensure that their interrogation policies complied with the President's stated view.

In fact, a secret statement of the President's views, which he signed on February 7, 2002, had a loophole that applied worldwide. "I . . . determine that none of the provisions of Geneva apply to our conflict with Al Qaeda in Afghanistan or elsewhere throughout the world," the President asserted. He also stated that he had "the authority under the Constitution to suspend Geneva as between the United States and Afghanistan, but I decline to exercise that authority at this time." In other words, detainees had no inherent protec-

tions under the Geneva Conventions—the condition of their im-
prisonment, good, bad, or otherwise, was solely at his discretion.

John Gordon had to know what he was up against in seeking a
high-level review of prison policies at Guantánamo, but he nonetheless did what amounted to the unthinkable inside the Bush White
House: he began showing the analyst's report to fellow N.S.C. members. Gordon's goal, apparently, was to rally support for a review from
his peers before bringing it to Rice's attention. At Gordon's request,
the C.I.A. analyst provided personal briefings to Elliott Abrams, at the
time the senior director for Democracy, Human Rights, and International Operations, and to John Bellinger, the N.S.C.'s counsel. Both
were supportive. But officials at two key posts—the White House
Counsel's office and the office of Vice President Dick Cheney—had
a different view. David Addington, the senior lawyer in Vice President
Cheney's office, made it clear to Gordon, the former White House
official said, that the prisoners at Guantánamo were all illegal combatants and thus not entitled to protections. The White House Counsel's office also did nothing to help Gordon.

Gordon persevered, the former White House official recalled,
and "We got it up to Condi."

As the C.I.A. analyst's report was making its way to Rice, in late
2002, there was a series of heated complaints about the interrogation tactics at Guantánamo from within the F.B.I., whose agents had
been questioning detainees in Cuba since the prison opened. A few
of the agents began telling their superiors what they had witnessed,
which, they believed, had little to do with getting good information.
"I was told," a senior intelligence official recalled, "that the military
guards were slapping prisoners, stripping them, pouring cold water
over them, and making them stand until they got hypothermia. The
agents were outraged. It was wrong and also dysfunctional." The
agents put their specific complaints in writing, the official told me,

and they were relayed, in e-mails and phone calls, to officials at the Department of Defense, including William J. Haynes II, the general counsel of the Pentagon. As far as day-to-day life for prisoners at Guantánamo was concerned, nothing came of it.

Further accounts of wrongdoing came in late 2002 from an Army Reserve lawyer who had served at Guantánamo and subsequently came to the F.B.I. to interview for a job. The officers running Guantánamo were violating the Geneva Conventions and the federal anti-torture statute, the lawyer told his interviewers. He explained that he and a colleague, also a lawyer, had written a detailed memorandum to the senior officers at Guantánamo, but they had received no response. They were urged to take their complaints to the lawyers in the Pentagon. Once again, nothing came of it, the intelligence official told me.

The unifying issue for General Gordon and his supporters inside the Administration was not the abuse of prisoners at Guantánamo, the former White House official told me: "It was about how many more people are being held there that shouldn't be. Have we really got the right people?" On that question, Gordon's effort got some support from a surprising source: Major General Michael Dunlavey, an Army reservist who was commanding general of the task force responsible for setting up interrogations at Guantánamo. Dunlavey had no sympathy for any prisoner who was linked to terrorism. In May 2004, after he returned home to Erie, Pennsylvania, he gave a speech to the local Rotary Club in which he said, according to an account in the *Erie Times-News*, "keeping a bag over a guy's head for three days, that's not right, but that's not torture." According to the newspaper, Dunlavey "likened the interrogation methods used by American soldiers to punishment he received as a child—missing dinner if he came home late, a spanking for talking back, being sent to his room without television if he was disobedient. . . . 'I guess [my mom] must be a war criminal,' Dunlavey said.'" But he, too, was frustrated by what he described to me as the "convoluted method" for processing people. "If the prisoners are not useful to me," Dunlavey explained, "there's no value in what you do."

When we spoke, Dunlavey, who in civilian life is a state judge, denied that elderly prisoners at Guantánamo had been abused, and said that Rice and others in the White House had been provided with photographs of old men, dressed in bright new hospital scrubs, undergoing what seemed to be top-notch medical treatment at the prison hospital. The problem, he said, was that "they *were* older than dirt. And my concern was, 'Please don't die of old age while you're here.' If they did die," Dunlavey added, with a laugh, "they'd have to be buried right away [under Muslim law] and we'd have enemies for life: 'Here's Great-Grandfather, the oldest guy in the village, who survived three generations, and the Americans dropped him off in a box.'"

The photographs, staged or not, were seen by some as evidence that something was very wrong at Guantánamo. "They were such old men," the former White House official told me. "It was hard to believe they were dangerous." The former official added that he was more than a little skeptical about the integrity of the photographs, since he knew what the C.I.A. analyst had found.

The briefing for Condoleezza Rice about problems at Guantánamo took place in the fall of 2002. It did not dwell on the question of torture or the possibility that some prisoners were being subjected to cruel, inhuman, or degrading treatment. The main issue, the former White House official told me, was simply, "Are we getting any intelligence? What is the process for sorting these people?" Rice agreed to call a high-level meeting in the White House situation room. Most significantly, she asked Secretary Rumsfeld to attend.

Rumsfeld, who was by then publicly and privately encouraging his soldiers in the field to get tough with captured prisoners, duly showed up, but he had surprisingly little to say. One participant in the meeting recalled that at one point Rice asked Rumsfeld "what the issues were, and he said he hadn't looked into it." Rice urged Rumsfeld to do so, and added, "Let's get the story right." Rumsfeld seemed to be in total agreement, and Gordon and his supporters left the meeting convinced, the former Administration official told me, that the Pentagon was going to deal with the issue.

Rice then called another White House meeting on the problems at Guantánamo. The Bush Administration's principals—Cabinet members and senior aides involved in military, intelligence, and national security affairs—were told to take part. But getting the story right did not seem to be a high priority for Rumsfeld. A newly appointed official, Marshall Billingslea, who was the acting assistant secretary of defense for Special Operations and Low-Intensity Conflict, or SOLIC, was ordered to prepare the briefing for the meeting. Billingslea, who was just thirty-one years old, had served as a specialist on disarmament for the Senate Foreign Relations Committee, then headed by Jesse Helms, the ultraconservative senator from North Carolina.

When he took the job, Billingslea made it clear to his colleagues that he knew a lot about arms control but not much about prison operations or international terrorism. He also knew that Guantánamo was in chaos, one involved Defense official said, with Dunlavey and a fellow commander at the base, Brigadier General Rick Baccus, of the Rhode Island National Guard, bitterly quarreling with each other over interrogation techniques and other management issues. Billingslea and his colleagues believed, the official told me, that "yes, we did have some pretty bad guys in there, but they were mixed in with people who weren't movers and shakers. The interrogations were going nowhere." It wasn't clear, the Defense official added, whether Guantánamo "was a detention facility or an interrogation facility." Shortly after coming on the job in August 2002, Billingslea had turned to a longtime Pentagon consultant and confided that the Bush Administration had not been getting useful intelligence from Cuba. "I recommended that they take a core group of prisoners and debrief them over a long time," the consultant told me. "The military's interrogators had no concept of what I was talking about—they were focussed on battlefield situations. We had to find a way to co-opt the prisoners. Billingslea agreed that there was no strategic purpose in what we were doing."

Billingslea also sought out a White House official before the next meeting and had a confidential discussion about how to proceed. Billingslea's initial instinct, or mandate from the Pentagon leadership, the official told me, seemed to be to minimize the extent of the problem at Guantánamo. "The message was, 'Trust us. We're working on it, but these guys are all enemy combatants.'" The White House official responded that such an approach would not be enough. "I told Billingslea," the White House official recalled, "you need to say, 'We've got a problem and here's how we're going to fix it.'"

Billingslea got the message. At the meeting before the principals, who included Colin Powell, the secretary of state, Billingslea acknowledged that "there was a separating the wheat from the chaff issue" at Guantánamo, the former White House official said, and then he "outlined a process for sorting through it." Such talk was not welcome in the Bush White House, and the meeting turned contentious. The former Administration official told me that "David Addington"—the lawyer in Cheney's office—"wanted to take off Billingslea's head for talking about the issue," and made negative remarks, saying, in essence, "Why are we doing this?"

Nothing changed. "The Pentagon went into a full-court stall," the former White House official recalled. "I trusted in the goodness of man and thought we got something to happen. I was naïve enough to believe that when a Cabinet member"—he was referring to Rumsfeld—"says he's going to take action, he will." Over the next few months, as the White House began planning for the coming war in Iraq, there were many more discussions about the continuing problems at Guantánamo and the lack of useful intelligence. No one in the Bush Administration would get far, however, if he was viewed as soft, in any way, on suspected Al Qaeda terrorism. "Why didn't Condi do more?" the official asked. "She made the same mistake I made. She got the secretary of defense to say he's going to take care of it." He and his colleagues inside the White House were also at fault, the official told me. "We didn't get it done either."

In a White House news conference in June 2004, at the height of the Abu Ghraib scandal, William Haynes, the Pentagon's general counsel, joined other senior Administration aides in assuring reporters that no prisoners in Iraq, Afghanistan, or Cuba had been tortured. He also responded to a question about how the government knew it had the right person in captivity by insisting that everyone in Guantánamo belonged there. "There is so much process at Guantánamo," Haynes said. All potential prisoners were screened by American authorities in Afghanistan, he added, before being sent to Cuba. Once there, he said, "there must be an additional determination that somebody is an enemy combatant, and then annually thereafter. . . . Everybody down there has been through all that."

There was, obviously, a disconnect between the reality of prison life in Guantánamo and how it was depicted to the public in carefully stage-managed news conferences and statements released by the Administration. American prison authorities have repeatedly assured the press and the public, for example, that the Al Qaeda and Taliban detainees were provided with a minimum of three hours of recreation every week. For the tough cases, however, according to a Pentagon adviser familiar with detainee conditions in mid-2002, at recreation time some prisoners would be strapped into heavy jackets, similar to straitjackets, with their arms locked behind them and their legs straddled by straps. Goggles were placed over their eyes and their heads were covered with a hood. The prisoner was then led at midday into what looked like a narrow fenced-in dog run—

the adviser told me that there were photographs of the procedure—and given his hour of recreation. The restraints forced him to move, if he chose to move, on his knees, bent over at a forty-five-degree angle. Most prisoners just sat and suffered in the heat.

Many journalists and congressional delegations who visited Guantánamo in 2002 nevertheless reported that they found nothing amiss. They were seeing what the military wanted them to see and allowed them to see—a virtual Potemkin village. A few months before the analyst's visit, a group of senators put together a scheduled visit to Guantánamo after hearing reports from within the military chain of command of prisoner abuse. The senators found all in order. "Everything was fine," one of the senators told me, with a shrug, adding that he and his colleagues were forbidden to talk to any prisoners and thus were unable to come to an independent judgment.

One of the Marines assigned to guard duty at Guantánamo in 2003, who has since left the military, told me, after being promised anonymity, that he and his enlisted colleagues at the base were encouraged by their squad leaders to "give the prisoners a visit" one or two times a month, when there were no television crews, journalists, or other outside visitors at the prison. "We tried to fuck with them as much as we could—inflict a little bit of pain. We couldn't do much," because of a fear of exposure, the former Marine, who also served in Afghanistan, said. "There were always newspeople there," he said. "That's why you couldn't send them back with a broken leg or so. And if somebody died, I'd get court-martialed." The roughing up of prisoners was sometimes spur-of-the-moment, the former Marine said. "A squad leader would say, 'Let's go—all the cameras on lunch break.'" One pastime was to put hoods on the prisoners and "drive them around the camp in a Humvee, making turns so they didn't know where they were." The prisoners would talk during the rides, the former Marine said, but "we didn't know what they were saying. I wasn't trying to get information. I was just having a little fun—

playing mind control." As far as he was concerned, the former Marine added, the prisoners at Guantámano were all terrorists: "I thought everybody was a bad guy." When I asked a senior F.B.I. official about the former Marine's account, he told me that agents assigned to interrogation duties at Guantánamo had described similar activities to their superiors at headquarters.

In 2003, investigators for the International Committee of the Red Cross made a series of tense visits to Guantánamo. The previous November, Army Major General Geoffrey Miller had relieved Generals Dunlavey and Baccus, unifying the command at Guantánamo. Baccus was seen by the Pentagon as soft—too worried about the prisoners' well-being. He objected to interrogation techniques and distributed Red Cross posters that reminded prisoners of their rights under the Geneva Conventions. I.C.R.C. inspection reports are traditionally private, but in June 2004, the *Washington Post* quoted a series of Pentagon memorandums on the Red Cross visits showing that the inspectors were increasingly troubled by conditions at the prison, and by their relationship with Miller, an artillery officer who had no experience in managing a prison.

In one report, written nearly two years after the prison opened, the I.C.R.C. sharply criticized the Bush Administration for continuing to hold prisoners in open-air cages, for keeping detainees in "excessive isolation," and for failing to establish a process for categorizing and releasing those prisoners who did not belong at Guantánamo. After another visit, in October 2003, the I.C.R.C. reported that it continued to be concerned by the lack of progress in key areas, including the establishment of a legal system for processing detainees; the report also complained that Miller and his subordinates were relying too heavily on isolation as a means of controlling the prisoners. The *Washington Post* reported that Miller "bristled at the comments, telling the Red Cross representatives that interrogation techniques were not their concern." He denied that isolation was used to punish those who refused to cooperate. Isolation, he said, was used to punish those who failed to follow prison rules or attempted to assault guards. (In Senate hearings after Abu Ghraib, it became known that Miller was permitted to use legally questionable interrogation techniques at Guantánamo, which could include, with approval, sleep deprivation, exposure to extremes of cold and heat, and placing prisoners in "stress positions" for agonizing lengths of time.)

After the October meeting, Christophe Girod, chief of the I.C.R.C. for the U.S. and Canada, publicly criticized Miller's continuing failure to repatriate detainees. There was "a worrying deterioration in the psychological health of a large number" of the detainees because of uncertainty about their fate, Girod said. "One cannot keep these detainees in this pattern, this situation, indefinitely." Girod said he was speaking out because the Red Cross's negotiations with the Bush Administration had been unproductive.

In May 2004, the *New York Times* reported that the F.B.I. had instructed its agents to avoid being present at interrogation sessions with suspected Al Qaeda members. The newspaper said the severe methods used to extract information would be prohibited in criminal cases, and therefore could compromise the agents in future legal proceedings against the suspects. "We don't believe in coercion," a senior F.B.I. official subsequently told me. "Our goal is to get information and we try to gain the prisoners' trust. We have strong feelings about it." The F.B.I. official added, "I thought Rumsfeld should have been fired long ago."

"They did it the wrong way," a Pentagon adviser on the war on terror told me, "and took a heavy-handed approach based on coercion, instead of persuasion—which actually has a much better track record. It's about rage and the need to strike back. It's evil, but it's also stupid. It's not torture but acts of kindness that lead to concessions. The persuasive approach takes longer but gets far better results."

*   *   *

The analyst's report resulted in one small victory, of sorts. On October 26, 2002, four of the captives at Guantánamo were released and returned home, three of them to Afghanistan. A senior Afghan official subsequently told newsmen in Kabul that the circumstances of their detainment were laughable. The *New York Times*, in a dispatch published on page A18, noted that one of the detainees, Faiz Muhammad, was "babbling at times like a child; the partially deaf, shriveled old man was unable to answer simple questions." He told the reporter that he wasn't angry at being detained: "They took away my old clothes and gave me new clothes." Another released prisoner, Jan Muhammad, said he remained mystified about how he ended up at Guantánamo. He explained that he was forced to fight by the Taliban and quickly surrendered to American soldiers, along with others. At some point, an Afghan warlord identified the whole group to the Americans as senior Taliban officials, and all were seized. "They came and took ten strong-looking people," Muhammad told the *New York Times*. "Only one of those ten was a Talib."

At a Pentagon briefing three days later, Victoria Clarke, the assistant secretary of defense for public affairs, assured reporters that the Pentagon was "definitely planning to release more from Guantánamo." Red Cross representatives, she said, "have a very strong and consistent presence at Guantánamo, and I'm sure they will have interviews with any and all detainees that may be leaving." Clarke added that "one of the best things that has happened over the last year, for instance, is the information we have been able to glean from detainees, including Guantánamo, to help prevent future attacks." The public talk from the Pentagon and the White House, when contrasted with what was really going on, amounted to strategic deception. The target of all the duplicity and double-talk was not, of course, Al Qaeda and other terrorist groups, but the American press corps, and the American people.

A few weeks after the four prisoners were released, the C.I.A. analyst was warmly greeted at the agency by Stephen Hadley, the senior deputy to Condi Rice. "You must feel good—to do interesting work and have it affect policy!" Hadley exclaimed, as the analyst later recounted to the former C.I.A. colleague. He said that he told Hadley, "You let four people out. I'd feel better if you'd actually done something" to improve conditions at the prison.

There was, we now know, a fantastical quality to the earnest discussions inside the White House in 2002 about the good and bad of the interrogation process at Guantánamo. Rice and Rumsfeld knew what many others involved in the prisoner discussions did not—that sometime in late 2001 or early 2002 the President had signed a top-secret finding, as required by law, authorizing the Defense Department to set up a specially recruited clandestine team of Special Forces operatives and others who would defy diplomatic niceties and international law and snatch—or assassinate, if necessary—identified "high-value" Al Qaeda operatives anywhere in the world. Equally secret interrogation centers would be set up in allied countries where harsh treatments were meted out, unconstrained by legal limits or public disclosure. The program was hidden inside the Defense Department as an "unacknowledged" special-access program, or SAP, whose operational details were known only to a few in the Pentagon, the C.I.A., and the White House.

The SAP owed its existence to Rumsfeld's oft-expressed desire to get the U.S. Special Forces community into the business of what he called, in public and internal communications, "manhunts," and his disdain for the Pentagon's senior generals. In the privacy of his office, Rumsfeld chafed over what he saw as the reluctance of the generals and admirals to act aggressively. By mid-2002, he and his senior civilian aides were exchanging secret memorandums on modifying the culture of the military leaders and finding ways to encourage them "to take greater risks." One memo spoke derisively of the generals in the Pentagon, and said, "Our prerequisite of perfection for 'actionable intelligence' has paralyzed us. We must accept that we may have to take action before every question can be answered." The defense secretary was told by his aides that he should "break the 'belt-and-suspenders' mindset within today's military . . . we 'over-plan' for every contingency. . . . We must be willing to accept the risks." With operations involving the death of foreign enemies, the memo went on, the planning should not be carried out in the military's normal channels: "The result will be decision by committee."

Rumsfeld's impatience with military protocol extended to questions about the treatment of prisoners caught in the course of its military operations. Soon after September 11th, he repeatedly made public his disdain for the Geneva Conventions. Complaints about the United States' treatment of prisoners, Rumsfeld said in early 2002, amounted to "isolated pockets of international hyperventilation."

One of Rumsfeld's goals was bureaucratic: to give the civilian leadership in the Pentagon, and not the C.I.A., the lead in fighting terrorism. Throughout the existence of the SAP, which eventually came to Abu Ghraib prison, a former senior intelligence official told me, "There was a periodic briefing to the National Security Council giving updates on results, but not on the methods." Did the White House ask about the process? The former officer said that he believed that they did, and that "they got the answers."

The creation of the SAP, and the need to provide legal protection for the people in it, could explain the confounding language of the President's secret February 7, 2002, statement on the treatment of the detainees at Guantánamo, in which he declared that when it came to Al Qaeda the Geneva Conventions were applicable only at his discretion. Some of the sweeping conclusions in other early memorandums from the Administration also relate to the potential problems presented by the SAP. For example, a Defense Department analysis written in March 2002, initially made public by the *Wall Street Journal,* concluded that the President's authority "to manage a military campaign" overrode any statutory or treaty prohibitions against torture: "Any effort by Congress to regulate the interrogation of unlawful combatants would violate the Constitution's sole vesting of the Commander-in-Chief authority in the President." The document also argued, amazingly, that a defendant "could negate a showing of specific intent . . . by showing that he had acted in good faith that his conduct would not amount to acts prohibited by the statute." Anthony Lewis, the legal commentator, noted later in the *New York Review of Books* that these and other memorandums "read like the advice of a mob lawyer to a mafia don on how to skirt the law and stay out of prison. Avoiding prosecution is literally a theme." Lewis said, "One remarkable suggestion is that an interrogator who harmed a prisoner could rely on the argument of 'self-defense' as a legal justification—defense not of himself but of the nation."

There were continuing protests by human rights groups about prisoner abuse at Guantánamo and at the military's main interrogation center at Bagram Air Base, in Afghanistan, but in the absence of photographs the complaints had little traction. Since early 2002, Human Rights Watch had publicly challenged the Administration's insistence that the Geneva Conventions did not apply to the prisoners captured in Afghanistan. But those complaints, too, had little impact. In a letter dated January 28, 2002, Kenneth Roth, the executive director of the group, acknowledged to Condoleezza Rice that many Al Qaeda members might not meet the criteria to be considered prisoners of war. But, he added, "the Taliban, as the de facto government of Afghanistan, was a Party" to the Geneva Conventions. Therefore, Roth pointed out, the Administration had an obligation to distinguish between Al Qaeda terrorists and the Taliban, and had failed to do so. Roth also made a broader argument: that the President was dead wrong in proclaiming that international law did not apply to the detainees at Guantánamo.

In February 2003, several weeks after the *Washington Post* reported on what it called the "brass-knuckled quest for information" from Al Qaeda and Taliban detainees in Afghanistan, Holly Burkhalter, the U.S. policy director of Physicians for Human Rights, and other human rights officials met with the Pentagon's William Haynes. "Haynes came in mad—he really looked angry," Burkhalter told me. "He started the meeting by saying, 'We don't torture' and then lectured us—'Those of you in the human rights community who suggest that what the United States does to detainees is torture are trivializing the meaning of torture.' His meaning was clear," Burkhalter added. "If you are calling what we do in our interrogations torture—keeping people awake and in binds—you are doing a disservice to the victims of real torture."

The definition of torture arose again, this time in the White House, in June 2003, three months after the American invasion of Iraq, when Roth was invited to meet with Rice and John Bellinger, the N.S.C. attorney. Roth's notes of the meeting, which he provided to me, showed that he told them that he welcomed President Bush's pledge to not rely on torture but asked that the White House go further. He noted that the United Nations International Day in Support of Victims of Torture was later that month, and suggested that the Administration take the occasion to publicly affirm that the United States would abide by requirements of federal law and the Convention Against Torture not to use cruel, inhuman, or degrading treatment.

It was a sticking point. "Torture isn't being used," Rice told Roth, according to the notes. But, she added, "I won't get into the details of the convention. I'm not competent." Bellinger then said, according to the notes, that "degrading" was a very subjective term. "It's hard to imagine that we won't be accused of it for blindfolding or even just incarcerating." Bellinger and Rice surely knew that the problems at Guantánamo went far beyond "blindfolding"—a euphemism for the practice of forcing prisoners to wear hoods. The President did issue the International Day statement sought by Roth. But Roth was subsequently troubled to find that the Administration had its own definitions of the unlawful practices in the various international conventions—definitions that were so narrow and extreme that the U.S. military could continue to use many coercive measures, such as stripping prisoners, putting them in stress positions, and depriving them of sleep.

In an interview with me in July 2004, Roth recalled, "I told Rice and Bellinger, in essence, that if you can't do it at your local precinct, you can't do it at Guantánamo." By the time of his meeting with Rice, Rumsfeld's SAP was in its third year of snatching or strong-arming suspected terrorists and questioning them in secret prison facilities in Singapore, Thailand, and Pakistan, among other sites. The White House was fighting terror with terror.

By late August of 2003, as we shall see, the war in Iraq was going badly and there was, once again, little significant intelligence being generated in the many prisons in Iraq. The President and his national security team turned for guidance to General Miller, the Guantánamo commander. Recounting that decision, one of the White House officials who had supported General Gordon's ill-fated effort to change prisoner policy asked me, rhetorically, "Why do I take a failed approach at Guantánamo and move it to Iraq?" The Administration's answer to the growing insurgency, and the lack of intelligence about it, however, was to get tough with the Iraqi men and women in detention—to treat them behind prison walls as if they had been captured on the battlefields of Afghanistan.

2. Photographs from a Prison

In the era of Saddam Hussein, Abu Ghraib, twenty miles west of Baghdad, was one of the world's most notorious prisons, with torture, weekly executions, and vile living conditions. As many as fifty thousand men and women—no accurate count is possible—were jammed into Abu Ghraib at one time, in twelve-foot-by-twelve-foot cells that were little more than human holding pits.

In the looting that followed the regime's collapse in April 2003, the huge prison complex, by then deserted, was stripped of everything that could be removed, including doors, windows, and bricks. The Coalition authorities had the floors tiled, cells cleaned and repaired, and toilets, showers, and a new medical center added. Abu Ghraib was now a U.S. military prison. Most of the prisoners, however—by the fall of 2003 there were several thousand, including women and teenagers—were civilians, many of whom had been picked up in random military sweeps and at highway checkpoints. They fell into three loosely defined categories: common criminals; security detainees suspected of "crimes against the Coalition"; and a small number of suspected "high-value" leaders of the insurgency against the Coalition forces.

In June 2003, Janis Karpinski, an Army Reserve brigadier general, was named commander of the 800th Military Police Brigade and put in charge of military prisons in Iraq. General Karpinski, the only female commander in the war zone, was an experienced operations and intelligence officer who had served with the Special Forces and in the 1991 Gulf War, but she had never run a prison system. Now she was in charge of three large jails, eight battalions, and thirty-four hundred Army reservists, most of whom, like her, had no training in handling prisoners.

General Karpinski, who had wanted to be a soldier since she was five, was a business consultant in civilian life, and was enthusiastic about her new job. In an interview in December 2003 with the *St. Petersburg Times*, she said that, for many of the Iraqi inmates at Abu Ghraib, "living conditions now are better in prison than at home. At one point we were concerned that they wouldn't want to leave."

A month later, General Karpinski was formally admonished and quietly suspended, and a major investigation into the Army's prison system, authorized by Lieutenant General Ricardo S. Sanchez, the senior commander in Iraq, was under way. A fifty-three-page report, which I obtained in April 2004, written by Major General Antonio M. Taguba and not meant for public release—portions of the report were classified secret—was completed in late February. Its conclusions about the institutional failures of the Army prison system were unequivocal. Specifically, Taguba found that between October and December of 2003 there were numerous instances of "sadistic, blatant, and wanton criminal abuses" at Abu Ghraib. This systematic and illegal abuse of detainees, Taguba reported, was perpetrated by soldiers of the 372nd Military Police Company, and also by members of the American intelligence community. (The 372nd was attached to the 320th Military Police Battalion, which reported to Karpinski's brigade headquarters.) Taguba's report listed some of the wrongdoing:

> Breaking chemical lights and pouring the phosphoric liquid on detainees; pouring cold water on naked detainees; beating detainees with a broom handle and a chair; threatening male detainees with rape; allowing a military police guard to stitch the wound of a detainee who was injured after being slammed against the wall in his cell; sodomizing a detainee with a chemical light and perhaps a broom stick, and using military working dogs to frighten and intimidate detainees with threats of attack, and in one instance actually biting a detainee.

There was stunning evidence to support the allegations, Taguba added—"detailed witness statements and the discovery of extremely graphic photographic evidence." Photographs and videos taken by the soldiers as the abuses were happening were not included in his report, Taguba said, because of their "extremely sensitive nature."

The photographs—several of which were broadcast on CBS's *60 Minutes II* on April 28, 2004, a few days before my account for *The*

New Yorker appeared—show leering G.I.s taunting naked Iraqi prisoners who are forced to assume humiliating poses. Six suspects—Staff Sergeant Ivan L. Frederick II, known as Chip, who was the senior enlisted man; Specialist Charles A. Graner; Sergeant Javal Davis; Specialist Megan Ambuhl; Specialist Sabrina Harman; and Private Jeremy Sivits—were, at the time, facing prosecution in Iraq, on charges that included conspiracy, dereliction of duty, cruelty toward prisoners, maltreatment, assault, and indecent acts. A seventh suspect, Private Lynndie England, had been reassigned to Fort Bragg, North Carolina, after becoming pregnant with Graner's child and was charged later.

In one photograph, Private England, a cigarette dangling from her mouth, is giving a jaunty thumbs-up sign and pointing at the genitals of a young Iraqi, who is naked except for a sandbag over his head, as he masturbates. Three other hooded and naked Iraqi prisoners are shown, hands reflexively crossed over their genitals. A fifth prisoner has his hands at his sides. In another, England stands arm in arm with Specialist Graner; both are grinning and giving the thumbs-up behind a cluster of perhaps seven naked Iraqis, knees bent, piled clumsily on top of each other in a pyramid. There is another photograph of a cluster of naked prisoners, again piled in a pyramid. Near them stands Graner, smiling, his arms crossed; Specialist Sabrina Harman stands in front of him, bending over, and she, too, is smiling. Then, there is another cluster of hooded bodies, with a female soldier standing in front, taking photographs. Yet another photograph shows a kneeling, naked, unhooded male prisoner, head momentarily turned away from the camera, posed to make it appear that he is performing oral sex on another male prisoner, who is naked and hooded.

Such dehumanization is unacceptable in any culture, but it is especially so in the Arab world. Homosexual acts are against Islamic law, and it is humiliating for men to be naked in front of other men, Bernard Haykel, a professor of Middle Eastern studies at New York University, explained. "Being put on top of each other and forced to masturbate, being naked in front of each other—it's all a form of torture," Haykel said.

Two Iraqi faces that do appear in the photographs are those of dead men. There is the battered face of prisoner No. 153399 and the bloodied body of another prisoner, wrapped in cellophane and packed in ice. There is a photograph of an empty room, splattered with blood.

The 372nd's abuse of prisoners seemed almost routine—a fact of Army life that the soldiers felt no need to hide. On April 9, 2004, at an Article 32 hearing (the military equivalent of a grand jury) in the case against Sergeant Frederick, at Camp Victory, near Baghdad, one of the witnesses, Specialist Matthew Wisdom, an M.P., told the courtroom what happened when he and other soldiers delivered seven prisoners, hooded and bound, to the so-called hard site at Abu Ghraib—seven tiers of cells where the inmates who were considered the most dangerous were housed. The men had been accused of starting a riot in another section of the prison. Wisdom said:

> SFC Snider grabbed my prisoner and threw him into a pile. . . . I do not think it was right to put them in a pile. I saw SSG Frederic [sic], SGT Davis and CPL Graner walking around the pile hitting the prisoners. I remember SSG Frederick hitting one prisoner in the side of its [sic] ribcage. The prisoner was no danger to SSG Frederick. . . . I left after that.

When he returned later, Wisdom testified:

> I saw two naked detainees, one masturbating to another kneeling with its mouth open. I thought I should just get out of there. I didn't think it was right. . . . I saw SSG Frederick walking towards me, and he said, "Look what these animals do when you leave them alone for two seconds." I heard PFC England shout out, "He's getting hard."

Wisdom testified that he told his superiors what had happened, and assumed that "the issue was taken care of." He said, "I just didn't want to be part of anything that looked criminal."

The abuses became public because of the outrage of Specialist Joseph M. Darby, an M.P. whose role emerged during the Article 32 hearing against Frederick. A government witness, Special Agent Scott Bobeck, who is a member of the Army's Criminal Investigation Division, or C.I.D., told the court, according to an abridged transcript made available to me, "The investigation started after SPC Darby . . . got a CD from CPL Graner. . . . He came across pictures of naked detainees." Bobeck said that Darby had "initially put an anonymous letter under our door, then he later came forward and gave a sworn statement. He felt very bad about it and thought it was very wrong."

Darby did what the world's most influential human rights groups could not. The International Committee of the Red Cross and Human Rights Watch had repeatedly complained during the previous year about the American military's treatment of Iraqi prisoners, with little response from the system. In one case, disclosed in April by the *Denver Post*, three Army soldiers from a military intelligence battalion were accused of assaulting a female Iraqi inmate at Abu Ghraib. After an administrative review, the three were fined "at least five hundred dollars and demoted in rank," the newspaper said.

Army commanders had a different response when they were presented with Darby's computer disk containing the graphic photographs. The images, it was soon clear, were being swapped from computer to computer throughout the 320th Battalion. The Army's senior commanders immediately understood they had a problem—a looming political and public relations disaster that would taint the United States and damage the war effort.

Darby gave the photographs to investigators on January 13, 2004. Frederick kept a running diary, addressed to his family, of what happened next. It began with a knock on his door by agents of the Army

C.I.D. at two-thirty in the morning of January 14th. "I was escorted . . . to the front door of our building, out of sight from my room," Frederick wrote, "while . . . two unidentified males stayed in my room. 'Are they searching my room?'" He was told yes. Frederick later formally agreed to permit the agents to search for cameras, computers, and storage devices.

On January 16th, three days after the Army received the pictures, U.S. Central Command (CENTCOM) issued a blandly worded five-sentence press release about an investigation into the mistreatment of prisoners. Secretary Rumsfeld said that it was then that he learned of the allegations. At some point soon afterward, Rumsfeld informed President Bush. On January 19th, General Sanchez ordered the secret investigation into Abu Ghraib. Two weeks later, General Taguba was ordered to conduct his inquiry.

The Army investigator said at the Article 32 hearing that Frederick and his colleagues had not been given any "training guidelines" that he was aware of. The M.P.s in the 372nd had been assigned to routine traffic and police duties upon their arrival in Iraq, in the spring of 2003. In October of 2003, the 372nd was ordered to prison-guard duty at Abu Ghraib. Frederick, at thirty-seven, was far older than his colleagues, and a natural leader. He had also worked for six years as a guard for the Virginia Department of Corrections. Bobeck explained:

> What I got is that SSG Frederick and CPL Graner were road M.P.s and were put in charge because they were civilian prison guards and had knowledge of how things were supposed to be run.

Bobeck also testified that witnesses had said that Frederick, on one occasion, "had punched a detainee in the chest so hard that the detainee almost went into cardiac arrest."

In letters and e-mails to family members, Frederick repeatedly noted that the military intelligence teams, which included C.I.A. officers and linguists and interrogation specialists from private defense contractors, were the dominant force inside Abu Ghraib. In one of the notes to his family, he said:

> I questioned some of the things that I saw . . . such things as leaving inmates in their cell with no clothes or in female underpants, handcuffing them to the door of their cell—and the answer I got was, "This is how military intelligence [MI] wants it done." . . . MI has also instructed us to place a prisoner in an isolation cell with little or no clothes, no toilet or running water, no ventilation or window, for as much as three days.

The military intelligence officers have "encouraged and told us, 'Great job,' they were now getting positive results and information," Frederick wrote. "CID has been present when the military working dogs were used to intimidate prisoners at MI's request." At one point, Frederick told his family, he pulled aside his superior officer, Lieutenant Colonel Jerry Phillabaum, the commander of the 320th M.P. Battalion, and asked about the mistreatment of prisoners. "His reply was 'Don't worry about it.'"

At the Article 32 hearing in April, the Army informed Frederick and his attorneys, Captain Robert Shuck, an Army lawyer, and Gary Myers, a civilian, that two dozen witnesses they had sought, including General Karpinski and all of Frederick's co-defendants, would not appear. Some had been excused after exercising their Fifth Amendment right; others were deemed to be too far away from the courtroom. "The purpose of an Article 32 hearing is for us to engage witnesses and discover facts," Gary Myers told me. "We ended up with a C.I.D. agent and no alleged victims to examine." After the hearing, the presiding investigative officer ruled that there was sufficient evidence to convene a court-martial against Frederick.

Myers, who was one of the military defense attorneys in the My

Lai prosecutions of the 1970s, told me in an interview in April 2004 that his client's defense would be that he was carrying out the orders of his superiors and, in particular, the directions of military intelligence. "I'm going to drag every involved intelligence officer and civilian contractor I can find into court," he said. "Do you really believe the Army relieved a general officer because of six soldiers? Not a chance." Similarly, Captain Robert Shuck, Frederick's military attorney, closed his defense at the April Article 32 hearing by saying that the Army was "attempting to have these six soldiers atone for its sins."

Frederick's defense was, of course, highly self-serving. But the complaints in his letters and e-mails home were reinforced by at least two internal Army reports—Taguba's and one by the Army's chief law enforcement officer, Provost Marshal Donald Ryder, a major general.

Early that fall, Taguba wrote, General Sanchez, apparently troubled by reports coming from Army jails in Iraq, had asked General Ryder to carry out a study of military prisons. The resulting study, which was still classified at the time the Taguba report became public, was filed on November 5, 2003, and concluded that there were potential human rights, training, and manpower issues, system-wide, that needed immediate attention. It also discussed serious concerns about the tension between the missions of the military police assigned to guard the prisoners and the intelligence teams who wanted to interrogate them. Army regulations limit intelligence activity by M.P.s to passive collection. But something had gone wrong at Abu Ghraib.

There was evidence dating back to the Afghanistan war, the Ryder report said, that M.P.s had worked with intelligence operatives: "Recent intelligence collection in support of Operation Enduring Freedom posited a template whereby military police actively set favorable conditions for subsequent interviews"—a euphemism for breaking the will of prisoners. "Such actions generally run counter to the smooth operation of a detention facility, attempting to maintain its population in a compliant and docile state." Ryder called for the establishment of procedures to "define the role of military police soldiers . . . clearly separating the actions of the guards from those of the military intelligence personnel." The officers running the war in Iraq had been put on notice.

Ryder undercut his warning, however, by concluding that the situation had not yet reached a crisis point. General Karpinski's brigade, Ryder reported, "has not been directed to change its facility procedures to set the conditions for MI interrogations, nor participate in those interrogations." Though some procedures were flawed, he said, he found "no military police units purposely applying inappropriate confinement practices." His investigation was at best a failure and at worst a cover-up.

Taguba, in his report, was polite but direct in refuting his fellow general. "Unfortunately, many of the systemic problems that surfaced during [Ryder's] assessment are the very same issues that are the subject of this investigation," he wrote. "In fact, many of the abuses suffered by detainees occurred during, or near to, the time of that assessment." The report continued: "Contrary to the findings of MG Ryder's report, I find that personnel assigned to the 372nd MP Company, 800th MP Brigade were directed to change facility procedures to 'set the conditions' for MI interrogations." Army intelligence officers, C.I.A. agents, and private contractors "actively requested that MP guards set physical and mental conditions for favorable interrogation of witnesses."

Taguba backed up his assertion by citing evidence from sworn statements to Army C.I.D. investigators. Specialist Harman, one of the accused M.P.s, testified that it was her job to keep detainees awake, including one hooded prisoner who was placed on a box with wires attached to his fingers, toes, and penis. She stated, "MI wanted to get them to talk. It is Graner and Frederick's job to do things for MI and OGA [other government agencies] to get these people to talk."

Sergeant Javal Davis, who was also one of the accused, told C.I.D. investigators, "I witnessed prisoners in the MI hold section . . . being made to do various things that I would question morally. . . . We were told that they had different rules." Taguba wrote, "Davis also stated that he had heard MI insinuate to the guards to abuse the inmates. When asked what MI said he stated: 'Loosen this guy up for us.' 'Make sure he has a bad night.' 'Make sure he gets the treatment.'" Military intelligence made these comments to Graner and Frederick, Davis said. "The MI staffs to my understanding have been giving Graner compliments . . . statements like, 'Good job, they're breaking down real fast. They answer every question. They're giving out good information.'"

When asked why he did not inform his chain of command about the abuse, Sergeant Davis answered, "Because I assumed that if they were doing things out of the ordinary or outside the guidelines, someone would have said something. Also the wing"—where the abuse took place—"belongs to MI and it appeared MI personnel approved of the abuse."

Another witness, Specialist Jason Kennel, who was not accused of wrongdoing, said, "I saw them nude, but MI would tell us to take away their mattresses, sheets, and clothes." (It was his view, he added, that if M.I. wanted him to do this, "they needed to give me paperwork.") Taguba also cited an interview with Adel L. Nakhla, an interpreter who was an employee of Titan, a civilian contractor. He told of one night when a "bunch of people from MI" watched as a group of handcuffed and shackled inmates were subjected to abuse by Graner and Frederick.

Taguba also got access to a classified report by General Geoffrey Miller, the Guantánamo commander. In late August 2003, Miller had brought a team of experts to Iraq to review the Army program.

His recommendations, filed in September, were radical: that Army prisons be geared, first and foremost, to interrogations and the gathering of information needed for the war effort. "Detention operations must act as an enabler for interrogation . . . to provide a safe, secure and humane environment that supports the expeditious collection of intelligence," Miller wrote. The military police on guard duty at the prisons should make support of military intelligence a priority.

General Sanchez agreed, and on November 19, 2003, his headquarters issued an order formally giving the 205th Military Intelligence Brigade tactical control over the prison. General Taguba fearlessly took issue with the Sanchez orders, which, he wrote in his report, "effectively made an MI Officer, rather than an MP officer, responsible for the MP units conducting detainee operations at that facility. This is not doctrinally sound due to the different missions and agenda assigned to each of these respective specialties."

Miller's concept, as it emerged in later Senate hearings, was to "Gitmoize" the prison system in Iraq—to make it more focussed on interrogation. While in Iraq, he briefed military commanders on the interrogation methods used in Cuba. A complete version of Miller's classified report, provided to some reporters in August 2004, made it clear that it had an ambitious goal: to turn Abu Ghraib into a center of intelligence for the Bush Administration's global war on terrorism. General Sanchez, he wrote, envisioned a system that could "drive the rapid exploitation of internees to answer . . . theater and national level counter terrorism requirements" and respond to the "needs of the Global War on Terrorism." Miller apparently believed that the prisoners in Iraq, if interrogated correctly, could provide strategic intelligence relevant to operations around the world. If his recommendations were put into effect immediately, the general claimed, "a significant improvement of actionable intelligence will be realized within thirty days."

It sounded good on paper, but Taguba, in his report, expressed well-founded skepticism. He noted that "the intelligence value of detainees held at . . . Guantánamo is different than that of the detainees/internees held at Abu Ghraib and other detention facilities in Iraq. . . . There are a large number of Iraqi criminals held at Abu Ghraib. These are not believed to be international terrorists or members of Al Qaeda." Taguba noted that Miller's advice appeared "to be in conflict" with other studies and with Army regulations that call for military police units to have control of the prison system. By placing military intelligence operatives in control instead, Miller's recommendations and Sanchez's change in policy undoubtedly played a role in the abuses at Abu Ghraib.

In late March, before the Abu Ghraib scandal became publicly known, General Miller was transferred from Guantánamo and named head of prison operations in Iraq. After the story broke on CBS, the Pentagon announced that Miller had arrived in Baghdad and was on the job. General Sanchez presented him to the media as the general who would clean up the Iraqi prison system and instill respect for the Geneva Conventions—a prisoner-of-war problem solver. "We have changed this—trust us," Miller told reporters in early May. "There were errors made. We have corrected those. We will make sure that they do not happen again."

General Taguba saved his harshest words for military intelligence officers and private contractors. He recommended that Colonel Thomas Pappas, the commander of one of the military intelligence brigades, be reprimanded and receive nonjudicial punishment, and that Lieutenant Colonel Steven Jordan, the former director of the Joint Interrogation and Debriefing Center, be relieved of duty and reprimanded. He further urged that Steven Stefanowicz, a civilian contractor with CACI International, a Virginia-based company, be fired from his Army job, reprimanded, and denied his security clearances for lying to the investigating team and allowing or ordering military policemen "who were not trained in interrogation techniques to facilitate interrogations by 'setting conditions' which were neither authorized" nor in accordance with Army regulations. "He clearly knew his instructions equated to physical abuse," Taguba wrote. He also recommended disciplinary action against a second contractor, John Israel.

"I suspect," Taguba concluded, that Pappas, Jordan, Stefanowicz, and Israel "were either directly or indirectly responsible for the abuse at Abu Ghraib," and strongly recommended immediate disciplinary action.

Private companies like CACI and Titan were, at the time, paying salaries of well over $100,000 for the dangerous work in Iraq, far more than the Army paid, and were permitted, as never before in U.S. military history, to handle sensitive jobs. Civilian employees at the prison were not bound by the Uniform Code of Military Justice, but they were bound by civilian law—though it is unclear whether American or Iraqi law would apply. (In a briefing in May 2004, General Miller confirmed that Stefanowicz had been reassigned to administrative duties. That month, a CACI spokeswoman declined to comment on any employee in Iraq, citing safety concerns, but said that the company had not heard anything directly from the government about Stefanowicz.)

Stefanowicz and his colleagues conducted most, if not all, of their interrogations in the Abu Ghraib facilities known to the soldiers as the Wood Building and the Steel Building. The interrogation centers were rarely visited by the M.P.s, a source familiar with the investigation said. Many of the most important prisoners—the suspected insurgency members deemed to be high-value detainees—were housed at Camp Cropper, near the Baghdad airport, but the pressure on soldiers to accede to requests from military intelligence was felt throughout the system.

Not everybody went along. In May 2004, I interviewed a company captain in a military police unit in Baghdad who told me about an incident the previous fall in which he was approached by a junior military intelligence officer who requested that his M.P.s keep a group of detainees awake around the clock until they began talking. "I said, 'No, we will not do that,'" the captain said. "The M.I. commander comes to me and says, 'What is the problem? We're stressed, and all we are asking you to do is to keep them awake.' I ask, 'How? You've received training on that, but my soldiers don't know how to do it. And when you ask an eighteen-year-old kid to keep someone awake, and he doesn't know how to do it, he's going to get creative.'" The M.I. officer took the request to the captain's commander, but, the captain said, "he backed me up."

"It's all about people. The M.P.s at Abu Ghraib were failed by their commanders—both low-ranking and high," the captain said. "The system is broken—no doubt about it. But the Army is made up of people, and we've got to depend on them to do the right thing."

———

In his report, Taguba singled out only three military men for praise. One of them, Master-at-Arms William J. Kimbro, a Navy dog handler, should be commended, Taguba wrote, because he "knew his duties and refused to participate in improper interrogations despite significant pressure from the MI personnel at Abu Ghraib." Elsewhere in the report it became clear what Kimbro would not do: American soldiers, Taguba said, used "military working dogs to frighten and intimidate detainees with threats of attack, and in one instance actually biting a detainee."

In the week after the scandal broke, I was given a second set of digital photographs, which had been in the possession of a member of the 320th. The reservist had returned home from a tour of duty at Abu Ghraib in the spring of 2003, inexplicably sullen and withdrawn. A family member, looking through files on a computer the soldier had had with her in Iraq, stumbled across images from the prison. More browsing led to a horrendous sequence that seemed to explain, or merely make comprehensible, the mental condition of the Iraqi veteran.

According to a time sequence embedded in the digital files, the photographs were taken by two different cameras over a twelve-minute period on the evening of December 12, 2003, two months after the military police unit was assigned to Abu Ghraib. One of them shows a young soldier, wearing a dark jacket over his uniform and smiling into the camera, in the corridor of the jail. In the background are two Army dog handlers, in full camouflage combat gear, restraining two German shepherds. The dogs are barking at a man who is partly obscured from the camera's view by the smiling soldier. Another image shows that the man, an Iraqi prisoner, is naked. His hands are clasped behind his neck and he is leaning against the door to a cell, contorted with terror, as the dogs bark a few feet away. Other photographs show the dogs straining at their leashes and snarling at the prisoner. In another, taken a few minutes later, the Iraqi is lying on the ground, writhing in pain, with a soldier sitting on top of him, knee pressed to his back. Blood is streaming from the inmate's leg. Another photograph is a close-up of the naked prisoner, from his waist to his ankles, lying on the floor. On his right thigh is what appears to be a bite or a deep scratch. There is another, larger wound on his left leg, covered in blood.

There had been at least one other report of violence involving American soldiers, an Army dog, and Iraqi citizens prior to this, although it was not in Abu Ghraib. Cliff Kindy, a member of the Christian Peacemaker Teams, a church-supported group that had been monitoring the situation in Iraq, told me that in November 2003 G.I.s unleashed a military dog on a group of civilians during a sweep in Ramadi, about thirty miles west of Falluja. At first, Kindy told me, "the soldiers went house to house, and arrested thirty people." (One of them was Saad al-Khashab, an attorney with the Organization for Human Rights in Iraq, who told Kindy about the incident.) While the thirty detainees were being handcuffed and laid on the ground, a firefight broke out nearby; when it ended, the Iraqis were shoved into a house. Khashab told Kindy that the American soldiers then "turned the dog loose inside the house, and several people were bitten."

When I asked retired Major General Charles Hines, who was commandant of the Army's military police school during a twenty-eight-year career in military law enforcement, about these reports, he reacted with dismay. "Turning a dog loose in a room of people? Loosing dogs on prisoners of war? I've never heard of it, and it would never have been tolerated," Hines said. He added that trained police dogs have long been a presence in Army prisons, where they are used for sniffing out narcotics and other contraband among the prisoners and, occasionally, for riot control. But, he said, "I would never have authorized it for interrogating or coercing prisoners. If I had, I'd have been put in jail or kicked out of the Army."

As the Army's investigation into Abu Ghraib deepened, it became clear that the use of unmuzzled dogs to frighten and intimidate prisoners was a routine practice—one that the prison guards believed had been authorized by senior commanders. Military investigative records, made public in June 2004 by the *Washington Post*, showed that dogs were repeatedly used during interrogations, and not always to elicit intelligence. One military intelligence witness, Specialist John Harold Ketzer, told Army investigators that he watched a dog team corner two male prisoners against a wall at Abu Ghraib, with one hiding behind the other and screaming. No interrogation was going on. "When I asked what was going on in the cell, the handler stated that . . . he and another of the handlers was having a contest to see how many detainees they could get to urinate on themselves."

Colonel Thomas Pappas, commander of the intelligence unit at Abu Ghraib, told the investigators that authorization had come from General Sanchez. But Sanchez, in an appearance in May 2004 before the Senate Armed Services Committee, denied doing so. Asked how a commander at Abu Ghraib had come to believe that there was authorization, the three-star general passed the buck. "You'd have to ask the commander," Sanchez told a senator.

Two months later, however, *USA Today* reported that it had obtained classified documents showing that Sanchez had issued orders the previous fall authorizing military interrogators to use dogs at their own discretion, without his prior approval. Sanchez's order required the dogs to be muzzled and in control of a handler when in interrogation rooms but put no restrictions on the use of dogs in other settings.

Taguba strongly suggested that there was a pattern of activity linking the interrogation process in Afghanistan and the abuses at Abu Ghraib. One parallel, not discussed by Taguba, was the handling of John Walker Lindh, who was accused of training with Al Qaeda terrorists and conspiring to kill Americans. A few days after his arrest, according to a federal court affidavit filed by his attorney, James Brosnahan, a group of armed American soldiers "blindfolded Mr. Lindh, and took several pictures of Mr. Lindh and themselves with Mr. Lindh. In one, the soldiers scrawled 'shithead' across Mr. Lindh's blindfold and posed with him. . . . Another told Mr. Lindh that he was 'going to hang' for his actions and that after he was dead, the soldiers would sell the photographs and give the money to a Christian organization." Some of the photographs later made their way to the American media. Lindh was stripped naked, bound to a stretcher with duct tape, and placed in a windowless shipping container. Once again, the affidavit said, "military personnel photographed Mr. Lindh as he lay on the stretcher." On July 15, 2002, Lindh agreed to plead guilty to carrying a gun while serving in the Taliban and received a twenty-year jail term. During that process, Brosnahan told me, "the Department of Defense insisted that we state that there was 'no deliberate' mistreatment of John." His client agreed to do so, but, the attorney noted, "Against that, you have that photograph of a naked John on that stretcher."

The photographing of prisoners, both in Afghanistan and in Iraq, seems to have been not random but, rather, part of the dehumanizing interrogation process. The *New York Times* subsequently published an interview with Hayder Sabbar Abd, who claimed, convincingly, to be one of the mistreated Iraqi prisoners in the Abu Ghraib photographs. Abd told Ian Fisher, the *Times* reporter, that his ordeal had been almost constantly recorded by cameras, which added to his humiliation. He remembered how the camera flashed repeatedly as soldiers told him to masturbate and beat him when he refused.

One of the questions that will be explored at any trial is why a group of Army Reserve military policemen, most of them from small towns, tormented their prisoners as they did, in a manner that was especially humiliating for Iraqi men. (Gary Myers, the attorney for Sergeant Frederick, asked me, "Do you really think a group of kids from rural Virginia decided to do this on their own? Decided that the best way to embarrass Arabs and make them talk was to have them walk around nude?")

The notion that Arabs are particularly vulnerable to sexual humiliation had become a talking point among pro-war Washington conservatives in the months before the March 2003 invasion of Iraq. One book that was frequently cited was *The Arab Mind*, a study of Arab culture and psychology, first published in 1973, by Raphael Patai, a cultural anthropologist who taught at, among other universities, Columbia and Princeton, and who died in 1996. The book includes a twenty-five-page chapter on Arabs and sex, depicting sex as a taboo vested with shame and repression. "The segregation of the sexes, the veiling of the women . . . and all the other minute rules that govern and restrict contact between men and women, have the effect of making sex a prime mental preoccupation in the Arab world," Patai wrote. Homosexual activity, "or any indication of homosexual leanings, as with all other expressions of sexuality, is never given any publicity. These are private affairs and remain in private." The Patai book, an academic told me, was "the bible of the neocons on Arab behavior." In their discussions, he said, two themes emerged—"one, that Arabs only understand force and, two, that the biggest weakness of Arabs is shame and humiliation."

The government consultant said that there may have been a serious goal, in the beginning, behind the sexual humiliation and the posed photographs. It was thought that some prisoners would do anything—including spying on their associates—to avoid dissemination of the shameful photos to family and friends. The government consultant said, "I was told that the purpose of the photographs was to create an army of informants, people you could insert back in the population." The idea was that they would be motivated by fear of exposure, and gather information about pending insurgency action, the consultant said. If so, it wasn't effective: the insurgency continued to grow.

The problems inside the Army prison system in Iraq were not hidden from senior commanders. During Karpinski's seven-month tour of duty, Taguba noted, there were at least a dozen officially reported incidents involving escapes, attempted escapes, and other serious security issues that were investigated by officers of the 800th M.P. Brigade. Some of the incidents had led to the killing or wounding of inmates and military police, and resulted in a series of "lessons learned" inquiries within the brigade. Karpinski invariably approved the reports and signed orders calling for changes in day-to-day procedures. But Taguba found that she did not follow up, doing nothing to insure that the orders were carried out. Had she done so, he added, "cases of abuse may have been prevented."

General Taguba further found that Abu Ghraib was filled beyond capacity, and that the M.P. guard force was significantly understaffed and short of resources. "This imbalance has contributed to the poor living conditions, escapes, and accountability lapses," he wrote. There were gross differences, Taguba said, between the actual number of prisoners on hand and the number officially recorded. A lack of proper screening also meant that many innocent Iraqis were being detained—in some cases indefinitely, it seemed.

Under the fourth Geneva Convention, an occupying power can jail civilians who pose an "imperative" security threat, but it must establish a regular procedure for insuring that only civilians who remain a genuine security threat be kept imprisoned. Prisoners have the right to appeal any internment decision and have their cases reviewed. In February 2004, Human Rights Watch complained to Rumsfeld that civilians in Iraq remained in custody month after month with no charges brought against them. Abu Ghraib had become, in effect, another Guantánamo.

The Taguba study noted that more than 60 percent of the civilian inmates at Abu Ghraib were deemed not to be a threat to society, which should have enabled them to be released. Karpinski's defense, Taguba said, was that her superior officers "routinely" rejected her recommendations regarding the release of such prisoners. But Karpinski was rarely seen at the prisons she was supposed to be running, Taguba wrote. He also found a wide range of administrative problems, including some that he considered "without precedent in my military career." The soldiers, he added, were "poorly prepared and untrained . . . prior to deployment, at the mobilization site, upon arrival in theater, and throughout the mission."

General Taguba spent more than four hours interviewing Karpinski, whom he described as extremely emotional: "What I found particularly disturbing in her testimony was her complete unwillingness to either understand or accept that many of the problems inherent in the 800th MP Brigade were caused or exacerbated by poor leadership and the refusal of her command to both establish and enforce basic standards and principles among its soldiers."

Taguba recommended that Karpinski and seven brigade military police officers and enlisted soldiers be relieved of command and formally reprimanded. No criminal proceedings were suggested for Karpinski; apparently, the loss of promotion and the indignity of a public rebuke were seen as enough punishment.

Taguba submitted his report on February 26, 2004. By then, according to testimony before the Senate by General Richard Myers, chairman of the Joint Chiefs of Staff, people "inside our building" had discussed the photographs. Myers, by his own account, had still not read the Taguba report or seen the photographs, yet he knew enough about the abuses to persuade *60 Minutes II* to delay its story.

At a Pentagon news conference on May 4th, Rumsfeld and Marine General Peter Pace, the vice chairman of the Joint Chiefs of Staff, insisted that the investigation into Abu Ghraib had moved routinely through the chain of command. If the Army had been slow, it was because of built-in safeguards. Pace told the journalists, "It's important to know that as investigations are completed they come up the chain of command in a very systematic way. So that the individual who reports in writing [sends it] up to the next level commander. But he or she takes time, a week or two weeks, three weeks, whatever it takes, to read all of the documentation, get legal advice [and] make the decisions that are appropriate at his or her level. . . . That way everyone's rights are protected and we have the opportunity systematically to take a look at the entire process."

In interviews, however, retired and active-duty officers and Pentagon officials said that the system had not worked. A senior Pentagon official said that many of the top generals in the Army were kept out of the loop on the Abu Ghraib allegations. The Pentagon official told me that many generals believe that, along with the civilians in Rumsfeld's office, General Sanchez and General John Abizaid, who was in charge of U.S. Central Command in Tampa, Florida, had done their best to keep the issue quiet in the first months of the year. The official chain of command flows from General Sanchez, in Iraq, to

Abizaid, and on to Rumsfeld and President Bush. "You've got to match action, or nonaction, with interests," the Pentagon official said. "What is the motive for not being forthcoming? They foresaw major diplomatic problems."

Within the Pentagon, there was a spate of finger pointing in the weeks after the pictures became public. One top general complained to a colleague that the commanders in Iraq should have taken C4, a powerful explosive, and blown up Abu Ghraib last spring, with all of its "emotional baggage" instead of turning it into an American facility. "This is beyond the pale in terms of lack of command attention," a retired major general told me, speaking of the abuses at Abu Ghraib. "Where were the flag officers? And I'm not just talking about a one-star," he added, referring to General Karpinski. "This was a huge leadership failure."

Since the scandal broke, senior generals in the chain of command have consistently denied any prior knowledge of wrongdoing in their public statements and congressional testimony. To prove a general wrong is a career-ending move for more junior officers, and those who have talked to me did so only after being assured of anonymity. One officer, who plays an important role in the difficult-to-prosecute war against the insurgents in Iraq, learned in November of 2003 that there was systematic abuse of prisoners at Abu Ghraib and elsewhere. He took that information to two of his superiors, General Abizaid, the CENTCOM commander, and his deputy, Air Force Lieutenant General Lance Smith. "I said there are systematic abuses going on in the prisons," the officer told me. "Abizaid just didn't say a thing. He looked at me—beyond me, as if to say, 'Move on. I don't want to touch this.'" Smith also said nothing. "They knew last year," the officer told me.

A military consultant with close ties to the Special Operations community told me in the summer of 2004 that he had been informed that some officers who were serving in Iraq had filed written complaints about prison abuse before the photographs were revealed. They were told, he said, that their papers had to be routed to General Sanchez. War crimes were committed and no action was taken, he added, in anger. "People were beaten to death. What do you call it when people are tortured and going to die and the soldiers know it, but do not treat their injuries?" He answered his own question: "Execution."

General Antonio Taguba suffered the fate of all truthtellers. "He's not regarded as a hero in some circles in the Pentagon," a retired Army major general said of Taguba. "He's the guy who blew the whistle, and the Army will pay the price for his integrity. The leadership does not like to have people make bad news public."

In his news conference on May 4th, the Tuesday after the first photographs appeared, Rumsfeld, when asked whether he thought the pictures and stories from Abu Ghraib were a setback for American policy in Iraq, still seemed to be in denial. "Oh, I'm not one for instant history," he said. By Friday the 7th, however, with editorials and some members of Congress calling for his resignation, Rumsfeld testified at length before the House and Senate and apologized for what he said was "fundamentally un-American" wrongdoing at Abu Ghraib. He also warned that more, and even uglier, disclosures were to come. He said that he had not actually looked at any of the photographs until they appeared in the press, and hadn't reviewed the Army's copies until the day before. When he did, they were "hard to believe," he said. "There are other photos that depict . . . acts that can only be described as blatantly sadistic, cruel, and inhuman." Later, he said, "It's going to get still more terrible, I'm afraid." Rumsfeld added, "I failed to recognize how important it was."

NBC News later quoted U.S. military officials as saying that the unreleased photographs showed American soldiers "severely beating an Iraqi prisoner nearly to death, having sex with a female Iraqi prisoner, and 'acting inappropriately with a dead body.' The officials said there also was a videotape, apparently shot by U.S. personnel, showing Iraqi guards raping young boys."

In my initial reporting, I saw more than fifty photographs depicting the abuses at Abu Ghraib. In the weeks that followed, other news organizations, notably the *Washington Post*, obtained and published more. An attorney involved in the case told me in July 2004 that one of the witness statements he had read described the rape of a boy by a foreign contract employee who served as an interpreter at Abu Ghraib. In the statement, which had not been made public, the lawyer told me, a prisoner stated that he was a witness to the rape, and that a woman was taking pictures. The witness further stated, according to the lawyer, that "the kid was making a lot of noise." In his report, General Taguba noted that the evidence he had assembled included videotapes as well as photographs. He also commented that certain members of the Iraqi work force "demonstrate questionable work ethics and loyalties, and are a potentially dangerous contingent within the Hard-Site." (The Red Cross counted 107 juveniles jailed in six American military prisons in Iraq during inspections it made in the first five months of 2004, but it was unable to get complete information about their ages and the conditions under which they were being held.)

Evidence of the traumatic impact of the abuses was conveyed to me by a senior Iraqi weapons scientist, now living abroad, in the spring of 2004. He told me that several women detained at Abu Ghraib had "passed messages to their families imploring them to smuggle poison to them to end their lives, while others have passed similar messages insisting that they must be killed immediately upon release from prison," the senior scientist reported. "Such is the code of honor in most parts of the Middle East. Innocent lives will be lost [so] their families can survive the shame."

The effort to get a complete picture of what happened at Abu Ghraib evolved into a sprawling set of related investigations, some of them hastily put together, including inquiries into dozens of suspicious deaths throughout the Army prison system. Investigators concerned with the role played not only by military and intelligence officials but also by C.I.A. agents and private-contract employees like the Iraqi interpreters. In a statement, the C.I.A. acknowledged that its Inspector General had an investigation under way into abuses at Abu Ghraib, which extended to the death of a prisoner, an Iraqi inmate named Manadel al-Jamadi. A photograph of Jamadi, depicting his battered body packed in ice, has circulated around the world.

In a letter to his family, Frederick wrote that in November 2003, an Iraqi prisoner (later identified as Jamadi) under the control of what the Abu Ghraib guards called "O.G.A.," or other government agencies—that is, the C.I.A. and its paramilitary employees—was brought to his unit for questioning. "They stressed him out so bad that the man passed away. They put his body in a body bag and packed him in ice for approximately twenty-four hours in the shower. . . . The next day the medics came and put his body on a stretcher, placed a fake IV in his arm and took him away." The dead Iraqi was never entered into the prison's inmate control system, Frederick recounted, "and therefore never had a number."

Subsequent testimony in the Abu Ghraib proceedings bore out much of Frederick's account. One witness, Specialist Bruce Brown, who was not a suspect, told of spraying "air freshener to cover the scent" of al-Jamadi's decaying body. Other witnesses testified that C.I.A. agents had delivered al-Jamadi, in a hood, to the prison for interrogation that was conducted—the witnesses disagreed on this—either by the C.I.A. operatives or by the C.I.A. and officers from military intelligence. After al-Jamadi's death, another witness testified, Colonel Pappas, the senior commander of military intelligence at Abu Ghraib, was involved in a discussion about what to do with the body. The immediate solution was to pack it in ice. The witness, Captain Donald Reese, commander of one of the involved military police companies, testified that he heard Pappas say at one point, "I'm not going down for this alone." By late July, Army investigators were looking into whether the officers and men participated in a conspiracy to commit murder.

As the international furor over Abu Ghraib grew, senior military officers, and President Bush, insisted that the actions of a few did not reflect the conduct of the military as a whole. Taguba's report, however, amounted to an unsparing study of collective wrongdoing and the failure of Army leadership at the highest levels. The picture he drew of Abu Ghraib was one in which Army regulations and the Geneva Conventions were routinely violated, and in which much of the day-to-day management of the prisoners was abdicated to Army military intelligence units and civilian contract employees.

No amount of apologetic testimony or political spin could mask the fact that, since the attacks of September 11th, President Bush and his top aides have seen themselves as engaged in a war against terrorism in which the old rules did not apply. Interrogating prisoners and getting intelligence, including by intimidation and torture, was the priority.

3. Crossing the Line

The roots of the Abu Ghraib scandal lie not in the criminal inclinations of a few Army reservists, but in the reliance of George Bush and Donald Rumsfeld on secret operations and the use of coercion—and eye-for-an-eye retribution—in fighting terrorism. Rumsfeld's most fateful decision, endorsed by the White House, came at a time of crisis in August 2003, when the defense secretary expanded the highly secret special-access program into the prisons of Iraq. Rumsfeld's decision embittered the American intelligence community, damaged the effectiveness of élite combat units, and hurt the prospects of the United States in the war on terror.

According to interviews with several past and present American intelligence officials, the Pentagon's operation—aspects of which were known inside the intelligence community by several code words, including Copper Green—encouraged physical coercion and sexual humiliation of Iraqi prisoners in an effort to generate more intelligence about the insurgency. A senior C.I.A. official confirmed the details of this account and said that the operation stemmed from Rumsfeld's long-standing desire to wrest control of clandestine and paramilitary operations from the C.I.A.

I was initially told of the SAP's existence by members of the intelligence community who were troubled by the program's prima facie violation of the Geneva Conventions; their concern was that such activities, if exposed, would eviscerate the moral standing of the United States and expose American soldiers to retaliation. After my article on the SAP was published, in May 2004, a ranking member of Congress confirmed its existence and further told me that President Bush had signed the mandated finding officially notifying Congress of the SAP. The legislator added that he had nonetheless been told very little about the program. Only a few members of the House and Senate leadership were authorized by statute to be informed of the program, and, even then, the legislators were provided with little more than basic budget information. It's not clear that the Senate and House members understood that the United States was poised to enter the business of "disappearing" people.

An indication of the importance of such programs to the Administration came from President Bush himself. In June 2002, the Administration took issue with a provision of the annual Pentagon appropriations bill that provided for thirty days advance notice to Congress before the start-up of a new SAP. "Situations may arise, especially in wartime," the White House said in a statement, "in which the President must promptly establish special-access controls on classified national security information." The President didn't get his way, and the thirty-day prohibition remained in the legislation. In October, President Bush, appearing testy, signed the bill, but essentially told the Congress that he could do what he wanted. "The U.S. Supreme Court has stated that the President's authority to classify and control access to information bearing on national security flows from the Constitution and does not depend upon a legislative grant of authority," the President said. He warned that he would construe the legislation "in a manner consistent with the constitutional authority of the President."

Rumsfeld, who testified about Abu Ghraib before the Senate in May, was precluded by law from explicitly mentioning highly secret matters in an unclassified session. But he conveyed the message that he was telling the public all that he knew about the story. He said, "Any suggestion that there is not a full, deep awareness of what has happened, and the damage it has done, I think, would be a misunderstanding." The senior C.I.A. official told me, when I asked about Rumsfeld's testimony and that of Stephen Cambone, his undersecretary for intelligence, "Some people think you can bullshit anyone."

The Abu Ghraib story began, in a sense, just weeks after the September 11th attacks, with the American bombing of Afghanistan. Almost from the start, the Administration's search for Al Qaeda members in the war zone, and its worldwide search for terrorists, came up against major command-and-control problems. For example, combat forces that had Al Qaeda targets in sight had to obtain legal clearance before firing on them. On October 7, 2001, the night the bombing began, an unmanned Predator aircraft tracked an automobile convoy that, American intelligence believed, contained Mullah Muhammad Omar, the Taliban leader. A lawyer on duty at the CENTCOM headquarters in Tampa, Florida, refused to authorize a strike. By the time an attack was approved, the target was out of reach. Rumsfeld was apoplectic over what he saw as a self-defeating hesitation to attack that was due to political correctness. One officer described him to me that fall as "kicking a lot of glass and breaking doors." In November 2001, the *Washington Post* reported that, as many as ten times since early October, Air Force pilots believed they'd had senior Al Qaeda and Taliban members in their sights but had been unable to act in time because of legalistic hurdles. There were similar problems throughout the world, as U.S. Special Forces units seeking to move quickly against suspected terrorist cells were compelled to get prior approval from local American ambassadors and brief their superiors in the chain of command.

After the Abu Ghraib abuses were revealed, a former senior intelligence official with direct information about the SAP gave me an account of how and why the top-secret program had begun. As the American-led hunt for Al Qaeda and Osama bin Laden began to stall, he said, it was clear that the American intelligence operatives in the field were failing to get useful intelligence in a timely manner. Osama bin Laden seemed far out of the reach of the United States. "The White House is asking," the former official recalled, "How can we put this together? We can't get it together." With the pressure mounting, some information was being delivered via the C.I.A. by friendly liaison intelligence services—allies of the United States in the Middle East and Southeast Asia—who were not afraid to get very rough with prisoners. Within a few weeks of the invasion of Afghanistan, the U.S. and allied troops were overwhelmed with prisoners. "We exceeded our capacity for interrogation and detention," the former intelligence official said. "Our allies would tell us," the former official recalled, " 'We pulled out teeth and fingers from a prisoner, but we got some good shit. He's dead now, but we don't care.' " The former official recounted, "The line gets blurred between using liaison officers to bust heads and getting American guys to do it." The tough tactics appealed to Rumsfeld and his senior civilian aides, however.

Rumsfeld then authorized the establishment of the highly secret program, which was given blanket advance approval to kill or capture and, if possible, interrogate high-value targets. The SAP—subject to the Defense Department's most stringent level of security—was set up, with an office in a secure area of the Pentagon. The program would recruit operatives and acquire the necessary equipment, including aircraft, and would keep its activities under wraps. The most successful U.S. intelligence operations during the Cold War had been SAPs, including the Navy's submarine penetration of underwater cables used by the Soviet high command and construction of the Air Force's stealth bomber. All the so-called black programs had one element in common: the secretary of defense, or his deputy, had to conclude that the normal military classification restraints did not provide enough security.

"Rumsfeld's goal was to get a capability in place to take on a high-value target—a standup group to hit quickly," the former senior intelligence official told me. "He got all the agencies together—the C.I.A. and the N.S.A.—to get pre-approval in place. Just say the code word and go." The operation had across-the-board approval from Rumsfeld and from Condoleezza Rice, the national security adviser.

The people assigned to the program worked by the book, the former intelligence official told me. They created code words and recruited, after careful screening, highly trained commandos and operatives from U.S. élite forces—Navy SEALs, the Army's Delta Force, and the C.I.A.'s paramilitary experts. They also asked some basic questions: "Do the people working the problem have to use aliases? Yes. Do we need dead drops for the mail? Yes. No traceability and no budget. And some special-access programs are never fully briefed to Congress."

In theory, the operation enabled the Bush Administration to respond immediately to time-sensitive intelligence: commandos crossed borders without visas and could interrogate terrorism suspects deemed too important for transfer to the military's facilities at Guantánamo. They carried out instant interrogations, often with the help of foreign intelligence services—using force if necessary—at secret C.I.A. detention centers scattered around the world. The intelligence would be relayed to the SAP command center in the Pentagon in real time, and sifted for those pieces of information critical to the "white," or overt, world.

Fewer than two hundred operatives and officials, including

Rumsfeld and General Myers, were "completely read into the program," the former intelligence official said. The goal was to keep the operation protected. "We're not going to read more people than necessary into our heart of darkness," he said. "The rules are 'Grab whom you must. Do what you want.'"

One Pentagon official who was deeply involved in the program was Stephen Cambone, the undersecretary of defense for intelligence. Cambone had worked closely with Rumsfeld in a number of Pentagon jobs since the beginning of the Administration, but this office, to which he was named in March 2003, was new; it was created as part of Rumsfeld's reorganization of the Pentagon. Cambone was unpopular among military and civilian intelligence bureaucrats in the Pentagon, essentially because he had little experience in running intelligence programs. He was known instead for his closeness to Rumsfeld. "Remember *Henry II*—'Who will rid me of this meddlesome priest?'" the senior C.I.A. official said to me with a laugh in May 2004. "Whatever Rumsfeld whimsically says, Cambone will do ten times that much."

Cambone was a strong advocate for war against Iraq. He chafed, as did Rumsfeld, at the C.I.A.'s inability, before the Iraq war, to state conclusively that Saddam Hussein harbored weapons of mass destruction. Cambone, who earned a doctorate in political science from Claremont Graduate University in 1982, had served as staff director for a 1998 committee, headed by Rumsfeld, that warned in its report of an emerging ballistic-missile threat and argued that intelligence agencies should be willing to go beyond the data at hand in their analyses. In the confirmation hearings for his intelligence post, Cambone told the Senate that consumers of intelligence assessments must ask questions of the analysts: "How they arrived at those conclusions and what the sources of the information were." This approach had been championed by Rumsfeld. It had been under attack, however, since the Administration's predictions about Iraq's weapons of mass destruction and the potential for insurgency failed to be realized, and the Pentagon civilians, like Cambone, were being widely accused of politicizing intelligence. (A month after the fall of Baghdad, Cambone was the first senior Pentagon official to publicly claim—wrongly, as it turned out—that a captured Iraqi military truck might be a mobile biological-weapons laboratory.)

Cambone's military assistant, Army Lieutenant General William G. Boykin, was also controversial. In the fall of 2003, he generated unwanted headlines after it was reported that, in a speech at an Oregon church, he had equated the Muslim world with Satan. After the scandal became public, I was repeatedly told that Boykin had been involved, on behalf of Cambone, in the policies that led to the abuse at Abu Ghraib.

Early in his tenure, Cambone provoked a bureaucratic battle within the Pentagon by insisting that he be given control of all special-access programs that were relevant to the war on terror. Those programs, which had been viewed by many in the Pentagon as sacrosanct, were monitored by Kenneth deGraffenreid, who had experience in counterintelligence. Cambone got control, and deGraffenreid subsequently left the Pentagon. Asked for comment on my story in May, a Pentagon spokesman said that he would "not discuss any covert programs" but that Cambone "had no involvement in the decision-making process regarding interrogation procedures in Iraq or anywhere else."

In mid-2003, the special-access program was regarded, at least in the Pentagon, as one of the success stories of the war on terror. "It was an active program," the former senior intelligence official, who has extensive knowledge of special-access programs, told me. The SAP was useful as long as it was under the control "of good, well-trained guys. But politics got involved, and decisions were based on speed, and not patience," the former official said. "It's a Greek tragedy. The guys are asking me, 'When do we start blowing the whistle? When do small transgressions and physical abuse become a bigger offense? When does it cross the line from abuse of prisoners to war crimes?'" he said.

"As this monster begins to take life," the former official recalled, "there's joy in the world. The monster is doing well—real well"—at least from the perspective of those involved who, according to the former officer, began to see themselves as "masters of the universe in terms of intelligence." However, some of the SAP's methods were troubling and could not bear close scrutiny.

"When you're in the heat of it," the former official noted, "guys do strange things that in retrospect they can't explain or condone. Guys are having pangs of conscience now—and they're scared shit-less" of a future investigation. "Once the crisis in Iraq is passed, somebody is going to start blowing the whistle. The good people are beginning to realize what they don't know."

On December 18, 2001, American operatives participated in what amounted to the kidnapping of two Egyptians, Ahmed Agiza and Muhammed al-Zery, who had sought asylum in Sweden. The Egyptians, believed by American intelligence to be linked to Islamic militant groups, were abruptly seized in the late afternoon and flown out of Sweden a few hours later on a U.S. government–leased Gulfstream 5 private jet to Cairo, where they underwent extensive, and brutal, interrogation. "Both were dirty," the former senior intelligence official said, "but it *was* pretty blatant."

The seizure of Agiza and Zery attracted little attention outside of Sweden, despite repeated complaints by human rights groups, until May 2004, when a Swedish television news magazine revealed that the Swedish government had cooperated after being assured that the exiles would not be tortured or otherwise harmed once they were sent to Egypt. Instead, according to the television report, enti-tled *The Broken Promise*, Agiza and Zery, in handcuffs and shackles, were driven to the airport by Swedish and, according to one wit-ness, American agents and turned over at plane-side to a group of

Americans wearing plain clothes whose faces were concealed. At that point, the report noted, "The two prisoners have their clothes cut from their bodies by scissors, without their handcuffs and shackles being loosened. The naked and chained prisoners have a suppository of unknown kind inserted into their anuses, and diapers are put on them. They are forcibly dressed in dark overalls. Their hands and feet are chained to a specially designed harness. On the plane, both men are blindfolded and hooded."

Once in Egypt, Agiza and Zery have reported through Swedish diplomats, family members, and attorneys, they were subjected to repeated torture by electrical shocks distributed by electrodes that were attached to the most sensitive parts of their bodies. Egyptian authorities eventually concluded, according to the documentary, that Zery had few ties to ongoing terrorism, and he was released from jail in October 2003, though he is still under official surveillance. Agiza was acknowledged by his attorneys to have been a member of Egyptian Islamic Jihad, a terrorist group outlawed in Egypt, and also was once close to Ayman al-Zawahiri, who is outranked in Al Qaeda only by Osama bin Laden. In April 2004, he was sentenced to twenty-five years in an Egyptian prison. His attorneys insist, nonetheless, that Agiza cut his ties to Zawahiri a decade ago and had publicly denounced the use of violence by Islamic radicals, including Al Qaeda. No evidence delineating a tie between Agiza and an act of terrorism has been made public.

Fredrik Laurin, a Swedish journalist who worked on *The Broken Promise*, extensively researched the leased Gulfstream jet that was used to ferry Zery and Agiza to Cairo. Laurin told me that he was able to track the aircraft to landings in Pakistan, Kuwait, Egypt, Germany, England, Ireland, Morocco, as well as the Washington, D.C., area. It also made visits to Guantánamo. The company told Laurin that the plane was leased almost exclusively to the U.S. government. Significantly, the records obtained by Laurin indicate that the Gulfstream apparently halted its overseas trips from May 5, 2004—the week after the Abu Ghraib scandal broke—until July 7, when it flew from Dulles Airport in suburban Washington to Cairo.

In public, the Swedish government has continued to maintain that it made the right decision. Kjell Jonsson, Zery's attorney, told me, "They did not tell the truth and so much is being kept secret, even now. I don't get access to the documents I need. Egypt wanted him"—referring to Zery—"but there is a legal procedure. Under Swedish law, if a state asks for extradition, the Swedish government must then ask the Swedish Supreme Court for its opinion. There is a procedure where both parties are heard."

In a statement issued in May 2004, Human Rights Watch urged the United Nations to convene an international inquiry to investigate the role of Sweden, Egypt, and the United States in the abduction and subsequent torture of the two men. "There must be a full accounting," Rachel Denber of Human Rights Watch said. "Otherwise, these cases will send yet another signal that when it comes to the 'war on terror' anything goes—including torture." As of summer 2004, the U.N. Office of the High Commissioner for Human Rights, which has the authority to initiate such an inquiry, had not done so.

International law prohibits the rendition, or forced return of any person, no matter what his status or suspected crime, to a foreign locale where he or she would be at risk of torture or mistreatment. The C.I.A., in testimony before Congress, acknowledged that before 2001 it engaged in about seventy "extraordinary renditions"—those deportations that were deemed too urgent to go through the usual legal process. Since September 11th, the Bush Administration has refused to discuss such forced returns, although there have been many published reports of uncooperative prisoners and others being shipped off to allies for extensive interrogation. During the Senate hearing into Abu Ghraib on May 11, 2004, Senator Edward M. Kennedy, Democrat of Massachusetts, repeatedly sought, without much success, to discuss the issue with Stephen Cambone. It was a dialogue of questions and nonresponsive or carefully caveated, and misleading, answers.

Kennedy cited published reports alleging that U.S. officials had transferred difficult detainees to governments that routinely torture prisoners, and then asked, "Can you assure the committee that the Administration is fully complying with all of the legal requirements and that all reports of U.S. officials engaging in the practice of rendering are false?"

CAMBONE: Sir, to the best of my knowledge, that is a true statement.

KENNEDY: [T]o your knowledge, the United States has not been involved in any rendering, any turning over of any personnel to any other country?

CAMBONE: No, no—you said that they were turned over for torture and mistreatment. We have returned, for example, individuals to the U.K. There may be three or four of them that have been returned from Gitmo.

KENNEDY: Have you turned over, to your knowledge, any suspects to Saudi Arabia, Jordan, Morocco, or Syria to gather information?

CAMBONE: From those people in D.O.D. [Department of Defense] custody, not that I'm aware of, sir . . . if there are, I will come back to you and tell you. As best I know, there are not any persons under our custody that have been transferred.

After the war began, in March 2003, the SAP was involved in a few assignments in Iraq, the former senior intelligence official said. C.I.A. and other American Special Forces operatives secretly teamed up to hunt for Saddam Hussein and—without success—for Iraqi weapons of mass destruction. But they weren't able to stop the evolving insurgency.

In the first months after the fall of Baghdad, Rumsfeld and his aides still had a limited view of the insurgency, seeing it as little more than the work of Baathist "dead-enders," criminal gangs, and foreign terrorists who were Al Qaeda followers. The Administration measured its success in the war by how many of those on its list of the fifty-five most wanted members of the old regime—reproduced on playing cards—had been captured. Then, in August 2003, terror bombings in Baghdad hit the Jordanian embassy, killing nineteen people, and the United Nations headquarters, killing twenty-three people, including Sergio Vieira de Mello, the head of the U.N. mission. On August 25th, less than a week after the U.N. bombing, Rumsfeld acknowledged, in a talk before the Veterans of Foreign Wars, that "the dead-enders are still with us." He went on: "There are some today who are surprised that there are still pockets of resistance in Iraq, and they suggest that this represents some sort of failure on the part of the Coalition. But this is not the case." Rumsfeld compared the insurgents with those true believers who "fought on during and after the defeat of the Nazi regime in Germany." A few weeks later—and five months after the fall of Baghdad—the defense secretary declared, "It is, in my view, better to be dealing with terrorists in Iraq than in the United States."

Inside the Pentagon, there was a growing realization that the war was going badly. The increasingly beleaguered and baffled Army leadership was telling reporters that the insurgents consisted of five thousand Baathists loyal to Saddam Hussein. "When you understand that they're organized in a cellular structure," General Abizaid declared, "that . . . they have access to a lot of money and a lot of ammunition, you'll understand how dangerous they are."

The American military and intelligence communities were having little success in penetrating the insurgency. One internal report prepared for the U.S. military, made available to me, concluded that the insurgents' "strategic and operational intelligence has proven to be quite good." According to the study:

Their ability to attack convoys, other vulnerable targets and particular individuals has been the result of painstaking surveillance
and reconnaissance. Inside information has been passed on to insurgent cells about convoy/troop movements and daily habits of
Iraqis working with coalition from within the Iraqi security services, primarily the Iraqi Police force which is rife with sympathy
for the insurgents, Iraqi ministries and from within pro-insurgent
individuals working with the CPA's so-called Green Zone.

The study concluded, "Politically, the U.S. has failed to date. Insurgencies can be fixed or ameliorated by dealing with what caused
them in the first place. The disaster that is the reconstruction of
Iraq has been the key cause of the insurgency. There is no legitimate government, and it behooves the Coalition Provisional Authority to absorb the sad but unvarnished fact that most Iraqis do
not see the Governing Council"—the Iraqi body appointed by the
C.P.A.—"as the legitimate authority. Indeed, they know that the
true power is the CPA."

By the fall of 2003, a military analyst told me, the extent of the
Pentagon's political and military misjudgments was clear. Rumsfeld's "dead-enders" now included not only Baathists but many marginal figures as well—thugs and criminals who were among the tens
of thousands of prisoners freed the previous fall by Saddam as part
of a prewar general amnesty. Their desperation was not driving the
insurgency; it simply made them easy recruits for those who were.
The analyst said, "We'd killed and captured guys who had been
given two or three hundred dollars to 'pray and spray'"—that is,
shoot randomly and hope for the best. "They weren't really insurgents but down-and-outers who were paid by wealthy individuals
sympathetic to the insurgency." In many cases, the paymasters were
Sunnis who had been members of the Baath Party. The analyst said
that the insurgents "spent three or four months figuring out how we
operated and developing their own countermeasures. If that meant

putting up a hapless guy to go and attack a convoy and see how the American troops responded, they'd do it." Then, the analyst said, "the clever ones began to get in on the action."

By contrast, according to the military report, the American and Coalition forces knew little about the insurgency: "Human intelligence is poor or lacking . . . due to the dearth of competence and expertise. . . . The intelligence effort is not coördinated since either too many groups are involved in gathering intelligence or the final product does not get to the troops in the field in a timely manner." The success of the war was at risk; something had to be done to change the dynamic.

The relationship between military policing and intelligence forces inside the Army prison system had reached a critical point. "This is a fight for intelligence," Brigadier General Martin Dempsey, commander of the 1st Armored Division, told a reporter at a Baghdad press briefing in November 2003. "Do I have enough soldiers? The answer is absolutely yes. The larger issue is, how do I use them and on what basis? And the answer to that is intelligence . . . to try to figure out how to take all this human intelligence as it comes in to us [and] turn it into something that's actionable."

The solution, endorsed by Rumsfeld and carried out by Stephen Cambone, was to get tough with those Iraqi prisoners who were suspected of being insurgents. The Army prison system would now be asked to play its part. A key figure, as we have seen, was Major General Geoffrey Miller, the commander of the detention and interrogation center at Guantánamo, who had been summoned to Baghdad in late August to review prison interrogation procedures. Rumsfeld and Cambone went a step beyond Gitmoizing, however: they expanded the scope of the SAP, bringing its unconventional methods to Abu Ghraib. The commandos were to operate in Iraq as they had in Afghanistan. The male prisoners could be treated roughly and exposed to sexual humiliation.

"They weren't getting anything substantive from the detainees in Iraq," the former intelligence official told me. "No names. Nothing that they could hang their hat on. Cambone says, I've got to crack this thing and I'm tired of working through the normal chain of command. I've got this apparatus set up—the black special-access program—and I'm going in hot. So he pulls the switch, and the electricity begins flowing last summer. And it's working. We're getting a picture of the insurgency in Iraq and the intelligence is flowing into the white world. We're getting good stuff"—so many in the Pentagon believed. "But we've got more targets than people who can handle them."

Cambone then made another crucial decision, the former intelligence official told me: not only would he bring the SAP's rules into the prisons; he would bring some of the Army military intelligence officers working inside the Iraqi prisons under the SAP's auspices. "So here are fundamentally good soldiers—military intelligence guys—being told that no rules apply," the former official said.

In a separate interview, a Pentagon consultant, who spent much of his career directly involved with special-access programs, spread the blame. "The White House subcontracted this to the Pentagon, and the Pentagon subcontracted it to Cambone," he said. "This is Cambone's deal, but Rumsfeld and Myers approved the program." When it came to the interrogation operation at Abu Ghraib, he said, Rumsfeld left the details to Cambone. Rumsfeld may not be personally culpable, the consultant added, "but he's responsible for the checks and balances. The issue is that, since 9/11, we've changed the rules on how we deal with terrorism and created conditions where the ends justify the means."

The pressure to learn about the insurgency mounted as the war foundered. "We're still not getting enough intelligence," the former senior intelligence official said. "So now we get our 'High Value' target lists and the Special Forces are given authority to kill on sight. The guys began to think, 'Shit, if I can shoot him [a high-value target] on the street, why can't I do what I want when he's under my control in prison.' Rank-and-file soldiers—not the Special Forces—are authorized to get tough. The seam between the special high-value targets and the general prison population begins to come apart." Within a few months, "we're bringing Reserve soldiers from Cumberland, Maryland, into the program. It was so bad," he said. "How are these guys from Cumberland going to know anything? The Army Reserve doesn't know what it's doing." The reservists he was referring to were the members of the 372nd Military Police Company.

Who was in charge of Abu Ghraib—whether military police or military intelligence—was no longer the only question that mattered. Hard-core special operatives, some of them with aliases, were working in the prison. The military police assigned to guard the prisoners wore uniforms, but many others—military intelligence officers, contract interpreters, C.I.A. officers, and the men from the special-access program—wore civilian clothes. It was not clear who was who, even to General Karpinski, then the commander of the 800th Military Police Brigade. "I thought most of the civilians there were interpreters, but there were some civilians that I didn't know," Karpinski told me. "I called them the disappearing ghosts. I'd seen them once in a while at Abu Ghraib and then I'd see them months later. They were nice—they'd always call out to me and say, 'Hey, remember me? How are you doing?'" The mysterious civilians, she said, were "always bringing in somebody for interrogation or waiting to collect somebody going out." Karpinski added that she had no idea who was operating in her prison system.

Military intelligence personnel assigned to Abu Ghraib repeatedly wore "sterile," or unmarked, uniforms or civilian clothes while on duty. "You couldn't tell them apart," a source familiar with the investigation said. The blurring of identities and organizations meant that it was impossible for the prisoners, or, significantly, the military policemen on duty, to know who was doing what to whom and who had the authority to give orders.

*   *   *

By fall, according to the former intelligence official, the senior leadership of the C.I.A. had had enough. "They said, 'No way. We signed up for the core program in Afghanistan—pre-approved for operations against high-value terrorist targets. And now you want to use it for cabdrivers, brothers-in-law, and people pulled off the streets'"—the sort of prisoners who populate the Iraqi jails. The C.I.A. balked, the former intelligence official said. "The C.I.A. said, 'We're not going to use our guys to do this. We've been there before,'" during the Vietnam War, when the agency ran the Phoenix assassination program, which spun out of control and led to the death of thousands of civilians. "The agency checks with their lawyers and pulls out," the official said, ending those of its activities in Abu Ghraib that related to the SAP. (In a later conversation, a senior C.I.A. official confirmed this account.)

The C.I.A.'s complaints were echoed throughout the intelligence community. There was fear that the situation at Abu Ghraib would lead to the exposure of the secret SAP, and thereby bring an end to what had been, before Iraq, a valued covert operation. "This was stupidity," a government consultant told me. "You're taking a program that was operating in the chaos of Afghanistan against Al Qaeda, a stateless terror group, and bringing it into a structured, traditional war zone. Sooner or later, the commandos would bump into the legal and moral procedures of a conventional war with an Army of a hundred and thirty-five thousand soldiers."

The former senior intelligence official blamed hubris for the Abu Ghraib disaster. "There's nothing more exhilarating for a pissant Pentagon civilian than dealing with an important national security issue without dealing with military planners, who are always worried about risk," he told me. "What could be more boring than needing the coöperation of logistical planners?" The former intelligence official told me he feared that one of the disastrous effects of the prison-abuse scandal would be the undermining of legitimate operations in the war on terror, which had already suffered from the draining of resources into Iraq. He portrayed Abu Ghraib as "a tumor" on the war on ter-ror. He said, "As long as it's benign and contained, the Pentagon can deal with the photo crisis without jeopardizing the secret program. As soon as it begins to grow, with nobody to diagnose it—it becomes a malignant tumor." He added, "We've never had a case where a special-access program went sour—and this goes back to the Cold War."

The exposure of the conditions at Abu Ghraib, and the inquiry that followed, presented a dilemma for the Pentagon. The C.I.D. had to be allowed to continue, the former intelligence official said. "You can't cover it up. You have to prosecute these guys for being off the reservation," he said, "so you hope that maybe it'll go away." The Pentagon's attitude in January 2004, he said, was "Somebody got caught with some photos. What's the big deal? Take care of it."

"This shit has been brewing for months," the Pentagon consult-ant who has dealt with SAPs told me. "You don't keep prisoners naked in their cell and then let them get bitten by dogs. This is sick." The consultant explained that he and his colleagues, all of whom had served for years on active duty in the military, had been appalled by Abu Ghraib. "We don't raise kids to do things like that. When you go after Mullah Omar, that's one thing. But when you give the authority to kids who don't know the rules, that's another."

4. The Gray Zone

In their testimony before Congress, Rumsfeld and Cambone strug-gled to convince the legislators that Miller's visit to Baghdad in late August had nothing to do with the subsequent abuse. Cambone sought to assure the Senate Armed Services Committee that the in-terplay between General Miller and General Sanchez had only a ca-sual connection to his office. Miller's recommendations, Cambone said, were made to Sanchez. His own role, he said, was mainly to in-sure that the "flow of intelligence back to the commands" was "efficient and effective." He added that Miller's goal was "to provide a safe, secure and humane environment that supports the expeditious collection of intelligence."

It was a hard sell. Senator Hillary Clinton, Democrat of New York, posed the essential question facing the senators:

> If, indeed, General Miller was sent from Guantánamo to Iraq for the purpose of acquiring more actionable intelligence from detainees, then it is fair to conclude that the actions that are at point here in your report [on abuses at Abu Ghraib] are in some way connected to General Miller's arrival and his specific orders, however they were interpreted, by those MPs and the military intelligence that were involved. . . . Therefore, I for one don't believe I yet have adequate information from Mr. Cambone and the Defense Department as to exactly what General Miller's orders were . . . how he carried out those orders, and the connection between his arrival in the fall of '03 and the intensity of the abuses that occurred afterward.

Sometime before the Abu Ghraib abuses became public, the former intelligence official told me, Miller was "read in"—that is, briefed—on the special-access operation. "His job is to save what he can," the former official said. "He's there to protect the program while limiting any loss of core capability."

One puzzling aspect of Rumsfeld's account of his initial reaction to news of the Abu Ghraib investigation was his lack of alarm and lack of curiosity. One factor may have been recent history: there had been many previous complaints of prisoner abuse from organizations like Human Rights Watch and the International Committee of the Red Cross, and the Pentagon had weathered them with ease. Rumsfeld told the Senate Armed Services Committee that he had not been provided with details of alleged abuses until late March, when he read the specific charges. "You read it, as I say, it's one thing. You see these photographs and it's just unbelievable. . . . It wasn't three-dimensional. It wasn't video. It wasn't color. It was quite a different thing." The former intelligence official said that, in his view, Rumsfeld and other senior Pentagon officials had not studied the photographs because "they thought what was in there was permitted under the rules of engagement." Instead, the photographs "turned out to be the result of the program run amok."

The former intelligence official made it clear that he was not alleging that Rumsfeld or General Myers knew that the specific nature of the atrocities in the photographs were committed. But, he said, "it was their permission granted to do the SAP, generically, and there was enough ambiguity, which permitted the abuses."

When I spoke to the former senior intelligence official, after the scandal broke, he said that the SAP was still active, and "the United States is picking up guys for interrogation." The program was protected by the fact that no one on the outside was allowed to know of its existence, and those who talked about it risked losing their clearances, which many retired military and intelligence personnel rely on to get work. In mid-June, the former official said, the Pentagon briefly disbanded the special-access team and, in a few days, reconstituted it, with new code words and new designators. The same rules of engagement were to be applied; suspected terrorists were fair game for the American operatives.

A government consultant with close ties to many conservatives defended the Administration's continued secrecy about the special-access program in Abu Ghraib. "Why keep it black?" the consultant asked. "Because the process is unpleasant. It's like making sausage—you like the result but you don't want to know how it was made. Also, you don't want the Iraqi public, and the Arab world, to know. Remember, we went to Iraq to democratize the Middle East. The last thing you want to do is let the Arab world know how you treat Arab males in prison."

In mid-2003, Rumsfeld's apparent disregard for the requirements of the Geneva Conventions while carrying out the war on terror had led a group of senior military legal officers from the Judge Advocate General's (JAG) Corps to pay two surprise visits within five months to Scott Horton, who was then chairman of the New York City Bar Association's Committee on International Human Rights. "They wanted us to challenge the Bush Administration about its standards for detentions and interrogation," Horton told me in May 2004. "They were urging us to get involved and speak in a very loud voice. It came pretty much out of the blue. The message was that conditions are ripe for abuse, and it's going to occur." The military officials were most alarmed about the growing use of civilian contractors in the interrogation process, Horton recalled. "They said there was an atmosphere of legal ambiguity being created as a result of a policy decision at the highest levels in the Pentagon. The JAG officers were being cut out of the policy formulation process." They told him that, with the war on terror, a fifty-year history of exemplary application of the Geneva Conventions had come to an end.

The mistreatment at Abu Ghraib may have done little to further American intelligence. Willie J. Rowell, who served for thirty-six years as an Army C.I.D. agent, told me that the use of force or humiliation with prisoners is invariably counterproductive. "They'll tell you what you want to hear, truth or no truth," Rowell said. "'You can flog me until I tell you what I know you want me to say.' You don't get righteous information."

Despite the promises of a full investigation into Abu Ghraib, it soon became clear that no one in the Pentagon or the White House wanted the investigation to go further. One of the Administration's early antagonists was, surprisingly, Senator John Warner, chairman of the Armed Services Committee. Warner, seventy-seven years old, was a loyal Republican and a staunch defender of George Bush and his war in Iraq. But he was also a former Marine officer and secretary of the Navy who was outraged by Abu Ghraib. In early May,

Warner had convened public hearings despite pressure from the White House. Warner's immediate targets were General Miller, who had been brought from Guantánamo to run the prison system in Iraq, and Stephen Cambone, who was summoned to testify before the committee on May 11th. In his opening statement, Warner was assured, eloquent, and categorical in his purpose:

> This mistreatment of prisoners represents an appalling and totally unacceptable breach of military regulations and conduct. The damage done to the reputation and credibility of our nation and the armed forces has the potential to undermine substantial gains and the sacrifices by our forces and their families and those of our allies fighting with us in the cause of freedom. . . .
>
> There must be a full accounting for the cruel and disgraceful abuse of Iraqi detainees consistent with our law and protections of the Uniform Military Code of Justice . . . I think it is important to confront these problems swiftly, assuring that justice is done and take the corrective action so that such abuses never happen again.

He didn't succeed. The problems weren't confronted, and no independent Committee investigation was authorized into the policies that led to Abu Ghraib. Warner had begun to backtrack. Within a few weeks, Democratic staff members were complaining about cover-up and egregious displays of party loyalty. "He means well," a Democratic Senate aide told me, speaking of Warner, "but people have convinced him that this will damage national security." (Warner also told an associate that the Pentagon had assured him that "the bad stuff was over" and the military leadership had it "under control.")

In a telephone interview, Warner acknowledged that "There's been a lot of pressure on me," but he said the Committee would continue its hearings. "I've had five public and five closed hearings since May," he said, "and we may have outside witnesses." At the time I first wrote about the secret program in *The New Yorker*, Lawrence Di Rita, a Pentagon spokesman, said, in a statement, that "No responsible official of the Department of Defense approved any program that could conceivably have been intended to result in such abuses as witnessed in the recent photos and videos." (It was a nondenial denial; *The New Yorker* article had not suggested that the SAP was created with the intent of producing the abuses seen in Abu Ghraib.) Warner told me that Donald Rumsfeld and other officials had repeated their denials to him. A Democratic aide subsequently explained that generally, in their classified testimony, Rumsfeld, Cambone, and others in the Bush Administration have not told the Armed Services Committee members much more than they've told the public, and that the senators had not pushed them to do so.

The always affable and gracious Warner is immensely popular with Democrats and Republicans in the intelligence community, the military, and the Senate. "He knows that people in the chain of command were culpable," the former senior intelligence official told me, "but he's drifting, and he wants to go down as the guy who doesn't read other people's mail. The stakes are too high. He'd rather have some bad guys and perpetrators go free than put national security at risk."

The Democratic senators and staff members of the Armed Services Committee quickly realized that the investigation into Abu Ghraib would be pro forma. In early May, when Rumsfeld appeared before the committee to express his dismay at the abuses, he had promised to provide committee members with all of the confidential Red Cross reports on the prison system in Iraq. The Pentagon dallied for ten weeks before delivering the documents to a secure committee room and then requiring that access to them be limited to senators only. No aides could join their senators, even those with top-security clearances, although by then many of the salient details of the Red Cross conclusions had been published in the *Wall Street Journal*. "I wrote a cover-up memo two months ago," a committee aide told me. In it, he said, he had explained to his senator that there was "no way the committee is going to do a good job. It took ten weeks to look at the Red Cross stuff? It was obvious to me that it was a trial balloon"—in other words, the Pentagon, which had been ordered by the committee to produce far more sensitive materials, was taking a measure of the senators' will. "They're setting markers for future stuff and they wanted to see how much we resisted."

Any doubt about Senator Warner's intentions ended in mid-July when he told reporters that he would not call any more witnesses until the Army completed the prosecutions of the military policemen at Abu Ghraib. At that point, the six remaining courts-martial weren't expected to begin trial until October 2004 at the earliest—assuring that future Abu Ghraib Senate hearings would not be held until after the presidential elections. There was little outcry. A week later, the committee was called to order to hear testimony from Lieutenant General Paul T. Mikolashek, the Army Inspector General who had completed one of many pending Pentagon investigations into the treatment of prisoners of war. Mikolashek, despite the evidence before him, somehow found that the demonstrated prisoner abuses in Iraq and Afghanistan were "not representative of policy, doctrine or soldier training. These abuses were unauthorized actions taken by a few individuals, coupled with the failure of a few leaders to provide adequate monitoring, supervision, and leadership." The report was challenged by a few Democratic senators and dismissed as a "whitewash" in editorials in the *New York Times* and the *Washington Post*, but there was little newspaper follow-up and, sadly, no public criticism from within the Army, although officers I talked to privately viewed the report with embarrassment. ("Nobody believes that," one experienced intelligence officer, who served in a sensitive post in Iraq, told me.) Many Republicans eagerly took the report at face value, in the hope that the nation had moved on. "This senator never doubted for a minute, and said so repeatedly at home and here, that no senior leader in the U.S. Army or in the government . . . would tolerate inhumanity or cruelty to prisoners,"

Senator James Talent, Republican of Missouri, told General Miko-lashek. "I never doubted it for a minute, and I am not surprised that that is what you concluded."

Another committee aide told me that none of the Democrats had been given an opportunity to review the Mikolashek report before the hearings. "If you were really aggressive about it, you wouldn't have anybody testify without the staff interviewing him first," the aide added. "To break through this Administration would take a concerted effort by a committee majority"—something that, given the Repub-lican control of the committee, wasn't about to happen.

In July 2004, I again spoke to Scott Horton, who has maintained contact with a network of JAG lawyers. He told me that Rumsfeld and his civilian deputies were pressuring the Army to conclude the pending investigations by late August, before the Republican Con-vention in New York. Horton added that the politics were blatant. Pentagon investigations, he said, "have a reputation for tending to whitewash, but even taking this into account, the current investiga-tions seem to be setting new standards." Rumsfeld's office had cir-cumscribed the investigators' charge and also placed tight controls on the documents to be made available. In other words, Horton said, "Rumsfeld has completely rigged the investigations. My friends say we should expect something much akin to the Army IG report—'just a few rotten apples.'"

Abu Ghraib won't go away, whether or not hearings take place. The Bush Administration's decisions regarding the treatment of prisoners have had enormous consequences: for the imprisoned civilian Iraqis, many of whom had nothing to do with the growing insurgency; for the integrity of the Army; and for the United States' reputation in the world.

———

In their dealings with outsiders about prison abuse, White House officials had a ready explanation: Someone in the military didn't get the message. In late May 2004, as the world was awash in the news from Abu Ghraib, Kenneth Roth, the executive director of Human Rights Watch, had a second disheartening meeting with Rice and John Bellinger, the N.S.C. attorney. The problem, Rice made clear, according to Roth's notes, was not the President's policies, which explicitly ruled out such abuse, but the "implementation of policy. There's obvious confusion in the military," Rice told Roth. "There's a need to clarify whether there's a need for better training, and there must be accountability"—not in the White House, again, but inside the military. "The military leadership," Rice added, "needs to learn where the breakdown was."

Torture, as the White House defined it, was not an option, the President had said, but Rice refused to be drawn into a discussion about what other interrogation techniques could be out of bounds. "The Administration can't overthrow the whole detention and interrogation facility," Rice said, according to Roth's notes.

"To this day," Roth said in late July 2004, "they cling to the fiction that there is a realm of coercion that does not violate the international prohibition against torture. Until the Administration formally abandons all forms of coercive interrogation, it is inviting the abuse that has become standard fare since September 11th."

Earlier, Roth had told me, "In an odd way, the sexual abuses at Abu Ghraib have become a diversion for the prisoner abuse and the violation of the Geneva Conventions that is authorized." Since September 11th, Roth added, the military has systematically used third-degree techniques around the world on detainees. "Some JAGs hate this and are horrified that the tolerance of mistreatment will come back and haunt us in the next war," Roth said. "We're giving the world a ready-made excuse to ignore the Geneva Conventions. Rumsfeld has lowered the bar."

The senior Pentagon consultant, who spent years in uniform, was in agreement with Kenneth Roth. The President, Rumsfeld, and Cambone, he said, "created the conditions that allowed transgressions to take place." He feared that Abu Ghraib had sent the message that the Pentagon was unable to handle its discretionary power. "When the shit hits the fan, as it did on 9/11, how do you push the pedal?" the consultant asked. "You do it selectively and with intelligence."

"You have to demonstrate that there are checks and balances in the system," he said. "When you live in a world of gray zones, you have to have very clear red lines."

II.

INTELLIGENCE FAILURE

1. How America's Spies Missed September 11th

During my three years of reporting on September 11th and its aftermath, one consistent theme has been a lack of timely and reliable intelligence about the other side—the Al Qaeda terrorists who planned and executed the hijackings, the Taliban in Afghanistan, and the insurgents who turned the neoconservatives' dreams about Iraq into a reality of daily violence and casualties. The problems were apparent long before the summer of 2004, when the 9/11 Commission and the Senate Intelligence Committee published their critiques. The intelligence community didn't have the essential information when it counted—in real time.

In late September 2001, after two weeks of around-the-clock investigation into the terrorist attacks on the World Trade Center and the Pentagon, the intelligence community was confused, divided, and unsure about how the terrorists operated, how many there were, and what they might do next. There was consensus on two issues, however: the attacks were brilliantly planned and executed, and the intelligence community was in no way prepared to stop them.

On September 23, 2001, Colin Powell told a television interviewer that "we will put before the world, the American people, a persuasive case" showing that Osama bin Laden was responsible for the attacks. "We are putting all of the information that we have together, the intelligence information, the information being generated by the F.B.I. and other law-enforcement agencies." But the widely anticipated white paper never appeared. The Administration justified the delay by telling the press that most of the information was classified and could not yet be released. A senior C.I.A. official told me at the time that the intelligence community had not yet developed enough solid information about the terrorists' operations, financing, and planning. "One day we'll know, but at the moment we don't know," the official said.

In those first chaotic days, investigators split into at least two factions. One, centered in the F.B.I., believed that the terrorists may not have been "a cohesive group," as one involved official put it, before they started training and working together on this operation. "These guys look like a pickup basketball team," he said. "A bunch of guys who got together." The F.B.I. was still trying to sort out the identities and backgrounds of the hijackers, and at that point the fact was, the official acknowledged, "we don't know much about them."

Initially, these investigators suspected that the suicide teams were simply lucky. "In your wildest dreams, do you think they thought they'd be able to pull off four hijackings?" the official asked. "Just taking out one jet and getting it into the ground would have been a success. These are not supermen." He argued that the most important advantage the hijackers had had, aside from the element of surprise, was history: in the past, most hijackings had ended up landing safely at a Third World airport, so pilots had been trained to coöperate.

The other view, centered in the Pentagon and the C.I.A., credited the hijackers with years of advance planning and practice and a deliberate after-the-fact disinformation campaign. "These guys were below everybody's radar—they're professionals," an official told me shortly after the attacks. "There's no more than five or six in a cell. Three men will know the plan; three won't know. They've been 'sleeping' out there for years and years." One military planner told me that many of his colleagues believed that the terrorists "went to ground and pulled phone lines" well before September 11th—that is, concealed traces of their activities. It was widely believed that the terrorists had a support team, and the fact that the F.B.I. was unable to track down fellow conspirators who were left behind in the United States immediately was seen as further evidence of careful planning. "Look," one person familiar with the investigation said, "if it were as simple and straightforward as a lucky one-off oddball operation, then the seeds of confusion would not have been sown as they were."

Many of the investigators wondered if some of the first clues that were uncovered about the terrorists' identities and preparations, such as flight manuals, were meant to be found. A former high-level intelligence official speculated at the time that "Whatever trail was left was left deliberately—for the F.B.I. to chase."

The attacks called into question what investigators thought they knew about Osama bin Laden's capabilities. "This guy sits in a cave in Afghanistan and he's running this operation?" one C.I.A. official asked. "It's so huge. He couldn't have done it alone." A senior military officer told me that because of the visas and other documentation needed to infiltrate team members into the United States, investigators were asking whether a major foreign intelligence service might also have been involved. "To get somebody to fly an airplane—to kill himself," the officer added, raised the possibility that "somebody paid his family a hell of a lot of money." A Justice Department official told me, "We're still running a lot of stuff out," adding that the F.B.I. has been inundated with leads.

"To me," the senior C.I.A. official added, "the scariest thing is that these guys"—the terrorists—"got the first one free. They knew that the standard operating procedure in an aircraft hijacking was to play for time. And they knew for sure that after this the security on airplanes was going to go way up. So whatever they've planned for the next round they had in place already."

The concern about a second attack was repeated by others involved in the investigation. Some in the F.B.I. suspected that the terrorists were following a war plan devised by the convicted conspirator Ramzi Ahmed Yousef, who was believed to have been the mastermind of the 1993 World Trade Center bombing. Yousef was involved in plans that called for, among other things, the releasing of poisons in the air and the bombing of the tunnels between New York City and New Jersey. The government's concern about the potential threat from hazardous-waste haulers was heightened by the Yousef case.

"Do they go chem/bio in one, two, or three years?" one senior general asked rhetorically. "We must now make a difficult transition from reliance on law enforcement to the preëmptive. That part is hard. Can we recruit enough good people?" In the years leading to September 11th, he said, "we've been hiring kids out of college who are computer geeks." He continued, "This is about going back to deep, hard dirty work, with tough people going down dark alleys with good instincts."

The C.I.A. of 2001 was not up to the job. Since the breakup of the Soviet Union, a decade earlier, the C.I.A. had become increasingly bureaucratic and unwilling to take risks, and had promoted officers who shared such values. ("The consciousness of kind," one former officer said.) It had steadily reduced its reliance on overseas human intelligence and cut the number of case officers abroad—members of the clandestine service, now known formally as the Directorate of Operations, or D.O., whose mission includes the recruitment of spies. (It used to be called the "dirty tricks" department.) Instead, the agency had relied on liaison relationships—reports from friendly intelligence services and police departments around the world—and on technical collection systems.

It wouldn't be easy to put agents back in the field. During the Cold War, the agency's most important mission was to recruit spies from within the Soviet Union's military and its diplomatic corps. C.I.A. agents were assigned as diplomatic or cultural officers at American embassies in major cities, and much of their work could be done at diplomatic functions and other social events. For an agent with such cover, the consequence of being exposed was usually nothing more than expulsion from the host country and temporary reassignment to a desk in Washington. Now, in Afghanistan or anywhere in the Middle East or South Asia, a C.I.A. operative would have to speak the local language and be able to blend in to be effective. The operative should seemingly have nothing to do with any Americans, or with the American Embassy, if there was one. The status is known inside the agency as "nonofficial cover," or NOC. Exposure could mean death.

At the time of the attacks, it's possible that there wasn't a single such officer operating today inside Islamic fundamentalist circles. In an essay published in the summer of 2001 in *The Atlantic*, Reuel Marc Gerecht, who served for nearly a decade as a case officer in the C.I.A.'s Near East Division, quoted one C.I.A. man as saying, "For Christ's sake, most case officers live in the suburbs of Virginia. We don't do that kind of thing." Another officer told Gerecht, "Operations that include diarrhea as a way of life don't happen."

The C.I.A.'s reputation was further undermined, after September 11th, by what proved to have been a series of wildly optimistic claims about the effectiveness of the agency's Counter Terrorism Center, which was set up in 1986 after a wave of international bombings, airplane hijackings, and kidnappings. The idea was to bring together experts from every American police agency, including the Secret Service, into a "fusion center," which would coördinate intelligence data on terrorism. In October 1998, after four men linked to bin Laden were indicted for their role in the bombings at the American embassies in Tanzania and Kenya, reporters for *Newsweek* were given a tour of the center. The indictments, *Newsweek* reported, "were intended as a clear message to bin Laden and his fugitive followers: the United States knows who they are and where to find them. . . . The story of how the C.I.A. and F.B.I., once bitter bureaucratic rivals, collaborated to roll up bin Laden's elusive network is a tale of state-of-the-art sleuthing—and just plain luck."

But in fact the C.T.C. was not authorized to recruit or handle agents overseas—that task was left to the D.O. and its stations in the Middle East, which had their own priorities. In 1986, Robert Baer, an Arabic speaker who was considered perhaps the best on-the-ground field officer in the Middle East, was drafted into the Counter Terrorism Center shortly after it was set up by its director, Duane ("Dewey") Clarridge. In his memoir, *See No Evil*, published in January 2002, Baer depicts what happened after he arrived, fresh from an assignment as a case officer in Khartoum:

> The first few months serving as a foot soldier in Dewey's war against terrorism were about as exhilarating as the spy business gets. . . . Dewey had a new presidential finding—authority to pretty much do anything he wanted against the terrorists. He had all the money he wanted. . . . It wasn't long before the politics of intelligence undermined everything Dewey tried to do. . . . It was too risky. A botched—or even a successful—operation would piss off a friendly foreign government. Someone might be thrown out of his cushy post, and sent home. Someone might even get killed. . . .
>
> We'd ask [the C.I.A. station in] Bonn to recruit a few Arabs and Iranians to track the Middle East émigré community in West Germany, and it would respond it didn't have enough officers. Once, we asked Beirut to meet a certain agent traveling to Lebanon, and it refused because of some security problem. Security was never *not* a problem in Beirut, for God's sake. Instead of fighting terrorists, we were fighting bureaucratic inertia, an implacable enemy. . . . After six months, [Dewey] could put his hands on only two Arabic speakers, one of whom was me.

In his memoir, Baer, who was awarded a Career Intelligence Medal after his resignation, also describes the "fatal malaise" that came over the Paris station of the C.I.A. in the early 1990s: new agents weren't being recruited, and "agents already on our books had lost their access, and no one seemed to care." C.I.A. surveillance apartments were closed and wiretaps turned off throughout the Middle East and Europe. "We'll never know the losses we had in terms of not capitalizing on the Soviet collapse," a retired official said. Former high-level Soviet officials with intelligence information or other data were rebuffed. "Walk-ins were turned away. It was stunning, and, as far as I knew, nobody fought it."

Little changed when Bill Clinton took office. The C.T.C. was bolstered with more money and more manpower after the World Trade Center bombing in 1993, but it remained a paper-shuffling unit whose officers were not required to be proficient in foreign languages. Baer, now assigned, at his request, to the tiny C.I.A. outpost in Dushanbe, Tajikistan, near the Afghanistan border, watched helplessly as Saudi-backed Islamic fundamentalists—the precursors of the Taliban—consolidated training bases and began to recruit supporters and run operations inside the frontier nations of the former Soviet Union.

Many of the C.I.A.'s old hands told me, in conversations soon after September 11th, that the C.T.C., despite its high profile, had not been an assignment of choice for a young and ambitious D.O. officer. The C.T.C. and two of the other major intelligence centers—dealing with narcotics and nuclear-nonproliferation issues—were so consumed by internecine warfare that the professional analysts found it difficult to do their jobs. "They're all fighting among each other," said one senior manager who took early retirement and whose last assignment was as the director of one of the centers. "There's no concentration on issues."

In 1995, the agency was widely criticized after the news came out that a paid informant in Guatemala had been involved in the murders of an American innkeeper and the Guatemalan husband of an American lawyer. The informant had been kept on the C.I.A. payroll even though his activities were known to the Directorate of Operations. John Deutch, the C.I.A.'s third director in three years, responded to the abuses, and to the public outcry, by issuing a directive calling for prior approval from headquarters before any person with criminal or human rights problems could be recruited. The approval, Deutch later explained, was to be based on a simple balancing test: "Is the potential gain in intelligence worth the cost that might be associated with doing business with a person who may be a murderer?"

The "scrub order," as it came to be known, was promulgated by Deutch and his colleagues with the best of intentions, and included provisions for case-by-case review. But in practice hundreds of "assets" were indiscriminately stricken from the C.I.A.'s payroll, with a devastating effect on anti-terrorist operations in the Middle East.

The scrub order led to the creation of a series of screening panels at C.I.A. headquarters. Before a new asset could be recruited, a C.I.A. case officer had to seek approval from a senior review panel. "It was like a cardiologist in California deciding whether a surgeon in New York City could cut a chest open," a former officer recalled. Potential agents were being assessed by officials who had no firsthand experience in covert operations. ("Americans hate intelligence—just hate it," Robert Baer recalls thinking.) In the view of the operations officers, the most important weapons in the war against international terrorism were being evaluated by men and women who, as one of the retired officers put it, "wouldn't drive to a D.C. restaurant at night because they were afraid of the crime problem."

Other bureaucratic panels began "multiplying like rabbits, one after another," a former station chief said. Experienced officers who were adamant about continuing to recruit spies found that obtaining approval before making a pitch had become a matter of going from committee to committee. "In the old days, they'd say, 'Go get them,'" the retired officer said. Yet another review process, known as A.V.S.—the asset validation system—was put in place. Another retired officer told me, "You'd have to write so much paper that guys would spend more time in the station writing reports than out on the street."

"It was mindless," a third officer said. "Look, we recruited assholes. I handled bad guys. But we don't recruit people from the Little Sisters of the Poor—they don't know anything." He went on: "What we've done to ourselves is criminal. There are a half-dozen good guys out there trying to keep it together."

"It did make the workday a lot easier," Robert Baer said of the edict. "I just watched CNN. No one cared." The C.I.A.'s vital South Group, made up of eight stations in Central Asia—all threatened by fundamentalist organizations, especially in Uzbekistan and Tajikistan, with links to the Taliban and bin Laden—had no agents by the mid-1990s, Baer said. "The agency was going away."

Unlike many senior officials at C.I.A. headquarters, Baer had lived undercover, in the 1980s, in Beirut and elsewhere in the Middle East, and he well understood the ability of terrorist organizations to cover their tracks. He told me that when the C.I.A. started to go after Islamic Jihad, a radical Lebanese group linked to a series of kidnappings in the Reagan years, the group's "people systematically went through documents all over Beirut, even destroying student records. They had the airport wired and could pick the Americans out. They knew whom they wanted to kidnap before he landed." The terrorists coped with the American ability to intercept conversations worldwide by constantly changing codes—often doing little more than changing the meanings of commonly used phrases. "There's a professional cadre out there," Baer said. Referring to the terrorists who struck on September 11th, he said, "These people are so damned good."

By 2001, the Directorate of Operations had been badly hurt by a series of resignations and retirements among high-level people, including four men whose names were little known to the public but who were widely respected throughout the agency: Douglas Smith, who spent thirty-one years in the clandestine service; William Lofgren, who at his retirement in 1996, was chief of the Central Eurasia Division; David Manners, who was chief of station in Amman, Jordan, when he left the agency in 1998; and Robert Baer, who left in 1997. All four repeatedly met with legislators and their staffs and testified before Congress in an effort to bring about changes, as did others. But nothing was done.

As it tried to respond to September 11th, the C.I.A. didn't have enough qualified case officers to staff its many stations and bases around the world. Two retired agents were brought back on a rotating basis to take temporary charge of the small base in Karachi, Pakistan, a focal point for terrorist activity. (Karachi was the site of the murder, in 1995, of two Americans, one of them a C.I.A. employee, allegedly in retaliation for the arrest in Pakistan of Ramzi Ahmed Yousef.) A retired agent was also running the larger C.I.A. station in Dacca, Bangladesh, a Muslim nation that could be a source of recruits. Other retirees ran C.I.A. stations in Africa.

Many people in the intelligence community, in their conversations with me after September 11th, complained bitterly about how difficult it was to work with the D.O., even during a crisis. "In order to work on a problem with D.O., you have to be in D.O.," a former senior scientist said. Other intelligence sources told me that the D.O.'s machinations led, at one point, to a feud with the National Security Agency over who would control the Special Collection Service, a joint undertaking of the two agencies that deploys teams of electronics specialists around the world to monitor diplomatic and other communications in moments of crisis. The S.C.S.'s highly secret operations, which produced some of the Cold War's most valuable data, were usually run from secure sites inside American embassies. Competence and sophistication were hindered by an absurd amount of bickering. A military man who was involved in a Middle East signals-intelligence operation in 1998 told me that he was not able to discuss the activity with representatives of the C.I.A. and the N.S.A. at the same time. "I used to meet with one in a safe house in Virginia, break for lunch, and then meet with the other," the officer said. "They wouldn't be in the same room."

"We'll never solve the terrorism issue until we reconstitute the D.O.," a former senior clandestine officer told me. "The first line of defense, and the most crucial line of defense, is human intelligence."

Faced with the failure to prevent the September 11th attacks, some members of the intelligence community I spoke to in the fall of 2001 were already raising questions about what lengths the C.I.A. should go to. In an interview, two former operations officers cited the tactics used in the late 1980s by the Jordanian security service, in its successful effort to bring down Abu Nidal, the Palestinian who led what was at the time "the most dangerous terrorist organization in existence," according to the State Department. Abu Nidal's group was best known for its role in two bloody gun and grenade attacks on check-in desks for El Al, the Israeli airline, at the Rome and Vienna airports in December 1985. At his peak, Abu Nidal threatened the life of King Hussein of Jordan—whom he called "the pygmy king"—and the king responded, according to the former intelligence officers, by telling his state security service, "Go get them."

The Jordanians did not move directly against suspected Abu Nidal followers but seized close family members instead—mothers and brothers. The Abu Nidal suspect would be approached, given a telephone, and told to call his mother, who would say, according to one C.I.A. man, "Son, they'll take care of me if you don't do what they ask." (To his knowledge, the official carefully added, all the suspects agreed to talk before any family members were actually harmed.) By the early 1990s, the group was crippled by internal dissent and was no longer a significant terrorist organization. (Abu

Nidal, who was in poor health, moved to Baghdad, where he died, an apparent suicide, in August 2002.) "Jordan is the one nation that totally succeeded in penetrating a group," the official added. "You have to get their families under control."

The official insisted that, when it came to bin Laden and his accomplices, "We need to do this—knock them down one by one. Are we serious about getting rid of the problem—instead of sitting around making diversity quilts?"

Such tactics defy the American rule of law, of course, and the C.I.A.'s procedures, and many experts doubt that they are even effective. Over the next few months, nonetheless, as Osama bin Laden and his operatives proved to be exceptionally elusive, Donald Rumsfeld and other civilian leaders in the Pentagon would increasingly come to share the belief that extraordinary means—actions that, in their view, were above the law—were required to deal with terrorism.

———

A few days after the attacks, Vice President Dick Cheney defended the C.I.A.'s director, George Tenet, on television, saying that it would be a "tragedy" to look for "scapegoats." President Bush subsequently added a note of support with a visit to C.I.A. headquarters. In an interview a week later, one top C.I.A. official also defended Tenet. "We know there's a lot of Monday-morning quarterbacking going on, but people don't understand the conditions that George inherited," he told me. "You can't penetrate a six-man cell when they're brothers and cousins—no matter how much Urdu you know." The official acknowledged that there was much dissatisfaction with the C.I.A.'s performance, but he said, "George has not gotten any word other than that the President has full confidence in him." He went on: "George wouldn't resign in a situation like this."

One Republican member of the Senate Intelligence Committee staff said soon after the attacks, however, that Senator Richard C.

Shelby of Alabama, who was the committee's chairman until early 2001, was convinced that the problem was at the top of the agency, and with Tenet. "We do have guys in the field with great ideas who are not supported by the establishment," the staff member said. But before September 11th none of the senior Democrats on the committee, he said, wanted to embarrass the director, George Tenet, by holding an inquiry or hearings into the various complaints. (Tenet had spent years working for the Democrats on the committee staff, and had served as a member of Bill Clinton's National Security Council staff before joining the C.I.A.'s management team.) One Democrat, however, blamed the process within the Senate committee, which, he said, neglected terrorism in favor of more politically charged issues. "Tenet's been briefing about bin Laden for years, but we weren't organized to consider what are threats to the United States. We're chasing whatever the hell is in the news at the moment."

In June 2001, Shelby, after a tour of the Persian Gulf and a series of intelligence briefings, told a *Washington Post* reporter that bin Laden was "on the run, and I think he will continue to be on the run, because we are not going to let up." He went on, "I don't think you could say he's got us hunkered down. I believe he's more hunkered down." After the 9/11 attacks, however, Shelby was among the first to suggest publicly that it was time for Tenet to go. "I think he's a good man, and he's done some good things, but there have been a lot of failures on his watch," Shelby told *USA Today*. Tenet, he said, lacked "the stature to control all the agencies. In a sense, he is in charge, but in reality he's not."

One friend and former colleague of Tenet's said that his refusal to urge the Senate leadership to deal with the hard issues was symptomatic of his problems as C.I.A. director. "He's a politician, too," that person said of Tenet. "That's why he shouldn't have been there, because he had no status to tell the senators, 'You don't know what you're talking about.'"

There were many officials in Washington who believed, in September 2001, that Tenet's days were numbered. "They've told him he's on his way out," one official said then. "He's trying to figure it out—whether to go gracefully or let it appear as if he's going to be fired." Even one of Tenet's close friends told me, "He's history." A White House adviser explained Cheney's public endorsement of Tenet that month by saying, "In Washington, your friends always stab you in the chest. Somebody has to take the blame for this." It was his understanding, he added, that "after a decent interval—whenever they get some traction on the problem—he will depart. I've heard three to six months."

It didn't happen. Tenet stayed on the job, and publicly loyal to George Bush, until June 2004, when he announced his resignation. I was told by his professional friends that family reasons—Tenet wanted to spend more time with his teenage son—were a major factor in his decision. But his friends also acknowledged that Tenet was aware that his reputation had been permanently scarred by the widespread belief, in and out of the agency, that in his dealings with the White House he had been far too deferential about Iraq. In other words, they believed that he had not played it straight. Tenet's resignation also came a few weeks before two reports, by the Senate Intelligence Committee and the bipartisan National Commission on Terrorist Attacks Upon the United States, were to be made public. (The 9/11 Commission, as it was called, had been created in November 2002 over initial objections from the White House.) Both reports were highly critical of the C.I.A.'s performance.

Former Senator Bob Kerrey of Nebraska, who served for four years as the Intelligence Committee's ranking Democrat before joining the 9/11 Commission, was initially one of Tenet's defenders. But Kerrey eventually told me that he no longer knew "how well we did our job" of legislative oversight. "Nobody with any responsibility can walk away from this. We missed something here."

Kerrey remained angry about U.S. policy toward Afghanistan in the years after its defeat of the Soviet Union. "The Cold War was over, and we shut down Afghanistan"—that is, virtually ceased intelligence operations. "From Bush to Clinton, what happened is one of the most embarrassing American foreign policy decisions, as bad as Vietnam," Kerrey said. He cited a botched 1996 C.I.A. plot to overthrow President Saddam Hussein of Iraq: "We also had a half-baked Iraqi operation and sent a signal that we're not serious."

Kerrey later brought his complaints to the televised hearings of the 9/11 Commission, where he emerged as the Commission's most caustic public questioner of the Bush Administration's handling of foreign policy and intelligence issues. He was especially effective in challenging witnesses about the attention they paid, or did not pay, to early warnings about the Al Qaeda threat.

2. Why the Government Didn't Know What It Knew

Colin Powell's promised white paper, if it had ever appeared, could have included an account of the top-secret Presidential Daily Brief given to President Bush on August 6, 2001, describing what was known about Al Qaeda's plans to attack American targets. The P.D.B., prepared by the C.I.A. at the President's request, was entitled "Bin Laden Determined to Strike in U.S." It warned that Al Qaeda hoped to "bring the fighting to America." But in October 2002, when evidence of bin Laden's involvement was made public—by proxy, in a white paper issued by the British prime minister, Tony Blair—there was no mention of the pre-attack warnings. In fact, the British paper stated, incorrectly, that no such information had been available before the attacks: "After 11 September we learned that, not long before, Bin Laden had indicated he was about to launch a major attack on America."

In addition to the August briefing, there was a prescient memorandum sent in July to F.B.I. headquarters from the Phoenix office warning of the danger posed by Middle Eastern students at American flight schools (Robert Mueller, the F.B.I. director, did not see the memo until a few days after September 11th), and there was what Condoleezza Rice, the President's national security adviser, called "a lot of chatter in the system."

The warnings about bin Laden's intentions and the worries about flight schools were not enough to spell out what would happen on September 11th. Nonetheless, the White House chose to keep secret the extent of what it did know in the months before the hijackings. What the President knew and when he knew it wasn't the only relevant question, however. The F.B.I., the C.I.A., and the other U.S. intelligence agencies have yet to effectively address what may be the most important challenge of September 11th: How does an open society deal with warnings of future terrorism? The Al Qaeda terrorists were there to be seen, but there was no system for seeing them.

One issue was the degree to which Al Qaeda owed its success not just to the failings of the C.I.A. but to the weakness of the F.B.I. and the bureau's chronic inability to synthesize intelligence reports, draw conclusions, and work with other agencies. These failings, it turns out, were evident long before George Bush took office.

The complaints about the F.B.I. were well known to the Senate Judiciary Committee, whose then chairman, Patrick Leahy, a Democrat from Vermont, had been urging extensive reform of the bureau for years. "These are not problems of money," Leahy said in July 2001, during confirmation hearings on the appointment of Robert Mueller as the new F.B.I. director. "We have poured a lot of money into the F.B.I. It is a management problem."

The F.B.I.'s computer systems, for example, have been in disarray for more than a decade, making it difficult, if not impossible, for analysts and agents to correlate and interpret intelligence. The

F.B.I.'s technological weakness also hinders its ability to solve crimes. In March 2002, Leahy's committee was told that photographs of the nineteen suspected hijackers could not be sent electronically in the days immediately after September 11th to the F.B.I. office in Tampa, Florida, because the F.B.I.'s computer systems weren't compatible. Robert Chiradio, the special agent in charge, explained at a hearing in March 2002, that "we don't have the ability to put any scanning or multimedia" into F.B.I. computer systems. The photographs had "to be put on a CD-ROM and mailed to me."

Part of the problem, former F.B.I. agents told me, was the longstanding practice by the F.B.I. leadership of "reprogramming" funds intended for computer upgrading. I. C. Smith, who was in charge of the F.B.I.'s budget for national security programs, explained that his department was "constantly raiding the technical programs" to make up for shortfalls in other areas—such as, in one case, the travel budget.

Mueller, who had been on the job for only a week before September 11th, acknowledged in a speech in April 2002 that many of the desktop computers at the F.B.I. were discards from other federal agencies that "we take as upgrades." He went on, "We have systems that cannot talk with other bureau systems, much less with other federal agencies. We're working to create a database . . . that we can use to share information and intelligence with the outside world. We hope to test it later next year"—that is, sometime in 2003. (In June of 2004, the *New York Times* reported that the system would not be fully deployed by the end of the year, and senior officials said they were unable to predict when the completed system would be installed.)

A preliminary 9/11 Commission report issued in 2004 noted that, even then, "Very few [FBI] field agents or analysts have access to Intelink, a worldwide web of information classified at the top secret level." It added, "Basic connectivity is still a problem for some

FBI field offices. The then-acting director of the Washington field office told us last August [of 2003] that he still could not e-mail anyone at the Department of Justice from his desk. He said that the Washington field office, which is the second largest field office in the country, still has only one Internet terminal on each floor."

Clearly, the agents in the field and their superiors at F.B.I. headquarters did not have the optimal tools to cope with the complex world of Middle Eastern terrorism—and the outpouring of intelligence data and warnings about activities inside the United States. The F.B.I. also found it extremely difficult to field undercover operatives inside the Islamic fundamentalist movement. Long after September 11th, the situation remained the same, intelligence officials told me. "They're incapable of it," one former intelligence official said, referring to the F.B.I.'s lack of experience in covert operations. "This is much scarier than the C.I.A.'s inability to penetrate overseas. We don't have eyes and ears in the Muslim communities. We're naked here."

Throughout the spring and early summer of 2001, intelligence agencies flooded the government with warnings of possible terrorist attacks against American targets, including commercial aircraft, by Al Qaeda and other groups. The warnings were vague but sufficiently alarming to prompt the F.A.A. to issue four information circulars, or I.C.s, to the commercial airline industry between June 22nd and July 31st, warning of possible terrorism. One circular, from late July, noted, according to Condoleezza Rice, that there was "no specific target, no credible info of attack to U.S. civil aviation interests, but terror groups are known to be planning and training for hijackings, and we ask you therefore to use caution."

For years, however, the airlines had essentially disregarded the F.A.A.'s information circulars. "I.C.s don't require special measures," a former high-level F.A.A. official told me. "To get the airlines to react, you have to send a Security Directive"—a high-priority message that, under F.A.A. regulations, mandates an immediate response. Without a directive, the American airline industry continued to operate in a business-as-usual manner.

Several weeks before the attacks, the actor James Woods, who was in the first-class section of a cross-country flight to Los Angeles, alerted a flight attendant to the suspicious behavior of four of his fellow passengers—well-dressed men who appeared to be Middle Eastern and were obviously travelling together. Woods told me later that the flight attendant said that she would file a report about the suspicious passengers. If she did, her report probably ended up in a regional Federal Aviation Authority office in Tulsa, or perhaps Dallas, according to Clark Onstad, the former chief counsel of the F.A.A., and disappeared in the bureaucracy. "If you ever walked into one of these offices, you'd see that they have no secretaries," Onstad told me. "These guys are buried under a mountain of paper, and the odds of this"—a report about suspicious passengers, even from a high-profile passenger like Woods—"coming up to a higher level are very low." When I spoke to him, eight months after the hijacking, Onstad said, the question "Where would you effectively report something like this so that it would get attention?" still had no practical answer.

After September 11th, the bureau found evidence that the terrorists from the four different planes had flown together earlier, in various combinations, to "check out flights," as one agent put it. The F.B.I. speculated that the hijackers flew on perhaps a dozen flights, together and separately, in the summer of 2001.

The hijackers' decision to risk flying together calls into question the characterization of the Al Qaeda terrorists as brilliant professionals—what I. C. Smith, who retired in 1998, after a twenty-five-year career at the F.B.I., much of it in counterintelligence, called "the superman scenario." In a rare public appearance, at Duke University in April 2002, James Pavitt, the C.I.A.'s deputy director for operations—the agency's top spymaster—spoke with awe about what he said was Al Qaeda's modus operandi:

The terror cells that we're going up against are typically small and all terrorist personnel . . . were carefully screened. The number of personnel who know vital information, targets, timing, the exact methods to be used, had to be smaller still. . . . Against that degree of control, that kind of compartmentation, that depth of discipline and fanaticism, I personally doubt—and I draw again upon my thirty years of experience in this business—that anything short of one of the knowledgeable inner-circle personnel or hijackers turning himself in to us would have given us sufficient foreknowledge to have prevented the horrendous slaughter that took place on the eleventh.

The point of operating in cells is to insure that if one person is caught he can expose only those in his own cell, because he knows nothing of the others. The entire operation is not put at risk. The Al Qaeda terrorists, it seemed, contrary to Pavitt's analysis, had violated a fundamental rule of clandestine operations. Far from working independently and maintaining rigid communications security, the terrorists, as late as the summer before the attacks, apparently mingled openly and had not yet decided which flights to target.

By the spring of 2002, many investigators had come to believe that the planning for September 11th appears to have been far more ad hoc than was at first assumed. A senior F.B.I. official insisted to me that the September 11th attacks were "carefully orchestrated and well planned," but he agreed that serious and potentially fatal errors were made by the terrorists. Another official said, "We early on thought that people on flight one did not know anything about flights two, three, and four, but we did find that there was cross-pollination in travel and coördination. If they're so good, why did they intermingle?" A third F.B.I. official said, "Are they ten feet tall? They're not."

The fact that the terrorists managed to bring down the World Trade Center may simply mean that seizing an airplane was easier than the American public has been led to believe. The real message of missed opportunities like the Woods flight may be that, even at a time when America's intelligence agencies had raised an alarm, chatter remained chatter—diffuse noise. There were no mechanisms to either dispose of leads, warnings, and suspicious incidents or effectively translate them into a plan for preventing Al Qaeda from attacking.

By 1990, in the wake of the terrorist bombing of Pan Am Flight 103, congressional committees had concluded that the F.A.A. needed more immediate access to current intelligence, and urged that an F.A.A. security official be assigned to the relevant offices in the C.I.A., the F.B.I., and the State Department. Leo Boivin, who was the agency's primary security analyst at the time, told me, "I started the program. Getting into the C.I.A. and State was no problem, but the F.B.I. effectively said no—that it wasn't going to happen. The bureau didn't want anybody in there, and we couldn't fight the bureau." In 1996, after the crash of TWA Flight 800, a commission directed by Vice President Al Gore also called for closer liaison. This time, according to Boivin, who retired the month before September 11th, the F.B.I. refused to give the F.A.A. security officer a building pass that would permit unfettered access to F.B.I. headquarters. "The problem with the intelligence community is that you didn't know what you didn't know," Boivin said. " 'If there is a problem,' the bureau would say, 'we'll tell you about it.' " The difficulties continued well after September 11th. Boivin said that the F.B.I. sought to get rid of the F.A.A.'s liaison man at headquarters, because, in Boivin's words, "he was seen as too pushy about trying to get information."

The airlines, always eager to trim operating expenses, successfully lobbied against many of the safety provisions recommended by the Gore commission, such as more stringent security checks on airline employees and tighter screening of passenger baggage. William Webster, the former F.B.I. director, served as the airlines' lobbyist. "The airlines never wanted to spend a lot of money on security," said David Plavin, who was on the Gore commission and is the president of Airports Council International, the lobbying arm of the nation's more than five hundred commercial airports. "They were always concerned that the government would stick them with the bill." Much of that worry, Plavin told me, was alleviated after September 11th with the passage of legislation creating the Transportation Security Administration, which puts the responsibility for security on the federal government, but the new legislation won't solve the most serious problem: bureaucratic infighting. "More than half a dozen federal agencies are involved in airline travel, and their inability to work with each other is notorious," Plavin said. "Protecting their own turf is what matters."

In the late 1990s, the C.I.A. obtained reliable information indicating that an Al Qaeda network based in northern Germany had penetrated airport security in Amsterdam and was planning to attack American passenger planes by planting bombs in their cargo, a former security official told me. The intelligence was good enough to warrant the dissemination of an F.A.A. Security Directive, and the C.I.A., working with German police, planned a series of successful preëmptive raids. "The Germans rousted a lot of people," the former official said. The F.A.A. and the C.I.A. worked closely together and the incident was kept secret. "While the threat was on, the F.A.A. was getting two or three C.I.A. briefings a day," the former official said. In contrast, in operations in which the F.B.I. took the lead, "the F.A.A. got nothing. The F.B.I. people said, 'If there is a threat, we'll tell you, but we're not going to tell you what's going on in the investigations.' The F.A.A. told them that it had much more information about threats in Hamburg and Beirut than in Detroit, and they said, 'That's the way it is.' They'd come and give a dog-and-pony show."

———

Not surprisingly, some F.B.I. agents have a different view of who was at fault for the failure to share information. In June 2004, I was contacted by Myron Fuller, a former special agent who retired in June 2001 after thirty years of service. In his last post, Fuller was in charge of two hundred F.B.I. employees in forty-six countries throughout Asia and the Pacific, including Afghanistan and Pakistan, whose primary mission was to stop international terrorism. Fuller told me that his team had unraveled a great deal about the threat from Islamic militants by the spring of 1999, but that no one in Washington seemed to be listening. In one instance, involving the 1997 assassination of four American businessmen, auditors for Union Texas Petroleum, and their driver in Karachi, Fuller told me, he was tipped off that F.B.I. headquarters had "information from the C.I.A. that revealed who was responsible for the auditor killings." He telephoned an F.B.I. assistant director, who confirmed that the data had been withheld for months because the C.I.A. "had asked that he not reveal this to anyone in the field." Fuller said that the information "revealed who killed the auditors and much more," including "a country that supported the act. It was possibly the trail to the planning of September 11th." Before the attacks, added Fuller, who is now a management consultant, "We had no global strategy, and we are not sure we have the right one now. If the terrorists have a strategy, shouldn't we?"

Similar stories flooded the 9/11 Commission, whose reports castigated members of the intelligence community for their institutional failures to work together. George Tenet, one Commission staff statement said, "was accountable for a community of loosely associated agencies and departmental offices that lacked the incentives to cooperate, collaborate, and share information." The report concluded, "as a result, a question remains: who is in charge of intelligence?"

———

Nonetheless, long before September 11th, the American intelligence community had a significant amount of information about specific terrorist threats to commercial airline travel in the United States, including the possibility that a plane could be used as a weapon. In 1994, an Algerian terrorist group hijacked an Air France airliner and threatened to crash it into the Eiffel Tower. In 1995, police in Manila broke up a terrorist operation that was planning to plant bombs with timing devices on as many as twelve American airliners. They also found information that led to the arrest of Ramzi Ahmed Yousef. Abdul Hakim Murad, one of Yousef's collaborators, told the Philippine police and, later, U.S. intelligence officers that he had earned his pilot's license in an American flight school and had been planning to seize a small plane, fill it with explosives, and fly it into C.I.A. headquarters. Murad confessed, according to an account published in the *Washington Post* in December 2001, that he had gone to the American flight school "in preparation for a suicide mission." In 1996, the F.B.I. director, Louis Freeh, asked officials in Qatar—a nation suspected of harboring Al Qaeda terrorists—for help in apprehending another alleged accomplice of Yousef, Khalid Sheikh Mohammed, who was then believed to be in Qatar. One of Freeh's diplomatic notes stated that Mohammed was involved in a conspiracy to "bomb U.S. airliners" and was also believed to be "in the process of manufacturing an explosive device."

In late December of 1999, a group of Al Qaeda terrorists armed with knives hijacked an Indian airliner and diverted it to Kandahar, Afghanistan. The hijackers maintained control of the passengers and crew by cutting the throat of a young passenger and letting the victim bleed to death, a tactic that the September 11th terrorists are believed to have used on flight attendants. (Shortly after the Indian hijacking, the F.B.I. opened a liaison office in New Delhi, and began to work closely with Indian security officials.) The F.A.A., in its annual report for the year 2000, warned that bin Laden and Al Qaeda posed "a significant threat to civil aviation." The F.A.A. had earlier noted, according to the *New York Times*, that there was a specific report from an exiled Islamic leader in Britain alleging that bin

Laden was planning to "bring down an airliner, or hijack an airliner to humiliate the United States."

The attendance of potential terrorists at flight-training schools in the United States was not a new phenomenon, either. As early as 1975, according to an unpublished Senate Foreign Relations Committee document, Raymond Winall, then the F.B.I.'s assistant director for intelligence, revealed that a suspected member of Black September, the Palestinian terrorist group responsible for the deaths of eleven Israeli athletes at the 1972 Olympics in Munich, had explained his presence in the United States by telling the F.B.I. that he had been admitted for pilot training—the same explanation for the presence here of a number of the September 11th terrorists. The suspect was indicted but fled the country before he could be arraigned. In the years that followed, according to Bill Carroll, a former district director for the Immigration and Naturalization Service, thousands of young Middle Easterners have obtained visas to enroll in flight-instruction programs.

In the spring and summer of 2002, there was a wave of media reports of warnings gone unheeded, and the Administration went on the offensive to minimize the political fallout. Vice President Dick Cheney warned against "incendiary rhetoric," and said that the criticism from Democrats about the missed messages was "thoroughly irresponsible of national leaders in a time of war." Other Cabinet members issued dire public warnings of increased terrorism threats—based not on specific information but on more "chatter" in various corners of the Islamic world. In interviews with me, senior F.B.I. counterterrorism officials had made a point of criticizing such vague warnings. "Is there some C.Y.A."—cover your ass—"involved when officials talk about threats to power supplies, or banks, or malls?" one senior F.B.I. official asked. "Of course there is."

"Puffing up the threat because of a political interest is a disservice," the official added. When such threats are unfulfilled, the result is that "the country lowers its guard. And that kind of flippancy is what we don't need now. The American people are going back to sleep."

Another F.B.I. official depicted the question of when to warn the public as a "lose-lose" situation. "Say we get a report that three Al Qaeda guys are driving up from Mexico to blow up an unspecified mall in Dallas," the official said. "What do you want to be told?" He added, "We know the power of the people. Do we want you calling us if your neighbor is turning in to his driveway at two in the morning?" The bureau responded to three hundred calls about suspicious packages between January 1st and September 10th of 2001. After September 11th, the official said, "we received fifty-four thousand calls and physically responded to fourteen thousand of them." Even months later, according to another official, scores of tips were arriving every day from overseas, many of them relayed by C.I.A. sources that are known to pay for such information. "And the C.I.A. is happy to forward them to us," he noted. "Then it's not the C.I.A.'s problem."

Stories of supposed terrorist sightings also became common inside the airline industry—a part of its post–September 11th folklore. One widely repeated tale involves a stewardess who flew with a man dressed as a captain—he had hitched a ride, as crew members often do. She later recognized him as Mohammed Atta. Many in the industry, it seems, know someone who knows someone who saw one or another of the September 11th terrorists in captain's uniforms in cockpit jumpseats.

In interviews several months after the attacks, three senior F.B.I. officials in charge of responding to terrorism threats did not defend the bureau's past performance and acknowledged that many of the longstanding complaints had merit. But they insisted that, since September 11th, many things had been done right. The F.B.I. had invested enormous resources in tracking the terrorists' travel activities, and much progress had been made in disrupting the international flow of money to Al Qaeda, they claimed. The officials admitted that there were questions about the reliability of some of the information that was collected in the days immediately after September 11th. One mystery was how many of the nineteen hijackers understood that the mission called for the immolation of all aboard.

The officials maintained that they had correctly established the true identity of all nineteen, by consulting records and going back to their countries of origin. Almost a year later, however, there were still questions about several of them. For example, the F.B.I. had identified one of the hijackers aboard United Airlines Flight 77, which crashed into the Pentagon, as Nawaf Alhazmi. A Maryland motel he had checked into under this name had a record of a New York driver's license number and a Manhattan address he had given. But the address turned out to be a hotel, which reported that it had no record of him. And the New York Department of Motor Vehicles said that the number was invalid, and that it had never issued a license to anyone named Nawaf Alhazmi. Similarly, Waleed Alshehri, who was aboard American Airlines Flight 11, was identified by the F.B.I. as a college graduate from Florida whose father was a Saudi diplomat. And yet, after the attacks, the diplomat told a Saudi Arabian newspaper that his son was still alive and working as a pilot for Saudi Arabian Airlines.

Saudi newspapers also reported that at least four men with the same names as those listed by the F.B.I. as hijackers had been victims of passport theft. A hijacker identified as Abdulaziz Alomari, who was also aboard Flight 11, was reported by the *Rocky Mountain News* to have the same name as a graduate of the University of Colorado, a man who did not resemble a photograph of the hijacker. That Alomari had been stopped by the Denver police several times for minor offenses while attending college and had given three different birth dates. One of the dates matches the birth date used by the hijacker. Investigators subsequently learned that in 1995 the Colorado student had reported a theft in his apartment; among the items stolen was his passport.

Another hijacker, who used the name Saeed Alghamdi and was aboard United Flight 93, was reported by *Newsday* soon after the hijackings to have taken the Social Security number of a Vermont woman who had been dead since 1965. The name is a common one in Saudi Arabia. At least four other men with that name have shown up on records at the flight school in Florida where Alghamdi was said by the F.B.I. to have trained. The school reported that it had trained more than sixteen hundred students with the first name Saeed and more than two hundred with the surname Alghamdi. Social Security officials also said that six of the nineteen hijackers were using identity cards belonging to other people.

In April 2002, police in Milan raided the apartment of Essid Sami Ben Khemais, the alleged head of an extremist group based in Italy that has been linked to Al Qaeda. A prosecutor's affidavit, the *Baltimore Sun* reported, described what was found: a cache of forged Tunisian and Yemeni passports, Italian identity cards, and photocopies of German driver's licenses. The prosecutor wrote, "One of the most essential illegal activities of the group is the procurement and use of false documents . . . to guarantee a new identity to the 'brothers' who must hide or escape investigation." The prosecutor further said that the police had recorded telephone conversations in which Khemais discussed with Al Qaeda members the mechanics of falsifying documents. (The preliminary report of the 9/11 Commission, which relied heavily on the work done by the F.B.I., did not discuss the possibility that some of the hijackers had been misidentified.)

In a conversation in mid-2002, a senior F.B.I. official explained, once again, that there had been "no breakthrough" inside the government, in terms of establishing how the September 11th suicide teams were organized and how they operated. "It's kind of obvious that we haven't wrapped anything up," a C.I.A. consultant told me at the time.

"Traditionally, when Americans have had a war, they go and find the enemy, defeat it on the battlefield, and come home to replant," a senior F.B.I. official said. The war against terrorism is a long-term struggle and has no borders. "We need maturity when it comes to protecting our society," the official went on. "We shouldn't profoundly change our system, but we need a balance. Democracy is a messy business." Meanwhile, the terrorists won't go away. Another senior F.B.I. official said, "They'd like nothing better than to regroup and come back."

"These guys were not superhuman," I. C. Smith, the former agent, told me, "but they were playing in a system that was more inept than they were. If you go back to the aircraft hijackings of the early 1970s, I can't recall a single instance where we caught a guy"—in advance—"who really intended to hijack a plane." But men like Mueller, Smith added, "can't afford to say that the terrorists stumbled through this."

In testimony before the Senate Judiciary Committee in May 2002, Robert Mueller emphasized how difficult it would have been to thwart the September 11th attacks, noting that fifty million people entered and left the United States in August 2001. "The terrorists took advantage of America's strengths and used them against us," he said. "And as long as we continue to treasure our freedoms we always will run some risk of future attacks." Mueller added, "We must refocus our missions and priorities. . . . we must improve how we hire, manage, and train our workforce, collaborate with others, and manage, analyze, share, and protect our information." He said, "I am more impatient than most, but we must do these things right, not simply fast."

Mueller had been given one of the most difficult jobs in government. He has been trying to reorganize a bureaucracy that has resisted change—and outsiders—for decades. He didn't praise the old days, and the old ways of doing business, in his public statements. A Senate aide told me in mid-2002 that Mueller's willingness to air the problems—even at the risk of adverse publicity—had won him few friends inside the Bush Administration. "He's had his hand slapped by the Justice Department," the official said, "and he's having problems with the White House."

"He inherited a mess," Senator Leahy said. "The F.B.I. has improved since the days of J. Edgar Hoover. It doesn't go around blackmailing members of Congress anymore. But it still has a 'We don't make mistakes or admit mistakes' culture." Mueller seemed to be committed to changing that attitude, Leahy told me. "Mueller's best defense—and his best offense—is to be as forthcoming with Congress as possible." The Senator added, "White Houses come and go, but he has a ten-year tenure."

In terms of personnel, however, the F.B.I. has a long way to go. The bureau, one of Mueller's aides said, was undergoing an enormous and painful change in its day-to-day approach to investigations. "The mission now is not just to put handcuffs on people and throw them into jail but to stop acts of terrorism in the future. A lot of people here are not prepared to radically change their way of doing business, and it's frustrating for many agents, with their black-and-white way of looking at the world. The F.B.I.'s priority now is to get information to prevent the next event—even if it means we lose the case." One inevitable problem is that the most significant of Mueller's changes—such as the recruitment and hiring of experts in foreign languages, area studies, and computer technology—will not pay dividends for years. "There hasn't been time to build up a cadre of people with the right skills," the aide said.

"The bureau is wonderful in solving crimes after they're committed," one C.I.A. man said. "But it's not good at penetration. We've got to do it." Another experienced C.I.A. operative was similarly skeptical about the rival agency's ability to transform itself. "They're cops," he said of the F.B.I. agents. "They spent their careers trying to catch bank robbers while we spent ours trying to rob banks."

Robert Baer said, "You wouldn't believe how bad it is. What saved the White House on Flight 93 was a bunch of rugby players"—who attacked the Al Qaeda hijackers, forcing the plane to crash in Pennsylvania, short of its target. "Is that what you're paying $30 billion for?" He was referring to the federal budget for intelligence. After the hijackings, the F.B.I. and the C.I.A. made an effort to improve coöperation, and C.I.A. personnel were assigned to F.B.I. offices. However, a 9/11 Commission staff statement, issued on April 14, 2004, while praising Mueller's efforts, said that the F.B.I. remained, as one White House aide told the commission, the "black hole" of information sharing. Throughout the intelligence community, the report added, "it is clear that gaps in intelligence sharing still exist. . . . We found that there is no national strategy for sharing information to counter terrorism."

Instead of results, the Administration delivered more jarring alerts from federal health agencies and the Office of Homeland Security depicting the far-reaching threat posed by biological warfare or the possible use of fissile materials by terrorists. One public health official who has participated in Homeland Security discussions described the group as being overwhelmed by the potential threat to the U.S. water supply, electrical grids, oil depots, and even the wholesale processing of milk. "Where do we start?" he said. "So many threats. We're like deer in the headlights."

3. The Twentieth Man

When I wrote about the case of Zacarias Moussaoui in September 2002, the real subject was Attorney General John Ashcroft. My sources inside the American intelligence community were appalled by Ashcroft's insistence that the Justice Department seek the death sentence for Moussaoui, who was under lock and key in an American jail on September 11th. The attorney general's intransigence ruled out a plea bargain. There was, of course, no love for Moussaoui, who admitted to being a member of Al Qaeda, but my sources told me there were electronic intercepts suggesting that the September 11th plotters did not think he could handle the job. Given that reliable information about Al Qaeda was hard to come by early in 2002, there were some in the F.B.I. and C.I.A. who believed that Moussaoui would tell what he did know about how Al Qaeda operated with the right inducement. But Ashcroft refused to reconsider, and an early chance to get reliable intelligence was missed.

———

Sometime in the mid-1990s—the exact date is not known—Zacarias Moussaoui, who is now facing trial as the alleged twentieth man in the September 11th aircraft hijackings, travelled to Chechnya with a childhood friend to join separatists in their fight against Russian control. At the time, young men from throughout the Muslim world were arriving in the region, which was regarded, after the Russian defeat in Afghanistan, as the site of a new jihad. Moussaoui was a Frenchman of Moroccan descent, and his friend was also from an immigrant family. Evidently, Moussaoui did not impress his superiors in the operation. When the Chechens decided that the foreign volunteers were more trouble than they were worth, Moussaoui was told to leave. (His friend was invited to stay, and was later killed, reportedly while filming combat scenes for an Islamic website.)

In February 2001, Moussaoui showed up at the Airman Flight School, in Norman, Oklahoma. He was now thirty-two, and had continued to travel in pursuit of fundamentalist causes. He had been in Afghanistan (where he is alleged to have spent time in an Al Qaeda training camp), in Pakistan, and in Malaysia, while maintaining a base of sorts at a radical mosque in north London. When he arrived in the United States, two weeks after returning to London from a trip to Pakistan, he told Customs he had $35,000 in cash. His sudden interest in flying had led him to pay $5,000, in advance, for a series of lessons that should have allowed him to earn a pilot's license. Over the next three months, Moussaoui took fifty-seven hours of flight instruction, far more than the twenty hours most students need before flying solo. But he left the school in late May without a license.

Moussaoui's foreign travels and his ties to Islamic fundamentalists had brought him to the attention of the French intelligence services. After Moussaoui was arrested in the United States on immigration charges in mid-August of 2001, the French gave the F.B.I. a dossier on him, which, according to an official who reviewed it, documented some of his contacts but provided no specific evidence against him. Nevertheless, the French report came to be viewed as an important missed warning. Americans wondered if the F.B.I. and other government agencies, with the "twentieth hijacker" in custody, had bungled the chance to put the pieces together and possibly stop the attacks.

The assumption of government bungling was predicated on the assumption that Moussaoui was indeed the twentieth hijacker. (There were five hijackers on each of the three planes that hit their targets, but only four on the flight that went down in Pennsylvania.) Early on, Moussaoui said in federal court that he was a member of Al Qaeda, but he denied any involvement in the hijackings. Many present and former F.B.I. and C.I.A. officials have told me that they believe he was a "wanna-be," as one put it, and far too volatile and unstable to handle a long-term undercover terrorist operation. Nevertheless, they said, Moussaoui may have had crucial knowledge about Al Qaeda. "He knew how the system worked and knew how to get in contact," a former C.I.A. official said. The real bungling, this official and others believe, has been the handling of Moussaoui since September 11th and the framing of the indictment against him. The case against Moussaoui, like the war on terrorism, was far more complex than the government revealed.

*　　*　　*

After his failure at the flight school in Oklahoma, Moussaoui decided to try again, this time in Minnesota. He arrived at the Pan Am International Flight Academy in Eagan, near St. Paul, on August 11, 2001. According to Clancy Prevost, his instructor, he seemed to be just another wealthy foreigner with a passion for flying—"friendly and amiable." Prevost, a former Navy and Northwest Airlines pilot, said, "I had a terrible time, because he had no knowledge. He knew nothing. He had no spatial skills. But he was a customer, and you wanted to give him his money's worth, and so it boiled down to me just telling him stories. We had lunch and shot the breeze. There was nothing to indicate that this guy was anything other than a genial businessman who liked to hang out with pilots and could tell the girls that he flew a 747."

Moussaoui became widely known in the press as the man who told his instructor that he wanted to learn only how to fly a plane in the air, not how to take off or land. According to Prevost, however, "He never said that. He did say, 'I want to take off from London Heathrow Airport and land at J.F.K., in New York.' But he wasn't skilled enough to do it, even in a simulator."

There was one disquieting note. After a few days of lessons, Prevost told Moussaoui that his goal as a flight instructor was to put the student in a position to take over a transoceanic flight in case of emergency. "He said, 'I'd rather take a parachute and jump out.'" Prevost was amused, and informed him that the cabin pressure would make it impossible for him to get the door open. He told Moussaoui a story, well known in pilot circles, about a fire started by passengers making tea on a butane stove in the main cabin of a Saudi Arabian airliner. As he remembered it, they were on a pilgrimage during Ramadan. The passengers, unable to get a door open, burned to death. "I asked about Ramadan—'What is that? Are you a Muslim?' Moussaoui said, 'I am nothing.'"

"He sort of flushed," Prevost continued. "It wasn't the right reaction. That's when I said to myself, 'Hey, wait a minute. What are we doing here? He's a nice guy, but he has no knowledge of airplanes. Professionally, we should check him out.'" Prevost reported his misgivings to the Pan Am administrators, who, after some hesitancy, called the F.B.I.

On August 16th, Moussaoui was arrested near the flight school by agents of the F.B.I. and the Immigration and Naturalization Service and charged with overstaying his visa. Like many immigration detainees, he was taken to the county jail. When the federal agents began to question him, he initially seemed willing to talk. (His English was good enough for him to have earned a master's degree in international business from South Bank University in London.) According to one of his court-appointed attorneys, he coöperated with the agents until he was asked whether he was planning an act of terrorism involving an airplane. "His answer was 'I want a lawyer,'" the attorney told me. He didn't get one. Instead, according to the attorney, the agents stopped the interrogation and decided, in effect, to handle the case as a visa matter. (Immigration detainees are not entitled to lawyers.) Over the next few days, however, the Minnesota agents tried to get F.B.I. headquarters to seek a special national security warrant, under the Foreign Intelligence Surveillance Act (FISA), for a secret search of Moussaoui's computer and personal belongings, on the ground that they had reason to believe he was a foreign agent. (Moussaoui had refused to give them access.) Headquarters turned the request down— a decision that later became controversial. There were no further attempts to interrogate him in late August and early September. Moussaoui's status didn't change until after September 11th, when, along with hundreds of other Muslim suspects, he was declared a material witness, and was sent to New York.

The charges against Moussaoui were announced on December 11, 2001, by Attorney General John Ashcroft, who described the indictment, handed down by a Virginia grand jury, as "a chronicle of evil." Moussaoui was charged "with undergoing the same training, receiving the same funding, and pledging the same commitment to kill Americans as the hijackers." There were six counts levelled against him: conspiracy to commit international terrorism; to commit aircraft piracy; to destroy aircraft; to use weapons of mass destruction; to murder federal employees; and to destroy property. The first four counts carried the death penalty.

The evidence that the government presented was, at that point, largely circumstantial. The search of Moussaoui's computer—a warrant was granted on the afternoon of September 11th—apparently yielded nothing that would have foretold the attack or tied him to it. The indictment depicted Moussaoui as having followed a pattern of activity similar to that of many of the hijackers. Like them, he spent months in flight training, he bought flight-deck videos for commercial airplanes from a pilots' store in Ohio, and he joined a gym. Two of the hijackers are also said to have visited the flight school in Oklahoma the year before Moussaoui did. In the fall of 2000, Moussaoui had been given a letter stating that he was being retained as a "marketing consultant" by Infocus Tech, a Malaysian company; the company's managing director was later linked in press reports to some of the hijackers.

The most specific evidence in the indictment linking Moussaoui to the September 11th conspirators was that, in August 2001, someone using the name of Ahad Sabet wired $14,000 to him from train stations in Hamburg and Düsseldorf. Ahad Sabet was the alias of Ramzi bin al-Shibh, a known Al Qaeda intermediary, who also funnelled money to at least one of the hijackers and was named as a co-conspirator in the Moussaoui indictment. He had sought four times before September 11th to get a visa to the United States, and, in a broadcast on Al Jazeera on the day after the anniversary of the attacks, he claimed that he was meant to be the twentieth hijacker. The indictment also notes that Moussaoui and al-Shibh were in London at the same time, in December 2000, just before Moussaoui flew to Pakistan. The government's theory is that al-Shibh's visa problems forced the conspirators to turn to Moussaoui.

If the government's case was to be built on the similarities between Moussaoui's activities and those of the known hijackers, it had to account for the fact that, though he shared their allegiance to Al Qaeda and its leader, Osama bin Laden, his behavior in the United States was strikingly different from theirs. The government found evidence of e-mails and meetings among the nineteen, but none between any of them and Moussaoui. The hijackers tried to fit in to American life—drinking in bars, for instance. Moussaoui, while in Oklahoma, remained largely aloof, although he was voluble about his Islamic beliefs. He criticized members of a mosque in Norman for not lowering their gaze when meeting women and for looking at lightly clad cheerleaders. "He went around making a nuisance of himself everywhere he went," Frank W. Dunham Jr., the federal public defender in charge of Moussaoui's defense team, said. "He was not flying under the radar by any means."

On March 28, 2002, Ashcroft announced that he had told Paul J. McNulty, the U.S. Attorney for the Eastern District of Virginia, to seek the death penalty for Moussaoui. If he was found guilty, the jury would then hear testimony and deliberate on the sentence in a separate penalty phase. In a notice of intent to the court, summarizing what the government would argue, McNulty wrote that death was warranted because Moussaoui, although not present on September 11th, intentionally and with premeditation participated in the act, in "an especially heinous, cruel and depraved manner" and with "reckless disregard for human life."

In pursuing the death penalty, the Justice Department set a high standard for itself. It accused Moussaoui of a level of involvement that included advance knowledge of the plans, and of the scope and intent of the mission. In this view, he wasn't just a candidate for the twentieth hijacker: he was one of the actual hijackers in all but the final execution, and was prevented from acting on his intentions only by his arrest.

A Justice Department official told me in an interview in the fall of 2002 that as the government made its case before the jury it would stress the "unspeakable horror of that day, and what followed." The prosecutors anticipated, he said, that Moussaoui's lawyers would attempt "to minimize his significance and nearness" to September 11th, and argue that he was "not worthy." But, the official added, "Everything we are aware of connects Moussaoui to September 11th, and that speaks volumes. Because there's nothing to compare to that crime—it's a crime of history. The path that Moussaoui took is the heart of the case, and, at the end of the day, a jury will hear evidence that supports the story the indictment tells."

The Justice Department official further told me that in the months after the terror attacks there was never a thought of plea bargaining with Moussaoui or indicting him on lesser charges that might be easier to prove. At the time, he said, the public and the federal government "were looking for the criminal justice system to do what it was designed to do—offer some justice for a great crime."

Those intelligence officials who were, at that point, skeptical of the government's case stressed to me that they did not believe that Moussaoui was in any way an innocent bystander. They believed that he remained in close contact with Al Qaeda, as the payment from al-Shibh suggested, and came to the United States prepared to do grievous harm, if asked. But months after Moussaoui's indictment, no evidence had yet been presented that the call from any handlers ever came.

The trial, presided over by Judge Leonie M. Brinkema, of the U.S. District Court in Alexandria, Virginia, was set for January 2003. Throughout the spring of 2002, Frank Dunham's team of attorneys became convinced that their client's mental condition, already precarious, was deteriorating under the stress of solitary confinement, and that he was becoming increasingly paranoid. Moussaoui, in turn, became angrier and angrier at their conduct of the case.

On April 22nd, Judge Brinkema permitted Moussaoui to speak at length at a pretrial hearing, and he stunned the court by railing against his lawyers and the American judicial system. He called for "the destruction of the United States of America," among other enemies of Islamic fundamentalism, and told the court that the United States was "orchestrating my sending to the safe haven, Bosnia style. Dead, injured. Judge, investigator, and the so-called defenders are all federal employees." His lawyers, he said, were "experienced in deception." He formally sought permission from Judge Brinkema to go pro se—to represent himself in court.

Moussaoui's outburst came during a hearing into his lawyers' protests over the conditions of his jailing. He had been held in solitary confinement, under extraordinary security conditions, which precluded unmonitored visits, telephone calls, or mail from anyone other than his attorneys. His cell was lit twenty-four hours a day. All visitors, including his attorneys, had to undergo F.B.I. clearance, and all written materials, even memorandums from his attorneys, were subject to search. Moussaoui was also not allowed any contact with journalists, because of the government's fear that he would communicate a coded message to Al Qaeda. In a memorandum, the Justice Department had defended the restrictions as necessary "to avoid the 'substantial risk' that the defendant will communicate with others outside the prison to facilitate or incite additional acts of terrorism." One of Moussaoui's attorneys later told me angrily that the prosecutors, despite their concern about the danger of unfettered communication, "let him talk in open court for fifty minutes and never said boo" when his outbursts appeared to be undermining his own defense.

Federal courts have consistently ruled that criminal defendants such as Moussaoui have the right to defend themselves if their waiver of counsel is "knowing, voluntary, and intelligent." Judge Brinkema relied in part on a report filed by Dr. Raymond Patterson, a court-appointed psychiatrist. Patterson found that many of Moussaoui's notes and letters to Judge Brinkema were "well-researched," and concluded that his decision to waive counsel was not the product of mental illness. He attributed much of Moussaoui's seemingly strange behavior to the "subculture" to which he belonged.

Two mental health experts retained by the defense, Dr. Xavier Amador of Columbia University, and Dr. William Stejskal of the University of Virginia, argued that Patterson's conclusions were unfounded and that Moussaoui needed further evaluation. After reading the papers, Judge Brinkema ruled from the bench on June 13th, without hearing testimony, that the defendant met the legal standard of competency.

Amador and Stejskal had not talked to Moussaoui. Instead, they had met three times with his mother, Aicha el-Wafi, who had travelled to Virginia from France (she was coöperating with the defense team, against her son's wishes), and reviewed his French academic records and data from French social services. The documents showed a family history of domestic violence and mental illness. Two of his siblings suffered from serious psychiatric disorders as adults; one was hospitalized with a diagnosis of schizophrenia.

El-Wafi, who divorced Moussaoui's father when the boy was two years old, told reporters that her son became involved with radical Islamic groups after moving from France to London in 1992. On a visit home in 1997, el-Wafi told the London *Observer*, Moussaoui, who as a child had exhibited little interest in religion, showed up in traditional Muslim dress and reprimanded her for not being religious enough. She blamed the mosque in London for turning her "carefree, happy boy" into someone "unrecognizable."

Farhad Khosrokhavar, a University of Paris sociologist, calls men like Moussaoui "the new martyrs": alienated young working-class Arabs from France who saw themselves as "not existing"—certainly not as Frenchmen or North Africans. They became attracted to radical Islam, and to the religious wars in Bosnia, Afghanistan, and Chechnya. Narbonne, the town near the Mediterranean where Moussaoui grew up, is an area of intense anti-immigrant sentiment. At school, he was placed, he believed, on a vocational track because of a bias against Arabs. Khosrokhavar, who interviewed more than a dozen convicted and would-be terrorists for a book published in France in 2002, depicts young men like Moussaoui as willing to "go to extremes in order to get out of this feeling of being 'less than nothing.'"

"Islam is the only plausible identity they can endorse," Khosrokhavar told me. "To accept their identity as French might mean accepting the inferiority they feel in their daily life as a second-rate citizen. The inevitable result is a hatred for France and, by extension, for the West." These young men, many of whom never learn to speak Arabic, became known to French human rights workers as *chair à canon*—cannon fodder—easily recruited zealots who were willing to fight, and die, for a religious cause about which, initially, they know little.

On May 21, 2002, Coleen Rowley, a staff lawyer at the F.B.I. office in Minneapolis, sent a letter of complaint to Robert Mueller, the F.B.I. director. It was made public in *Time* and prompted a wave of news accounts and congressional hearings into whether clues to the impending attacks had been missed before September 11th. Rowley's letter was primarily a complaint about the refusal of F.B.I. headquarters, after Moussaoui's arrest, to endorse the Minneapolis office's request for the special FISA warrant to search his belongings. At the time, FISA, which created a secret federal court to hear spy cases, required the government to show probable cause that the target was either working for an international terrorist organization, for a foreign intelligence organization—a Russian mole inside the C.I.A., for example—or was aiding or abetting a foreign power. Seven District Court judges are appointed to the panel, on a rotating basis, by the Chief Justice of the United States. The FISA court has issued some thirteen thousand warrants, a thousand in 2000 alone; at the time of the September 11th attacks, it had been known to have turned down only one request. F.B.I. headquarters concluded, however, that the flight instructor's apprehensions and the suspicions of the French did not meet the FISA standard.

Rowley acknowledged that her F.B.I. colleagues had another option. They could have taken their evidence to the U.S. Attorney in Minneapolis and asked that office to seek a routine criminal search warrant from a federal judge. However, Rowley wrote, she thought that, "for a lot of reasons including just to play it safe," the U.S. Attorney's office "might turn us down."

Since FISA was introduced, in 1978, civil libertarians have worried that the government would use the warrants, which allow secret wiretapping, as a mechanism for circumventing constitutional prohibitions on unreasonable searches and seizures. (The Fourth Amendment requires that "no Warrants shall issue, but upon probable cause, supported by Oath or affirmation, and particularly describing the place to be searched, and the persons or things to be seized.") Evidence uncovered by a FISA warrant can be introduced in criminal cases, but the warrants themselves can be granted only for intelligence investigations. After Congress expanded FISA's reach, in 1994, by allowing physical searches of homes and computers in addition to electronic surveillance, criminal investigators had increased incentive to use the act—as Rowley apparently hoped to do—as an expedient alternative to going before an ordinary judge. Coleen Rowley's letter, describing how the Minneapolis office of the F.B.I. went to the FISA court before even consulting with the local U.S. Attorneys' Office, did nothing to discourage that view.

Jonathan Turley, a leading FISA critic who teaches law at George Washington University, described Rowley's letter as "the first time I've seen in writing what we've been seeing for years: you go to FISA when you can't make a criminal case. We've long suspected that FISA is routinely used in cases where there is no evidence of probable cause. Rowley is the very personification of the fears that led to the opposition to FISA." Turley, who served as defense counsel in a number of national security and espionage cases before moving to academia, has written that the United States' federal law enforcement officials "are gradually shifting searches from the Fourth Amendment process to a secure court that is neither mentioned nor consistent with the Constitution."

In the spring of 2002, John Ashcroft issued new guidelines declaring that the passage of the U.S.A. Patriot Act after September 11th enabled federal authorities to seek FISA warrants "primarily for a law enforcement purpose, so long as a significant foreign intelligence purpose remains." Given the constitutional concerns about the abuse of the FISA process, many law enforcement professionals were distressed by the widespread assumption—stemming from Rowley's public complaints—that headquarters had erred seriously in not pursuing the FISA warrant to search Moussaoui's belongings.

Little of that feeling showed, as Mueller publicly thanked Rowley for her letter and later assured members of the Senate Judiciary Committee that there would be no retaliation. "Rowley's rewriting history a little bit here," an intelligence official who reviewed the French material told me in the fall of 2002. "There's nothing in the French intelligence reports that connects Moussaoui as an agent of a foreign power." He added, "It's not that the French didn't think he was a bad person—we think that, too. The question is, was there something the French had that gets up over the FISA threshold? It's not there." (This official and others did acknowledge that many of Rowley's generalized complaints dealing with the F.B.I.'s antiquated computer systems and the centralized control in Washington had much merit.)

"The people in the Minneapolis office are dying to tell their side," B. Todd Jones, a former U.S. Attorney for the Minnesota District, told me, "but Rowley's been painted as Joan of Arc."

*   *   *

In the summer of 2002, Moussaoui filed a stream of handwritten
motions that suggested the extent of his mental decay. They contained some glimpses of acute intelligence and awareness, but more
often Moussaoui veered into angry ramblings. He insisted, in one
motion, that the F.B.I. "will kill Zacarias Moussaoui to silence him."
In another, he claimed that the F.B.I. was concealing the fact that he
and the nineteen hijackers were under surveillance the entire time
he was in the United States—which, he said, proved his innocence.
The F.B.I., he claimed, had even placed a "bug" in an electric fan in
his apartment in Oklahoma. In a motion filed on July 15th, he asked
Brinkema to force the F.B.I. to turn over the fan, which he called
"hidden concrete evidence of their coverup operation."

  Although Moussaoui had won the right to defend himself, Judge
Brinkema decided that the federal defenders should stay on as
standby counsel, and Moussaoui's relationship with them soured
further. Whenever his mental health came under question, he became outraged. The lawyers I spoke with pointed to this as one of
the fundamental problems in the defense of clients who may be
mentally ill. Moussaoui's attempt to plead guilty, at a procedural
hearing on July 18, 2002, came after Judge Brinkema objected to
the defendant's insistence that he would not accept any documents,
even exculpatory ones, from his former attorneys. As an accused terrorist, Moussaoui does not have the clearance to see any of the government's classified evidence against him—only his court-appointed
attorneys could do so, on his behalf. "If you choose not to accept
that information," the judge told Moussaoui, "you proceed at your
own risk and will not be allowed to complain down the road that
you were denied a fair trial."

  Faced with the prospect of having to work with the federal defenders, Moussaoui abruptly announced that he wanted to plead
guilty. "You allow them to do this and to speak, and I will be soon
removed from my defense," he told the judge. "I will be certainly

gagged during trial and you will carry on your so-called justice." One week later, after Judge Brinkema informed him that he could not, as he had assumed, plead guilty to the conspiracy charges and then argue in the penalty phase of the trial that he had had nothing to do with the September 11th attacks, Moussaoui changed his mind. He had clearly failed to grasp that, as Judge Brinkema explained, "what you will not be able to do during the penalty phase of this trial is to come in and say that you were not . . . guilty of the offense." Moussaoui responded, "That's your—your interpretation!"

Moussaoui's confusion and inability to understand the consequences of a guilty plea prompted his attorneys once again to raise the question with Judge Brinkema of his competency to defend himself. In late July, Amador and Stejskal, the mental health experts, told Judge Brinkema that they had observed "a marked deterioration in his mental state since he was permitted to proceed pro se." Moussaoui's motions, they added, were filled with "repetitive ruminations" about the F.B.I., the C.I.A., and "S.S. Judge Brinkema."

In August, Moussaoui responded with renewed rancor to the efforts of Frank Dunham and the other federal defenders on his behalf. He delivered a document to the judge entitled "DUNHAM MIND YOUR OWN PIG BUZINESS." The goal of his motion, he wrote, was to "keep mad, out of control standby herd of blood suckers out of . . . PURE PRO SE LAND." At the same time, according to a memorandum filed by the standby attorneys, Moussaoui was refusing to forward to the judge a series of vital pretrial motions, including one dealing with the suppression of government evidence.

On August 16th, Judge Brinkema granted a defense motion to delay the trial until January 2003, but she stuck to her decision to permit Moussaoui to defend himself. Two weeks later, however, the judge, citing Moussaoui's "irrelevant, inflammatory, and insulting rhetoric," ordered the sealing of all future pleadings from him "containing threats, racial slurs, calls to action . . . or other irrelevant and inappropriate information." When news organizations protested, the prosecutors warned that Moussaoui was "presumably attempting to communicate" in code with Al Qaeda.

Moussaoui's frenetic behavior in and out of court, one former public defender who has observed the case told me, was "providing ammunition for the military-tribunal crowd"—those who argue that civilian courts are not equal to the challenge of bringing international terrorists to justice. The case also contributed to discontent within the F.B.I. over what some saw as a politicized Justice Department more eager to have splashy court victories than to protect intelligence resources. An intelligence official confirmed the dispute, and depicted the Bush Administration as still looking for "the right balance between the prosecution of crime, its prevention, and intelligence."

That balance, by all indications, has yet to be struck in the Moussaoui case. He remains the only man to be indicted in an American court for the deaths of some three thousand people. Moussaoui's lawyers, and some F.B.I. officials, were bewildered at the government's failure to pursue a plea bargain. Frank Dunham, who was a federal prosecutor in northern Virginia before becoming a federal public defender, told me, "I've never been in a conspiracy case where the government wasn't interested in knowing if the defendant had any information—to see if there wasn't more to the conspiracy."

Any talks on a plea bargain would have hinged on Ashcroft's willingness to forgo the death penalty in return for coöperation, something several officials said he was unwilling to do. "We've been blocked by Justice," the senior F.B.I. official said. "It's very frustrating." Others who are familiar with the case believe that the government has simply overreached.

Moussaoui was certainly connected to Al Qaeda, but his real value to the United States may have been as a witness and not as a stand-in for the dead hijackers, who are beyond punishment. That potential appears to have been traded away for the sake of a high-profile prosecution that would be politically and emotionally satisfying.

"This man stands accused of one of the worst crimes committed on American soil," Martín Sabelli, a former public defender in San Francisco who has written on the pro se issue, told me in the fall of 2002. "This is precisely the kind of case where we must be most alert and most certain that the adversarial process actually involves adversaries—not Goliath on one side and a slingless David on the other. It appears that Moussaoui is not competent to represent himself, because he doesn't seem to understand the fundamentals of the charges against him, but I am starting to feel that the rest of us are crazier—that is, we are not competent to construct a legal system in which lives are in the balance. For all our expertise and professionalism, we may let this man talk himself to death to soothe our sense of vulnerability."

On September 11, 2002, Ramzi bin al-Shibh was arrested by Pakistani forces, after a yearlong hunt, in a shoot-out in Karachi. He was turned over to the United States for questioning and brought to an undisclosed military base, and is expected to be tried by a military tribunal. Al-Shibh's capture complicated the Moussaoui trial. According to Edward B. MacMahon Jr., one of Moussaoui's attorneys, the defense, which had so far been denied access to captured Al Qaeda members, planned to seek testimony from him.

"They're gearing up," Eugene R. Fidell, an expert on military law, said at the time. "This is going to take months to sort out, especially if al-Shibh has exculpatory material, and both sides are probably going to ask for an extension of time. Al-Shibh has to be made available, but what if he takes the Fifth? Judge Brinkema is going to have a moment of truth," Fidell told me. "It's the highest-stakes poker you could imagine."

———

Fidell had it right. On March 1, 2003, Khalid Sheikh Mohammed, a suspected ringleader of September 11th, was arrested in

Rawalpindi, Pakistan. Over the next year the Moussaoui defense team would insist that their client had a constitutional right to interrogate al-Shibh and Khalid Sheikh Mohammed to seek exculpatory information. The Bush Administration refused to produce any of its captured Al Qaeda members, arguing that any defense access to the prisoners would endanger national security.

In October 2003, Judge Brinkema ruled that the federal prosecutors, without providing such access, could not seek the death penalty for Moussaoui, nor could they allege that he had any link to September 11th. *Time* magazine depicted the government's case at the time as being "a shambles." Judge Brinkema's decision was reversed in April 2004 by the conservative federal appeals court in Richmond, Virginia, which ordered the trial judge to work out a compromise that would enable Moussaoui to have access to the testimony of the Al Qaeda witnesses he wanted while preserving the government's right to continue to interrogate them without interruption. The court did not say how to get it done. Prosecutors were also allowed, once again, to pursue the death penalty, but that ruling was placed in legal limbo after a hearing in June 2004, when questions arose about an agreement that would have given the defense "neutral summaries" of detainee interrogations. Federal prosecutors acknowledged the government had had "input" into the summaries. The question of how to proceed was left, once again, to the appeals courts in Richmond. The trial, scheduled for January 2003, when I first wrote about it, has now been indefinitely delayed.

Moussaoui has continued to deteriorate and, after filing a stream of irrational pleadings last fall, he became increasingly agitated and was stripped of the right to defend himself. Since then, he has met only sporadically with his attorneys.

III.

THE OTHER WAR

1. Afghanistan's Secret Battles

Early on the morning of October 20, 2001, more than one hundred Army Rangers parachuted into a Taliban-held airbase sixty miles southwest of Kandahar, in southern Afghanistan. The air war in Afghanistan had been under way for two weeks, and the American bombs had done much to boost morale throughout the United States—and to boost the popularity of President George Bush. The night jump by the Rangers was the first direct American ground assault of the war. A military cameraman videotaped the action with the aid of a night-vision lens, and his grainy, green-tinted footage of determined commandos and billowing parachutes dominated the television news that night. The same morning, a second Special Operations unit, made up largely of Rangers and a reinforced Delta Force squadron, struck at a complex outside Kandahar which included a house used by Mullah Omar, the Taliban leader whose life had been spared on the first night of the air war, so Donald Rumsfeld and his aides believed, thanks to a clumsy and far too cautious military command structure.

In a Pentagon briefing later that day, General Richard Myers, the new chairman of the Joint Chiefs of Staff, reported that the Special Operations forces "were able to deploy, maneuver, and operate inside Afghanistan without significant interference from Taliban forces." He stated that the soldiers did meet resistance at both sites, but overcame it. "I guess you could characterize it as light," he said. "For those experiencing it, of course, it was probably not light." He concluded, "The mission over all was successful. We accomplished our objectives." Myers also told reporters that the commandos were "refitting and repositioning for potential future operations against terrorist targets" in Afghanistan. But at a second briefing, two days later, he refused to say whether commando operations would continue. "Some things are going to be visible, some invisible," he said.

Visible or not, the public did not get the full story. There was disdain among Delta Force soldiers, a number of senior officers told me, for what they saw as the staged nature of the assault on the airfield, which had produced such exciting television footage. "It was sexy stuff, and it looked good," one general said. But the operation was something less than the Pentagon suggested. The Rangers' parachute jump took place only after an Army Pathfinder team—a specialized unit that usually works behind enemy lines—had been inserted into the area and had confirmed that the airfield was clear of Taliban forces. "It was a television show," one informed source told me. "The Rangers were not the first in."

Some of the officials I spoke with argued that the parachute operation had value, even without enemy contact, in that it could provide "confidence building" for the young Rangers, many of whom had joined the Army out of high school and had yet to be exposed to combat. "The Rangers come in and the choppers come in and everybody feels good about themselves," a military man who served alongside the Special Forces said. Nonetheless, he asked, "Why would you film it? I'm a big fan of keeping things secret—and this was being driven by public opinion."

In the case of the assault on Mullah Omar's complex, Myers did not tell the press that there had been a near-disaster and that, in its wake, the Pentagon was rethinking future Special Forces operations inside Afghanistan. Delta Force, which prides itself on stealth, had been counterattacked by the Taliban, and some of the Americans had had to fight their way to safety. Twelve Delta members were wounded, three of them seriously.

Delta Force, which is based at Fort Bragg, North Carolina, has a mystique unmatched by any other unit of the Army. Its mere existence is classified, and, invariably, its activities are described to the public only after the fact. *Black Hawk Down*, a book by Mark Bowden about the Special Forces disaster in Mogadishu, Somalia, in 1993, in which eighteen Rangers and Delta Force members were killed, took note of Delta's special status. "They operated strictly in secret," Bowden wrote.

> You'd meet this guy hanging out at a bar around Bragg, deeply tanned, biceps rippling, neck wide as a fireplug, with a giant Casio watch and a plug of chaw under his lip, and he'd tell you he worked as a computer programmer for some army contract agency. They called each other by their nicknames and eschewed salutes and all the other traditional trappings of military life. Officers and noncoms in Delta treated each other as equals. Disdain for normal displays of army status was the unit's signature. They simply transcended rank.

On combat missions, Bowden wrote, Delta Force soldiers disliked working with the younger, far less experienced Rangers.

Referring to the October 20th raid on the Mullah Omar complex, some Delta members told a colleague that it was a "total goat fuck"—military slang meaning that everything that could go wrong did go wrong. According to a report in the London *Observer*, the complex included little more than potholed roads, the brick house used by Mullah Omar, and a small protective garrison of thatched huts. The Pentagon had intelligence reports indicating that the

Mullah sometimes spent the night there; a successful mission could result in his death or capture and might, at a minimum, produce valuable intelligence. Delta had hoped to do what it did best: work a small team of four to six men on the ground into the target area—the phrase for such reconnaissance is "snoop and poop"—and attack with no warning. (One senior intelligence officer said that a member of Delta Force had told him, "We take four guys, and if we lose them, that's what we get paid for.") CENTCOM's attack plan called, instead, for an enormous assault on the Mullah's complex. The mission was initiated by at least one AC-130 gunship, which poured thousands of rounds into the surrounding area but deliberately left the Mullah's house unscathed.* The idea was that any Taliban intelligence materials would thus be left intact, or that, with a bit of luck, Omar would perhaps think he was safe and spend the night. A reinforced company of Rangers—roughly two hundred soldiers—was flown by helicopter into a nearby area, to serve as a blocking force in case Delta ran into heavy resistance.

Chinook helicopters, the Army's largest, then flew to a staging area and disgorged the reinforced Delta squadron—about a hundred soldiers—and their six-by-six assault vehicles, with specially mounted machine guns. The Delta team stormed the complex and found little of value: no Mullah and no significant documents.

"As they came out of the house, the shit hit the fan," one senior officer recounted. "It was like an ambush. The Taliban were firing light arms and either R.P.G.s"—rocket-propelled grenades—"or mortars." The chaos was terrifying. A high-ranking officer who has had access to debriefing reports told me that the Taliban forces were firing grenades, and that they seemed to have an unlimited supply. Delta Force, he added, found itself in "a tactical firefight, and the Taliban had the advantage." Almost immediately, several Americans

*In my original story on the battle, I erroneously reported that sixteen AC-130s were involved.

were hit, and the team evacuated. The soldiers broke into separate units—one or more groups of four to six men each and a main force that retreated to the waiting helicopters. According to established procedures, the smaller groups were to stay behind to provide fire cover. Army gunships then arrived on the scene and swept the compound with heavy fire.

The Delta team was forced to abandon one of its objectives—the insertion of an undercover team into the area—and the stay-behind soldiers fled to a previously determined rendezvous point, under a contingency plan known as an E. & E., for escape and evasion. One of the Chinook helicopters smashed its undercarriage while pulling away from the grenades and the crossfire, leaving behind a section of the landing gear. The Taliban later displayed this as a trophy, claiming, falsely, that a helicopter had been shot down. (According to the Pentagon, the helicopter had come "into contact with a barrier.")

The failed 1993 Special Forces attack in Mogadishu, with its enduring image of a slain American dragged through the city's streets, had created a furor, and led to allegations that the soldiers had been sent in without adequate combat support. The CENTCOM planners were unquestionably eager to avoid the same mistake, and their anxiety was perhaps heightened by the fact that the attacks would be the first of the ground war. But the resulting operation was criticized by many with experience in Special Operations as far too noisy ("It would wake the dead," one officer told me) and far too slow, giving the Taliban time to organize their resistance. One Delta Force soldier told a colleague that the planners "think we can perform fucking magic. We can't. Don't put us in an environment we weren't prepared for. Next time, we're going to lose a company."

Delta Force has long complained about a lack of creativity in the Army leadership, but the unexpectedness and the ferocity of the Taliban response "scared the crap out of everyone," a senior military officer told me, and triggered a review of commando tactics and procedures at CENTCOM, at MacDill Air Force Base, in Florida, the headquarters for the war in Afghanistan. "This is no war for Special Operations," one officer said—at least, not as orchestrated by CENTCOM and its commander, General Tommy R. Franks, of the Army, on October 20th.

In the briefings after the raids, Defense Secretary Donald Rumsfeld and General Myers gave no indication of the intensity of the resistance near Mullah Omar's house. Rumsfeld also chastised the Pentagon press corps for relying on unnamed military sources in filing the first reports on the raids before the commandos had returned. Rumsfeld said, "You can be certain that I will answer your questions directly when I can and that we'll do our best to give you as much information as we can safely provide." He added, "This is a very open society, and the press knows—you know—almost as much as exists and almost as soon as it exists. And the idea that there is some great iceberg out there that's not known, below water . . . it's just not true."

In the days that followed, as details of the raids filtered through the military system, the Pentagon gave no hint of the bitter internal debate they had provoked. There was evidence, however, that something had gone wrong. On Sunday, October 21st, the day after the raids, the London *Sunday Telegraph* reported that the United States had requested the immediate assignment to Afghanistan of the entire regiment of Britain's élite commando units, the Special Air Service, or S.A.S. American officials told me that month that British military authorities assigned to CENTCOM were urging the Pentagon to forgo its airborne operations inside Afghanistan and bring the war to the Taliban by establishing a large firebase in Afghanistan. The British position, one officer explained, was "We should tell the Taliban, 'We're now part of your grid square' "—that is, in the Taliban's territory. " 'What are you going to do about it?' "

In the after-action arguments in the following weeks, many of the senior officers in Delta Force were "still outraged," as one military man described it. The Pentagon could not tell the American people the details of what really happened at Kandahar, he added angrily, "because it doesn't want to appear that it doesn't know what it's doing." Another senior military officer told me, "This is the same M.O. that they've used for ten years." He dismissed CENTCOM's planning for the Afghanistan mission as "Special Ops 101," and said, "Franks is clueless." Of Delta Force the officer said, "These guys have had a case of the ass since Mogadishu. They want to do it right and they train hard. Don't put them on something stupid." He paused, and said, "We'll get there, but it's going to get ugly."

On October 26th, Abdul Haq, an Afghan guerrilla leader who was a hero in the war against the Soviets and had become one of the most prominent operatives in the war against the Taliban, was killed. According to press reports, Haq was ambushed and executed after a two-day standoff in eastern Afghanistan. Haq was said by the Taliban to have been on a mission for the United States, and to have been carrying large amounts of money—presumably to be used to induce Taliban commanders to defect. An Afghan press report subsquently quoted a Taliban spokesman, who said that fifty of Haq's supporters, possibly including "foreigners," had also been surrounded.

Haq's death was a major setback to the American anti-Taliban effort. One of Haq's close friends, Kurt Lohbeck, a former stringer for CBS television who covered the Afghan-Soviet war for years, acknowledged in a telephone interview that week that Haq, who prided himself on his independence, had been on a temporary assignment for the C.I.A. at the time of his death, although he "never worked with them, for them, or loved them." Lohbeck told me, "He had two or three top Taliban people who were willing to defect, and he was going in with C.I.A. support and money to get these guys." Instead, he was double-crossed by the Taliban. "I'm furious at the C.I.A.," Lohbeck said. "They didn't provide operational security."

As October ended and Osama bin Laden continued to elude the American forces, there was talk in the Pentagon and the White House of lowered expectations. A high-level former intelligence official talked about how the air attacks had "contained" bin Laden and the Taliban leadership, rather than about the prospect of actually capturing him. Bin Laden, one senior general told me, might not be dead, "but he's hiding in a cave at six thousand feet freezing his ass off." A former State Department official added, "What worries me is if, a month from now, bin Laden gets on Al Jazeera and thumbs his nose at us. It'd be a huge loss of prestige for the United States."

A senior official I spoke to at that point, less than a month into the war, acknowledged that there were serious problems in the effort thus far, but said, "It's like reading a six-hundred-page murder mystery. It's solved on the last few pages, but you have to read five hundred and ninety-eight pages to get there."

2. The Getaway

In November 2001, the Northern Alliance, supported by American Special Forces troops and emboldened by the highly accurate American bombing, forced thousands of Taliban and Al Qaeda fighters to retreat inside the hill town of Kunduz, in northern Afghanistan. Trapped with them were Pakistani Army officers, intelligence advisers, and volunteers who were fighting alongside the Taliban. Pakistan had been the Taliban's staunchest military and economic supporter in its long-running war against the Northern Alliance, and many in the Pakistani military have close personal and religious ties to the Taliban dating back to their war against the Soviet Union. Many of the fighters had fled earlier defeats at Mazar-i-Sharif, to the west; Taloqan, to the east; and Pul-i-Khumri, to the south. The road to Kabul, a potential point of retreat, was blocked and was targeted by American bombers. Kunduz offered safety from the bombs and a chance to negotiate painless surrender terms, as Afghan tribes often do.

Surrender negotiations began immediately, but the Bush Administration heatedly—and successfully—opposed them. On November 25th, the Northern Alliance took Kunduz, capturing some four thousand of the Taliban and Al Qaeda fighters. The next day, President Bush said, "We're smoking them out. They're running, and now we're going to bring them to justice."

Even before the siege ended, however, a puzzling series of reports appeared in the *New York Times* and in other publications, quoting Northern Alliance officials who claimed that Pakistani airplanes had flown into Kunduz to evacuate the Pakistanis there. American and Pakistani officials refused to confirm the reports. On November 16th, when journalists asked Rumsfeld about the reports of rescue aircraft, he was dismissive. "Well, if we see them, we shoot them down," he said. Five days later, Rumsfeld declared, "Any idea that those people should be let loose on any basis at all to leave that country and to go bring terror to other countries and destabilize other countries is unacceptable." At a Pentagon news conference on Monday, November 26th, the day after Kunduz fell, General Myers was asked about the reports. The general did not directly answer the question but stated, "The runway there is not usable. I mean, there are segments of it that are usable. They're too short for your standard transport aircraft. So we're not sure where the reports are coming from."

Pakistani officials also debunked the rescue reports, and continued to insist, as they had throughout the Afghanistan war, that no Pakistani military personnel were in the country. Anwar Mehmood, the government spokesman, told newsmen at the time that reports of a Pakistani airlift were "total rubbish. Hogwash."

In interviews in the next months, however, American intelligence officials and high-ranking military officers told me that Pakistanis were indeed flown to safety, in a series of nighttime airlifts that were approved by the Bush Administration. The Americans also said that what was supposed to be a limited evacuation apparently

slipped out of control, and, as an unintended consequence, an unknown number of Taliban and Al Qaeda fighters managed to join in
the exodus. "Dirt got through the screen," a senior intelligence official told me.

Pakistan's leader, General Pervez Musharraf, who seized power in
a 1999 coup, had risked his standing with the religious fundamentalists—and perhaps his life—by endorsing the American attack on
Afghanistan and the American support of the Northern Alliance. At
the time of Kunduz, his decision looked like an especially dangerous
one. The initial American aim in Afghanistan had been not to eliminate the Taliban's presence there entirely but to undermine the
regime and Al Qaeda while leaving intact so-called moderate Taliban elements that would play a role in a new postwar government.
This would insure that Pakistan would not end up with a regime on
its border dominated by the Northern Alliance. By mid-November
2001, it was clear that the Northern Alliance would quickly sweep
through Afghanistan. There were fears that once the Northern Alliance took Kunduz, there would be wholesale killings of the defeated fighters, especially the foreigners.

Musharraf won American support for the airlift by warning that
the humiliation of losing hundreds—and perhaps thousands—of
Pakistani Army men and Pakistani Inter-Services Intelligence, or
I.S.I., operatives would jeopardize his political survival. "Clearly,
there is a great willingness to help Musharraf," an American intelligence official told me. A C.I.A. analyst said that it was his understanding that the decision to permit the airlift was made by the
White House and was indeed driven by a desire to protect the Pakistani leader. According to a former high-level American defense official, the airlift was approved because of representations by the
Pakistanis that "there were guys—intelligence agents and underground guys—who needed to get out."

Once under way, a senior American defense adviser said, the airlift became chaotic. "Everyone brought their friends with them," he said, referring to the Afghans with whom the Pakistanis had worked, and whom they had trained or had used to run intelligence operations. "You're not going to leave them behind to get their throats cut." Recalling the last-minute American evacuation at the end of the Vietnam War, in 1975, the adviser added, "When we came out of Saigon, we brought our boys with us." He meant South Vietnamese nationals. " 'How many does that helicopter hold? Ten? We're bringing fourteen.' "

Some C.I.A. analysts believed that bin Laden himself had eluded American capture early in the war with help from elements of Pakistani intelligence. In late October, one senior Administration official had told me that, despite the bombings and the efforts by C.I.A. operatives in the area to persuade Taliban commanders to defect, "People in my building wonder why there hasn't been a truly significant defection." In a subsequent interview, a former C.I.A. officer provided one reason for that failure. The agency, he said, had few or no people in the field who spoke fluent Pashto, the language of the Taliban, and had been forced to rely on Pakistani I.S.I. officers to communicate its offers to potential defectors. Thus, he said, "the same Pakistani case officers who built up the Taliban are doing the translating for the C.I.A. It's like using the Gottis to translate a conversation with the Lucheses." Another intelligence officer depicted the language situation in Afghanistan as "madness." He added, "Our biggest mistake is allowing the I.S.I. to be our eyes and ears."

The airlift "made sense at the time," the C.I.A. analyst said. "Many of the people they spirited away were the Taliban leadership"—who Pakistan hoped could play a role in a postwar Afghan government. According to this person, "Musharraf wanted to have these people to put another card on the table" in future political negotiations. "We were supposed to have access to them," he said, but "it didn't happen," and the rescued Taliban remained unavailable to American intelligence.

None of the American intelligence officials I spoke with were able to say with certainty how many Taliban and Al Qaeda fighters were flown to safety or may have escaped from Kunduz by other means. Operatives in India's main external intelligence unit—known as RAW, for Research and Analysis Wing—reported extensively on the Pakistani airlift out of Kunduz. RAW has excellent access to the Northern Alliance and a highly sophisticated ability to intercept electronic communications. An Indian military adviser boasted that when the airlift began, "we knew within minutes." In interviews in New Delhi soon after the airlifts, Indian national security and intelligence officials repeatedly told me that the airlift had rescued not only members of the Pakistani military but Pakistani citizens who had volunteered to fight against the Northern Alliance, as well as non-Pakistani Taliban and Al Qaeda. Brajesh Mishra, India's national security adviser, said his government had concluded that five thousand Pakistanis and Taliban—he called it "a ballpark figure"—had been rescued.

According to RAW's senior analyst for Pakistani and Afghan issues, the most extensive rescue efforts took place on three nights at the time of the fall of Kunduz. Indian intelligence had concluded that eight thousand or more men were trapped inside the city in the last days of the siege, roughly half of whom were Pakistanis. (Afghans, Uzbeks, Chechens, and various Arab mercenaries accounted for the rest.) At least five flights were specifically "confirmed" by India's informants, the RAW analyst told me, and many more were believed to have taken place.

In the Indian assessment, thirty-three hundred prisoners surrendered to a Northern Alliance tribal faction headed by General Abdul Rashid Dostum. A few hundred Taliban were also turned over to other tribal leaders. That left between four and five thousand men unaccounted for. "Where are the balance?" the intelligence officer asked. According to him, two Pakistani Army generals were on the flights.

The Bush Administration may have done more than simply acquiesce in the rescue effort: at the height of the standoff, according to both a C.I.A. official and a military analyst who has worked with the Delta Force, the American commando unit that was destroying Taliban units on the ground, the Administration ordered CENTCOM to set up a special air corridor to help insure the safety of the Pakistani rescue flights from Kunduz to the northwest corner of Pakistan, about two hundred miles away. The order left some members of the Delta Force deeply frustrated. "These guys did Desert Storm and Mogadishu," the military analyst said. "They see things in black-and-white. 'Unhappy' is not the word. They're supposed to be killing people." The airlift also angered the Northern Alliance, whose leadership, according to Reuel Gerecht, a former Near East operative for the C.I.A., had sought unsuccessfully for years to "get people to pay attention to the Pakistani element" among the Taliban. The Northern Alliance was eager to capture "mainline Pakistani military and intelligence officers" at Kunduz, Gerecht said. "When the rescue flights started, it touched a raw nerve."

December of 2001 turned out to be the high point of the American involvement in Afghanistan. The armies of the Northern Alliance, supported by American airpower and Special Forces troops, took Kabul, forcing the Taliban from power. At a conference of various Afghan factions held in Bonn, the Administration's candidate, Hamid Karzai, was named chairman of the interim government. (His appointment as president was confirmed six months later at a carefully orchestrated Afghan tribal council, known as a Loya Jirga.) It was a significant achievement, but there were major flaws in the broader accord. There was no agreement on establishing an international police force, no procedures for collecting taxes, no strategy for disarming either the many militias or individual Afghans, and no resolution with the Taliban.

"The game against bin Laden is not over," one analyst told me in January 2002. The analyst said that he had concluded that "he's out. We've been looking for bombing targets for weeks and weeks there but can't identify them."

That January, Donald Rumsfeld told journalists that he believed bin Laden was still in Afghanistan. At the same time, in an interview with me, a senior C.I.A. official cautioned that there were a variety of competing assessments inside the agency as to bin Laden's whereabouts. "We really don't know," he said. "We'll get him, but anybody who tells you we know where he is is full of it."

———

There's always a story that wasn't written, and it almost always should have been. The one that follows is about an American military operation in March of 2002 in the mountains of Afghanistan that border Pakistan. At the time, there was already frustration in the military and the press about progress in Afghanistan. Osama bin Laden was still at large and the Taliban, far from being smashed, had retreated into the mountains. The Pentagon presented the engagement to the public as an example of American resolve and of its determination to extend the ground war to even the most fortified Al Qaeda redoubt. The Bush Administration's spin carried the day with the American press.

During my reporting, I was told that the operation was far more troubled than the Pentagon had let on. I discussed what I was learning with retired Army General Wesley Clark, the former NATO commander who later became a Democratic candidate for president. Clark knew about what had happened in the mountains—his contacts inside the Army remained excellent—and, as usual, had a distinctive take on it. Two years later, I bumped into Clark at a television studio, and he surprised me by asking why the story hadn't made it into the pages of *The New Yorker.* I mumbled some answer and the former general gave me a withering glance. He then told me, in emphatic terms, that I should have made sure that the story got out and that, in his view, if the public had understood the lack of resources the Army had in Afghanistan it "might have saved some lives later."

———

In the weeks before the U.S. Army launched a ground assault on entrenched Al Qaeda forces in the Shah-i-Kot mountains of eastern Afghanistan, on March 2, 2002, a bruising interservice dispute over tactics broke out, according to a group of active duty and retired military and intelligence officials. The attack, code-named Operation Anaconda, praised as a triumph by the Pentagon, resulted in eight American dead and forty wounded, in addition to an unknown number of casualties among Afghans working with Americans.

The plan, as devised by officers at CENTCOM, headed at the time by Army General Tommy Franks, called for American and Afghan forces to drive in truck convoys up the main mountain road leading east from the town of Gardez into the Shah-i-Kot Valley, where a large contingent of Al Qaeda and Taliban fighters had gathered in the previous months. A former high-level intelligence officer told me that senior Marine Corps officers objected vigorously to the proposed assault, and when the plans were not altered, the Marines took the dramatic step of withdrawing from active participation in the operation.

The dispute between the Marines and CENTCOM had its beginnings in December 2001, officials said, when General Franks made it known that he might order a reinforced company of Marines, then assigned to the guarding of an airfield near Kandahar, to begin searching caves near Tora Bora, with the support of the Army. A CENTCOM spokesman told newsmen on December 26th that the Marines "are trained to accomplish missions such as that, and if he"—Franks—"feels the need to call these folks, he will do so." The company of Marines, part of a self-contained Marine Expeditionary

Unit, never went to Tora Bora. Donald Rumsfeld subsequently dismissed the issue in a press conference at the Pentagon: "The stuff you're reading about in the paper, that there was a decision to send in five hundred Marines, then a decision to not send in five hundred Marines, that's all newspaper talk."

In fact, military and intelligence officials said, Franks' proposal to shift some of the Marines to Tora Bora was bitterly resisted at the time by the Marines, who have insisted since World War II on operating in self-contained units. Eventually, the Marines and CENT-COM worked out an extraordinary written memorandum of understanding (M.O.U.) that outlined the conditions under which the Marines would operate. It set the terms of the engagement. "It's all about what is the mission," a Pentagon consultant said. "We're not the Army," a former Marine planner told me. "We don't only do ground operations. We're not the Air Force. We don't do air only. We go in with our armor, our artillery, our close air support. We beat everybody because we do it all together."

CENTCOM's insistence on using Marines in what the Marines saw as the high-risk Anaconda attack revived the interservice conflict. One glaring problem, officials told me, was the lack of intelligence. The CENTCOM planners were unable to tell the Marines, a former high-level intelligence official said, whether the Al Qaeda would "fight or run away. It drove the Marines nuts," the former official added. "How dumb can you be? They said, 'Maybe they'll fight or maybe they'll run away.' The Marines said, 'Fuck you. We're not going to do it. These are young kids at risk.' That's why I love the Marines."

"If you try and make us do it," the former officer quoted a Marine as saying, "we will go public and expose the whole mess"— including the existence of the memorandum of understanding. The CENTCOM command was told that "the public will come out on our side." The Marines were not included in the final plan.

Yet another point of tension was the initial refusal of CENT-COM to alter its attack plan to include a last-minute report by a

SEAL team that uncovered an additional cave system in the Shah-i-Kot Valley. The complex appeared to be occupied by Al Qaeda. The SEALs noted that the caves "needed to be targeted, but CENT-COM didn't want to slow down the attack," the former official said. The planners had worked out strike details to the minute, he added, and "their mindset is that you guys have to execute it, even when on-the-ground realities force changes. The colonels [at CENT-COM] still didn't want to change it." The former official said that the SEALs insisted that "They could not proceed further until you bomb." Their complaints had little effect, he said, until Air Force Lieutenant General T. Michael "Buzz" Moseley, the CENTCOM air commander, intervened and said, "We can do it." He said, "Ultimately, reason prevailed. The very idea that there would be a debate over this is shocking to me."

The actions of General Franks and the Army commander on the ground in Afghanistan, Major General Frank Hagenbeck, were seen as confounding, and hostile, by many in the Air Force. Months after the operation, I obtained a copy of an Air Force PowerPoint briefing on Anaconda that essentially accused the Army of endangering soldiers by cutting the Air Force out of the planning process. "The exclusion of the air component was deliberate and resulted in a suboptimal joint operation," the briefing said. The study noted that "Airman and soldiers were put at risk" at the helicopter landing zones, where combat troops of the 10th Mountain and 101st Airborne Divisions were to be disgorged, because the Army had refused to authorize premission bombing raids that would suppress and perhaps eliminate enemy fire. Air Force planners were told, the study noted, that Generals Franks and Hagenbeck rejected the advance bombing because they "wanted to retain the element of surprise. . . . We thought that we could do it on our own." The Air Force briefing, which was presented at the Air Combat Command in Langley, Virginia, concluded dryly that "surprise was problematic"—it was already known through the region that an attack was coming. A senior Air Force planner later told me, angrily, that General Franks simply did not want to use airpower.

A Pentagon official told me that key aspects of the battle plan, as briefed in advance by CENTCOM, were set not by the Joint Chiefs of Staff but by civilian officials in the Office of the Secretary of Defense—for example, the insistence on using a small force. The Pentagon consultant added that the various Special Forces units on the scene—including Navy SEAL teams and Delta Force—had been routinely going around the military chain of command and placing calls directly to the White House office of Wayne Downing, a retired general who ran Special Forces during the Gulf War and became a presidential adviser on combating terrorism after September 11th. "You need an adult supervisor to say, 'Stop all the bullshit,'" the consultant said. The retired intelligence officer depicted the system at CENTCOM as "broken. Everybody is intimidated and uncertain about how to proceed."

Subsequent events justified the Marines' caution. The first trucks to head up the highway, filled with Afghan fighters who had been through a brief course of training by American Special Forces, were devastated by mortar fire at a fixed point along the road, with as many as forty injured or dead. The Al Qaeda forces had "registered" their mortar fire—that is, calibrated it in advance to hit certain areas on the highway—to great effect, the Pentagon official said. The Afghans retreated and then balked when ordered to go back up the mountain, a former C.I.A. official said: "They knew that the first wave had been blown away."

The former C.I.A. official said, "It was clear that the opposition had time to set up mortar traps and line of fire. It was clear that they were ready for our advance, and they'd been ready for two months and were going to fight to the end. We knew they were there, but it doesn't appear that we knew about their mortar emplacements or their mortar alleys."

The Pentagon consultant explained that CENTCOM had failed, in its advance planning, to "systematically eat up sections of land, grid by grid," with mortar and artillery attacks. "This is all about jumping on the back of trucks, going up a hill, and saying, 'Oh shit, they're shooting at us.'" (The former C.I.A. official said, "You don't have to be a military man to understand that before you attack on the ground, you have to pave the highway with lead.")

General Franks said in a press conference on March 4th, "One, I think, wants to be very careful about just arbitrarily bombing." Anaconda was a job for the conventional Army, Franks said. "At the end of the day, the sure way to do work against the enemy is to put people on the ground, and that's what we've done in this case, and that's the reason we did it that way."

The American ground attack was synchronized with a helicopter assault high up in the mountains. Helicopters dropped two companies of troops from the 10th Mountain Division, 2nd Brigade, into a designated landing zone at one end of the valley; they were to serve as a blocking force to engage and destroy the Al Qaeda forces who, if things went as planned, would flee from the Special Forces and Afghan ground assault. The Americans instead came under fire as they tumbled from the helicopters—once again, from registered mortar rounds—and suffered immediate casualties. At that point, a former C.I.A. counterterrorism official told me, "There was a complete breakdown at the tactical level. It was a disaster." A former Marine officer added, "The chain of command froze. Young soldiers cried and threw down their weapons. There was a total unit failure." The landing zone was littered with weapons, backpacks, night-vision goggles, and radios as the soldiers fled down the mountain to safety.

Retired General Wesley Clark defended the soldiers. He criticized the senior Army leadership for sending troops into combat with little training and poor intelligence. "So some night-vision goggles were lost—who cares? What would be worse? To have people killed or some night goggles lost?" Clark said. "The fact that a bunch of guys got un-hinged is not good. But most of them were fine."

Far more distressing, Clark added, was that the 10th Mountain Division's 2nd Brigade was not adequately prepared when it was sent into combat. "It's been a travesty for years," Clark said. "You've got half-assed units all over the place. It's a function of trying to do things on the cheap. And who suffers? The kids."

A former senior intelligence officer confirmed that manpower and training weaknesses inside the 10th Mountain were widely known among the military leadership in Afghanistan. Some weeks before the March offensive, the former officer said, senior sergeants from Delta Force were assigned to the 2nd Brigade to serve as last-minute training officers. The Delta Force instructors found that the soldiers "didn't know about perimeter security," the former officer said. "They didn't know how to clear their weapons." The Army brass was warned, " 'They're dead meat if they go out there.' "

Seven of the eight American fatalities in Anaconda were mem-bers of a Special Operations team whose mission, along with other Special Forces units, was to flush the Al Qaeda from their hideouts and into range of the waiting Army units. That aspect of the attack plan was disrupted early on the first morning when a SEAL jumped off a helicopter in order to help American soldiers on the ground and found himself alone and under attack by Al Qaeda gunmen. The SEAL, armed with a handgun, defended himself courageously but futilely. A squad of his Special Forces colleagues flew to his rescue—unaware that he was already dead. One of their helicopters, straining to maintain speed and maneuverability in the high alti-tude, was severely damaged by ground fire. Over the next twelve hours, six more Americans died and eleven were injured before hel-icopters were permitted to risk the ground fire and fly to the scene of the stranded rescuers.

What took place during those hours "remains cloaked in confusion," the *Los Angeles Times* later reported. I was told that the survivors were saved not by fellow Americans but by a team of Australian S.A.S. commandoes who, operating under cover, had climbed high above the battle scene a few days earlier to help coördinate air strikes and provide strategic reconnaissance in the mountains. "The S.A.S. actually came out of their mission and attacked and drove off the Afghans," a former Marine officer said. "We would have lost the entire team." A Pentagon official subsequently confirmed the Australian help, which was never made public. "The Army doesn't want to talk about it because they're embarrassed," the official said, though he added that they were also grateful for the help. The former C.I.A. counterterrorism official provided another reason for the silence: "A lot of people know about this, but think it's not patriotic to blow the lid off."

Pentagon officials had little to say about Afghan claims, made to reporters on the scene, of high casualties along the highway. In the days and weeks after the battle, the Army did its best to turn Operation Anaconda into a success story. Several reporters were provided with briefings and access to soldiers from the 10th Mountain Division, some of whom told the truth about the chaos and panic on that first morning. One of the few detailed accounts appeared in a dispatch by Charles Clover in the London *Financial Times*, on March 11, 2002: "In many cases, the men had to run for their lives, often blowing up their packs with shoulder-fired missiles so they could run faster. They could hear Al Qaeda troops laughing at them when they tried to hit them with machine guns and rifles. Few of the U.S. troops ever got close enough to their adversaries to find out who they were fighting."

But most reporters shared the Army's need to emphasize the positive. A lengthy *Los Angeles Times* account, published March 24th, accurately noted that "a large piece of the plan . . . had ended in a rout," with heavy casualties. But the division's commanders, the *Times* said, "were not discouraged." It quoted Lieutenant Colonel David Gray, the division's operations officer, as saying: "It was a scary situation, but from our position, what that air assault did for us was identify where the decisive point on the battlefield was. We found the enemy on the first day." It was a novel way to describe an ambush.

There was much lingering bitterness. Wesley Clark told me, speaking of the Marines, "You don't have the choice to turn down a mission. They shouldn't have the option." The Air Force planner said, "The Army is talking about showing resolve because it sent a bunch of kids with no plan and no idea how to fight a war up a mountain, and they died."

Anaconda officially ended on March 18th. Over the next two weeks, the Army forces regrouped and, aided by heavy bombing, managed to dislodge the Al Qaeda and Taliban fighters and overrun the cave and tunnel hideouts. There were widespread press and Afghan reports stating that the vast majority of Al Qaeda and Taliban had avoided the brunt of the American attack by simply going across the mountains to Pakistan—as they had months before, at Kunduz. The Army commanders in Afghanistan praised the operation as a significant battle that demonstrated American resolve; and claimed that at least seven hundred Al Qaeda members and their allies had been killed. However, according to *Newsweek*, fewer than ten bodies were found in the mountains at battle's end.

At the time of Anaconda, the cost of the war in Afghanistan was already far greater than the public knew. The former senior intelligence official told me that the C.I.A. and military services had paid many millions of dollars to the leadership of the Northern Alliance and other tribal factions in Afghanistan for their continued support in the war. In mid-November 2001, a top officer of the Northern Alliance received an early-morning payoff of $1 million from the C.I.A. before committing his troops to a battle against the Taliban near Mazar-i-Sharif. His forces were routed and retreated. The C.I.A. paid him another million in the afternoon to regroup his forces and compel them to return to the battlefield. A 2002 analysis by Desmond Ball, an intelligence expert at the Australian National University in Canberra, concluded that the United States had assembled nearly fifty intelligence, communications, navigation, and meteorological satellites to support its operations in Afghanistan, at a total cost of $25 billion. Billions more for additional highly classified satellite systems have been added to the defense budget.

The former C.I.A. counterterrorism official told me that many in the agency had envisioned Operation Anaconda as a last hurrah in terms of a direct American role in Afghanistan. "The bottom line was to do this and get out," the officer said. "This was seen as an exit scenario." The former official, who spent time early in 2002 working inside the agency's clandestine station in Kabul, said that there were growing concerns about security—even in Kabul, where the men and women on duty at the American Embassy and in the nearby C.I.A. station had to check with security officials before venturing out. Conditions elsewhere in Afghanistan were much worse, the operative said, as various tribal clans struggled for dominance. He added, "The house of cards"—the Taliban regime—"fell apart earlier than expected, and we had no idea what to do afterward."

One night in Kabul, the former C.I.A. counterterrorism official recalled, a senior agency officer had confessed over drinks that he was "overwhelmed at how ignorant people at the top are"—and how difficult it was to get information directly into the system. "They're basing everything on briefings that convey a gist of a gist of a gist. The guys at the top are as ignorant as they could be, but at the top loyalty is more important than effectiveness." When he returned to the United States, he said, he, too, was dismayed at the disconnect between the perceptions of the operatives in Afghanistan and how the situation was understood in Washington. "My concern is that the President and even Cheney are not getting all the right advice. What's going on is difficult to deal with, and we"—the C.I.A. men and women in the field—"are having to deal with decisions that are made before anybody checks out all the facts. There's no endgame in terms of where they expect to get and what's supposed to be there," the former official said.

"It's far beyond being scary," he went on. "There is a total failure of the war against terrorism—in spades."

In interviews in early 2002, a number of past and present military and intelligence officials—men who are far from dissidents—questioned whether the Administration had a coherent endgame for the Afghan war. They also questioned the Administration's belief that a crushing victory over the remnants of the Al Qaeda forces still in Afghanistan would be decisive in the war against terrorism. "We've lost sight of our objective"—stopping the spread of terrorism—"and redoubled our efforts," a former high-level intelligence official told me. "Now we're mopping up elements that aren't important. We're getting sucked in just like the Russians did."

The Pentagon consultant, who retired from active duty as a senior commander, told me that Anaconda raised serious issues of command and control: "Who in the hell is in charge?" But he added that flaws in the chain of command would probably not be "a lethal issue" in terms of the overall American war effort in Afghanistan. "There's not enough of them to be worried about. We will drop more ordnance on them than we did in Iwo Jima in World War II," he said. "It's a good thing that it's a third-rate enemy." He was not as confident, he added, of the system's ability to cope in a real crisis, and feared that the inevitable result would be future terrorism attacks in the United States. "In Bush One, Powell and Cheney formed a coherent unit and worked as a team," the defense consultant said. In contrast, the current Administration "is not a coherent group. Too much infighting."

The Pentagon consultant went on: "What I don't know is if they know how this is going to end in Afghanistan." At one meeting, he said, he asked a senior Administration official—a Cabinet officer deeply involved in the war against terrorism—about his strategic vision for Afghanistan. The official had no immediate answer. The consultant said that he pressed him, asking, "Where do you want this to come out?" The Cabinet officer eventually said, vaguely, that he wanted "the good guys to come out ahead." The Bush Administration had "lost focus, and military activity is becoming disconnected from political mandates," the consultant said. "This is the blind leading the blind."

3. A Power Base of Warlords

On December 18, 2002, Donald Rumsfeld gave an upbeat assessment of Afghanistan's future to CNN's Larry King. "They have elected a government. . . . The Taliban are gone. The Al Qaeda are gone. The country is not a perfectly stable place, and it needs a great deal of reconstruction funds," Rumsfeld said. "There are people who are throwing hand grenades and shooting off rockets and trying to kill people, but there are people who are trying to kill people in New York or San Francisco. So it's not going to be a perfectly tidy place." Nonetheless, he said, "I'm hopeful. I'm encouraged." And he added, "I wish them well."

A year and a half later, the Taliban were still a force in many parts of Afghanistan, and the country continued to provide safe haven for members of Al Qaeda. American troops, more than ten thousand of whom remained, were heavily deployed in the mountainous areas near Pakistan, still hunting for Osama bin Laden and Mullah Omar. Hamid Karzai, the U.S.-backed president, exercised little political control outside Kabul and was struggling to undercut the authority of local warlords, who effectively controlled the provinces. Heroin production was soaring, and outside of Kabul and a few other cities, people were terrorized by violence and crime. A report by the United Nations Development Program, made public in March 2004, stated that the nation was in danger of once again becoming a "terrorist breeding ground" unless there was a significant increase in development aid. The turmoil in Afghanistan was becoming a political issue in the presidential campaign, as the Bush Administration's general conduct of the war on terrorism was being challenged by Richard A. Clarke, the former National Security Council terrorism adviser, in his memoir *Against All Enemies*, and in contentious hearings before the 9/11 Commission. The Bush Administration still consistently invoked Afghanistan as a success story—an example of the President's determination. However, it was making this claim in the face of renewed warnings, from international organizations, from allies, and from within its own military—notably a Pentagon-commissioned report that was left in bureaucratic limbo when its conclusions proved negative—that the situation there was deteriorating rapidly.

In his book, Clarke depicts the victory in Afghanistan as far less decisive than the Administration has portrayed it, and he sharply criticizes the Pentagon's tactics, especially the decision to rely on airpower, and not U.S. troops on the ground, in the early weeks. The war began on October 7, 2001, but, he wrote, not until seven weeks later did the United States "insert a ground force unit (Marines) to take and hold a former al Qaeda and Taliban facility. . . . The late-November operation did not include any effort by U.S. forces to seal the border with Pakistan, snatch the al Qaeda leadership, or cut off the al Qaeda escape."

Clarke told me in an interview in April 2004 that the Administration viewed Afghanistan as a military and political backwater—a detour along the road to Iraq, the war that mattered most to the President. Clarke and some of his colleagues, he said, had repeatedly warned the national security leadership that, as he put it, "you can't win the war in Afghanistan with such a small effort." Clarke continued: "There were more cops in New York City than soldiers on the ground in Afghanistan. We had to have a security presence coupled with a development program in every region and stay there for several months."

In retrospect, Clarke said, he believes that the President and his men did not respond for three reasons: "One, they did not want to get involved in Afghanistan like Russia did. Two, they were saving forces for the war in Iraq. And, three, Rumsfeld wanted to have a laboratory to prove his theory about the ability of small numbers of ground troops, coupled with airpower, to win decisive battles." The result, Clarke told me, was that "the U.S. has succeeded in stabilizing only two or three cities. The president of Afghanistan is just the mayor of Kabul."

Deputy Assistant Secretary of Defense Joseph Collins, a Pentagon expert on Afghanistan, acknowledged that it was only since the end of 2003 that "significant money began to flow" into Afghanistan for reconstruction and security. "We found in the security area we were doing the right thing, but not fast enough," he told me. The resurgence of the Taliban and Al Qaeda, Collins said, did not begin until early last year. They had begun to realize that encouraging instability was the key to undermining Karzai's regime—and that the way to do it was "not to fight our soldiers but U.N. officials and aid workers." In the long run, he added, "these tactics are self-defeating—in Afghanistan and in Iraq."

Clarke's view of what went wrong was buttressed by an internal military analysis of the Afghanistan war that was completed in early 2004. A little over a year earlier, the Defense Department's office of Special Operations and Low-Intensity Conflict (SOLIC) had asked Hy Rothstein, a retired Army colonel and leading military expert in unconventional warfare, to examine the planning and execution of the war in Afghanistan. The understanding was that he would focus on Special Forces. As part of his research, Rothstein travelled to

Afghanistan and interviewed many senior military officers, in both Special Forces and regular units. He also talked to dozens of junior Special Forces officers and enlisted men who fought there. His report was a devastating critique of the Administration's strategy. He wrote that the bombing campaign was not the best way to hunt down Osama bin Laden and the rest of the Al Qaeda leadership, and that there was a failure to translate early tactical successes into strategic victory. In fact, he wrote, the victory in Afghanistan was not, in the long run, a victory at all.

In March 2004, I visited Rothstein in his office at the Naval Postgraduate School, in Monterey, California, where he is a senior lecturer in defense analysis. A fit, broad-shouldered man in his early fifties, he served more than twenty years in the Army Special Forces, including three years as the director of plans and exercises for the Joint Special Operations Command at Fort Bragg, before retiring, in 1999. His associates depicted him as anything but a dissident. "He puts boots on the ground," Robert Andrews, a former head of SOLIC, told me, referring to Rothstein's missions in Central America, for which he earned a decoration for valor, and in the former Yugoslavia. Rothstein agreed to speak to me, with some reluctance, only after I had obtained his report independently, and he would not go into details about his research. "They asked me to do this," he said of the Pentagon, "and my purpose was to make some things better. All I want people to do is to look at the paper and not at me. I'll tell you the good and the bad."

The report describes a wide gap between how Donald Rumsfeld represented the war and what was actually taking place. Rumsfeld had told reporters at the start of the Afghanistan bombing campaign, Rothstein wrote, that "you don't fight terrorists with conventional capabilities. You do it with unconventional capabilities." Nonetheless, Rothstein wrote, the United States continued to emphasize bombing and conventional warfare while "the war became increasingly unconventional," with Taliban and Al Qaeda fighters "operating in small cells, emerging only to lay land mines and launch nighttime rocket attacks before disappearing once again." Rothstein added:

> What was needed after December 2001 was a greater emphasis on U.S. special operations troops, supported by light infantry, conducting counterinsurgency operations. Aerial bombardment should have become a rare thing. . . . The failure to adjust U.S. operations in line with the post-Taliban change in theater conditions cost the United States some of the fruits of victory and imposed additional, avoidable humanitarian and stability costs on Afghanistan. . . . Indeed, the war's inadvertent effects may be more significant than we think. By the end of 2001, the Afghan war had essentially become a counterinsurgency.

At this point, it was important to turn to a specific kind of unconventional warfare: "The Special Forces were created to deal with precisely this kind of enemy," Rothstein wrote. "Unorthodox thinking, drawing on a thorough understanding of war, demography, human nature, culture and technology are part of this mental approach. . . . Unconventional warfare prescribes that Special Forces soldiers must be diplomats, doctors, spies, cultural anthropologists, and good friends—all before their primary work comes into play."

Instead, Rothstein said, "the command arrangement evolved into a large and complex structure that could not (or would not) respond to the new unconventional setting." The result has been "a campaign in Afghanistan that effectively destroyed the Taliban but has been significantly less successful at being able to achieve the primary policy goal of ensuring that al Qaeda could no longer operate in Afghanistan."

Rothstein wrote that Rumsfeld routinely responded to criticism about civilian casualties by stating that "some amount" of collateral damage "is inevitable in war." It is estimated that more than a thousand Afghan civilians were killed by bombing and other means in the early stages of the war. Rothstein suggested that these numbers could have been lower, and that further incidents might have been avoided if Special Forces had been allowed to wage a truly unconventional war that reduced the reliance on massive firepower. The Administration's decision to treat the Taliban as though all its members identified with, and would fight for, Al Qaeda was also a crucial early mistake. "There were deep divisions within the Taliban that could have been exploited through a political-military effort, which is the essence of unconventional warfare," Rothstein said. "A few months of intensive diplomatic, intelligence and military preparations between Special Forces and anti-Taliban forces would have made a significant difference."

The conditions under which the post-Taliban government came to power gave "warlordism, banditry and opium production a new lease on life," Rothstein wrote, and left a power vacuum in Afghanistan. He concluded, "Defeating an enemy on the battlefield and winning a war are rarely synonymous. Winning a war calls for more than defeating one's enemy in battle." In 1975, Rothstein recalled, when Harry G. Summers, an Army colonel who later wrote a history of the Vietnam War, told a North Vietnamese colonel, "You never defeated us on the battlefield," the colonel replied, "That may be so, but it is also irrelevant."

Rothstein delivered his report in January 2004. It was returned to him, with the message that he had to cut it drastically and soften his conclusions. Months later, when I spoke to him, he had heard nothing further. "It's a threatening paper," one military consultant told me. The Pentagon, asked for comment, confirmed that Rothstein was told "we did not support all of his conclusions," and said that he would eventually be sent notes. In addition, the Pentagon's Joseph Collins told me, "There may be a kernel of truth in there, but our experts found the study rambling and not terribly informative." In interviews,

however, a number of past and present Bush Administration officials
have endorsed Rothstein's key assertions. "It wasn't like he made it up,"
a former senior intelligence officer said. "The reason they're petrified
is that it's true, and they didn't want to see it in writing."

The Administration had, by then, turned its attention to Iraq, and
seemed eager to put Afghanistan behind it. In interviews with academics, aid workers, and nongovernmental organization officials, I
was repeatedly told that, as the United States began its buildup in
the Gulf, security and political conditions throughout Afghanistan
eroded. In the early summer of 2002, a military consultant, reflect-
ing the views of several American Special Forces commanders in the
field, provided the Pentagon with a briefing, warning that the Taliban and Al Qaeda were adapting quickly to American tactics. "His
decision loop has tightened, ours has widened," the briefing said,
referring to the Taliban. "He can see us, but increasingly we no
longer see him." Only a very few high-level generals listened, and
the briefing changed nothing. By then, some of the most highly
skilled Americans were being diverted from Afghanistan. Richard
Clarke noted in his memoir, "The U.S. Special Forces who were
trained to speak Arabic, the language of al Qaeda, had been pulled
out of Afghanistan and sent to Iraq." Some C.I.A. paramilitary
teams were also transferred to Iraq.

The United States continued to pay off and work closely with
local warlords, many of whom were involved in heroin and opium
trafficking. Their loyalty was not for sale but for rent. Warlords like
Hazrat Ali in eastern Afghanistan, near the Pakistan border, and
Mohammed Fahim had been essential to the United States' initial
military success, and, at first, they had promised to accept Karzai.
Hazrat Ali would be one of several commanders later accused of
double-crossing American troops in an early, unsuccessful sweep for
Al Qaeda in 2002. Fahim, who became the defense minister in December 2001, was deeply involved in a number of illicit enterprises.

In January of 2003, Paul Wolfowitz, the deputy secretary of defense, made a fifteen-hour visit to Kabul and announced, "We're clearly moving into a different phase, where our priority in Afghanistan is increasingly going to be stability and reconstruction. There's no way to go too fast. Faster is better." There was talk of improving security and rebuilding the Afghan National Army in time for presidential and parliamentary elections, but little effort to provide the military and economic resources. "I don't think the Administration understood about winning hearts and minds," a former Administration official told me.

The results of the postwar neglect are stark. A leading scholar on Afghanistan, Barnett R. Rubin, wrote, in the April 2004 issue of *Current History*, that Afghanistan "does not have functioning state institutions. It has no genuine army or effective police. Its ramshackle provincial administration is barely in contact with, let alone obedient to, the central government. Most of the country's meager tax revenue has been illegally taken over by local officials who are little more than warlords with official titles." The goal of American policy in Afghanistan "was not to set up a better regime for the Afghan people," Rubin wrote. "The goal instead was to get rid of the terrorist threat against America." The United States enlisted the warlords in its war against terrorism, and "the result was an Afghan government created at Bonn that rested on a power base of warlords."

One military consultant with extensive experience in Afghanistan told me, "The real action is at the village level, but we're not there. And we need to be there 24/7. Now we are effectively operating above the conflict. It's the same old story as in Vietnam. We can't hit what we can't see." He added, "From January 2002 on, we were in the process of snatching defeat from the jaws of victory."

In the summer of 2003, a coalition of seventy-nine human rights and relief organizations wrote an open letter to the international community calling for better security in Afghanistan and warning that the presidential elections there, then scheduled for June 2004, were imperilled. The letter noted, "For the majority of the Afghan people, security is precarious and controlled by regional warlords, drug traffickers or groups with terrorist associations. The situation is getting worse, and there is no comprehensive plan in place to halt the spiral of violence." Statistics compiled by CARE International showed that eleven aid workers were murdered in four incidents during a three-week period ending in early March 2004, and the rate of physical assaults on aid workers in Afghanistan more than doubled in January and February compared with the same period in the previous year. Such attacks, a CARE policy statement suggested, inevitably led to cutbacks in Afghan humanitarian and reconstruction programs. In early 2003, for example, according to the *Chicago Tribune*, there were twenty-six humanitarian agencies at work in Kandahar, the main Afghan city in the south. By early 2004, there were fewer than five.

Even one of the most publicized achievements of the post-Taliban government, the improvements in the lives of women, has been called into question. Judy Benjamin, who served as the gender adviser to the U.S. Agency for International Development mission in Kabul in 2002 and 2003, told me, in an interview in March 2004, "The legal opportunities have improved, but the day-to-day life for women, even in Kabul, isn't any better. Girls are now legally permitted to go to school and work, but when it comes to the actual family practice, people are afraid to let them go out without burkas." Conditions outside Kabul are far worse, she said. "Families do not allow females to travel—to go to jobs or to school. You cannot go on many roads without being held up by bandits. People are saying they were safer under the Taliban system, which is why the Taliban are getting more support—the lack of safety."

Nancy Lindborg, the executive vice president of Mercy Corps, one of the major N.G.O.s at work in Afghanistan, had a similar view. Outside of Kabul, she said, "everywhere I go, from Kunduz to Kandahar,

I see no change for most women, and security for everybody has fallen apart since November of 2002." The Pentagon's announcements of increased commitments to security and reconstruction were viewed "as a big charade," Lindborg said. "The United States has left Afghanistan to fester for two years."

The humanitarian community is not alone in its concern. In February 2004, Vice Admiral Lowell E. Jacoby, the head of the Defense Intelligence Agency, acknowledged during a Senate Intelligence Committee hearing that the growing Taliban insurgency was targeting humanitarian and reconstruction organizations. Over all, he said, Taliban attacks had "reached their highest levels since the collapse of the Taliban government."

Heroin was among the most immediate—and the most intractable—social, economic, and political problems. "The problem is too huge for us to be able to face alone," Hamid Karzai declared at an international donors' conference in Berlin in April 2004, as he appealed for more aid. "Drugs in Afghanistan are threatening the very existence of the Afghan state." Drug dealing and associated criminal activity produced about $2.3 billion in revenue in 2003, according to an annual survey by the United Nations Office on Drugs and Crime, a sum that was equivalent to half of Afghanistan's legitimate gross domestic product. "Terrorists take a cut as well," the U.N. report noted, adding that "the longer this happens, the greater the threat to security within the country."

The U.N. report, published in the fall of 2003, found that opium production, which, following a ban imposed by the Taliban, had fallen to 185 metric tons in 2001, had soared to 3600 tons—a twentyfold increase. The report declared the nation to be "at a crossroads: either (i) energetic interdiction measures are taken now . . . or (ii) the drug cancer in Afghanistan will keep spreading and metastasise into corruption, violence and terrorism—within and beyond the country's borders." Afghanistan was once again, the U.N. said, producing three-quarters of the world's illicit opium, with no evidence of a cutback in sight, even though there has been a steady stream of reports from Washington about drug interdictions. The report said that poppy cultivation had continued to spread and was reported in twenty-eight of the nation's thirty-two provinces.

Most alarmingly, according to a U.N. survey, nearly 70 percent of farmers intended to increase their poppy crops in 2004, most of them by more than half. Only a small percentage of farmers were planning any reduction, despite years of international pressure. Many of the areas that the U.N. report identified as likely to see increased production are in regions where the United States has a major military presence. Despite such statistics, the American military has, for the most part, looked the other way, essentially because of the belief that the warlords can deliver the Taliban and Al Qaeda. One senior N.G.O. official told me, "Everybody knows that the U.S. military has the drug lords on the payroll. We've put them back in power. It's gone so terribly wrong." (The Pentagon's Joseph Collins told me, "Counternarcotics in Afghanistan has been a failure." Collins said that the 2004 crop was estimated to be the second largest on record.)

The easy availability of heroin also represents a threat to the well-being of American troops. Since the fall of 2002, a number of active-duty and retired military and C.I.A. officials have told me about increasing reports of heroin use by American military personnel in Afghanistan, many of whom have been there for months, with few distractions. A former high-level intelligence officer told me that the problem wasn't the Special Forces or Army combat units who were active in the field but "the logistical guys"—the truck drivers and the food and maintenance workers who are stationed at the military's large base at Bagram, near Kabul. However, I was also told that there were concerns about heroin use within the Marines. In the spring of 2004, the former intelligence officer told me that while G.I.s assigned to Bagram were nominally confined to the base, for security reasons, the drugs were relayed to the users by local Afghans hired to handle menial duties. The Pentagon's senior leadership has a "head-in-the-sand attitude," he said. "There's no desire to expose it and get enforcement involved. This is hard shit," he added, speaking of heroin.

The Pentagon, asked for comment that April, denied that there was concern about drug use at Bagram, but went on to acknowledge that "disciplinary proceedings were initiated against some U.S. military personnel in Afghanistan for suspected drug use." Asked separately about the allegations against Marines, the Pentagon said that some Marines had been removed from Afghanistan to face disciplinary proceedings, but blamed alcohol and marijuana rather than heroin.

The drug lords traditionally processed only hashish inside the Afghan borders and shipped poppies to heroin-production plants in northern Pakistan and elsewhere. A senior U.N. narcotics official told me that since 2002 "most of the heroin has been processed in Afghanistan, as part of a plan to keep profits in-country." Only a fraction of what is produced in Afghanistan is used there, the narcotics official said. Nonetheless, a U.S. government relief official told me, the "biggest worry" is that the growth in local production will increase the risk of addiction among G.I.s. A former C.I.A. officer who served in Afghanistan also said that the agency's narcotics officials were independently investigating military drug use.

Afghanistan began to regain the Bush Administration's attention in the spring of 2004, in part because the worsening situation in Iraq has increased the need for a foreign policy success. State Department and intelligence officials who had worked in Kabul told me that their understanding, as of April, was that Afghanistan's presidential and parliamentary elections, which had already been rescheduled for September, had to be held before the American presidential elections on November 2nd. The upside to the political timetable was a new commitment of American reconstruction funds—more than $2 billion, a fourfold increase over the previous year—for schools, clinics, and road construction in Afghanistan. "Why are we getting aid money now?" the U.S. government relief official said to me, with a laugh. "We've been asking for two years and no one in their right mind thought about getting all this."

In insisting that elections be held by the fall, the Administration was overriding the advice of many of its allies and continuing to bank heavily on Hamid Karzai. The international conference in Berlin bolstered Karzai's regime, and his prospects in elections, by promising to provide more than $4 billion in aid and low-cost loans in the next year—although that figure includes more than $1 billion previously pledged. Half of the contributions came from the Bush Administration. Secretary of State Colin Powell praised Karzai for having turned Afghanistan from "a failed state, ruled by extremists and terrorists, to a free country with a growing economy and emerging democracy."

Nonetheless, Hamid Karzai appeared unsure of himself and totally dependent on the United States for security and finances. One of Karzai's many antagonists was his own defense minister, Mohammed Fahim. In 2003, the Bush Administration was privately given a memorandum by an Afghan official and American ally, warning that Fahim was working to undermine Karzai and would use his control over money from illegal businesses and customs revenue to do so. Fahim was also said to have recruited at least eighty thousand men into new militias.

The United States' toleration of warlords such as Fahim and General Abdul Rashid Dostum—an alleged war criminal and gunrunner who, after being offered millions of dollars by Washington, helped defeat the Taliban in the fall of 2001—mystifies many who have long experience in Afghanistan. "Fahim and Dostum are part of the problem, and not the solution," said Milt Bearden, who ran the C.I.A.'s Afghan operations during the war with the Soviet Union. "These people have the clever gene and they can get us to do their fighting for them. They just lead us down the path," Bearden said. "How wonderful for them to have us knock off their opposition with American airplanes and Special Forces."

The wild card may be the Taliban. The former Taliban foreign minister, Wakil Ahmed Muttawakil, who spent months in American custody, repeatedly offered to open a channel to the Taliban leadership for extended talks. "But the Administration only wants to get help in finding Osama bin Laden," a Democratic Senate aide said. "Its only concern is tactical information." The Taliban's influence grew in early 2004 throughout the south and east of Afghanistan, in defiance of—or, perhaps, because of—continued American air and ground assaults, which inevitably result in civilian casualties.

At the same time, in an effort to strengthen Karzai, the American military command was trying to reduce its own reliance on some regional warlords. One target was Ismail Khan, the popular independent governor of Herat, a large province in western Afghanistan, adjacent to Iran. Khan, a bitter enemy of the Taliban, supported the initial American invasion of Afghanistan after September 11th. He then defied the central government and refused to hand over to Kabul most of the tax and customs revenue. (Herat is an ancient trade center.) Khan personified how difficult it was for the United States to separate its enemies from its allies in Afghanistan. "If Mohammed Fahim is a government minister and Ismail Khan is a warlord," one American official told me, "you're abusing the language." The official's point was that Khan had provided better security and more stability for the local population than was found in other Afghan provinces, and international observers believed that he would probably win a provincial election. But he treated Herat as a private fiefdom and alarmed many in the Bush Administration with his vocal support of Iran; in the fall of 2003, he was quoted as calling it "the best model of an Islamic country in the world."

One regional expert told me that in the spring of 2003, during a brief visit by Donald Rumsfeld to Kabul, Karzai—who was always apprehensive about Ismail Khan—raised the question of how to remove him. "He asked Rumsfeld for his support," the expert recalled. "Rumsfeld wished him good luck but said the United States could not get involved. So Karzai got cold feet." The issue was revisited again the following February, a former C.I.A. consultant told me, by the American military command at Bagram. Sometime that month, the American command put out a request to its intelligence components for a new operational plan for Khan. The former C.I.A. consultant learned from within the intelligence community that there was agreement that Khan had to be neutralized. Asked what that meant, he said that he was told, "Khan had to be eliminated— we've got to end his influence." (The Pentagon denied that there was such a plan.)

On March 21, 2004, an armed conflict erupted in Herat between Khan's forces and those loyal to the central government. Accounts of what happened vary widely; it was not immediately clear who started what. According to an account by U.N. workers in Afghanistan, filed to headquarters in New York, tensions had been mounting between Khan and one of his bitter rivals, General Abdul Zaher Naibzadah, over control of the Afghan military's Herat garrison. Khan's son heard reports that there had been an assassination attempt on his father and drove to the general's house, where Naibzadah's bodyguards gunned him down, along with others. According to the U.N. dispatch, Ismail Khan took violent revenge on his attackers, burning down the local headquarters of the Afghan militia and killing scores. (Some press accounts put the death toll of the subsequent daylong battle at a hundred or more; other accounts, emanating from Kabul, said that fewer than two dozen were killed.) The U.N. account included reports that a personal phone call from Karzai to Khan was necessary to defuse the situation. In the next days, a division of the Afghan National Army, sent by the central government, moved into Herat to restore order.

There is no evidence that the American commanders were

involved in any attempt on Khan's life, the C.I.A. consultant told me. But according to some officials, Americans were attached to Afghan military units that were present in Herat. "We clearly had embedded American trainers and advisers with the Afghan troops," the consultant said. "They knew what was going on." The result, the U.N. reported, was that Khan "may become even more intractable in his dealing with the central government." The American-endorsed plan to challenge Khan's leadership and strengthen Karzai's national standing inside Afghanistan, it seemed, had served to make Khan a more determined enemy.

The U.S. government relief official told me of spending weeks travelling through Afghanistan—including the south and the east, areas with few ties to the central government in Kabul. "They'd say, 'We don't like the Taliban, but they did bring us security you haven't been able to give us,'" the official said. "They perceived that we were allied with the bad guys—the warlords—because of our war on terrorism." The official recalled being asked constantly about the American war in Iraq. "They were concerned about Iraq, and wanted to know, 'Are you going to stay?' They remembered how we left"—after the American-sponsored defeat of the Soviet Union in Afghanistan. "They'd say, 'You guys are going to leave us, like you did in 1992. If we had confidence in the staying power of America, we'd deal with you.'" The official concluded, "Iraq, in their mind, meant that America had bigger priorities."

A U.N. worker who was helping to prepare for elections in Afghanistan told me that American aid funds, whatever the Administration's motives in supplying them, were essential for the country's future. "We've got a golden window of opportunity that will close on November 2nd"—the date of the American Presidential election. It was a cynical process, he added. "A key factor in holding the election will be the noninterference of the various drug-dealing warlords around the nation, and stemming the drug trade will not be a priority." The message he was getting from the warlords, the U.N. worker said, was that if the United States attempted a "hard and heavy" poppy eradication program, the warlords would disrupt the elections.

The U.N. worker added that among Afghans President Karzai was perceived as "a weak leader with very little street credibility." He told me that, again and again, when he met with village elders as part of his work, "the old people say, 'Hamid is a good man. He doesn't kill people. He doesn't steal things. He doesn't sell drugs. How could you possibly think he could be a leader of Afghanistan?' "

IV.

THE IRAQ HAWKS

I wrote two articles in late 2001 and early 2002 for *The New Yorker* depicting the Bush Administration's bitter infighting over the need to overthrow Saddam Hussein and the link, if any, between Iraq and the war on terror. The accounts below show that the fight to set the agenda on Iraq was no secret, and that neoconservatives like Richard Perle, who got his way in Iraq, had difficulty listening to, or learning from, their critics. The future missteps in Iraq were predictable and perhaps inevitable. Perle, as we shall see, had problems of his own.

1. The Early Fight to Take On Saddam Hussein

In November of 1993, Ahmad Chalabi, the leader of the Iraqi National Congress, an opposition group devoted to the overthrow of Saddam Hussein, presented the Clinton Administration with a detailed, four-phase war plan entitled "The End Game," along with an urgent plea for money to finance it. "The time for the plan is now,"

Chalabi wrote. "Iraq is on the verge of spontaneous combustion. It only needs a trigger to set off a chain of events that will lead to the overthrow of Saddam." It was a message that Chalabi would repeat, with increasing effectiveness, for the next ten years.

Chalabi, who was born into a wealthy Shiite banking family, hadn't lived in Iraq for decades. He had emigrated to England with his parents in 1958, when he was thirteen years old, and earned a doctorate in mathematics from the University of Chicago. In 1992, he had been convicted in absentia of bank fraud in Jordan. (He has always denied any wrongdoing.) Chalabi received money and authorization from the Clinton Administration to put his plan into effect, however, and by October 1994, a small C.I.A. outpost had been set up in an area in northern Iraq controlled by the Kurds. Chalabi's headquarters were nearby. His plan called for simultaneous insurrections in Basra, the largest city in southern Iraq, which is dominated by disaffected Shiites (Saddam is a Sunni, as were many of his followers), and in Mosul and Kirkuk, Kurdish cities in the north. Massive Iraqi military defections would follow. "We called it Chalabi's rolling coup," Bob Baer, the C.I.A. agent in charge, recounted.

At the time, Baer has written in his memoir *See No Evil*, "the C.I.A. didn't have a single source in Iraq. . . . Not only were there no human sources in-country, the C.I.A. didn't have any in the neighboring countries—Iran, Jordan, Turkey, and Saudi Arabia— who reported on Iraq. Like the rest of the U.S. government, its intelligence-gathering apparatus was blind when it came to Iraq."

In March 1995, Chalabi's insurrection was launched, and failed dramatically. "There was nothing there," Baer told me. "No one moved except one Kurdish leader acting on his own—three days too late. Nothing happened." As far as recruiting agents from inside the Iraqi military, "Chalabi didn't deliver a single lieutenant, let alone a colonel or a general."

Baer emphasized that, as he put it, "Chalabi was trying." Even so, Baer said, "he was bluffing—he thought it was better to bluff and try to win. But he was forced to play bridge with no trump cards." Baer went on, "He always thought it was a psychological war, and that if Clinton would stand up and say, 'It's time for the guy to go,' people would do it."

Chalabi had written in his war plan that if there was "no movement" and if Saddam was permitted to export oil, "then the psychology of the people will turn. Saddam will appear to open [for] them hope for the future. At that point he will have escaped." A month after the failed insurrection, the United Nations Security Council allowed Iraq to resume oil sales under its Oil for Food program, insuring a flow of money to the regime. By late 1996, the Iraqi Army had all but driven Chalabi's operation out of northern Iraq. A hundred and thirty Iraqi National Congress members were executed.

Chalabi managed to maintain his hold on the I.N.C., despite repeated charges from his coalition's members of mismanagement, self-aggrandizement, and corruption. After his failure in the field, his plans were essentially written off by the State Department and the C.I.A., and he moved his anti-Saddam base to London. America's goal would be to pursue Saddam's removal by military or political coup, and not by open rebellion. "I don't see an opposition group that has the viability to overthrow Saddam," Marine Corps General Anthony Zinni, then the commander of CENTCOM, who later served as the U.S. special envoy to the Middle East, told a Senate committee in 1998. "Even if we had Saddam gone, we could end up with fifteen, twenty, or ninety groups competing for power."

Chalabi bore his fall from official favor gracefully. Disdainful of the Clinton Administration, which he felt had abandoned him in northern Iraq, he took his campaign to the press and to Congress. The I.N.C. soon emerged as a rallying point for political conservatives and for many of the former senior officials who had run the Gulf War for the first President Bush.

In February of 1998, forty prominent Americans—including

Caspar Weinberger, Frank Carlucci, and Donald Rumsfeld, all former secretaries of defense—signed an open letter to President Clinton warning that Saddam Hussein still posed an immediate threat,
because he had a stockpile of biological and chemical weapons.
They urged that the government once again consider fostering a
popular uprising against the Iraqi government. Echoing Chalabi's
1993 war plan, the letter writers argued that Saddam's weakness was
his lack of popular support: "He rules by terror. The same brutality
which makes it unlikely that any coups or conspiracies can succeed
makes him hated by his own people. . . . Iraq today is ripe for a
broad-based insurrection." Their first two recommendations were
that the I.N.C. be recognized as the provisional government of Iraq
and be reinstalled in northern Iraq. Another recommendation urged
the Clinton Administration to release Iraqi assets frozen at the time
of the Gulf War, which total more than $1.5 billion, to help fund
the provisional government.

The letter, like similar pleas from congressional Republicans,
failed to persuade the Democrats in the White House. Eight months
later President Clinton, under pressure from Congress, signed the
Iraq Liberation Act, which allocated $97 million for training and
military equipment for the Iraqi opposition. Because of continued
skepticism within the government, the I.N.C. had, as of late 2001,
received less than $1 million of that money, but the State Depart-
ment provided the group with roughly $10 million in routine oper-
ating funds. (That fall, the State Department Inspector General
conducted a review into how the I.N.C. had handled two grants that
totalled more than $4 million. The review found that the I.N.C.'s
accounting practices and internal controls were inadequate, and
raised questions about more than $2 million in expenses.)

According to one of Chalabi's advisers, the I.N.C.'s war plan before September 11th revolved around training, encouraging defectors,
and American enforcement of the no-fly zone in southern Iraq. The
idea was to recruit two hundred instructors and put them to work

training a force of five thousand or more dissident Iraqis, reinforced by soldiers of fortune, some of whom, inevitably, would be retired Americans who had served in Special Forces units. The United States would also be asked to institute a no-drive zone, backed up by air strikes, to protect the insurgents from attack by Iraqi tanks.

A Chalabi adviser explained, "You insert this force into southern Iraq"—the site of most of Iraq's oil fields—"perhaps at an abandoned airbase west of Basra, and you sit there and let Saddam come to you. And if he doesn't come, you go home and say we failed. This is not the Bay of Pigs." On the other hand, the adviser said, "if the insurgent force took Basra—that's the end. You don't have to go to Baghdad. You tie up his oil and he'll collapse."

During the 2000 presidential campaign, George W. Bush and Al Gore both promised support for the opposition to Saddam—Bush said he would "take him out"—if he continued to develop weapons of mass destruction. After the election, Condoleezza Rice, the national security adviser, made it clear, according to a former government official, that Iraq, in her view, was not a priority for the new Administration. "Her feeling was that Saddam was a small problem—chump change—that we needed to wall him into a corner so we could get on with the big issues: Russia, China, NATO expansion, a new relationship with India and, down the road, with Africa," the former official said.

But for others in the Administration, getting rid of Saddam Hussein and his regime had been a major priority since the end of the first Gulf War. Several of the people who signed the 1998 open letter to Clinton urging American support for Iraqi insurgents had taken positions of authority in the Bush Administration, including Defense Secretary Donald Rumsfeld; his deputy, Paul Wolfowitz; and Douglas Feith, an undersecretary of defense for policy.

The Pentagon's conservative and highly assertive civilian leadership, assembled by Wolfowitz, gained extraordinary influence, especially after September 11th. These civilians were the most vigorous advocates for taking action against Saddam Hussein and for the use of preëmptive military action to combat terrorism. Preëmption would emerge as the overriding idea behind the Administration's foreign policy.

One of the drafters of the 1998 letter was Richard Perle, who was an assistant secretary of defense under Ronald Reagan and a longtime conservative foreign policy adviser in Washington. In the Bush Administration, Perle was named chairman of the Defense Policy Board, which advised the Pentagon on strategic issues. He turned the then-obscure board into a bully pulpit from which to advance the overthrow of Saddam Hussein and the policy of preëmption. There was a close personal bond, too, between Chalabi and Wolfowitz and Perle, dating back many years. Their relationship deepened after the Bush Administration took office, and Chalabi's ties extended to others in the Administration, including Rumsfeld, Feith, and I. Lewis Libby, Vice President Dick Cheney's chief of staff. For years, Chalabi has had the support of prominent members of the American Enterprise Institute and other conservatives. Chalabi had some Democratic supporters, too, including James Woolsey, the former head of the C.I.A.

In the early summer of 2001, a career official assigned to a Pentagon planning office undertook a routine evaluation of the assumption, adopted by hawks like Wolfowitz and Feith, that the I.N.C. could play a major role in a coup d'état to oust Saddam Hussein. He also analyzed their assumption that Chalabi, after the coup, would be welcomed by Iraqis as a hero. An official familiar with the evaluation described how it subjected that scenario to the principle of what planners call "branches and sequels"—that is, "plan for what you expect not to happen." The official said, "It was a 'what could go wrong' study. What if it turns out that Ahmad Chalabi is not so popular? What's Plan B if you discover that Chalabi and his boys don't have it in them to accomplish the overthrow?"

The people in the policy offices didn't seem to care. When the official asked about the analysis, he was told by a colleague that the new Pentagon leadership wanted to focus not on what could go wrong but on what would go right. He was told that the study's exploration of options amounted to planning for failure. "Their methodology was analogous to tossing a coin five times and assuming that it would always come up heads," the official told me. "You need to think about what would happen if it comes up tails."

In late 2001, Perle and Woolsey inspired a surge of articles and columns calling for the extension of the Afghan war into Iraq. Their arguments provide an early glimpse of what would become a national debate over the imminence of the threat from Iraq. In November, at a meeting in Philadelphia of the Foreign Policy Research Institute, a conservative think tank, Perle said, "The question in my mind is: Do we wait for Saddam and hope for the best? Do we wait and hope he doesn't do what we know he is capable of, which is distributing weapons of mass destruction to anonymous terrorists, or do we take preëmptive action? . . . What is essential here is not to look at the opposition to Saddam as it is today, without any external support, without any realistic hope of removing that awful regime, but to look at what could be created with the power and authority of the United States."

The Pentagon officials were at odds with the leaders of the State Department, who were far more restrained in their planning, and accused the Pentagon leadership of confusing dissent with disloyalty; Pentagon officials, in turn, accused Secretary of State Colin Powell and his deputy, Richard Armitage, of a loss of nerve. Armitage, who was one of the signatories of the 1998 letter, had become, in private, an opponent of the revised Chalabi plan. "I've got to believe that Wolfowitz and Feith are angry" at Armitage, one friend of all three men told me at the time. "They feel he's betrayed a fundamental conviction they shared."

One of Armitage's supporters in the internal debate, a former high-level intelligence official, wondered scornfully if the Perle circle's enthusiasm for Chalabi's plan grew out of their unease with the decision of the first Bush Administration in early 1991 not to seek Saddam's demise at the end of the Gulf War. "It's the revenge of the nerds," he said in an interview in late 2001. "They won in Afghanistan when everybody said it wouldn't work, and it's got them in a euphoric mood of cockiness. They went against the established experts on the Middle East who said it would lead to fundamental insurrections in Saudi Arabia and elsewhere. Not so, and anyone who now preaches any approach of solving problems with diplomacy is scoffed at. They're on a roll."

Armitage viewed the I.N.C.'s eagerness to confront Saddam as ill-considered, the former official told me. "We have no idea what could go wrong in Iraq if the crazies took over that country," the former official said. "Better the devil we know than the one we don't." He described Armitage as confident, at that point, that he could block the plan, and frustrated by the amount of time he has been forced to spend on the issue. "Dick says no way. He's going to win it." Otherwise, he added, "he knows it's going to be a political disaster."

A senior State Department official depicted Chalabi as "totally charming," but said that the Administration had no intention of allowing "a bunch of half-assed people to send foreigners into combat." Of Chalabi and his supporters in and out of government, the senior official said, "Who among them has ever smelled cordite? These are pissants who can't get the President's ear and have to blame someone else. We're not going to let them lead others down the garden path." The I.N.C., he added, is not the only Iraqi opposition group being funded by the Bush Administration.

Secretary of State Colin Powell, known to be skeptical of the I.N.C., "backed away from the infighting" in late 2001, a senior general explained, and left it to Armitage, his trusted colleague, "to stall them off four or five months. There's a lot of ways to squeeze

Saddam without using military force." More focussed sanctions would be one logical step, but that November the Bush Administration agreed to delay for six months its insistence on "smart sanctions," which would enable the United Nations to crack down on "dual-use" goods, which could be employed for military or civilian purposes, while allowing medicine, food, and other essentials to flow. At the time, the Iraqi regime exported an estimated two million barrels of oil daily under the Oil for Food program. Major purchasers included ExxonMobil, Chevron, and other American companies, who routinely bought the oil through third parties. As many as eight hundred thousand barrels of that oil a day ended up in the U.S. market.

The United States' early success in routing the Taliban improved Chalabi's standing with some members of the defense community. By December 2001, Chalabi had given the Bush Administration an updated war plan, which called not only for bombing but for the deployment of thousands of American Special Forces troops.

There was a second significant addition to the plan: it envisioned the participation of Iran, which fought a protracted war with Iraq during the 1980s. It was believed that the government of President Mohammad Khatami, the United States' newfound partner in the war against the Taliban, would permit I.N.C. forces and their military equipment to cross the Iranian border into southern Iraq. In an interview in late 2001, an I.N.C. official told me that, months earlier, the Treasury Department's Office of Foreign Assets Control had given the organization special approval to open a liaison office in Tehran. (American companies are forbidden under federal sanctions law to do business with Iran.) The office opened in April 2001. "We did it with U.S. government money, and that's what convinced them in Tehran," the I.N.C. official told me. "They took it as a sign from the United States of a common interest—getting rid of Saddam. The way to get to him is through Iran."

Once inside Iraq, according to this scenario, the I.N.C. would establish a firebase and announce the creation of a provisional Iraqi government, which the Bush Administration would quickly recognize. Nearly two-thirds of the Iraqi population are Shiites, and the United States and the I.N.C. saw them as potential allies in a political uprising. The United States would then begin an intense bombing campaign, as it did in Afghanistan, and airlift thousands of Special Forces troops into southern Iraq. At the same time, I.N.C. supporters in the north, in the areas under Kurdish control, would begin signalling that they were about to attack. According to the plan, dissent would quickly break out inside the Iraqi military, and Saddam Hussein would be confronted with a dilemma: whether to send his élite forces south to engage the Americans or, for his own protection, keep all his forces nearby to guard against an invasion from the north.

This attack plan was worked out with the help of a retired four-star Army general, Wayne Downing, and a former C.I.A. officer, Duane ("Dewey") Clarridge, who served as unpaid consultants to the I.N.C. Downing was appointed by President Bush in October 2001 to be the deputy national security adviser for combatting terrorism. Downing, who ran a Special Forces command during the Gulf War, was convinced that the I.N.C., with airpower and a small contingent of well-trained Special Forces, could do the job inside Iraq. He was privy to one of the most astonishing engagements of the Gulf War: In mid-February of 1991, a Delta Force troop of sixteen men on night patrol south of Al-Qaim, near the Syrian border in western Iraq, was overrun by a large enemy force, and the Iraqis wounded two Americans. The Delta troops, operating from heavily armed vehicles, counterattacked with grenade launchers and machine guns (a maneuver known as Final Protective Fire) and killed or wounded an estimated one hundred and eighty Iraqis, with no further injury to themselves. One American veteran of the Gulf War told me, "In the west"—where Delta operated—"there was little opposition, and we had freedom of movement"; that is, the troops were operating on their own. "Downing loved it."

"They believe they have found the perfect model, and it works," a defense analyst said of the updated war plan. "The model is bombing, a modest insertion of Special Forces, plus an uprising." Similarly, Tim McCarthy, a former United Nations weapons inspector, acknowledged that "the one thing the I.N.C. has going for it is that, once someone puts their stake down, the Iraqis will have to go after them. Saddam will have to send his Hammurabi after them"—the Iraqi Army's élite armored-tank division. Once Saddam made his move, McCarthy said, his forces would be exposed to American air strikes, "and then they are toast."

Chalabi's revised war plan, augmented and modified by a Pentagon planning group authorized by Paul Wolfowitz, made its way to the Joint Chiefs of Staff for evaluation. It left some military men cold, and prompted a debate about the lessons learned from Afghanistan and how they could be applied to Saddam. "There's no question we can take him down," a former government official told me in December 2001. "But what do you need to do it? The J.C.S. is feeling the pressure. These guys are being squeezed so hard."

Some of the concerns were articulated by Robert Pape, a University of Chicago political scientist who has written widely on airpower. "The lesson from Afghanistan is less than meets the eye," Pape told me. "Airpower is becoming more effective, but the real lesson is that you need significant ground forces to make the strategy effective. The Taliban, which controlled fifty thousand troops, were thinly dispersed and never in total control of the country. We don't have an armed opposition already in Iraq like the Northern Alliance"—America's strongest ally in Afghanistan.

A former senior State Department official also depicted the I.N.C. proposal as "highly risky, because two things they can't control have to happen. There's got to be an uprising against Saddam, and our allies have to join us in-country." A senior intelligence official similarly debunked the notion that what worked in Afghanistan would necessarily work in Iraq as equivalent to "taking the show from upstate New York to Broadway."

The military's response was cautious and bureaucratic. A former official told me that the Joint Chiefs ordered their staff to "come up with a counterproposal," which in December 2001, was still in the planning stages. An Air Force consultant told me that the I.N.C. was not included in that planning, adding, "Everything is going to happen inside Iraq, and Chalabi is going to be on the outside."

Generals and admirals were among the most outspoken critics of Chalabi's proposals. In his years of planning at CENTCOM, General Zinni concluded, according to a Clinton Administration official, that a prudent and successful invasion of Iraq would involve the commitment of two corps—at least six combat divisions, or approximately a hundred and fifty thousand soldiers—as well as the ability to fly bombing missions from nearby airfields. In an essay published in 2000 in the U.S. Naval Institute Proceedings, Zinni, who was on the eve of retirement, wrote about what it would take to "drive a stake" through the heart of someone like Saddam:

> You must have the political will—and that means the will of the administration, the Congress, and the American people. All must be united in a desire for action. Instead, however, we try to get results on the cheap. There are congressmen today who want to fund the Iraqi Liberation Act, and let some silk-suited, Rolex-wearing guys in London gin up an expedition. We'll equip a thousand fighters and arm them with ninety-seven million dollars' worth of AK-47s and insert them into Iraq. And what will we have? A Bay of Goats, most likely.

One of the officials involved in the Pentagon's planning said that he, too, had doubts about the efficacy of an I.N.C. armed insurrection, even one backed up by American warplanes and Special Forces. "If you go to war and don't address the root political problem, why bother?" he asked. "All we're going to get is another tyrant in five years. If this is the war to end all jihads, it's got to have a broad-based political agenda behind it."

One of Zinni's close aides told me, "Our question was 'What about the day after?' How do you deal with the long-term security aspects of Iraq? For example, do you take the Republican Guard"— the military unit most loyal to Saddam—"and disarm it? Or is it preferable to turn it from having a capability to protect Saddam to a capability to protect Iraq? You've got Kurds in the north, Arab Shia in the south, and the Baath Party in the middle, with great internal tribal divisions. There's potential for civil war. Layer on external opposition and you've got a potential for great instability. I'm a military planner and plan for the worst case. As bad as this guy is, a stable Iraq is better than instability."

When I asked James Woolsey, the former C.I.A. director, about these concerns, he said, "Iraq has its tribal factions and regional loyalties, but it also has a very sophisticated and intellectual infrastructure of highly educated people. There's no reason they couldn't establish a federalized—or loosely federalized—democracy."

"The issue is not how nice it would be to get rid of Saddam," a former senior Defense Department official told me. "Everybody in the Middle East would be delighted to see him go. The problem is feasibility."

As 2001 ended, the senior Administration official told me that he believed that President Bush had not yet decided what to do about Iraq. Until he did, he said, the State Department would continue to give financial support to opposition groups, including the I.N.C. In a *Washington Post* interview earlier that fall, Condoleezza Rice used a football metaphor to indicate that all options remain open. "We will be calling audibles every time we come to the line," she told columnist Jim Hoagland.

There is evidence that Saddam Hussein was rattled by the war talk in Washington. "The Iraqis are scared to death," one intelligence source said. The intelligence community, according to a former official, had also received hints—however hard to credit—that the Iraqis might be willing to join in the hunt for Osama bin Laden. Conciliatory messages were relayed through diplomatic channels in Canada and eventually reached the White House.

Inside the Administration, there was a general consensus on one issue, officials told me: opposition to a renewed U.N. inspection regime in Iraq. The inspectors had been withdrawn in late 1998, after seven years of contentious and sometimes very successful inspections, and Iraq was refusing to accept a new wave of inspectors. "I've been told that senior U.S. officials have little faith in the viability of the new inspection regime," one disarmament expert told me.

A retired flag officer described the Administration's approach as deterrence: "We have to make sure that Saddam knows that if he sticks his head up he'll get whacked."

2. Getting Closer

In the early spring of 2002, the Bush Administration remained sharply divided about Iraq. There was widespread agreement that Saddam Hussein should be overthrown, but no agreement about how to get it done. The President had given his feuding agencies a deadline of April 15, 2002, to come up with a "coagulated plan," as one senior State Department official put it, for ending the regime. The President was meeting that month with Tony Blair, the British prime minister, whose support for the Iraqi operation was considered essential.

There was strong debate over how many American troops would be needed, whether Baghdad should be immediately targeted, which Iraqi opposition leader should be installed as the interim leader, and— most important—how the Iraqi military would respond to an attack:

Would it retreat, and even turn against Saddam? Or would it stand and fight?

The normal planning procedures were marginalized, according to many military and intelligence officials I spoke to at the time. These usually included a series of careful preliminary studies under the control of the National Security Council and the Joint Chiefs of Staff. But I was told that there was far less involvement by the Joint Chiefs and their chairman, Air Force General Richard Myers. As one senior Administration consultant put it, the military's planning for Iraq was operating "under V.F.R. direct"—that is, under visual flight rules, an air-traffic controllers' term for proceeding with minimal guidance.

The dispute between the Pentagon and the State Department had become even more personal. "It's the return of the right-wing crazies, crawling their way back," one of Armitage's associates said, referring to Wolfowitz's team. "The knives are out." The senior State Department official angrily told me that he would "meet them"—his "pissant" detractors in the Pentagon—"anytime, anywhere." In return, one of those detractors depicted the State Department's behavior as "unbelievably personal and vitriolic. Their attitude is that we're yahoos—especially those of us who come from the far right. The American Enterprise Institute"—a conservative think tank in Washington—"is like Darth Vader's mother ship for them."

Senior State Department officials were particularly displeased with William Luti, the deputy assistant secretary of defense for Near East and South Asian affairs. Luti, a retired Navy captain and Gulf War combat veteran who served on Vice President Dick Cheney's staff in the summer of 2001, was seen by people at State as so obsessed with an immediate overthrow of Saddam that he hadn't thought through the consequences. Luti's supporters, however, included Richard Perle.

In previous administrations, such interagency fights were often resolved by the national security adviser. But under Condoleezza Rice the National Security Council's ability to intervene had been diminished by a series of resignations and reassignments, some of them said to be the result of internal bickering. That March, the N.S.C. had no senior Iraq expert on its staff. Bruce Riedel, the long-time ranking expert on the Middle East, had recently moved overseas on a sabbatical, and the person who had filled in as the N.S.C.'s Iraq expert, an intelligence officer on loan from the C.I.A., went back to the agency after only a few months at the White House. A third regional expert had left the N.S.C. after a series of policy disputes with civilian officials in the Pentagon. In the absence of a replacement, a former official told me, the N.S.C. had been forced to "farm out" papers on important issues to the C.I.A. and the State Department.

Wayne Downing, the former general—and I.N.C. consultant—brought in by President Bush as a deputy national security adviser on combating terrorism, had begun to fill the planning void created by N.S.C.'s lack of high-level expertise on Iraq. Downing hired Linda Flohr, a twenty-seven-year veteran of the C.I.A.'s clandestine service who, after retiring in 1994—her last assignment was for the top-secret Iraqi Operations Group—went to work for the Rendon Group, a public relations firm that was retained by the C.I.A. in 1991 to handle press issues related to the Iraqi opposition, including Chalabi and the I.N.C. The firm, headed by John Rendon, who once served as executive director of the Democratic National Committee, was paid close to $100 million by the C.I.A. over the next five years, according to an I.N.C. official. In the fall of 2001, the Rendon Group was retained by the Defense Department to give advice on how to counter what the government considered to be "disinformation" about the American war effort in Afghanistan. The firm was also retained by the Pentagon's Office of Strategic Influence, which was eliminated in February 2002, after the *New York Times* reported that it would provide foreign reporters with "news items, possibly even false ones." (Rendon's contract with the Pentagon was not cancelled, however.) Flohr also worked for a private business—it manufactured bulletproof vests—founded by Oliver North, the former Marine and Reagan Administration N.S.C. aide who was fired for his role in the Iran-contra scandal.

The Iraq hawks and their opponents were preoccupied with disputes over Chalabi's potential usefulness. The civilian leadership in the Pentagon continued to insist that only the I.N.C. could lead the opposition. At the same time, a former Administration official told me, "Everybody but the Pentagon and the office of the Vice President wants to ditch the I.N.C." The I.N.C.'s critics noted that Chalabi, despite years of effort and millions of dollars in American aid, was intensely unpopular among many elements in Iraq. "If Chalabi is the guy, there could be a civil war after Saddam's overthrow," one former C.I.A. operative told me at the time.

A former high-level Pentagon official added, "There are some things that a president can't order up, and an internal opposition is one. Show me a Northern Alliance"—the opposition group in Afghanistan that, with United States help, scored early victories against the Taliban—"and then we can argue about what it will cost to back it up." A former station chief for the C.I.A. in the Middle East told me, "It would be ridiculous to tie our wagon to Chalabi. He's got no credibility in the region."

The C.I.A. and the State Department accelerated their efforts to forge a coalition of former Iraqi military men and opposition groups, with the goal of convincing the steadfast Chalabi supporters that a new approach could work—without I.N.C. involvement. Iraqi opposition factions were now meeting regularly in London, and the long-sought concept of a broad opposition, without Chalabi, was "gaining mass," a former C.I.A. operative said, in part because of what other Iraqis saw as Chalabi's arrogance and high-handedness. According to one intelligence official Chalabi had "succeeded in galvanizing the opposition against him." The key participants, known to some C.I.A. officials as the "gang of four," included representatives from the fiercely anti-Saddam Patriotic Union of Kurdistan; its archrival, the Kurdistan Democratic Party; the pro-Iran Supreme Council for Islamic Revolution in Iraq, a Shiite resistance group; and the British-based Iraqi National Accord, headed by Iyad Allawi, a neurologist who left Iraq in the 1970s.

Within six months of September 11th, Allawi and a number of former Iraqi military officers attended meetings—more like auditions—with C.I.A. officials in various hotels in suburban Virginia. Allawi's credentials included his two decades of anti-Saddam activities, as the founder of the Iraqi National Accord. But his role as a Baath Party operative while Saddam struggled for control in the 1960s and 1970s—Saddam became president in 1979—was much less well known. "Allawi helped Saddam get to power," an American intelligence officer told me. "He was a very effective operator and a true believer." Reuel Gerecht, the former C.I.A. officer, added, "Two facts stand out about Allawi. One, he likes to think of himself as a man of ideas; and, two, his strongest virtue is that he's a thug."

In early 2004, one of Allawi's former medical school classmates, Dr. Haifa al-Azawi, published an essay in an Arabic newspaper in London raising questions about his character and his medical bona fides. Al-Azawi depicted Allawi as a "big husky man . . . who carried a gun on his belt and frequently brandished it, terrorizing the medical students." Allawi's medical degree, she wrote, "was conferred upon him by the Baath party." Allawi moved to London in 1971, ostensibly to continue his medical education; there he was in charge of the European operations of the Baath Party organization and the local activities of the Mukhabarat, its intelligence agency, until 1975.

"If you're asking me if Allawi has blood on his hands from his days in London, the answer is yes, he does," Vincent Cannistraro, the former C.I.A. officer, told me. "He was a paid Mukhabarat agent for the Iraqis, and he was involved in dirty stuff." A Cabinet-level Middle East diplomat told me that Allawi was involved with a Mukhabarat "hit team" that sought out and killed Baath Party dissenters throughout Europe. (Allawi's office did not respond to a request for comment.)

At some point, for reasons that are not clear, Allawi fell from favor, and the Baathists organized a series of attempts on his life. The third attempt, by an axe-wielding assassin who broke into his home near London in 1978, resulted in a year-long hospital stay.

The C.I.A.'s brightest prospect, officials told me at the time, was Nizar Khazraji, a former Iraqi Army chief of staff who defected in the mid-1990s. As a Sunni and a former combat general, Khazraji was viewed by the C.I.A. as being far more acceptable to the Iraqi officer corps than Chalabi, who has no formal military background. Chalabi's advocates in the Pentagon pointed out that he was not only a Shiite, like the majority of Iraqis, but also, as one scholar put it, "a completely Westernized businessman"—which is one of the reasons the State Department doubted whether he can gain support among Iraqis.

Chalabi and his allies responded by endorsing a public relations campaign against Khazraji, alleging that he was involved in a war crime—the 1988 Iraqi gassing of a Kurdish town, a claim Khazraji denied—and suggesting that he might be a double agent. (In November of 2002, Khazraji was indicted for war crimes in Denmark, where he was living, and placed under house arrest. He subsequently disappeared.)

"There's a huge firestorm over Chalabi that's preventing us from reaching out to the Iraqi military," a former C.I.A. operative told me in early 2002. "It's mind-boggling for an outsider to understand the impasse."

More than five hundred thousand American soldiers took part in the first Gulf War, and, in early 2002, military planners at CENT-COM, in Tampa, were insisting that at least six combat divisions—roughly a hundred and fifty thousand troops—would be needed for another invasion. In an article published in the March/April 2002 issue of *Foreign Affairs*, Kenneth Pollack, the director of Persian

Gulf affairs for the N.S.C. during the Clinton Administration, provided the following assessment:

> Some light infantry will be required in case Saddam's loyalists fight in Iraq's cities. Air-mobile forces will be needed to seize Iraq's oil fields at the start of hostilities and to occupy the sites from which Saddam could launch missiles against Israel or Saudi Arabia. And troops will have to be available for occupation duties once the fighting is over. All told, the force should total roughly two hundred thousand to three hundred thousand people; for the invasion, between four and six divisions plus supporting units, and for the air campaign seven hundred to a thousand aircraft and anywhere from one to five carrier battle groups. . . . Building up such a force in the Persian Gulf would take three to five months, but the campaign itself would take probably about a month, including the opening air operations.

The hawks in and around the Administration, including Paul Wolfowitz and Richard Perle, were arguing, however, that any show of force would immediately trigger a revolt against Saddam within Iraq, and that it would quickly expand. When I spoke to Perle in early 2002, he dismissed the widely publicized concerns expressed by Iraq's regional neighbors, who expect prolonged civil war and chaos if the Iraqi Army stood and fought. "Arabs are like most people," Perle told me. "They like winners, and will go with the winners all the time." And General Downing, who ran a Special Forces command during the Gulf War, criticized the Pentagon for its elaborate planning and heavy-force requirements, telling his I.N.C. colleagues that if five thousand troops could do the job, the Pentagon would insist on at least five times as many.

A key player in the discussion of troop needs was Army General Tommy Franks, who, as the head of CENTCOM, would be in charge of a war in Iraq—and had been directing the increasingly difficult operation in Afghanistan. In early 2002, senior Administration offi-

cials told me that Franks was still following in the path of his predecessor, General Zinni, and insisting, despite pressure from civilians in
the Pentagon, on an intense and careful American buildup in the region before Iraq could be attacked. "Franks is hanging tough," one
of Armitage's associates told me in February 2002. Marine Corps planners were depicted as less sanguine than their counterparts in the other
Armed Services about the ability of a smaller American force to topple the regime. "The Army and Air Force are ready to go," Armitage's
associate continued. "So it's 'Let's go work on the Marines.' The
Marines are digging in and are not going to go"—that is, not going
to lower estimates of the forces needed.

"We've got a bunch of people involved who think it's going to be
easy. We're set up for a big surprise," one recently retired senior
military officer, who drafted CENTCOM battle studies with the
Marine leadership, said at the time. A former U.S. ambassador in
the Middle East told me, "If we have to have three months of
bombing, with civilian casualties, we'll have real problems with the
Arab world." Scott Ritter, the former Marine who led U.N. inspection teams into Iraq during the 1990s—and insisted before the war
that Iraq had no significant W.M.D.s—said that the Iraqi Army
could respond to an invasion by dispersing into the countryside. In
that case, Ritter asked, "What will we do? Flatten the towns?"

In the first months of 2002, Chalabi and his Pentagon supporters were telling journalists that an attack could come as early as that
spring. Any objections from France and Russia, Saddam's major oil-
trading partners, would be assuaged, a senior I.N.C. official told
me, by assurances that they would be given access to the extraordi-
narily rich oil fields in southern Iraq. Chalabi had been in contact
with American oil companies, the official added, in an effort to insure that the fields got into quick production and provided a source
of revenue for the new interim government that the I.N.C. hoped
to lead. The French and Russian oil companies "would have to go as
junior partners to Americans."

The senior State Department official told me at the time, however, "The President has a time line, but it doesn't fit what those boys tell you. The last thing we want to do is hit Baghdad and have Al Qaeda hit Chicago. We'd look real bad." The official added, "When we go to Iraq, we will do it right. There's a before and after, and we want to get the after right." A high-ranking intelligence official similarly noted, referring to Afghanistan, "We aren't done where we are now, and we got plenty to do where we are without biting off something else." A former intelligence official put the issue more vividly. "We're a powerful boa constrictor, and we're now squeezing out these terrorists," he said. "Let's digest these rats we've swallowed before we get another one."

Israel, an enthusiastic allied booster of an American war with Iraq, also posed one of the most vexing stumbling blocks. Special security commitments had to be made, and they were—in secret. The ostensible theme of Israeli Prime Minister Ariel Sharon's official visit to Washington in early February 2002 was the Palestinian conflict, but there was an important private agenda for the White House: briefing Israel about the President's determination to overthrow Saddam and persuading its leadership to delay a response, as it did during the 1991 Gulf War, in the event of an Iraqi Scud missile attack. Israel is within range of Scuds coming from western Iraq. Thirty-nine Scuds struck Israel in 1991. Despite extensive air and ground searches by United States military commanders, and despite repeated public assurances to the contrary, there was no evidence that American Special Forces troops were able to find and destroy any mobile Scud launchers in the Gulf War.

During Sharon's visit, American and Israeli officials told me, the prime minister and Binyamin Ben-Eliezer, the Israeli defense minister, reached an understanding with Washington on advance notice of any impending invasion, and also urged that the Bush Administration do what was necessary—placing a large number of troops on

the ground in western Iraq, for example—in order to destroy potential Scud launching sites at the outset of an attack.

But the Israeli leaders refused to give the White House an assur-
ance that Israel would not retaliate. A senior Israeli official told me,
shortly after the meeting, "We basically said that the United States
should assume, in its considerations, that if Israel is to be hit, Israel
will hit back. We took a hit in 1991 and did not hit back because we
could have ruined the United States–Arab coalition. Our lack of retaliation was seen in the West as very smart, but in the Arab world it
had a serious negative effect on Israel's deterrence posture. If someone thinks it can hit Israel and not be hit ten times as strongly back,
it is a serious issue. It won't happen again. Our message is clear—if
a Scud hits Tel Aviv with a dirty warhead and you have dozens of
people killed, does anyone really expect Israel to sit there? Will they
dare ask us not to respond?"

In the talks, the Bush Administration let the Israeli side know
that it anticipated that the Iraqi leadership would arm its mobile
Scuds with biological and chemical warheads. "No one discounts
the possibility of biological warfare," the Israeli official said, "but we
believe it is more likely to be delivered by Iraqi aircraft, and not
Scuds, and therefore is not as much of a threat. No Iraqi aircraft
reached Israel in 1991, and Saddam does not have as much as he did
then—and we're a lot better in anti-aircraft defenses." However, he
added, "If Saddam believes that a regime change is the goal of an
American invasion, and he is the target, it's all for broke."

One of Richard Armitage's associates described the threat to Israel, and Israel's ability to counterattack, as factors that could not be
dismissed in the war planning, given Israel's known nuclear capability: "If Saddam goes against Israel big time and they come on our
side big time, we've got the whole Arab-speaking world against us,
instead of just Muslim terrorists."

When I interviewed him at the time, Richard Perle took issue
with the Israeli concern about an Iraqi bombardment. Because of

the strong likelihood of devastating retaliation by Israel, he argued, Saddam would consider attacking only if his options ran out. "The doomsday scenario is that in desperation Saddam sends weapons of mass destruction toward Israel," Perle told me. "If you assume it's a desperation move, you have to ask yourself to what extent will Saddam's maniacal orders be carried out"—presuming that Iraqi troops and citizens, encouraged by the American attacks and bombing, would rebel against the leadership. "If you get that order and you're managing a Scud unit, do you carry it out? If you do, you're hanged or you're dead. By the time Saddam does that"—order the attack on Israel—"he's done anyway.

"Nobody's going to say that it's without risk," Perle added, referring to a U.S. attack. "From Israel's point of view, are they going to get safer in time? If the Israeli leadership is already deterred by what Saddam threatens now, what happens when he gets nuclear weapons?" Echoing the view of Wolfowitz and many of his colleagues in the Pentagon, Perle said, "The moment Saddam is challenged effectively, he's history."

Some Administration supporters, however, saw little evidence of long-range thinking. "The central American premise is that you deal with Iraq and everything else will fall in place," said Geoffrey Kemp in an interview in early 2002. Kemp, who had been the N.S.C.'s ranking expert on the Near East during the first Reagan Administration, was then examining options for the Middle East after Saddam in his capacity as director of Regional Strategic Programs at the Nixon Center. " 'Syria comes to terms. The Saudis will conform. Iran will be surrounded by American forces, and the mullahs will have to make concessions to the moderates. There will be a settlement between Israel and Palestine. The end of Saddam will lead to an economic renaissance in Iraq.' I'd say fantastic—if it happens."

Kemp went on, "Whatever happens, Bush cannot afford to fail. At the end of the day, we must have a stable, pro-Western government in Baghdad. But it's important also that you look at the worst case. One nightmare would be that Saddam used weapons of mass destruction against Israel and you'd end up with a U.S.-Israeli war against Iraq. No one knows how much it will cost. You could have an interruption in oil supplies. Meanwhile, you've still got Afghanistan. The whole purpose of going in is to cleanse Iraq of all weapons of mass destruction capability. If Saddam is gone and his sons dispatched, you will still need two things: complete coöperation of whoever is running the show and inspection teams to cleanse every bedroom and every crevice in the palaces. Iraq is a proud country that has been humiliated, and it's madness to think that these people, while hating Saddam, are in love with the United States. Latent nationalism will emerge, and there will be those who want to hold on to whatever weapons they've held back. The danger is that these capabilities could pop up somewhere else—in control of some small army group with its own agenda."

In mid-March 2002, Vice President Cheney went on an extended trip to the Middle East—where a significant and largely unpublicized buildup of American military forces was already under way. Officially, the Pentagon said at the time that about five thousand American troops were stationed in Kuwait, but a senior Administration consultant told me that by mid-February there were, in fact, many times that number on duty there, along with an extensive offshore Navy presence. The military buildup, intelligence officials explained, was designed to protect Kuwait and other allied nations in the Gulf in case Saddam chose to strike first.

The President's "axis of evil" language in the 2002 State of the Union Message and the steadily expanding American arsenal had prompted many anxious diplomatic inquiries from the Middle East and Europe. One of Cheney's goals was to explain the U.S. position to allies and attempt to build a coalition for another invasion of Iraq—a daunting task. The only likely ally at that point was Tony Blair's Britain.

With regard to the attack on Iraq, not everyone on the inside was sure that the President could get what he wanted: a successful overthrow with few American casualties and a new, pro-Western regime. "We've got a great way to get it started," a former intelligence official said before Cheney's trip. "But how do we finish it?" As for Bush's eagerness to get rid of Saddam, he said, "It's a snowball rolling downhill, gaining momentum on its own. It's getting bigger and bigger, but nobody knows what they're going to do."

———

There was little doubt among some White House insiders about what the President wanted to do, and about when he had made his decision. "I arrived at the White House in early 2002, and began attending N.S.C. meetings with the President," a former National Security Council staff member told me. "Whenever the President would talk about Iraq, it was always something we knew we wanted to happen." White House talking points always noted that no decision had been made, the N.S.C. staff member added, but all involved knew it was a done deal. As of February 2002, he said, "the decision to go to war was taken."

The undeclared decision had a devastating impact on the continuing struggle against terrorism. The Bush Administration took many intelligence operations that had been aimed at Al Qaeda and other terrorist groups around the world and redirected them to the Persian Gulf. Linguists and special operatives were abruptly reassigned, and several ongoing anti-terrorism intelligence programs were curtailed.

In May 2002, the United Nations reviewed economic sanctions against Iraq. The new "smart" sanctions sought by the Bush Administration would make it harder for Iraq to buy dual-use goods—materials with both civil and military functions—but permit more medicine and other needed materials to flow into Iraq, easing the strain on the population. At any time, of course, the sanctions could be dropped if Iraq first accepted a renewal of United Nations inspections of its suspected nuclear, chemical, and biological weapons sites. The American plan, officials agreed, was to make so many demands—complete access to palaces, for example—that it would be almost impossible for Saddam to agree. The Europeans, especially the French, were known to be trying to persuade Saddam to "open up," as a senior Administration consultant put it, to another U.N. inspection plan and "not give the United States an excuse to bomb."

The coming war meant money—lots of it—would be spent, and made. Some of the most ardent advocates of the war against Iraq were also the most eager to profit from it.

3. Richard Perle Goes to Lunch

At the peak of his deal-making activities, in the 1970s, the Saudi-born businessman Adnan Khashoggi brokered billions of dollars in arms and aircraft sales for the Saudi royal family, earning hundreds of millions in commissions and fees. Though never convicted of wrongdoing, he was repeatedly involved in disputes with federal prosecutors and the Securities and Exchange Commission, and in recent years he has been in litigation in Thailand and Los Angeles, among other places, concerning allegations of stock manipulation and fraud. During the Reagan Administration, Khashoggi was one of the middlemen between Oliver North in the White House and the mullahs in Iran in what became known as the Iran-contra scandal. Khashoggi subsequently claimed that he lost $10 million that he had put up to obtain embargoed weapons for Iran which were to be bartered (with presidential approval) for American hostages. The scandals of those times seemed to feed off each other: a congressional investigation revealed that Khashoggi had borrowed much of the money for the weapons from the Bank of Credit and Commerce

International (B.C.C.I.), whose collapse, in 1991, defrauded thousands of depositors and led to years of inquiry and litigation.

Khashoggi is still brokering. In January of 2003, he arranged a private lunch, in France, to bring together Harb Saleh al-Zuhair, a Saudi industrialist whose family fortune included extensive holdings in construction, electronics, and engineering companies throughout the Middle East, and Richard Perle.

Perle had served as a foreign policy adviser in George W. Bush's presidential campaign, but he chose not to take a senior position in the Administration. In mid-2001, however, he accepted an offer from Rumsfeld to chair the Defense Policy Board. Its members (there are around thirty of them) are primarily highly respected former government officials, retired military officers, and academics, including former secretaries of defense and heads of the C.I.A., who serve without pay. The board members meet several times a year at the Pentagon to review and assess the country's strategic defense policies. They may be outside the government, but they have access to classified information and to senior policy makers, and also give advice on such matters as weapons procurement. Most of the board's proceedings are confidential.

Perle was also a managing partner in a venture capital company called Trireme Partners L.P., which was registered in November 2001—two months after the September 11th attacks—in Delaware. Trireme's main business, according to a two-page letter that one of its representatives sent to Khashoggi the following November, was to invest in companies dealing in technology, goods, and services that are of value to homeland security and defense. The letter argued that the fear of terrorism would increase the demand for such products in Europe and in countries like Saudi Arabia and Singapore.

The letter mentioned the firm's government connections prominently: "Three of Trireme's Management Group members currently advise the U.S. Secretary of Defense by serving on the U.S. Defense Policy Board, and one of Trireme's principals, Richard Perle, is chairman of that Board." The two other Defense Policy Board members associated with Trireme were Henry Kissinger, the former secretary of state (who was, in fact, only a member of Trireme's advisory group and was not involved in its management), and Gerald Hillman, an investor and a close business associate of Perle's who handled matters in Trireme's New York office. The letter said that $45 million had already been raised, including $20 million from Boeing; the purpose, clearly, was to attract more investors, such as Khashoggi and Zuhair.

As chairman of the board, Perle was considered to be a special government employee and therefore subject to a federal code of conduct. Those rules bar a special employee from participating in an official capacity in any matter in which he has a financial interest. "One of the general rules is that you don't take advantage of your federal position to help yourself financially in any way," a former government attorney who helped formulate the code of conduct told me. The point, the attorney added, was to "protect government processes from actual or apparent conflicts."

Advisory groups like the Defense Policy Board enable knowledgeable people outside government to bring their skills and expertise to bear, in confidence, on key policy issues. Because such experts are often tied to the defense industry, however, there are inevitable conflicts. One board member told me that most members were active in finance and business, and on at least one occasion a member had left a meeting when a military or an intelligence product in which he had an active interest had come under discussion.

When I contacted members of the Defense Policy Board to ask about Perle and Trireme, for a story that was to run in March 2003, four of them told me that the board, which had met shortly before, on February 27th and 28th, had not been informed of Perle's involvement in the company. One board member, upon being told of Trireme and Perle's meeting with Khashoggi, exclaimed, "Oh, get out of here. He's the chairman! If you had a story about me setting up a company for homeland security, and I've put people on the board with whom I'm doing that business, I'd be had"—a reference to Gerald Hillman, who had almost no senior policy or military experience in government before being offered a post on the policy board. "Seems to me this is at the edge of or off the ethical charts. I think it would stink to high heaven."

Hillman, a former McKinsey consultant, stunned at least one board member at the February 2003 meeting when he raised questions about the validity of Iraq's existing oil contracts. "Hillman said the old contracts are bad news; he said we should kick out the Russians and the French," the board member told me. "This was a serious conversation. We'd become the brokers. Then we'd be selling futures in the Iraqi oil company. I said to myself, 'Oh, man. Don't go down that road.'" (Hillman denied making such statements at the meeting.)

Larry Noble, the executive director of the Washington-based Center for Responsive Politics, a nonprofit research organization, said of Perle's Trireme involvement, "It's not illegal, but it presents an appearance of a conflict. It's enough to raise questions about the advice he's giving to the Pentagon and why people in business are dealing with him." Noble added, "The question is whether he's trading off his advisory committee relationship. If it's a selling point for the firm he's involved with, that means he's a closer—the guy you bring in who doesn't have to talk about money, but he's the reason you're doing the deal."

Perle's association with Trireme was not his first exposure to the link between high finance and high-level politics. He was born in New York City, graduated from the University of Southern California in 1964, and spent a decade in Senate staff jobs before leaving government in 1980 to work for a military consulting firm. The next year, he was back in government, as assistant secretary of defense. In 1983, he was the subject of a *New York Times* investigation into an allegation that he recommended that the Army buy weapons from an Israeli company from whose owners he had, two years earlier, accepted a $50,000 fee. Perle later acknowledged that he had accepted the fee, but vigorously denied any wrongdoing. He had not recused himself in the matter, he explained, because the fee was for work he had done before he took the Defense Department job. He added, "The ultimate issue, of course, was a question of procurement, and I am not a procurement officer." He was never officially accused of any ethical violations in the matter. Perle served in the Pentagon until 1987 and then became deeply involved in the lobbying and business worlds. Among other corporate commitments, he now serves as a director of a company doing business with the federal government: the Autonomy Corporation, a British firm that recently won a major federal contract in homeland security. When I asked him about that contract, Perle told me that there was no possible conflict, because the contract was obtained through competitive bidding, and "I never talked to anybody about it."

One former high-level intelligence official spoke with awe of Perle's ability to "radically change government policy," even though he is a private citizen. "It's an impressive achievement that an outsider can have so much influence and has even been given an institutional base for his influence."

Perle's authority in the Bush Administration was buttressed by close association, politically and personally, with many important Administration figures, including Wolfowitz and Douglas Feith. In 1989, Feith created International Advisors Incorporated, a lobbying firm whose main client was the government of Turkey. The firm retained Perle as an adviser between 1989 and 1994. Feith got his current position, according to a former high-level Defense Department official, only after Perle personally intervened with Rumsfeld, who was skeptical about him. He and Perle share the same views on many foreign policy issues. Both have been calling for Saddam Hussein's removal for years, long before September 11th, had struggled with the State Department over Iraq, and were energetic supporters of Chalabi. They also worked together, in 1996, to prepare a list of policy initiatives for Benjamin Netanyahu, shortly after his election as the Israeli prime minister. The suggestions included working toward regime change in Iraq.

Perle has also been an outspoken critic of the Saudi government, and Americans who are in its pay. He has often publicly rebuked former American government officials who are connected to research centers and foundations that are funded by the Saudis, and told the *National Review* in the summer of 2002, "I think it's a disgrace. They're the people who appear on television, they write op-ed pieces. The Saudis are a major source of the problem we face with terrorism. That would be far more obvious to people if it weren't for this community of former diplomats effectively working for this foreign government." In August 2002, the Saudi government was dismayed when the *Washington Post* revealed that the Defense Policy Board had received a briefing on July 10th from a Rand Corporation analyst named Laurent Murawiec, who depicted Saudi Arabia as an enemy of the United States and recommended that the Bush Administration give the Saudi government an ultimatum to stop backing terrorism or face seizure of its financial assets in the United States and its oil fields. Murawiec, it was later found, was a former editor of the *Executive Intelligence Review*, a magazine controlled by Lyndon H. LaRouche Jr., the perennial presidential candidate, conspiracy theorist, and felon. According to *Time*, it was Perle himself who had invited Murawiec to make his presentation.

Perle's hostility to the politics of the Saudi government did not stop him from meeting with potential Saudi investors for Trireme. Khashoggi and Zuhair told me that they understood that one of Trireme's objectives was to seek the help of influential Saudis to win homeland-security contracts with the Saudi royal family for the businesses it financed. The profits for such contracts could be substantial. Saudi Arabia had already spent nearly $1 billion to survey and demarcate its eight-hundred-and-fifty-mile border with Yemen, and the second stage of that process would require billions more. Trireme apparently turned to Adnan Khashoggi for help.

In February 2003, I spoke with Khashoggi, who, at sixty-seven years old, was recovering from open-heart surgery at his penthouse apartment overlooking the Mediterranean in Cannes. "I was the intermediary," he said. According to Khashoggi, he was first approached by a Trireme official named Christopher Harriman. Khashoggi said that Harriman, an American businessman whom he knew from his jet-set days, when both men were fixtures on the European social scene, sent him the Trireme pitch letter. (Harriman would not answer my calls for comment.) Khashoggi explained that before Christmas he and Harb Zuhair, the Saudi industrialist, had met with Harriman and Gerald Hillman in Paris and had discussed the possibility of a large investment in Trireme.

Zuhair was interested in more than the financial side; he also wanted to share his views on war and peace with someone who had influence with the Bush Administration. Though a Saudi, he had been born in Iraq, and he hoped that a negotiated "step-by-step" solution could be found to avoid war. Zuhair recalls telling Harriman and Hillman, "If we have peace, it would be easy to raise a hundred million. We will bring development to the region." Zuhair's hope, Khashoggi told me, was to combine opportunities for peace with opportunities for investment. According to Khashoggi, Hillman and Harriman said that such a meeting could be arranged. Perle emerged, by virtue of his position on the policy board, as a natural catch; he was "the hook," Khashoggi said, for obtaining the investment from Zuhair. Khashoggi said that he agreed to try to assemble potential investors for a private lunch with Perle.

The lunch took place on January 3, 2003, at a seaside restaurant in Marseilles. (Perle had a vacation home in the south of France.) Those who attended the lunch differed about its purpose. According to both Khashoggi and Zuhair, there were two items on the agenda. The first was to give Zuhair a chance to propose a peaceful alternative to war with Iraq; Khashoggi said that he and Perle knew that such an alternative was far-fetched, but Zuhair had recently returned from a visit to Baghdad and was eager to talk about it. The second, more important item, according to Khashoggi and Zuhair, was to pave the way for Zuhair to put together a group of ten Saudi businessmen who would invest $10 million each in Trireme.

"It was normal for us to see Perle," Khashoggi told me. "We in the Middle East are accustomed to politicians who use their offices for whatever business they want. I organized the lunch for the purpose of Harb Zuhair to put his language to Perle. Perle politely listened, and the lunch was over." Zuhair, in a telephone conversation with me, recalled that Perle had made it clear at the lunch that "he was above the money. He said he was more involved in politics, and the business is through the company"—Trireme. Perle, throughout the lunch, "stuck to his idea that 'we have to get rid of Saddam,'" Zuhair said. When we spoke in early March 2003, to the knowledge of Zuhair, no Saudi money had yet been invested in Trireme.

In my first telephone conversation with Gerald Hillman, in mid-February of 2003, before I knew of the involvement of Khashoggi and Zuhair, he assured me that Trireme had "nothing to do" with the Saudis. "I don't know what you can do with them," he said. "What we saw on September 11th was a grotesque manifestation of their ideology. Americans believe that the Saudis are supporting terrorism. We have no investment from them, or with them." (A few weeks later, he acknowledged that he had met with Khashoggi and Zuhair, but said that the meeting had been arranged by Harriman and that he hadn't known that Zuhair would be there.) Perle, he insisted in February, "is not a financial creature. He doesn't have any desire for financial gain."

Perle, in a series of telephone interviews in the same period, acknowledged that he had met with two Saudis at the lunch in Marseilles, but he did not divulge their identities. (At that point, I still didn't know who they were.) "There were two Saudis there," he said. "But there was no discussion of Trireme. It was never mentioned and never discussed." He firmly stated, "The lunch was not about money. It just would never have occurred to me to discuss investments, given the circumstances." Perle added that one of the Saudis had information that Saddam was ready to surrender. "His message was a plea to negotiate with Saddam."

When I asked Perle whether the Saudi businessmen at the lunch were being considered as possible investors in Trireme, he replied, "I don't want Saudis as such, but the fund is open to any investor, and our European partners said that, through investment banks, they had had Saudis as investors." Both Perle and Hillman stated categorically that there were, at that point, no Saudi investments.

Khashoggi professed to be amused by the activities of Perle and Hillman as members of the policy board. As Khashoggi saw it, Trireme's business potential depended on a war in Iraq taking place. "If there is no war," he told me, "why is there a need for security? If there is a war, of course, billions of dollars will have to be spent." He commented, "You Americans blind yourself with your high integrity and your democratic morality against peddling influence, but they were peddling influence."

When Perle's lunch with Khashoggi and Zuhair, and his connection to Trireme, became known to a few ranking members of the Saudi royal family, they reacted with anger and astonishment. The meeting in Marseilles left Perle, one of the kingdom's most vehement critics, exposed to a ferocious counterattack.

Prince Bandar bin Sultan, who has served as the Saudi ambassador to the United States for twenty years, told me that he had got wind of Perle's involvement with Trireme and the lunch in Marseilles. Prince Bandar, who is in his early fifties, is a prominent member of the royal family (his father is the defense minister). He said that he was told that the contacts between Perle and Trireme and the Saudis were purely business, on all sides. After the 1991 Gulf War, Prince Bandar told me, Perle had been involved in an unsuccessful attempt to sell security systems to the Saudi government, "and this company does security systems." (Perle confirmed that he had been on the board of a company that attempted to make such a sale but said he was not directly involved in the project.)

"There is a split personality to Perle," Prince Bandar said. "Here he is, on the one hand, trying to make a hundred-million-dollar deal, and, on the other hand, there were elements of the appearance of blackmail—'If we get in business, he'll back off on Saudi Arabia'—as I have been informed by participants in the meeting."

As for Perle's meeting with Khashoggi and Zuhair, and the assertion that its purpose was to discuss politics, Prince Bandar said, "There has to be deniability, and a cover story—a possible peace initiative in Iraq—is needed. I believe the Iraqi events are irrelevant. A business meeting took place."

Zuhair, however, was apparently convinced that, thanks to his discussions with Trireme, he would have a chance to enter into a serious discussion with Perle about peace. A few days after the meeting in Paris, Hillman had sent Khashoggi a twelve-point memorandum, dated December 26, 2002, setting the conditions that Iraq would have to meet. "It is my belief," the memorandum stated, "that if the United States obtained the following results it would not go to war against Iraq." Saddam would have to admit that "Iraq has developed, and possesses, weapons of mass destruction." He then would be allowed to resign and leave Iraq immediately, with his sons and some of his ministers.

Hillman sent Khashoggi a second memorandum a week later, the day before the lunch with Perle in Marseilles. "Following our recent discussions," it said, "we have been thinking about an immediate test to ascertain that Iraq is sincere in its desire to surrender." Five more steps were outlined, and an ambitious final request was made: that Khashoggi and Zuhair arrange a meeting with Prince Nawaf Abdul Aziz, the Saudi intelligence chief, "so that we can assist in Washington."

Both Khashoggi and Zuhair were skeptical of the memorandums. Zuhair found them "absurd," and Khashoggi told me that he thought they were amusing, and almost silly. "This was their thinking?" he recalled asking himself. "There was nothing to react to. While Harb was lobbying for Iraq, they were lobbying for Perle."

In my initial conversation with Hillman, he said, "Richard had nothing to do with the writing of those letters. I informed him of it afterward, and he never said one word, even after I sent them to him. I thought my ideas were pretty clear, but I didn't think Saddam would resign and I didn't think he'd go into exile. I'm positive Richard does not believe that any of those things would happen." Hillman said that he had drafted the memorandums with the help of his daughter, a college student. Perle, for his part, told me, "I didn't write them and didn't supply any content to them. I didn't know about them until after they were drafted."

The views set forth in the memorandums were, indeed, very different from those held by Perle, who had said publicly that Saddam would leave office only if he were forced out, and from those of his fellow hard-liners in the Bush Administration. Given Perle's importance in American decision-making, and the risks of relying on a deal-maker with Adnan Khashoggi's history, questions remain about Hillman's drafting of such an amateurish peace proposal for Zuhair. Prince Bandar's assertion—that the talk of peace was merely a pretext for some hard selling—is difficult to dismiss.

Hillman's proposals, meanwhile, took on an unlikely life of their own. A month after the lunch, the proposals made their way to *Al Hayat*, a Saudi-owned newspaper published in London. If Perle had ever intended to dissociate himself from them, he did not succeed. The newspaper, in a dispatch headlined "WASHINGTON OFFERS TO AVERT WAR IN RETURN FOR AN INTERNATIONAL AGREE-

MENT TO EXILE SADDAM," characterized Hillman's memorandums as "American" documents and said that the new proposals bore Perle's imprimatur. The paper said that Perle and others had attended a series of "secret meetings" in an effort to avoid the pending war with Iraq, and "a scenario was discussed whereby Saddam Hussein would personally admit that his country was attempting to acquire weapons of mass destruction and he would agree to stop trying to acquire these weapons while he awaits exile."

A few days later, the Beirut daily *Al Safir* published Arabic translations of the memorandums themselves, attributing them to Richard Perle. The proposals were said to have been submitted by Perle, and to "outline Washington's future visions of Iraq." Perle's lunch with two Saudi businessmen was now elevated by *Al Safir* to a series of "recent American-Saudi negotiations" in which "the American side was represented by Richard Perle." The newspaper added, "Publishing these documents is important because they shed light on the story of how war could have been avoided." The documents, of course, did nothing of the kind.

When Perle was asked whether his dealings with Trireme might present the appearance of a conflict of interest, he said that anyone who saw such a conflict would be thinking "maliciously." But Perle, in crisscrossing between the public and the private sectors, put himself in a difficult position—one not uncommon to public men. He was credited with being the intellectual force behind a war that not everyone wanted and that many suspect, unfairly or not, of being driven by American business interests. There is no question that Perle believed that removing Saddam from power was the right thing to do. At the same time, he set up a company that stood to gain from a war. In doing so, he gave ammunition not only to the Saudis but to his other ideological opponents as well.

———

Perle responded to my account of his business dealings, which appeared in *The New Yorker* in March 2003, by comparing me to a terrorist and announcing that he planned to sue for libel. In November 2003, the Pentagon released a heavily redacted Inspector General's report that acknowledged that Perle "with few exceptions . . . engaged in the outside activities that were attributed to him"—that is, he served as an agent for private firms seeking federal contracts. But the I.G. report ruled that Perle did not violate federal statutes barring such representation because those laws restricted only special government employees who worked sixty days a year or more. Perle, as chairman of the Defense Policy Board, logged only eight days a year, the I.G. said. On "the more elusive" question of whether Perle violated government ethical rules or appeared to do so, the I.G. ruled that there was an "insufficient basis" to conclude that Perle's business activities amounted to a violation.

Perle soon became enmeshed in a series of financial scandals that involved possible conflicts of interest, as in the Trireme affair, as well as possible violations of U.S. Security and Exchange Commission disclosure rules. A few weeks after my story appeared, Perle resigned as chairman of the Defense Policy Board; a year later, he resigned as a board member. No libel suit has been filed.

V.

WHO LIED TO WHOM?

1. March 2003: "These Documents . . . Are in Fact Not Authentic"

On September 24, 2002, as Congress prepared to vote on the resolution authorizing President George W. Bush to wage war in Iraq, a group of senior intelligence officials, including George Tenet, the director of Central Intelligence, briefed the Senate Foreign Relations Committee on Iraq's weapons capability. It was an important presentation for the Bush Administration. Some Democrats were publicly questioning the President's claim that Iraq still possessed weapons of mass destruction that posed an immediate threat to the United States. Just the day before, former Vice President Al Gore had sharply criticized the Administration's advocacy of preëmptive war, calling it a doctrine that would replace "a world in which states consider themselves subject to law" with "the notion that there is no law but the discretion of the President of the United States." A few Democrats were also considering putting an alternative resolution before Congress.

According to two of those present at the briefing, which was highly classified and took place in the committee's secure hearing room, Tenet declared, as he had done before, that a shipment of high-strength aluminum tubes that was intercepted on its way to Iraq had been meant for the construction of centrifuges that could be used to produce enriched uranium. The suitability of the tubes for that purpose had been disputed, but this time the argument that Iraq had a nuclear program under way was buttressed by a new and striking assertion: the C.I.A. had recently received intelligence showing that, between 1999 and 2001, Iraq had attempted to buy five hundred tons of uranium oxide from Niger, one of the world's largest producers. This form of uranium ore, known as "yellow-cake," can be used to make fuel for nuclear reactors. It can also be converted, if processed differently, into weapons-grade uranium. Five tons can produce enough for a bomb.

On the same day, in London, Tony Blair's government made public a dossier containing some of the information that the Senate committee was being given in secret—that Iraq had sought to buy "significant quantities of uranium" from an unnamed African country, "despite having no active civil nuclear power programme that could require it." The allegation attracted immediate attention; a headline in the London *Guardian* declared, "AFRICAN GANGS OFFER ROUTE TO URANIUM."

Two days later, Secretary of State Colin Powell, appearing before a closed hearing of the Senate Foreign Relations Committee, also cited Iraq's attempt to obtain uranium from Niger as evidence of its persistent nuclear ambitions. The testimony from Tenet and Powell helped to mollify the Democrats, and two weeks later the resolution passed overwhelmingly, giving the President a congressional mandate for a military assault on Iraq. (William Harlow, the C.I.A. spokesman, initially denied that Tenet had briefed the senators on Niger when my story appeared, in March 2003. I learned later that an internal Senate investigation was launched to identify my source.)

A former high-level intelligence official told me that the information on Niger was judged serious enough to include in the President's Daily Brief, one of the most sensitive intelligence documents in the American system. Its information is supposed to be carefully analyzed, or "scrubbed." Distribution of the two- or three-page early-morning report, which is prepared by the C.I.A., is limited to the President and a few other senior officials. The P.D.B. is not made available, for example, to any members of the Senate or House Intelligence Committees. "I don't think anybody here sees that thing," a State Department analyst told me. "You only know what's in the P.D.B. because it echoes—people talk about it."

On December 19, 2002, Washington, for the first time, publicly identified Niger as the alleged seller of the nuclear materials, in a State Department position paper that rhetorically asked, "Why is the Iraqi regime hiding their uranium procurement?" Both Iraq and Niger denied the charge. President Bush cited the uranium deal, along with the aluminum tubes, in his State of the Union message, on January 28, 2003, while crediting Britain as the source of the information: "The British government has learned that Saddam Hussein recently sought significant quantities of uranium from Africa." He commented, "Saddam Hussein has not credibly explained these activities. He clearly has much to hide."

Then the story fell apart. On March 7th, less than two weeks before the war against Iraq began, Mohamed ElBaradei, the director general of the International Atomic Energy Agency, in Vienna, told the U.N. Security Council that the documents involving the Niger-Iraq uranium sale were fakes.

"The I.A.E.A. has concluded, with the concurrence of outside experts, that these documents . . . are in fact not authentic," ElBaradei said. One senior I.A.E.A. official went further. He told me, "These documents are so bad that I cannot imagine that they came from a serious intelligence agency. It depresses me, given the low quality of the documents, that it was not stopped. At the level it reached, I would have expected more checking."

The I.A.E.A. had first sought the documents last fall, shortly after the British government released its dossier. After months of pleading by the I.A.E.A., the United States turned them over to Jacques Baute, a Frenchman who is the director of the agency's Iraq Nuclear Verification Office. It took Baute's team only a few hours to determine that the documents were fake. The agency had been given about a half-dozen letters and other communications between officials in Niger and Iraq, many of them written on letterheads of the Niger government. The problems were glaring. One letter, dated October 10, 2000, was signed with the name of Allele Habibou, a Niger minister of foreign affairs and coöperation, who had been out of office since 1989. Another letter, allegedly from Tandja Mamadou, the president of Niger, had a signature that had obviously been faked and a text with inaccuracies so egregious, the senior I.A.E.A. official said, that "they could be spotted by someone using Google on the Internet." Baute, according to the I.A.E.A. official, "confronted the United States with the forgery: 'What do you have to say?' They had nothing to say."

When asked about the forgery during a television interview two days after ElBaradei's report, Colin Powell dismissed the subject by saying, "If that issue is resolved, that issue is resolved." A few days later, at a House hearing, he denied that anyone in the U.S. government had anything to do with the forgery. "It came from other sources," Powell testified. "It was provided in good faith to the inspectors." On March 8th, an American official who had reviewed the documents was quoted in the *Washington Post* as explaining, simply, "We fell for it."

The forgery became the object of widespread, and bitter, questions in Europe and elsewhere about the credibility of the United States. But it initially provoked only a few news stories in the United States, and little sustained questioning about how the White House could endorse such an obvious fake. Vice President Cheney responded to ElBaradei's report mainly by attacking the messenger. On March 16th,

Cheney, appearing on *Meet the Press*, stated emphatically that the United States had reason to believe that Saddam Hussein had reconstituted his nuclear-weapons program. He went on, "I think Mr. ElBaradei, frankly, is wrong. And I think if you look at the track record of the International Atomic Energy Agency on this kind of issue, especially where Iraq's concerned, they have consistently underestimated or missed what it was Saddam Hussein was doing. I don't have any reason to believe they're any more valid this time than they've been in the past." Three days later, the war in Iraq began.

What went wrong? How did such an obvious fraud manage to move, without significant challenge, through the top layers of the American intelligence community and into the most sacrosanct of presidential briefings? Who permitted it to go into the President's State of the Union speech? Was the Administration lying to itself? Or did it, in this and other cases, deliberately give Congress and the public what it knew to be bad information? When and how did the message—the threat posed by Iraq—become more important than the integrity of the intelligence-vetting process?

2. Into the Intelligence Stovepipe

They call themselves, self-mockingly, the Cabal—a small cluster of policy advisers and analysts who were based in the Pentagon's Office of Special Plans. In the debate leading up to the Iraq war, their operation, which was conceived by Paul Wolfowitz, brought about a crucial change of direction in the American intelligence community. These advisers and analysts, who began their work in the days after September 11, 2001, produced a skein of intelligence reviews that have helped to shape public opinion and American policy toward Iraq. They relied on data gathered by other intelligence agencies and also on information provided by Ahmad Chalabi's Iraqi National Congress. By the fall of 2002, the operation rivalled both the

C.I.A. and the Pentagon's own Defense Intelligence Agency, the D.I.A., as President Bush's main source of intelligence regarding Iraq's possible possession of stockpiles of weapons of mass destruction and connection with Al Qaeda.

The director of the Special Plans operation was Abram Shulsky, a scholarly expert in the works of the political philosopher Leo Strauss. Shulsky had quietly worked on intelligence and foreign policy issues for three decades; he was on the staff of the Senate Intelligence Committee in the early 1980s and, during the Reagan Administration, served in the Pentagon under Richard Perle, who was then an assistant secretary of defense, after which he joined the Rand Corporation. The Office of Special Plans was overseen by Undersecretary of Defense William Luti, the retired Navy captain who was an early advocate of military action against Iraq. As the Administration moved toward war and policy-making power shifted toward the civilians in the Pentagon, Luti took on increasingly important responsibilities. W. Patrick Lang, the former chief of Middle East intelligence at the D.I.A., said that the Pentagon had "banded together to dominate the government's foreign policy, and they've pulled it off. They're running Chalabi. The D.I.A. has been intimidated and beaten to a pulp. And there's no guts at all in the C.I.A."

The hostility went both ways. A Pentagon official who worked for Luti told me, in April 2003, "I did a job when the intelligence community wasn't doing theirs. We recognized the fact that they hadn't done the analysis. We were providing information to Wolfowitz that he hadn't seen before. The intelligence community is still looking for a mission like they had in the Cold War, when they spoon-fed the policy makers."

A Pentagon adviser who had worked with Special Plans similarly told me, in an interview that spring, that in his view Shulsky and Luti had simply "won the policy debate." He said, "they beat 'em—they cleaned up against State and the C.I.A. There's no mystery why they won—because they were more effective in making their argument. Luti is smarter than the opposition. Wolfowitz is smarter. They out-argued them. It was a fair fight. They persuaded the President of the need to make a new security policy. Those who lose are so good at trying to undercut those who won." He added, "I'd love to be the historian who writes the story of how this small group of eight or nine people made the case and won."

Special Plans was created in order to find evidence of what Wolfowitz and his boss, Defense Secretary Donald Rumsfeld, believed to be true—that Saddam Hussein had close ties to Al Qaeda, and that Iraq had an enormous arsenal of chemical, biological, and possibly even nuclear weapons. Iraq's possible possession of weapons of mass destruction had been a matter of concern to the international community since before the first Gulf War. Saddam Hussein had used chemical weapons in the past. At some point, he assembled thousands of chemical warheads, along with biological weapons, and made a serious attempt to build a nuclear-weapons program. What was in dispute was how much of that capacity, if any, survived the 1991 war and the years of U.N. inspections, no-fly zones, and sanctions that followed. In addition, since September 11th there had been recurring questions about Iraq's ties to terrorists. A February 2003 poll showed that 72 percent of Americans believed it was likely that Saddam was personally involved in September 11th, although no good evidence of such a connection had been presented.

Rumsfeld had long complained about the limits of American intelligence. In the late 1990s, he had chaired a commission on ballistic-missile programs that criticized the unwillingness of intelligence analysts "to make estimates that extended beyond the hard evidence they had in hand." Even before September 11th, Richard Perle was making a similar argument about the intelligence community's knowledge of Iraq's weapons. At a Senate Foreign Relations subcommittee hearing in March 2001, he said, "Does Saddam now have weapons of mass destruction? Sure he does. We know he has chemical weapons. We know he has biological weapons. . . . How far he's gone on the nuclear-weapons side I don't think we really know. My guess is it's further than we think. It's always further than we think, because we limit ourselves, as we think about this, to what we're able to prove and demonstrate. . . . And, unless you believe that we have uncovered everything, you have to assume there is more than we're able to report."

By the fall of 2002, Rumsfeld was in a public fight with the C.I.A. over the agency's inability to document significant direct ties between Al Qaeda and Iraq. He and his allies believed that the C.I.A. was simply unable to perceive the reality of the situation in Iraq. "The agency was out to disprove linkage between Iraq and terrorism," the Pentagon adviser told me. "That's what drove them. If you've ever worked with intelligence data, you can see the ingrained views at C.I.A. that color the way it sees data." The goal of Special Plans, he said, was "to put the data under the microscope to reveal what the intelligence community can't see. Shulsky's carrying the heaviest part."

In October 2002, an article in the *New York Times* reported that Rumsfeld had ordered up an intelligence operation "to search for information on Iraq's hostile intentions or links to terrorists" that might have been overlooked by the C.I.A. When Rumsfeld was asked about the story at a Pentagon briefing, he was initially vague. "I'm told that after September 11th a small group, I think two to start with, and maybe four now . . . were asked to begin poring over this mountain of information that we were receiving on intelligence-type things." He went on to say, "You don't know what you don't know. So in comes the daily briefer"—from the C.I.A.— "and she walks through the daily brief. And I ask questions. 'Gee, what about this?' or 'What about that? Has somebody thought of this?'" At the same briefing, Rumsfeld said that he had already been informed that there was "solid evidence of the presence in Iraq of Al Qaeda members." (In its report, the 9/11 Commision found that there was no evidence of an operational link between Iraq and Al Qaeda.)

A former high-level intelligence officer told me, "Rumsfeld's got to discredit the C.I.A.'s analyses to make his intelligence more reliable." Another former C.I.A. officer said that Rumsfeld "wants his own G.R.U."—a reference to the former Soviet military intelligence agency. "He does not want to be dependent on the C.I.A. for intelligence to prepare the battlefield for his troops."

One internal Pentagon memorandum from December 2001, went so far as to suggest that terrorism experts in the government and outside it had deliberately "downplayed or sought to disprove" the link between Al Qaeda and Iraq. "For many years, there has been a bias in the intelligence community" against defectors, the memorandum said. It urged that two analysts working with Shulsky be given the authority to "investigate linkages to Iraq" by having access to the "proper debriefing of key Iraqi defectors."

In its search for new intelligence, the Office of Special Plans turned to Chalabi's Iraqi National Congress, which constantly sought out Iraqi defectors. The office developed a close working relationship with the I.N.C. and became a conduit for intelligence reports from the I.N.C. to officials in the White House. This strengthened its position in disputes with the C.I.A. and gave the Pentagon's pro-war leadership added leverage in its constant disputes with the State Department—despite well-founded doubts about the I.N.C. In the mid-1990s, the C.I.A. had secretly funnelled millions of dollars annually to the I.N.C. Those payments ended around 1996, a former C.I.A. Middle East station chief told me, essentially because the agency had doubts about Chalabi's integrity.

"You had to treat them with suspicion," another former Middle East station chief said of Chalabi's people. "The I.N.C. has a track record of manipulating information because it has an agenda. It's a political unit—not an intelligence agency."

*　　　*　　　*

The I.N.C. was not alone in misrepresenting and manipulating intelligence. The White House was also twisting facts and ignoring unwanted evidence as it strove to convince Americans of the pending nuclear threat from Saddam Hussein. One of the more glaring cases involved Iraq's most celebrated defector, General Hussein Kamel. In August 1995, Kamel, who was in charge of Iraq's weapons program, defected to Jordan, with his brother, Colonel Saddam Kamel. They brought with them crates of documents containing detailed information about Iraqi efforts to develop weapons of mass destruction—much of which was unknown to the U.N. inspection teams that had been on the job since 1991—and were interviewed at length by the U.N. inspectors. In 1996, Saddam Hussein lured the brothers back with a promise of forgiveness, and then had them killed. The Kamels' information became a major element in the Bush Administration's campaign to convince the public of the failure of the U.N. inspections. In October 2002, in a speech in Cincinnati, the President cited the Kamel defections as the moment when Saddam's regime "was forced to admit that it had produced more than thirty thousand liters of anthrax and other deadly biological agents. . . . This is a massive stockpile of biological weapons that has never been accounted for, and is capable of killing millions." A couple of weeks earlier, Vice President Cheney had declared that Hussein Kamel's story "should serve as a reminder to all that we often learned more as the result of defections than we learned from the inspection regime itself."

The full record of Hussein Kamel's interview with the inspectors reveals, however, that he also said that Iraq's stockpile of chemical and biological warheads, which were manufactured before the 1991 Gulf War, had been destroyed, in many cases in response to ongoing inspections. The interview, on August 22, 1995, was conducted by Rolf Ekeus, then the executive chairman of the U.N. inspection teams, and two of his senior associates—Nikita Smidovich and Maurizio Zifferaro. "You have an important role in Iraq,"

Kamel said, according to the record, which was assembled from notes taken by Smidovich. "You should not underestimate yourself. You are very effective in Iraq." When Smidovich noted that the U.N. teams had not found "any traces of destruction," Kamel responded, "Yes, it was done before you came in." He also said that Iraq had destroyed its arsenal of warheads. "We gave instructions not to produce chemical weapons," Kamel explained later in the debriefing. "I don't remember resumption of chemical-weapons production before the Gulf War. Maybe it was only minimal production and filling. . . . All chemical weapons were destroyed. I ordered destruction of all chemical weapons. All weapons—biological, chemical, missile, nuclear—were destroyed."

Kamel also cast doubt on the testimony of Dr. Khidhir Hamza, an Iraqi nuclear scientist who defected in 1994. Hamza settled in the United States with the help of the I.N.C. and would become a highly vocal witness concerning Iraq's alleged nuclear ambitions. Kamel told the U.N. interviewers, however, that Hamza was "a professional liar." He went on, "He worked with us, but he was useless and always looking for promotions. He consulted with me but could not deliver anything. . . . He was even interrogated by a team before he left and was allowed to go."

After his defection, Hamza became a senior fellow at the Institute for Science and International Security, a Washington disarmament group, whose president, David Albright, was a former U.N. weapons inspector. In 1998, Albright told me, he and Hamza sent publishers a proposal for a book tentatively entitled *Fizzle: Iraq and the Atomic Bomb*, which described how Iraq had failed in its quest for a nuclear device. There were no takers, Albright said, and Hamza eventually "started exaggerating his experiences in Iraq." The two men broke off contact. In 2000, Hamza published *Saddam's Bombmaker*, a vivid account claiming that by 1991, when the Gulf War began, Iraq was far closer than had been known to the production of a nuclear weapon.

In a speech on November 14, 2001, as the Taliban were being routed in Afghanistan, Richard Perle cited Hamza's account, including his claim that Saddam Hussein, in response to the 1981 Israeli bombing of the Osirak nuclear reactor, near Baghdad, had ordered future nuclear facilities to be dispersed at four hundred sites across the nation. "Every day," Perle said, these sites "turn out a little bit of nuclear materials." He told his audience, "Do we wait for Saddam and hope for the best, do we wait and hope he doesn't do what we know he is capable of . . . or do we take some preëmptive action?"

In May 2003, when I spoke to Jeff Stein, a Washington journalist who collaborated on the book, he told me that Hamza's account was "absolutely on the level, allowing for the fact that any memoir puts the author at the center of events, and therefore there is some exaggeration." James Woolsey, the former head of the C.I.A., also told me that month, "I think highly of him and I have no reason to disbelieve the claims that he's made." At the time, Hamza could not be reached for comment; he had just returned to Iraq as a member of a group of exiles designated by the Pentagon to help rebuild the country's infrastructure. He was to be responsible for atomic energy. (Hamza's contract with the Coalition Provisional Authority was not renewed in 2004.)

The advantages and disadvantages of relying on defectors has been a perennial source of dispute within the American intelligence community—as Shulsky himself noted in a 1991 textbook on intelligence that he co-authored. Despite their importance, he wrote, "it is difficult to be certain that they are genuine. . . . The conflicting information provided by several major Soviet defectors to the United States . . . has never been completely sorted out; it bedeviled U.S. intelligence for a quarter of a century." Defectors can provide unique insight into a repressive system. But such volunteer sources, as Shulsky writes, "may be greedy; they may also be somewhat unbalanced people who wish to bring some excitement into their lives;

they may desire to avenge what they see as ill treatment by their government; or they may be subject to blackmail." There is a strong incentive to tell interviewers what they want to hear.

A retired C.I.A. officer described for me some of the questions that would normally arise in vetting a source: "Does dramatic information turned up by an overseas spy square with his access, or does it exceed his plausible reach? How does the agent behave? Is he on time for meetings?" The vetting process is especially important when one is dealing with foreign reports—sensitive intelligence that can trigger profound policy decisions. In theory, no request for action should be taken directly to higher authorities—a process known as "stovepiping"—without the information on which it is based having been subjected to rigorous scrutiny.

The intelligence community was in full retreat, and the Office of Special Plans circumvented the vetting process. In the spring of 2002, the former White House official told me, Rumsfeld and Wolfowitz began urging the President to release more than $90 million in federal funds to Chalabi that had been authorized by the 1998 Iraq Liberation Act but not dispersed because of State Department questions about I.N.C. accounting practices. "The Vice President came into a meeting furious that we hadn't given the money to Chalabi," the former official recalled. Cheney said, "Here we are, denying him money, when they"—the Iraqi National Congress—"are providing us with unique intelligence on Iraqi W.M.D.s."

With the Pentagon's support, Chalabi's group worked to put defectors with compelling stories in touch with reporters in the United States and Europe. The resulting articles had dramatic accounts of advances in weapons of mass destruction or told of ties to terrorist groups. In some cases, these stories were disputed in analyses by the C.I.A. Misstatements and inconsistencies in I.N.C. defector accounts were also discovered after the final series of U.N. weapons inspections, which ended a few days before the American assault. Dr. Glen Rangwala, a lecturer in political science at Cambridge University, compiled and examined the information that had been made public at the time of the invasion and concluded that the U.N. inspections had failed to find evidence to support the defectors' claims.

For example, many newspapers published extensive interviews with Adnan Ihsan Saeed al-Haideri, a civil engineer who, with the I.N.C.'s help, fled Iraq in 2001, and subsequently claimed that he had visited twenty hidden facilities that he believed were built for the production of biological and chemical weapons. One, he said, was underneath a hospital in Baghdad. Haideri was a source for Secretary of State Colin Powell's claim, in his presentation to the United Nations Security Council on February 5, 2003, that the United States had "firsthand descriptions" of mobile factories capable of producing vast quantities of biological weapons. The U.N. teams that returned to Iraq in November 2002 were unable to verify any of Haideri's claims. In a statement to the Security Council in March, on the eve of war, Hans Blix, the United Nation's chief weapons inspector, noted that his teams had physically examined the hospital and other sites with the help of ground-penetrating radar equipment. "No underground facilities for chemical or biological production or storage were found so far," he said.

Almost immediately after September 11th, the I.N.C. began to publicize the stories of defectors who claimed that they had information connecting Iraq to the attacks. In an interview on October 14, 2001, conducted jointly by the *New York Times* and the public television program *Frontline*, Sabah Khodada, an Iraqi Army captain, said that the September 11th operation "was conducted by people who were trained by Saddam," and that Iraq had a program to instruct terrorists in the art of hijacking. Another defector, who was identified only as a retired lieutenant general in the Iraqi intelligence service, said that in 2000 he witnessed Arab students being given lessons in hijacking on a Boeing 707 parked at an Iraqi training camp near the town of Salman Pak, south of Baghdad.

In separate interviews with me in the spring of 2003, however, a former C.I.A. station chief and a former military intelligence analyst said that the camp near Salman Pak had been built not for terrorism training but for counterterrorism training. In the mid-1980s, Islamic terrorists were routinely hijacking aircraft. In 1986, an Iraqi airliner was seized by pro-Iranian extremists and crashed, after a hand grenade was triggered, killing at least sixty-five people. (At the time, Iran and Iraq were at war, and the United States favored Iraq.) Iraq then sought assistance from the West, and got what it wanted from Britain's MI6. The C.I.A. offered similar training in counterterrorism throughout the Middle East. "We were helping our allies everywhere we had a liaison," the former station chief told me. Inspectors recalled seeing the body of an airplane—which appeared to be used for counterterrorism training—when they visited a biological-weapons facility near Salman Pak in 1991, ten years before September 11th. It is, of course, possible for such a camp to be converted from one purpose to another. The former C.I.A. official noted, however, that terrorists would not practice on airplanes in the open. "That's Hollywood rinky-dink stuff," the former agent said. "They train in basements. You don't need a real airplane to practice hijacking. The 9/11 terrorists went to gyms. But to take one back you have to practice on the real thing."

Salman Pak was overrun by American troops on April 6, 2003. Neither the camp nor the former biological facility has yielded evidence to substantiate the claims made before the war.

Throughout 2002, reports were flowing from the Pentagon directly to the Vice President's office, and then on to the President, with little prior evaluation by intelligence professionals. When analysts did get a look at the reports, they were troubled by what they found. "They'd pick apart a report and find out that the source had been wrong before, or had no access to the information provided," Greg Thielmann, an expert on disarmament with the State Department's Bureau of Intelligence and Research, told me. "There was considerable skepticism throughout the intelligence community about the reliability of Chalabi's sources, but the defector reports were coming all the time. Knock one down and another comes along. Meanwhile, the garbage was being shoved straight to the President."

A routine settled in: the Pentagon's defector reports, classified "secret," would be funnelled to newspapers, but subsequent analyses of the reports by intelligence agencies—scathing but also classified—would remain secret. "It became a personality issue," a Pentagon consultant said of the Bush Administration's handling of intelligence. "My fact is better than your fact. The whole thing is a failure of process. Nobody goes to primary sources."

A former Bush Administration intelligence official recalled a case in which Chalabi's group, working with the Pentagon, produced a defector from Iraq who was interviewed overseas by an agent from the D.I.A. The agent relied on an interpreter supplied by Chalabi's people. In the summer of 2002, the D.I.A. report, which was classified, was leaked. In a detailed account, the London *Times* described how the defector had trained with Al Qaeda terrorists in the late 1990s at secret camps in Iraq, how the Iraqis received instructions in the use of chemical and biological weapons, and how the defector was given a new identity and relocated. A month later, however, a team of C.I.A. agents went to interview the man with their own interpreter. "He says, 'No, that's not what I said,'" the former intelligence official told me. "He said, 'I worked at a fedayeen camp; it wasn't Al Qaeda.' He never saw any chemical or biological training." Afterward, the former official said, "the C.I.A. sent out a piece of paper saying that this information was incorrect. They put it in writing." But the C.I.A. rebuttal, like the original report, was classified. "I remember wondering whether this one would leak and correct the earlier, invalid leak. Of course, it didn't."

The former intelligence official went on, "One of the reasons I left was my sense that they were using the intelligence from the C.I.A. and other agencies only when it fit their agenda. They didn't like the intelligence they were getting, and so they brought in people to write the stuff. They were so crazed and so far out and so difficult to reason with—to the point of being bizarre. Dogmatic, as if they were on a mission from God." He added, "If it doesn't fit their theory, they don't want to accept it."

Shulsky's work, and that of his colleagues, had deep theoretical underpinnings. In his academic and think-tank writings, Shulsky, the son of a newspaperman—his father, Sam, wrote a nationally syndicated business column—has long been a critic of the American intelligence community. During the Cold War, his area of expertise was Soviet disinformation techniques. Like Wolfowitz, he was a student of Leo Strauss's, at the University of Chicago. Both men received their doctorates under Strauss in 1972. Strauss, a refugee from Nazi Germany who arrived in the United States in 1937, was trained in the history of political philosophy, and became one of the foremost conservative émigré scholars. He was widely known for his argument that the works of ancient philosophers contain deliberately concealed esoteric meanings whose truths can be comprehended only by a very few, and would be misunderstood by the masses. The Straussian movement has many adherents in and around the Bush Administration. In addition to Wolfowitz, they include William Kristol, the editor of the *Weekly Standard*, and Stephen Cambone.

Strauss's influence on foreign policy decision making (he never wrote explicitly about the subject himself) is usually discussed in terms of his tendency to view the world as a place where isolated liberal democracies live in constant danger from hostile elements abroad, and face threats that must be confronted vigorously and with strong leadership. How Strauss's views might be applied to the intelligence-gathering process is less immediately obvious. As it happens, Shulsky himself explored that question in a 1999 essay, written with Gary Schmitt, entitled "Leo Strauss and the World of Intelligence (By

Which We Do Not Mean *Nous*)"—in Greek philosophy the term *nous* denotes the highest form of rationality. In the essay, Shulsky and Schmitt write that Strauss's "gentleness, his ability to concentrate on detail, his consequent success in looking below the surface and reading between the lines, and his seeming unworldliness . . . may even be said to resemble, however faintly, the George Smiley of John le Carré's novels." Echoing one of Strauss's major themes, Shulsky and Schmitt criticize the United States' intelligence community for its failure to appreciate the duplicitous nature of the regimes it deals with, its susceptibility to social science notions of proof, and its inability to cope with deliberate concealment.

The agency's analysts, Shulsky and Schmitt argue, "were generally reluctant throughout the Cold War to believe that they could be deceived about any critical question by the Soviet Union or other Communist states. History has shown this view to have been extremely naïve." They suggested that political philosophy, with its emphasis on the variety of regimes, could provide an "antidote" to the C.I.A.'s failings, and would help in understanding Islamic leaders, "whose intellectual world was so different from our own."

Strauss's idea of hidden meaning, Shulsky and Schmitt added, "alerts one to the possibility that political life may be closely linked to deception. Indeed, it suggests that deception is the norm in political life, and the hope, to say nothing of the expectation, of establishing a politics that can dispense with it is the exception."

Robert Pippin, the chairman of the Committee on Social Thought at Chicago and a critic of Strauss, told me, "Strauss believed that good statesmen have powers of judgment and must rely on an inner circle. The person who whispers in the ear of the king is more important than the king. If you have that talent, what you do or say in public cannot be held accountable in the same way." Another Strauss critic, Stephen Holmes, a law professor at New York University, put the Straussians' position this way: "They believe that your enemy is deceiving you, and you have to pretend to agree, but secretly you follow your own views." Holmes added, "The whole story is complicated by Strauss's idea—actually Plato's—that philosophers need to tell noble lies not only to the people at large but also to powerful politicians."

When I asked one of Strauss's staunchest defenders, Joseph Cropsey, professor emeritus of political science at Chicago, about the use of Strauss's views in the area of policy making, he told me that common sense alone suggested that a certain amount of deception is essential in government. "That people in government have to be discreet in what they say publicly is so obvious—'If I tell you the truth I can't but help the enemy.'" But there is nothing in Strauss's work, he added, that "favors preëmptive action. What it favors is prudence and sound judgment. If you could have got rid of Hitler in the 1930s, who's not going to be in favor of that? You don't need Strauss to reach that conclusion."

Some former intelligence officials believe that Shulsky and his superiors were captives of their own convictions, and were merely deceiving themselves. Vincent Cannistraro, the former chief of counterterrorism operations and analysis at the C.I.A., worked with Shulsky at a Washington think tank after his retirement. He said, in an interview in the spring of 2003, "Abe is very gentle and slow to anger, with a sense of irony. But his politics were typical for his group—the Straussian view." The group's members, Cannistraro said, "reinforce each other because they're the only friends they have, and they all work together. This has been going on since the 1980s, but they've never been able to coalesce as they have now. September 11th gave them the opportunity, and now they're in heaven. They believe the intelligence is there. They want to believe it. It has to be there."

The rising influence of the Office of Special Plans in the year before the war was accompanied by a decline in the influence of the C.I.A. and the D.I.A. "Feith and Luti see everybody not 100 percent with them as 100 percent against them—it's a very Manichaean world," a defense consultant said. A former C.I.A. expert who spent the past decade immersed in Iraqi-exile affairs said of the Special Plans people, "They see themselves as outsiders. There's a high degree of paranoia. They've convinced themselves that they're on the side of angels, and everybody else in the government is a fool."

The neoconservatives in the Pentagon's Office of Special Plans were not alone in bypassing the checks and balances of the intelligence community. A few months after George Bush took office, Greg Thielmann, of the State Department's Bureau of Intelligence and Research (I.N.R.), was assigned to be the daily intelligence liaison to John Bolton, the Undersecretary of State for Arms Control and International Security, who is a prominent conservative. Thielmann understood that his posting had been mandated by Secretary of State Colin Powell, who thought that every important State Department bureau should be assigned a daily intelligence officer. "Bolton was the guy with whom I had to do business," Thielmann said. "We were going to provide him with all the information he was entitled to see. That's what being a professional intelligence officer is all about."

But, Thielmann told me, "Bolton seemed to be troubled because I.N.R. was not telling him what he wanted to hear."

Thielmann soon found himself shut out of Bolton's early-morning staff meetings. "I was intercepted at the door of his office and told, 'The Undersecretary doesn't need you to attend this meeting anymore.'" When Thielmann protested that he was there to provide intelligence input, the aide said, "The Undersecretary wants to keep this in the family."

Eventually, Thielmann said, Bolton demanded that he and his staff have direct electronic access to sensitive intelligence, such as foreign-agent reports and electronic intercepts. In previous administrations, such data had been made available to undersecretaries only after it was analyzed, usually in the specially secured offices of

I.N.R. The whole point of the intelligence system in place, according to Thielmann, was "to prevent raw intelligence from getting to people who would be misled." Bolton, however, wanted his aides to receive and assign intelligence analyses and assessments using the raw data. In essence, the undersecretary would be running his own intelligence operation, without any guidance or support. "He surrounded himself with a hand-chosen group of loyalists, and found a way to get C.I.A. information directly," Thielmann said.

In a subsequent interview, Bolton acknowledged that he had changed the procedures for handling intelligence, in an effort to extend the scope of the classified materials available to his office. "I found that there was lots of stuff that I wasn't getting and that the I.N.R. analysts weren't including," he told me. "I didn't want it filtered. I wanted to see everything—to be fully informed. If that puts someone's nose out of joint, sorry about that." Bolton told me that he wanted to reach out to the intelligence community but that Thielmann had "invited himself" to his daily staff meetings. "This was my meeting with the four assistant secretaries who report to me, in preparation for the Secretary's 8:30 A.M. staff meeting," Bolton said. "This was within my family of bureaus. There was no place for I.N.R. or anyone else—the Human Resources Bureau or the Office of Foreign Buildings."

Bolton and his Special Plans colleagues may not have been consciously distorting intelligence. What was taking place, however, was much more systematic—and potentially just as troublesome. Kenneth Pollack, a former National Security Council expert on Iraq, whose book *The Threatening Storm* generally supported the use of force to remove Saddam Hussein, told me that what the Bush people did was "dismantle the existing filtering process that for fifty years had been preventing the policy makers from getting bad information. They created stovepipes to get the information they wanted directly to the top leadership. Their position is that the professional bureaucracy is deliberately and maliciously keeping information from them.

"They always had information to back up their public claims, but it was often very bad information," Pollack continued. "They were forcing the intelligence community to defend its good information and good analysis so aggressively that the intelligence analysts didn't have the time or the energy to go after the bad information." (Commenting on Rumsfeld's control over the D.I.A., one former senior official told me, in early 2002, "If it became known that Rummy wanted them to link the government of Tonga to 9/11, within a few months they would come up with sources who'd do it.")

A former C.I.A. task force leader who was a consultant to the Bush Administration said that many analysts in the C.I.A. were convinced that the Chalabi group's defector reports on weapons of mass destruction and Al Qaeda had produced little of value, but said that the agency was "not fighting it." He said that the D.I.A. had studied the information as well. "Even the D.I.A. can't find any value in it."

In interviews, former C.I.A. officers and analysts described the agency as increasingly demoralized. One former officer said of Tenet, "George knows he's being beaten up, and his analysts are terrified. George used to protect his people, but he's been forced to do things their way." Because the C.I.A.'s analysts were on the defensive, they wrote "reports justifying their intelligence rather than saying what's going on. The Defense Department and the Office of the Vice President write their own pieces, based on their own ideology. We collect so much stuff that you can find anything you want."

The Administration eventually got its way, a former C.I.A. official said. "The analysts at the C.I.A. were beaten down defending their assessments. I've never seen a government like this."

3. Behind the "Mushroom Cloud"

In the fall of 2001, the Bureau of Intelligence and Research undertook a major review of Iraq's progress in developing W.M.D.s. The review was presented to Secretary of State Powell in December 2001; according to Greg Thielmann, who was one of the analysts who worked on the study, "It basically said that there is no persuasive evidence that the Iraqi nuclear program is being reconstituted." This was not entirely welcome news. Members of the Administration were already beginning to articulate what would become its most compelling argument for going to war with Iraq: the possibility that, with enough time, Saddam Hussein would be capable of attacking the United States with a nuclear weapon.

In fact, the best case for the success of the U.N. inspection process in Iraq was in the area of nuclear arms. In October 1997, the International Atomic Energy Agency issued a definitive report declaring Iraq to be essentially free of nuclear weapons. The I.A.E.A.'s inspectors said, "There are no indications that there remains in Iraq any physical capability for the production of amounts of weapon-usable nuclear material of any practical significance." The report noted that Iraq's nuclear facilities had been destroyed by American bombs in the 1991 Gulf War.

The study's main author, Garry Dillon, a British nuclear-safety engineer who spent twenty-three years working for the I.A.E.A. and retired as its chief of inspection, told me that it was "highly unlikely" that Iraq had been able to maintain a secret or hidden program to produce significant amounts of weapons-usable material, given the enormous progress in the past decade in the technical ability of I.A.E.A. inspectors to detect radioactivity in ground locations and in waterways. "This is not kitchen chemistry," Dillon said. "You're talking factory scale, and in any operation there are leaks."

The Administration could offer little or no recent firsthand intelligence to contradict the I.A.E.A.'s 1997 conclusions. During the

Clinton years, there had been a constant flow of troubling intelligence reports on Iraqi weapons of mass destruction, but most were in the context of worst-case analyses—what Iraq could do without adequate United Nations inspections—and included few, if any, reliable reports from agents inside the country. The inspectors left in 1998. The Bush Administration was receiving new reports from defectors, but those accounts could not be corroborated by the available intelligence.

In the fall of 2001, however, soon after the September 11th attacks, the C.I.A. had received an intelligence report from Italy's Military Intelligence and Security Service, or SISMI, about a public visit that Wissam al-Zahawie, then the Iraqi ambassador to the Vatican, had made to Niger and three other African nations two and a half years earlier, in February 1999. The visit had been covered at the time by the local press in Niger and by a French press agency. The American ambassador, Charles O. Cecil, filed a routine report to Washington on the visit, as did British intelligence. There was nothing untoward about the Zahawie visit. "We reported it because his picture appeared in the paper with the president," Cecil, who is now retired, told me. There was no article accompanying the photograph, only the caption, and nothing significant to report. At the time, Niger, which had sent hundreds of troops in support of the American-led Gulf War in 1991, was actively seeking economic assistance from the United States. None of the contemporaneous reports, as far as is known, made any mention of uranium, although Niger is a major exporter of yellowcake. But now, apparently as part of a larger search for any pertinent information about terrorism, SISMI dug the Zahawie trip report out of its files and passed it along, with a suggestion that Zahawie's real mission was to arrange the purchase of yellowcake.

What made the two-and-a-half-year-old report stand out in Washington was its relative freshness. A 1999 attempt by Iraq to buy uranium ore, if verified, would seem to prove that Saddam had been working to reconstitute his nuclear program—and give the lie to the I.A.E.A. and to intelligence reports inside the American government that claimed otherwise.

The SISMI report, however, was unpersuasive. Inside the American intelligence community, it was dismissed as amateurish and unsubstantiated. One former senior C.I.A. official told me that the initial report from Italy contained no documents but only a written summary of allegations. "I can fully believe that SISMI would put out a piece of intelligence like that," a C.I.A. consultant told me, "but why anybody would put credibility in it is beyond me." No credible documents have emerged since to corroborate it. The intelligence report was quickly stovepiped to those officials who had an intense interest in building the case against Iraq, including Vice President Dick Cheney. "The Vice President saw a piece of intelligence reporting that Iraq was attempting to buy uranium," Cathie Martin, the spokeswoman for Cheney, told me. Sometime after he first saw it, Cheney brought it up at his regularly scheduled daily briefing from the C.I.A., Martin said. "He asked the briefer a question. The briefer came back a day or two later and said, 'We do have a report, but there's a lack of details.'" The Vice President was further told that it was known that Iraq had acquired uranium ore from Niger in the early 1980s but that that material had been placed in secure storage by the I.A.E.A., which was monitoring it. "End of story," Martin added. "That's all we know."

According to a former high-level C.I.A. official, however, Cheney was dissatisfied with the response, and asked the agency to review the matter once again. It was the beginning of what turned out to be a year-long tug-of-war between the C.I.A. and the Vice President's office.

As the campaign to build a case against Iraq intensified, a former aide to Cheney told me, the Vice President's office, run by his chief of staff, Lewis "Scooter" Libby, became increasingly secretive when it came to intelligence about Iraq's W.M.D.s. As with Wolfowitz and

Bolton, there was a reluctance to let the military and civilian analysts on the staff vet intelligence. "It was an unbelievably closed and small group," the former aide told me. Intelligence procedures were far more open during the Clinton Administration, he said, and professional staff members had been far more involved in assessing and evaluating the most sensitive data. "There's so much intelligence out there that it's easy to pick and choose your case," the former aide told me. "It opens things up to cherry-picking." ("Some reporting is sufficiently sensitive that it is restricted only to the very top officials of the government—as it should be," Cathie Martin said.)

By early 2002, the SISMI intelligence—still unverified—had begun to play a role in the Administration's warnings about the Iraqi nuclear threat. On January 30th, the C.I.A. published an unclassified report to Congress that stated, "Baghdad may be attempting to acquire materials that could aid in reconstituting its nuclear-weapons program." A week later, Colin Powell told the House International Relations Committee, "With respect to the nuclear program, there is no doubt that the Iraqis are pursuing it."

The C.I.A. assessment reflected both deep divisions within the agency and the position of its director, George Tenet, which was far from secure; the agency had been sharply criticized, after all, for failing to provide any effective warning of the September 11th attacks. In the view of many C.I.A. analysts and operatives, the director was too eager to endear himself to the Administration hawks and improve his standing with the President and the Vice President. Senior C.I.A. analysts dealing with Iraq were constantly being urged by the Vice President's office to provide worst-case assessments on Iraqi weapons issues. "They got pounded on, day after day," one senior Bush Administration official told me, and received no consistent backup from Tenet and his senior staff. "Pretty soon you say 'Fuck it.'" And they began to provide the intelligence that was wanted.

* * *

In late February 2002, the C.I.A. persuaded retired Ambassador Joseph Wilson to fly to Niger to discreetly check out the story of the uranium sale. Wilson, who was working as a business consultant, had excellent credentials: he had been deputy chief of mission in Baghdad, had served as a diplomat in Africa, and had worked in the White House for the National Security Council. He was known as an independent diplomat who had put himself in harm's way to help American citizens abroad. Wilson told me he was informed at the time that the mission had come about because the Vice President's office was interested in the Italian intelligence report. Before his departure, he was summoned to a meeting at the C.I.A. with a group of government experts on Iraq, Niger, and uranium. He was shown no documents but was told, he said, that the C.I.A. "was responding to a report that was recently received of a purported memorandum of agreement"—between Iraq and Niger—"that our boys had gotten." He added, "It was never clear to me, or to the people who were briefing me, whether our guys had actually seen the agreement, or the purported text of an agreement."

Wilson's trip to Niger, which lasted eight days, produced nothing. He learned that any memorandum of understanding to sell yellowcake would have required the signatures of Niger's prime minister, foreign minister, and minister of mines. "I saw everybody out there," Wilson said, and no one had signed such a document. "If a document purporting to be about the sale contained those signatures, it would not be authentic." Wilson also learned that there was no uranium available to sell: it had all been pre-sold to Niger's Japanese and European consortium partners. Wilson returned to Washington and made his report. It was circulated, he said, but "I heard nothing about what the Vice President's office thought about it."

By early March 2002, a former White House official told me, it was understood by many in the White House that the President had already decided, in his own mind, to go to war. In late summer, the White House sharply escalated the nuclear rhetoric. There were at least two immediate targets: the midterm congressional elections and the pending vote on a congressional resolution authorizing the President to take any action he deemed necessary in Iraq, to protect America's national security.

On August 7, 2002, Vice President Cheney, speaking in California, said of Saddam Hussein, "What we know now, from various sources, is that he . . . continues to pursue a nuclear weapon." On August 26th, Cheney suggested that Saddam had a nuclear capability that could directly threaten "anyone he chooses, in his own region or beyond." He added that the Iraqis were continuing "to pursue the nuclear program they began so many years ago." On September 8th, he told a television interviewer, "We do know, with absolute certainty, that he is using his procurement system to acquire the equipment he needs in order to enrich uranium to build a nuclear weapon." The President himself, in his weekly radio address on September 14th, stated, "Saddam Hussein has the scientists and infrastructure for a nuclear-weapons program, and has illicitly sought to purchase the equipment needed to enrich uranium for a nuclear weapon." There was no confirmed intelligence for the President's assertion.

The government of the British Prime Minister, Tony Blair, President Bush's closest ally, was also brought in. As Blair later told a British government inquiry, he and Bush had talked by telephone that summer about the need "to disclose what we knew or as much as we could of what we knew." Blair loyally took the lead: on September 24th, the British government issued a dossier dramatizing the W.M.D. threat posed by Iraq. In a foreword, Blair proclaimed that "the assessed intelligence has established beyond doubt that Saddam . . . continues in his efforts to develop nuclear weapons." The dossier noted that intelligence—based, again, largely on the SISMI report—showed that Iraq had "sought significant quantities of uranium from Africa." A subsequent parliamentary inquiry determined that the published statement had been significantly toned down after the C.I.A. warned its British counterpart not to include the claim in the dossier, and in the final version Niger was not named, nor was SISMI.

The White House, meanwhile, had been escalating its rhetoric. In a television interview on September 8th, Condoleezza Rice, addressing questions about the strength of the Administration's case against Iraq, said, "We don't want the smoking gun to be a mushroom cloud"—a formulation that was taken up by hawks in the Administration. And, in a speech on October 7th, President Bush said, "Facing clear evidence of peril, we cannot wait for the final proof—the smoking gun—that could come in the form of a mushroom cloud."

At that moment, in early October 2002, a set of documents suddenly appeared that promised to provide solid evidence that Iraq was attempting to reconstitute its nuclear program. The first notice of the documents' existence came when Elisabetta Burba, a reporter for *Panorama*, a glossy Italian weekly owned by the publishing empire of Prime Minister Silvio Berlusconi, received a telephone call from an Italian businessman and security consultant whom she believed to have been connected to Italian intelligence. He told her that he had information connecting Saddam Hussein to the purchase of uranium in Africa. She considered the informant credible. In 1995, when she worked for the magazine *Epoca*, he had provided her with detailed information, apparently from Western intelligence sources, for articles she published dealing with the peace process in Bosnia and with an Islamic charity that was linked to international terrorism. The information, some of it in English, proved to be accurate. *Epoca* had authorized her to pay around $4,000 for the documents—a common journalistic practice in Italy. Now, years later, "he comes to me again," Burba told me. "I knew he was an informed person, and that he had contacts all over the world, including in the Middle East. He deals with investment and security issues." When Burba met with the man, he showed her the

Niger documents and offered to sell them to her for about $10,000.

The documents he gave her were photocopies. There were twenty-two pages, mostly in French, some with the letterhead of the Niger government or embassy, and two on the stationery of the Iraq Embassy to the Holy See. There were also telexes. When Burba asked how the documents could be authenticated, the man produced what appeared to be a photocopy of the codebook from the Niger embassy, along with other items. "What I was sure of was that he had access," Burba said. "He didn't receive the documents from the moon."

The documents dealt primarily with the alleged sale of uranium, Burba said. She informed her editors, and shared the photocopies with them. She wanted to arrange a visit to Niger to verify what seemed to be an astonishing story. At that point, however, *Panorama*'s editor-in-chief, Carlo Rossella, who is known for his ties to the Berlusconi government, told Burba to turn the documents over to the American Embassy for authentication. Burba dutifully took a copy of the papers to the embassy on October 9th.

A week later, Burba travelled to Niger. She visited mines and the ports that any exports would pass through, spoke to European businessmen and officials informed about Niger's uranium industry, and found no trace of a sale. She also learned that the transport company and the bank mentioned in the papers were too small and too ill-equipped to handle such a transaction. As Ambassador Wilson had done eight months earlier, she concluded that there was no evidence of a recent sale of yellowcake to Iraq. The *Panorama* story was dead, and Burba and her editors said that no money was paid. The documents, however, were now in American hands. They were also just what Administration hawks had been waiting for.

Two former C.I.A. officials provided slightly different accounts of what happened next. "The embassy was alerted that the papers were coming," the first former official told me, "and it passed them directly to Washington without even vetting them inside the embassy." Once the documents were in Washington, they were forwarded by the C.I.A. to the Pentagon, he said. "Everybody knew at every step of the way that they were false—until they got to the Pentagon, where they were believed."

The second former official, Vincent Cannistraro, who served as chief of counterterrorism operations and analysis, told me that copies of the Burba documents were given to the American Embassy, which passed them on to the C.I.A.'s chief of station in Rome, who forwarded them to Washington. Months later, he said, he telephoned a contact at C.I.A. headquarters and was told that "the jury was still out on this"—that is, on the authenticity of the documents.

The former high-level intelligence official told me that some senior C.I.A. officials were aware that the documents weren't trustworthy. "It's not a question as to whether they were marginal. They can't be 'sort of' bad, or 'sort of' ambiguous. They knew it was a fraud—it was useless. Everybody bit their tongue and said, 'Wouldn't it be great if the Secretary of State said this?' The Secretary of State never saw the documents." He added, "He's absolutely apoplectic about it." A former intelligence officer told me that questions about the authenticity of the Niger documents were raised inside the government by analysts at the Department of Energy and the State Department's I.N.R. However, these warnings were not heeded.

George Tenet clearly was ambivalent about the information: in early October, he intervened to prevent the President from referring to Niger in a speech in Cincinnati. But Tenet then seemed to give up the fight, and Saddam's desire for uranium from Niger soon became part of the Administration's public case for going to war. On December 7th, the Iraqi regime provided the U.N. Security Council with a twelve-thousand-page series of documents in which it denied having a W.M.D. arsenal. Very few in the press, the public, or the White House believed it. In a January 23rd op-ed column in the *New York Times*, entitled "Why We Know Iraq Is Lying," Condoleezza Rice wrote that the "false declaration . . . fails to account for or explain Iraq's efforts to get uranium from abroad." On January 26th, Secretary Powell, speaking at the World Economic Forum in Davos, Switzerland, asked, "Why is Iraq still trying to procure uranium?" Two days later, President Bush described the alleged sale in his State of the Union address, saying, "The British government has learned that Saddam Hussein recently sought significant quantities of uranium from Africa."

President Bush's State of the Union speech had startled Elisabetta Burba, the Italian reporter. She had been handed documents and had personally taken them to the American Embassy, and she now knew from her trip to Niger that they were false. Later, Burba revisited her source. "I wanted to know what happened," she said. "He told me that he didn't know the documents were false, and said he'd also been fooled."

Burba, convinced that she had the story of the year, wanted to publish her account immediately after the President's speech, but Carlo Rossella, *Panorama*'s editor-in-chief, decided against it. Rossella explained to me, "When I heard the State of the Union statement, I thought to myself that perhaps the United States government has other information. I didn't think the documents were that important—they weren't trustable." (Eventually, in July, after her name appeared in the press, Burba published an account of her role. She told me that she was interviewed at the American consulate in Milan by three agents for the F.B.I. in early September 2003.)

The State of the Union speech was confounding to many members of the intelligence community, who could not understand how such intelligence could have got to the President without vetting. A former intelligence official told me that his colleagues were also startled by the speech. "They said, 'Holy shit, all of a sudden the President is talking about it in the State of the Union address!' They began to panic. Who the hell was going to expose it?"

When I first wrote about the forgery, Harlow, the C.I.A. spokesman, said that the agency had not obtained the actual documents until after the President's State of the Union speech and therefore had been unable to evaluate them in a timely manner. This was incorrect, as the C.I.A. later admitted. True or not, Harlow's original statement put the C.I.A. in an unfortunate position: it was, essentially, copping a plea of incompetence. And it didn't explain why the agency left the job of revealing the embarrassing forgery to the I.A.E.A.

In its July 2004 report into prewar intelligence on Iraq's weapons, the Republican-led Senate Intelligence Committee revealed, without any comment, that it took the C.I.A. more than three weeks to translate the documents that were in French, and another few days before it issued an internal report warning that the papers "could be fraudulent." On March 11th, four days after ElBaradei publicly debunked the Niger documents at the United Nations, the agency forwarded an assessment to Donald Rumsfeld agreeing with the I.A.E.A. findings. (The senior I.A.E.A. investigators, as we have seen, took only a few hours, with the aid of Google, to determine that the papers were fake.) The C.I.A. assessment also informed Rumsfeld that the other available information on the attempted Iraq purchase of Nigerian ore was "fragmentary and unconfirmed." Amazingly, the assessment then concluded, "we are concerned that these reports may indicate Baghdad has attempted to secure an unreported source of uranium yellowcake for a nuclear weapons program." In the C.I.A.'s view, apparently, the lack of reliable intelligence was not evidence of a lack of an active Iraqi nuclear program, but evidence that Iraq was especially devious and deceptive in masking its nuclear efforts.

However, the committee's report, widely depicted in press reports as an unqualified indictment of the agency's prewar estimates, also showed—perhaps inadvertently—the extent to which the C.I.A., like an abused child, was extremely sensitive to the desires and wants of the White House. In its analysis of the Niger episode, the report reproduced a series of documents in which the C.I.A.'s Center for Weapons Intelligence, Nonproliferation, and Arms Control massaged the available intelligence in an effort to please the office of Vice President Cheney. The center repeatedly minimized or ignored expressions of skepticism from other agencies, most notably the State Department's I.N.R., forwarding assessments suggesting that there was credible evidence, from third-party reports, of Iraq's desire to purchase uranium ore from Niger. In its conclusion, the committee somehow found that "it was reasonable" for analysts to conclude that Iraq may have been seeking uranium from Africa. There was little to the committee's report to support such a conclusion. But the committee deferred for months—undoubtedly until after the election—publication of its continuing analysis of the White House's use, or misuse, of the intelligence.

In March 2003, I met with a group of senior I.A.E.A. officials in Vienna, site of the organization's headquarters. In an interview over dinner, they told me that they had not even known the papers existed until the previous month, a few days after the President's speech. The I.A.E.A. had been asking Washington and London for their evidence of Iraq's pursuit of African uranium, without receiving any response, ever since the previous September, when word of it turned up in the British dossier. After Niger was specified in the State Department's fact sheet of December 19, 2002, the I.A.E.A. became more insistent. "I started to harass the United States," recalled Jacques Baute. Mark Gwozdecky, the I.A.E.A.'s spokesman, added, "We were asking for actionable evidence, and Jacques was getting almost nothing."

On February 4, 2003, while Baute was on a plane bound for New York to attend the United Nations Security Council meeting on the Iraqi weapons dispute, the U.S. Mission in Vienna suddenly briefed members of Baute's team on the Niger papers, but still declined to hand over the documents. "I insisted on seeing the documents myself," Baute said, "and was provided with them upon my arrival in New York." The next day, Secretary Powell made his case for going to war against Iraq before the Security Council. The presentation did not mention Niger, a fact that did not escape Baute. I.A.E.A. officials told me that they were puzzled by the timing of the American decision to provide the documents—which Baute had quickly concluded were fake.

Over the next few weeks, I.A.E.A. officials conducted further investigations. There were the obvious problems, the evidence of a clumsy forgery that should have been obvious to anyone with a few reference tools. There were also factors, like those identified by Wilson and Burba, that made not only the papers but the deal they described implausible. For example, the large quantity of uranium involved should have been a warning sign. Niger's yellowcake comes from two uranium mines controlled by a French company, with its entire output presold to nuclear power companies in France, Japan, and Spain. "Five hundred tons can't be siphoned off without anyone noticing," an I.A.E.A. official told me. They also got in touch with American and British officials to inform them of the findings, and give them a chance to respond. Nothing was forthcoming, and so the I.A.E.A.'s director general, Mohamed ElBaradei, publicly described the fraud at his next scheduled briefing to the U.N. Security Council, in New York on March 7th. Then the war began, and, for a time, the tale of the African-uranium-connection forgery sank from view.

Who actually fabricated the Niger papers? When we spoke in the spring of 2003, a few weeks after the forgery was exposed, the I.A.E.A. official told me that his agency had not been able to answer that question. "It could be someone who intercepted faxes in Israel, or someone at the headquarters of the Niger foreign ministry in Niamey. We just don't know," the official said. "Somebody got old letterheads and signatures and cut and pasted."

Forged documents and false accusations have been an element in U.S. and British policy toward Iraq at least since the fall of 1997, after an impasse over U.N. inspections put the British and the Americans on the losing side in the battle for international public opinion. A former Clinton Administration official told me that London had resorted to, among other things, spreading false information about Iraq. The British propaganda program—part of its Information Operations, or I/Ops—was known to a few senior officials in Washington. "I knew that was going on," the former Clinton Administration official said of the British efforts. "We were getting ready for action in Iraq, and we wanted the Brits to prepare."

Over the next year, a former American intelligence officer told me, at least one member of the U.N. inspection team who supported the American and British position arranged for dozens of unverified and unverifiable intelligence reports and tips—data known as inactionable intelligence—to be funnelled to MI6 operatives and quietly passed along to newspapers in London and elsewhere. "It was intelligence that was crap, and that we couldn't move on, but the Brits wanted to plant stories in England and around the world," the former officer said. There was a series of clandestine meetings with MI6, at which documents were provided, as well as quiet meetings, usually at safe houses in the Washington area. The British propaganda scheme eventually became known to some members of the U.N. inspection team. "I knew a bit," one official still on duty at U.N. headquarters acknowledged in March 2003, "but I was never officially told about it."

In addition to speculation about MI6, press reports in the United States and elsewhere have suggested other possible sources: the Iraqi exile community, the French. One theory, favored by some journalists in Rome, is that SISMI produced the false documents and passed them to *Panorama* for publication.

Another explanation was provided by a former senior intelligence official. "Somebody deliberately let something false get in there," he said in March 2003, when I first wrote about the forgery. "It could not have gotten into the system without the agency being involved. Therefore it was an internal intention. Someone set someone up." In interviews in subsequent months, he said that he had been told that a small group of disgruntled retired C.I.A. clandestine operators were to blame.

"The agency guys were so pissed at Cheney," the former officer said. "They said, 'O.K., we're going to put the bite on these guys.'" My source said that he was first told of the fabrication late in 2002, at one of the many holiday gatherings in the Washington area of past and present C.I.A. officials. "Everyone was bragging about it— 'Here's what we did. It was cool, cool, cool.'" These retirees, he said, had superb contacts among current officers in the agency and were informed in detail of the SISMI intelligence. The thinking, he said, was that the documents would be endorsed by Iraq hawks at the top of the Bush Administration, who would then look foolish when intelligence officials pointed out that they were obvious fakes. But the tactic backfired, he said, when the papers won widespread acceptance within the Administration. "It got out of control."

Like all large institutions, C.I.A. headquarters, in Langley, Virginia, is full of water-cooler gossip, and a retired clandestine officer told me in the summer of 2003 that the story about a former operations officer involved in faking the documents was making the rounds. "What's telling," he added, "is that the story, whether it's true or not, is believed"—an extraordinary commentary on the level of mistrust, bitterness, and demoralization within the C.I.A. under the Bush Administration.

On March 14, 2003, Senator Jay Rockefeller, of West Virginia, the senior Democrat on the committee, formally asked Robert Mueller, the F.B.I. director, to investigate the forged documents. Rockefeller had voted for the resolution authorizing force in the fall of 2002. Now he wrote to Mueller, "There is a possibility that the fabrication of these documents may be part of a larger deception campaign aimed at manipulating public opinion and foreign policy regarding Iraq." He urged the F.B.I. to ascertain the source of the documents, the skill level of the forgery, the motives of those responsible, and "why the intelligence community did not recognize the documents were fabricated."

Months later, with the investigation still open, a senior F.B.I. official told me, "This story could go several directions. We haven't gotten anything solid, and we've looked." He said that the F.B.I. agents assigned to the case are putting a great deal of effort into the investigation. But "somebody's hiding something, and they're hiding it pretty well." What was generally agreed upon, as the former senior intelligence official told me, was that "something as bizarre as Niger raises suspicions everywhere."

The increasingly bitter debate over the value and integrity of the W.M.D. intelligence came to a halt in March 2003 when President Bush authorized the war against Iraq. After a few weeks of fighting, Saddam Hussein's regime collapsed, leaving American forces to declare victory against a backdrop of disorder and uncertainty about the country's future.

The subsequent failure to find weapons of mass destruction in places where the Pentagon's sources confidently predicted they would be found reanimated the debate on the quality of the office's intelligence. A former high-level intelligence official told me that American Special Forces units had been sent into Iraq in mid-March of 2003, before the start of the air and ground war, to investigate sites suspected of being missile or chemical- and biological-weapon storage depots. "They came up with nothing," the official said. "Never found a single Scud."

A number of false alarms followed, but no evidence of the weapons Americans had been led to expect. On April 22, 2003,

Hans Blix, hours before he asked the U.N. Security Council to send his team back to Iraq, told the BBC, "I think it's been one of the disturbing elements that so much of the intelligence on which the capitals built their case seemed to have been so shaky."

There was, in contrast, little self-doubt or second-guessing in the Pentagon over the failure to immediately find the weapons. The Pentagon adviser to Special Plans told me in May 2003 that the delay "means nothing. We've got to wait to get all the answers from Iraqi scientists who will tell us where they are." Similarly, the Pentagon official who works for Luti said that month, "I think they're hidden in the mountains or transferred to some friendly countries. Saddam had enough time to move them." There were suggestions from the Pentagon that Saddam might be shipping weapons over the border to Syria.

"It's bait and switch," the former high-level intelligence official explained. "Bait them into Iraq with weapons of mass destruction. And, when they aren't found, there's this whole bullshit about the weapons being in Syria."

In Congress, a senior legislative aide told me, a month and a half after the war began, "Some members are beginning to ask and to wonder, but cautiously." For the moment, he said, "the members don't have the confidence to say that the Administration is off base." He also commented, "For many, it makes little difference. We vanquished a bad guy and liberated the Iraqi people. Some are astute enough to recognize that the alleged imminent W.M.D. threat to the United States was a pretext. I sometimes have to pinch myself when friends or family ask with incredulity about the lack of W.M.D., and remind myself that the average person has the idea that there are mountains of the stuff over there, ready to be tripped over. The more time elapses, the more people are going to wonder about this, but I don't think it will sway U.S. public opinion much. Everyone loves to be on the winning side."

If the American advance didn't uncover stashes of weapons of mass destruction, it did turn up additional graphic evidence of the brutality of the regime. But Saddam Hussein's cruelty was documented long before September 11th, and was not the principal reason the Bush Administration gave to the world for the necessity of war. Former Senator Bob Kerrey had been a strong supporter of the President's decision to overthrow Saddam. "I do think building a democratic secular state in Iraq justifies everything we've done," Kerrey told me. "But they've taken the intelligence on weapons and expanded it beyond what was justified." Speaking of the hawks, he said, "It appeared that they understood that to get the American people on their side they needed to come up with something more to say than 'We've liberated Iraq and got rid of a tyrant.' So they had to find some ties to weapons of mass destruction and were willing to allow a majority of Americans to incorrectly conclude that the invasion of Iraq had something to do with the World Trade Center. Overemphasizing the national security threat made it more difficult to get the rest of the world on our side. It was the weakest and most misleading argument we could use." Kerrey added, "It appears that they have the intelligence. The problem is, they didn't like the conclusions."

More than a year after Joseph Wilson travelled to Africa to investigate the Niger allegation, he revived the story. He was angered by what he saw as the White House's dishonesty about Niger, and in early May 2003, he casually mentioned his mission, and his findings, during a brief talk about Iraq at a political conference in suburban Washington sponsored by the Senate Democratic Policy Committee. (Wilson is a Democrat.) Another speaker at the conference was *New York Times* columnist Nicholas Kristof, who got Wilson's permission to mention the Niger trip in a column. A few months later, on July 6th, Wilson wrote about the trip himself on the *Times* op-ed page. "I gave them months to correct the record," he told me, speaking of the White House, "but they kept on lying."

The White House responded by blaming the intelligence community for the Niger reference in the State of the Union address. Condoleezza Rice told a television interviewer on July 13th, "Had there been even a peep that the agency did not want that sentence in or that George Tenet did not want that sentence . . . it would have been gone." Five days later, a senior White House official went a step further, telling reporters at a background briefing that they had the wrong impression about Joseph Wilson's trip to Niger and the information it had yielded. "You can't draw a conclusion that we were warned by Ambassador Wilson that this was all dubious," the unnamed official said, according to a White House transcript. "It's just not accurate."

But Wilson's account of his trip forced a rattled White House to acknowledge, for the first time, that "this information should not have risen to the level of a Presidential speech." It also triggered retaliatory leaks to the press by White House officials that exposed Wilson's wife as a C.I.A. operative—and led to an F.B.I. investigation. By the summer of 2004, Attorney General John Ashcroft had appointed a federal prosecutor from Chicago to look into the leaks, and many senior members of the Administration, including the President, had been questioned.

Among the best potential witnesses on the subject of Iraq's actual nuclear capabilities are the men and women who worked in the Iraqi weapons industry and for the National Monitoring Directorate, the agency set up by Saddam to work with the United Nations and I.A.E.A. inspectors. More than six months after the invasion, many of the most senior weapons-industry officials, even those who voluntarily surrendered to U.S. forces, were still being held in captivity at the Baghdad airport and other places, away from reporters. Their families had been told little by American authorities. Desperate for information, they called friends and other contacts in America for help. One Iraqi émigré who heard from the scientists' families was Shakir al Kha Fagi, who left Iraq as a young man and ran a successful business in the Detroit area. "The people in intelligence and in the W.M.D. business are in jail," he said. "The Americans are hunting them down one by one. Nobody speaks for them, and there's no American lawyer who will take the case."

Not all the senior scientists were in captivity, however. Jafar Dhia Jafar, a British-educated physicist who coördinated Iraq's efforts to make the bomb in the 1980s, and who had direct access to Saddam Hussein, fled Iraq in early April, before Baghdad fell, and, with the help of his brother, Hamid, the managing director of a large energy company, made his way to the United Arab Emirates. Jafar refused to return to Baghdad, but he agreed to be debriefed by C.I.A. and British intelligence agents. There were some twenty meetings, involving as many as fifteen American and British experts. The first meeting, on April 11th, began with an urgent question from a C.I.A. officer: "Does Iraq have a nuclear device? The military really want to know. They are extremely worried." Jafar's response, according to the notes of an eyewitness, was to laugh. The notes continued:

> Jafar insisted that there was not only no bomb, but no W.M.D., period. "The answer was none." . . . Jafar explained that the Iraqi leadership had set up a new committee after the 91 Gulf war, and after the UNSCOM [United Nations] inspection process was set up . . . and the following instructions [were sent] from the Top Man [Saddam]—"give them everything."

The notes said that Jafar was then asked, "But this doesn't mean all W.M.D.? How can you be certain?" His answer was clear: "I know all the scientists involved, and they chat. There is no W.M.D."

Jafar also explained why Saddam had decided to give up his valued weapons:

Up until the 91 Gulf war, our adversaries were regional. . . .
But after the war, when it was clear that we were up against the
United States, Saddam understood that these weapons were re-
dundant. "No way we could escape the United States." Therefore, the W.M.D. warheads did Iraq little strategic good.

Jafar had his own explanation, according to the notes, for one of
the enduring mysteries of the U.N. inspection process—the six-
thousand-warhead discrepancy between the number of chemical
weapons thought to have been manufactured by Iraq before 1991
and the number that were accounted for by the U.N. inspection
teams. It was this discrepancy which led Western intelligence officials and military planners to make the worst-case assumptions.
Jafar told his interrogators that the Iraqi government had simply
lied to the United Nations about the number of chemical weapons
used against Iran during the brutal Iran-Iraq war in the 1980s. Iraq,
he said, dropped thousands more warheads on the Iranians than it
acknowledged. For that reason, Saddam preferred not to account
for the weapons at all.

There are always credibility problems with witnesses from a defeated regime, and anyone involved in the creation or concealment
of W.M.D.s would have a motive to deny it. But a strong endorsement of Jafar's integrity came from an unusual source—Jacques
Baute, of the I.A.E.A., who spent much of the past decade locked in
a struggle with Jafar and the other W.M.D. scientists and techni-
cians of Iraq. "I don't believe anybody," Baute told me, "but, by and
large, what he told us after 1995 was pretty accurate."

In June 2003, the Senate Intelligence Committee began its politically charged investigation into the disparity between the Bush Administration's prewar assessment of Iraq's weapons of mass
destruction and what was actually discovered. A few months later,
an intelligence official told me that the committee's preliminary

findings were disquieting. "The intelligence community made all kinds of errors and handled things sloppily," he said. The problems range from a lack of quality control to different agencies' reporting contradictory assessments at the same time.

One finding, the official went on, was that the intelligence reports about Iraq provided by the United Nations inspection teams and the I.A.E.A., were far more accurate than the C.I.A. estimates. "Some of the old-timers in the community are appalled by how bad the analysis was," the official said. "If you look at them side by side, C.I.A. versus United Nations, the U.N. agencies come out ahead across the board."

In early October 2003, David Kay, the former U.N. inspector who is the head of the Administration's Iraq Survey Group, made his interim report to Congress on the status of the search for Iraq's W.M.D.s. "We have not yet found stocks of weapons," Kay reported, "but we are not yet at the point where we can say definitively either that such weapon stocks do not exist or that they existed before the war." In the area of nuclear weapons, Kay said, "Despite evidence of Saddam's continued ambition to acquire nuclear weapons, to date we have not uncovered evidence that Iraq undertook significant post-1998 steps to actually build nuclear weapons or produce fissile material."

Kay was widely seen as having made the best case possible for President Bush's prewar claims of an imminent W.M.D. threat. But what he found fell drastically short of those claims, and the report was regarded as a blow to the Administration. President Bush, however, saw it differently. He told reporters that he felt vindicated by the report, in that it showed that "Saddam Hussein was a threat, a serious danger."

The President's response raised the question of what, if anything, the Administration learned from the failure to find significant quantities of W.M.D.s in Iraq. Any president depends heavily on his staff for the vetting of intelligence and a reasonable summary and analysis of the world's day-to-day events. The ultimate authority in the

White House for such issues lies with the President's national security adviser—in this case, Condoleezza Rice. The former White House official told me, "Maybe the Secretary of Defense and his people are short-circuiting the process, and creating a separate channel to the Vice President. Still, at the end of the day all the policies have to be hashed out in the interagency process, led by the national security adviser." What happened instead, he said, "was a real abdication of responsibility by Condi."

Vice President Cheney remained unabashed about the Administration's reliance on the Niger documents, despite the revelation of their forgery. In a September 2003 interview on *Meet the Press*, Cheney claimed that the British dossier's charge that "Saddam was, in fact, trying to acquire uranium in Africa" had been "revalidated." Cheney went on: "So there may be a difference of opinion there. I don't know what the truth is on the ground. . . . I don't know Mr. Wilson. I probably shouldn't judge him."

The Vice President also defended the way in which he had involved himself in intelligence matters: "This is a very important area. It's one that the President has asked me to work on. . . . In terms of asking questions, I plead guilty. I ask a hell of a lot of questions. That's my job."

VI.

THE SECRETARY AND THE GENERALS

1. Driving to Baghdad

The war against Iraq began on March 19, 2003. In its first week, the ground campaign against Saddam Hussein faltered, with attenuated supply lines and a lack of immediate reinforcements, and the first reaction in the Pentagon was anger.

Several senior war planners complained to me in interviews at the time that Secretary of Defense Donald Rumsfeld and his inner circle of civilian advisers, who had been chiefly responsible for persuading President Bush to lead the country into war, had insisted on micromanaging the war's operational details. Rumsfeld's team took over crucial aspects of the day-to-day logistical planning—traditionally, an area in which the uniformed military excels—and Rumsfeld repeatedly overruled the senior Pentagon planners on the Joint Staff, the operating arm of the Joint Chiefs of Staff. "He thought he knew better," one senior planner said. "He was the decision maker at every turn."

On at least six occasions, the planner told me, when Rumsfeld and his deputies were presented with operational plans—the Iraqi assault was designated Plan 1003—he insisted that the number of ground troops be sharply reduced. Rumsfeld's faith in precision bombing and his insistence on streamlined military operations has had profound consequences for the ability of the Armed Forces to fight effectively overseas. "They've got no resources," a former high-level intelligence official said. "He was so focussed on proving his point—that the Iraqis were going to fall apart." (At the time, Rumsfeld did not respond to a request for comment.)

The critical moment, one planner said, came in the fall of 2002, during the buildup for the war, when Rumsfeld decided that he would no longer be guided by the Pentagon's most sophisticated war-planning document, the TPFDL—time-phased forces deployment list—which is known to planning officers as the tip-fiddle (tip-fid, for short). A TPFDL is a voluminous document describing the inventory of forces that are to be sent into battle, the sequence of their deployment, and the deployment of logistical support. "It's the complete applecart, with many pieces," Roger J. Spiller, the George C. Marshall professor of military history at the U.S. Command and General Staff College, said. "Everybody trains and plans on it. It's constantly in motion and always adjusted at the last minute. It's an embedded piece of the bureaucratic and operational culture." A retired Air Force strategic planner remarked, "This is what we do best—go from A to B—and the tip-fiddle is where you start. It's how you put together a plan for moving into the theatre." Another former planner said, "Once you turn on the tip-fid, everything moves in an orderly fashion." A former intelligence officer added, "When you kill the tip-fiddle, you kill centralized military planning. The military is not like a corporation that can be streamlined. It is the most inefficient machine known to man. It's the redundancy that saves lives."

The TPFDL for the war in Iraq ran to forty or more computer-generated spreadsheets, dealing with everything from weapons to toilet paper. When it was initially presented to Rumsfeld in 2002 for his approval, it called for the involvement of a wide range of forces from the different armed services, including four or more Army divisions. Rumsfeld rejected the package, because it was "too big," the Pentagon planner said. He insisted that a smaller, faster-moving attack force, combined with overwhelming air power, would suffice. Rumsfeld further stunned the Joint Staff by insisting that he would control the timing and flow of Army and Marine troops to the combat zone. Such decisions are known in the military as R.F.F.s—requests for forces. He, and not the generals, would decide which unit would go when and where.

The TPFDL called for the shipment in advance, by sea, of hundreds of tanks and other heavy vehicles—enough for three or four divisions. Rumsfeld ignored this advice. Instead, he relied on the heavy equipment that was already in Kuwait—enough for just one full combat division. The 3rd Infantry Division, from Fort Stewart, Georgia, the only mechanized Army division that was active inside Iraq in the first week of the war, thus arrived in the Gulf without its own equipment.

"Those guys are driving around in tanks that were pre-positioned. Their tanks are sitting in Fort Stewart," the planner said. "To get more forces there we have to float them. We can't fly our forces in, because there's nothing for them to drive. Over the past six months, you could have floated everything in ninety days— enough for four or more divisions."

The planner added, "This is the mess Rumsfeld put himself in, because he didn't want a heavy footprint on the ground."

Plan 1003 was repeatedly updated and presented to Rumsfeld, and each time, according to the planner, Rumsfeld said, "You've got too much ground force—go back and do it again." In the planner's view, Rumsfeld had two goals: to demonstrate the efficacy of precision bombing and to "do the war on the cheap." Rumsfeld and his two main deputies for war planning, Paul Wolfowitz and Douglas Feith, "were so enamored of 'shock and awe' that victory seemed assured," the planner said. "They believed that the weather would always be clear, that the enemy would expose itself, and so precision bombings would always work."

Rumsfeld's personal contempt for many of the senior generals and admirals who were promoted to top jobs during the Clinton Administration was widely known. He was especially critical of the Army, with its insistence on maintaining costly mechanized divisions. In his off-the-cuff memorandums, or "snowflakes," as they're called in the Pentagon, he chafed about generals having "the slows"—a reference to Lincoln's characterization of General George McClellan. "In those conditions—an atmosphere of derision and challenge—the senior officers do not offer their best advice," a high-ranking general who served for more than a year under Rumsfeld said. One witness to a meeting recalled Rumsfeld confronting General Eric Shinseki, the Army Chief of Staff, in front of many junior officers. "He was looking at the Chief and waving his hand," the witness said, "saying, 'Are you getting this yet? Are you getting this yet?'"

Gradually, Rumsfeld succeeded in replacing those officers in senior Joint Staff positions who challenged his view. "All the Joint Staff people now are handpicked, and churn out products to make the Secretary of Defense happy," the planner said. "They don't make military judgments—they just respond to his snowflakes."

In the months leading up to the war, a split developed inside the military, with the planners and their immediate superiors warning that the war plan was dangerously thin on troops and matériel, and the top generals—including General Tommy Franks, the head of the U.S. Central Command, and Air Force General Richard Myers, the chairman of the Joint Chiefs of Staff—supporting Rumsfeld. After Turkey's parliament astonished the war planners in early March by denying the United States permission to land the 4th Infantry Division in Turkey, Franks initially argued that the war ought to be delayed until the troops could be brought in by another route, a former intelligence official said. "Rummy overruled him."

Many of the present and former officials I spoke to were critical of Franks for his perceived failure to stand up to his civilian superiors. A former senator told me that Franks was widely seen as a commander who "will do what he's told." A former intelligence official asked, "Why didn't he go to the President?" A Pentagon official recalled that one senior general used to prepare his deputies for meetings with Rumsfeld by saying, "When you go in to talk to him, you've got to be prepared to lay your stars on the table and walk out. Otherwise, he'll walk over you."

In early February 2003, according to a senior Pentagon official, Rumsfeld appeared at the Army Commanders' Conference, a biannual business and social gathering of all the four-star generals. Rumsfeld was invited to join the generals for dinner and make a speech. All went well, the official told me, until Rumsfeld, during a question-and-answer session, was asked about his personal involvement in the deployment of combat units, in some cases with only five or six days' notice. To the astonishment and anger of the generals, Rumsfeld denied responsibility. "He said, 'I wasn't involved,'" the official said. "'It was the Joint Staff.'"

"We thought it would be fence mending, but it was a disaster," the official said of the dinner. "Everybody knew he was looking at these deployment orders. And for him to blame it on the Joint Staff—" The official hesitated a moment, and then said, "It's all about Rummy and the truth."

According to a dozen or so military men I spoke to, Rumsfeld simply failed to anticipate the consequences of protracted warfare. He put Army and Marine units in the field with few reserves and an insufficient number of tanks and other armored vehicles. (The military men said that the vehicles that they did have had been pushed too far and were malfunctioning.) Supply lines—inevitably, they say—quickly became overextended and vulnerable to attack, creating shortages of fuel, water, and ammunition that first week. Pentagon officers spoke contemptuously of the Administration's optimistic press briefings. "It's a stalemate now," the former intelligence official told me at the time. "It's going to remain one only if we can maintain our supply lines. The carriers are going to run out of JDAMs"—the satellite-guided bombs that were striking targets in Baghdad and elsewhere with extraordinary accuracy. Much of the supply of Tomahawk guided missiles had been expended. "The Marines are worried as hell," the former intelligence official went on. "They're all committed, with no reserves, and they've never run the LAVs"—light armored vehicles—"as long and as hard" as they had in their first week in Iraq. There were serious maintenance problems as well. "The only hope is that they can hold out until reinforcements come."

The 4th Infantry Division—the Army's most modern mechanized division—whose equipment spent weeks waiting in the Mediterranean before being diverted to the overtaxed American port in Kuwait, was not expected to be operational until the end of April. The 1st Cavalry Division, in Texas, was ready to ship out, the planner said, but by sea it would take weeks to reach Kuwait. "All we have now is front-line positions," the former intelligence official told me. "Everything else is missing."

That first week, as plans for an assault on Baghdad stalled, the six Republican Guard divisions expected to provide the main Iraqi defense had yet to have a significant engagement with American or British soldiers. The shortages forced CENTCOM to "run around looking for supplies," the former intelligence official said. The immediate goal, he added, was for the Army and Marine forces "to hold tight and hope that the Republican Guard divisions get chewed up" by bombing. The planner agreed, saying, "The only way out now is back, and to hope for some kind of a miracle—that the Republican Guards commit themselves," and thus become vulnerable to American air strikes. "Hope," a retired four-star general subsequently told me, "is not a course of action."

On March 28th, the Army's senior ground commander, Lieutenant General William S. Wallace, said to reporters, "The enemy

we're fighting is different from the one we war-gamed against."
(One senior Administration official commented to me, speaking of
the Iraqis, "They're not scared. Ain't it something? They're not
scared.") At a press conference the next day, Rumsfeld and Myers
were asked about Wallace's comments, and defended the war plan—
Myers called it "brilliant" and "on track." They pointed out that the
war was only a little more than a week old.

Scott Ritter, the former Marine and United Nations weapons
inspector, noted that much of the bombing had, at first, little effect,
or was counterproductive. For example, the bombing of Saddam's
palaces freed up a brigade of special guards who had been assigned
to protect them. "Every one of their homes—and they are scattered
throughout Baghdad—is stacked with ammunition and supplies,"
Ritter told me.

"This is tragic," one senior planner said bitterly. "American lives
are being lost." The former intelligence official told me, "They all said,
'We can do it with air power.' They believed their own propaganda."
The high-ranking former general described Rumsfeld's approach to
the Joint Staff war planning as "McNamara-like intimidation by in-
tervention of a small cell"—a reference to Secretary of Defense Robert
S. McNamara and his aides, who were known for their challenges to
the Joint Chiefs of Staff during the Vietnam War. The former high-
ranking general compared the Joint Chiefs of Staff to the Stepford
wives. "They've abrogated their responsibility," he said.

Perhaps the biggest disappointment the first week of the war was
the failure of the Shiite factions in southern Iraq to support the
American and British invasion. Various branches of the Al Dawa
faction, which operate underground, had been carrying out acts of
terrorism against the Iraqi regime since the 1980s. But Al Dawa had
also been hostile to American interests. Some in American intelligence had implicated the group in the 1983 bombing of the Marine
barracks in Beirut, which cost the lives of two hundred and forty-

one Marines. Nevertheless, in the months before the war the Bush Administration courted Al Dawa by including it among the opposition groups that would control postwar Iraq. "Dawa is one group that could kill Saddam," a former American intelligence official told me at the time. "They hate Saddam because he suppressed the Shiites. They exist to kill Saddam." He said that if, as it then appeared, they had decided to stand with the Iraqi regime it would be a "disaster" for the United States. "They're like hard-core Vietcong."

There were also reports that week that Iraqi exiles, including fervent Shiites, were crossing into Iraq by car and bus from Jordan and Syria to get into the fight on the side of the Iraqi government. Robert Baer, the former C.I.A. Middle East operative, told me in a telephone call from Jordan, "Everybody wants to fight. The whole nation of Iraq is fighting to defend Iraq. Not Saddam. They've been given the high sign, and we are courting disaster. If we take fifty or sixty casualties a day and they die by the thousands, they're still winning. It's a jihad, and it's a good thing to die. This is no longer a secular war." There were press reports of mujahideen arriving from Pakistan, Afghanistan, and Algeria for "martyrdom operations."

There had been an expectation before the war that Iran, Iraq's old enemy, would side with the United States in this fight. Ahmed Chalabi's I.N.C. had been in regular contact with the Supreme Council for Islamic Revolution in Iraq, or SCIRI, an umbrella organization for Shiite groups who oppose Saddam. The organization had been based in Iran and has close ties to Iranian intelligence. Chalabi had repeatedly predicted that the Tehran government would provide support, including men and arms, if an American invasion of Iraq took place. Before the week was out, however, it became clear that that was unlikely. In a press conference on Friday, Rumsfeld warned Iranian militants against interfering with American forces and accused Syria of sending military equipment to the Iraqis. A Middle East businessman who has long-standing ties in Jordan and

Syria—and whose information I have always found reliable—told me that week that the religious government in Tehran "is now backing Iraq in the war. There isn't any Arab fighting group on the ground in Iraq who is with the United States," he said.

———

Within days after publication of my story on the first week of the war in *The New Yorker,* the U.S. Army's 3rd Infantry Division made its highly successful dash—some called it a "hail Mary pass"—across the desert to the outskirts of Baghdad. In a few more days, a suddenly quiet Baghdad fell and the giant statue of Saddam Hussein was pulled down, with the help of an American tank, before a worldwide television audience. The complaints about the lack of troops and reliance of air power seemed flat-out wrong, and were ridiculed by Rumsfeld and his subordinates. The Iraqi Army and its vaunted Republican Guard had collapsed—so it seemed at first. And then wholesale looting of government offices, businesses, and private homes began, and there were not enough American troops on the ground to stop it. The next few days saw the first inklings of a well-armed insurgency; once again, there were not enough troops on the ground to stop it. The Bush Administration, it turned out, had won a major battle, but still had a war to fight.

Just how little we in the United States understood about the nature of the insurgency became clear to me in December 2003, when I spent three days in Syria with Ahmad Sadik, an Iraqi Air Force brigadier general who served in signals intelligence during the Iran-Iraq war. Sadik, whose English is excellent, was reassigned in the early 1990s to work with the United Nations inspectors who, over their seven years inside Iraq, we now know, successfully dismantled, destroyed, or otherwise accounted for the Iraqi arsenal of chemical, biological, and nuclear weapons. I was eventually introduced to

Sadik and, after many e-mail exchanges—his information about what had taken place and what would take place in Iraq proved accurate—we arranged to meet at a hotel in Damascus.

Sadik told me that he'd been interrogated by three American intelligence officers in June of 2003, but he was not jailed, although some of his acquaintances were. Nor, he said, was he quizzed intensely about his experiences as a senior communications intelligence officer. Over the next few months, he told me, he learned from former colleagues and internal planning documents—many of the regime's most sensitive offices were ransacked after its collapse and some material was published in the Arabic press—that Saddam had drawn up plans for a widespread insurgency in 2001, soon after George Bush's election brought into office many of the officials who had directed the 1991 Gulf War. Huge amounts of small arms and other weapons were stockpiled around the country for use by insurgents. In January of 2003, as the long-expected Coalition invasion appeared imminent, Saddam issued a four-page document ordering his secret police, the Mukhabarat, to respond to an attack by immediately breaking into key government offices and ministries, destroying documents, and setting buildings on fire. He also ordered the Mukhabarat to arrange for the penetration of the various Iraqi exile groups that would be brought into Iraq, with U.S. help, in the aftermath of the invasion.

One of the war's most critical dates, according to Sadik, was April 7, 2003, as American troops were moving at will on the outskirts of Baghdad and were obviously prepared for rough door-to-door urban warfare. American commanders had feared, and planned for, a drawn-out siege of Baghdad. Instead, the troops, who included members of the Baath Party hierarchy, the Special Republican Guard, the Special Security Organization, and the Mukhabarat, were ordered to return to their homes and initiate the resistance from there. "In my neighborhood," Sadik recalled, "there were roadblocks on every street corner, guarded by well-armed forces.

They were there at six P.M. on April 7th and gone by six the next morning. Fighting the U.S. Army head-to-head is useless." (A former high-level American intelligence official had told me months earlier that the American signal intelligence community had reported that Baghdad had suddenly gone quiet on the evening of April 7th—Saddam loyalists had stopped chatting on satellite phones and other devices and simply melted away overnight. It was only then, the former official said, that it was clear that there would be no bitter fighting in the city.)

Sadik further told me that Saddam, in his 2001 directive, had ordered three insurgency divisions to be set up, each to operate underground under the direct control of a handpicked Iraqi official. The divisions were to contain two to four thousand members, organized in small cells of three to four. The first division, Sadik said, commanded by Izzat al-Douri, one of Saddam's deputies, "was composed of Baathists not publicly known at the time." Their mission was to operate independently in small cells, while hiding out in well-fortified safe houses. The second division, under the command of Taha Yassin Ramadan, was composed of Baath Party members whose assignment was to back up the first division by providing operating instructions via a series of carefully screened dead drops. Ramadan was captured by Kurdish troops in Mosul in August, but his capture, Sadik said, did not lead to an unraveling of the operations because Ramadan, by the very nature of the compartmentalized process, did not know which cell was operating where. The third division was composed of technocrats—"doctors, lawyers, engineers, administrators," Sadik said, "and the people who run the country—the power plants, the water, the sewage, in the Ministry of Commerce and the Ministry of Finance." The technocrats also had left Baghdad overnight on April 7th, Sadik said. Saddam's instructions to his underground was explicit, Sadik said: "They were never to come forward at the same time."

In his view, Sadik said, Saddam patterned his insurgency on the methods that had been used by Al Dawa. Saddam responded to an Al Dawa assassination attempt in 1980 against Tariq Aziz, his deputy prime minister, by executing Ayatollah Mohammad Baqir al-Sadr, an Al Dawa leader who was, at the time, one of the most important Shiites in Iraq. (Baqir al-Sadr's nephew, Moqtada al-Sadr, emerged in early 2004 as a major opponent of the American occupation.) Thirty thousand Iraqis of Iranian ancestry, many of them innocents, were expelled from Iraq, at Saddam's insistence, but he was unable to eradicate Al Dawa, and the group continued its hit-and-miss attacks against the Iraqi leadership. "The Dawa party used dead drops and operated via courier," Sadik told me. "There was no real communication between the cells, and the Iraqi security people had no idea what to do. They had never seen this before." When they were captured, the Al Dawa members had little information to give, and thus proved resistant to the most extreme torture. "They did not know anything. It was so effective," Sadik said.

In our conversations, Sadik made it clear that Saddam's preplanning was only one of many factors in the growing insurrection. There also were thousands of Iraqi nationalists and religious leaders —people who had struggled against the Saddam regime—who chose within days after the fall of Baghdad to resist the American occupation. The ultimate enemy, Sadik told me, was the occupation itself: the failure of the American occupiers to understand the Iraqis and the increasingly harsh tactics of the American troops as they sought to quell the continuing violence. "People reacted to what they saw before them," Sadik said. Even the most ordinary of American charities led to unintended consequences. For example, on the night before Thanksgiving in November 2003, American soldiers suddenly appeared in his neighborhood, leaving the safety of their Humvees to knock on doors and fling cooked turkeys into each home. The soldiers clearly meant well, but "no one explained anything about the holiday. Everybody came outside and asked, 'What's this? Why are we getting this?' The authorities had done nothing to prepare us," he said.

"That's how they do everything in Baghdad," Sadik went on, with obvious exasperation, as he recalled the chaotic street scene. "They don't explain anything."

———

We now know that the Bush Administration decided in late 2001 or early in 2002 to assassinate, capture, or otherwise "disappear" suspected Al Qaeda and terrorist operatives wherever they could be found, in secrecy, with no due process. But in late 2002, when I first began to report for *The New Yorker* on Donald Rumsfeld's obsession with "manhunts," and even in late 2003, when I wrote a second story on the subject, the formal existence of such programs seemed hard to credit. I was on the edge, as the accounts that follow make clear, but I did not perceive that there was an organized, top-secret program to simply eliminate the opposition, real or otherwise. Some operatives on the inside were trying to tell me, but I just didn't have the whole story.

In one interview in late 2002, a recently retired Special Forces operative, a colonel who served on high-level planning staffs at the Pentagon, warned me that the civilians running the Pentagon were no longer trying to "avoid the gray area." He went on, "It is not unlawful, but ethics is about what we ought to do in our position as the most powerful country in human history. Strategic deception plans, global assassinations done by the military—all will define who we are and what we want to become as a nation. Unintended consequences are huge." He added, "The perception of a global vigilante force knocking off the enemies of the United States cannot be controlled by any strategic deception plan."

The first sign of something new turned up in Yemen.

2. Manhunts

Sometime on Sunday, November 3, 2002, an unmanned American Predator reconnaissance aircraft, flying out of a base in Djibouti, fired a Hellfire missile at an automobile in Yemen. The passenger was believed to be an Al Qaeda leader named Qaed Salim Sinan al-Harethi. A joint American and Yemeni intelligence team had been tracking al-Harethi, and the order to fire was not given until the car was isolated, far from any other traffic—and from any witnesses—as it sped through a vast tract of desert in Marib Province. Al-Harethi was in the car, along with five other men. All of them were killed.

The operation entailed a high level of technical coöperation and trust between the Americans and the Yemenis. The joint intelligence team, working out of a situation room in Yemen—a Yemeni official would say only that the site was not visible from the air—had been tracing al-Harethi's satellite telephone calls for weeks. Al-Harethi clearly was aware of the danger and frequently changed telephones and numbers; five cell phones were found on his body. Yemeni security officials arrived at the scene shortly after the blast—a helicopter had been standing by—and removed the bombed-out car. They took the bodies to a military hospital in Sanaa, Yemen's capital, where American officials collected DNA samples for processing at a military laboratory in the United States.

By the next day, Bush Administration officials had begun informing journalists that the Predator had made its first Al Qaeda kill outside Afghanistan. Some journalists were also told that al-Harethi, long sought for a role in the bombing of the U.S.S. *Cole* in Aden Harbor in the fall of 2000, was on a list of "high-value" targets whose elimination, by capture or death, had been called for by President Bush.

The Hellfire was meant for al-Harethi, but, Yemeni and American officials told reporters, the five passengers in the car had terrorist ties as well. Four of them belonged to the Aden-Abyan Islamic Army, an outlawed terrorist sect that had links to Al Qaeda, and the fifth had been identified as Kamal Derwish, an Arab American who grew up near Buffalo and, according to the F.B.I., recruited American Muslims to attend Al Qaeda training camps. There was no indication that American or Yemeni officials knew in advance who was in the car with al-Harethi. The Yemeni official told me that there was no thought of blockading the highway and attempting to capture al-Harethi and his passengers, because he had evaded earlier attempts and because "it was suspected that they were going to a target." The official said, "From past experience, this was the most effective way."

The intelligence about al-Harethi that day had been superb. The Yemeni official told me, however, that earlier there had been two intelligence "mistakes" that almost resulted in targeting innocent Bedouins. In one case, the joint intelligence center found a group of Bedouins whose armed pickup trucks—pickups are the main mode of travel in the desert—included at least one vehicle that was mounted with a heavy machine gun. The Americans were about to hit the truck with a Predator, the Yemeni official said, "but we had someone tracking it, too. He was asked by phone, 'Who are those people?' He said, 'Bedouins. Not Al Qaeda.'"

The Yemeni official also said that the al-Harethi operation had produced valuable diplomatic information. For example, the car bearing al-Harethi and his colleagues had Saudi plates, which led investigators to believe that al-Harethi had been shuttling back and forth along Yemen's border with Saudi Arabia. According to the official, al-Harethi had obtained operating funds from Saudis. Apparently, they weren't the only suppliers of cash for the terrorists. Al-Harethi's last known satellite telephone call, an hour before the Predator struck, was to a number in the United Arab Emirates, an American ally that is also known to be a center of support for Muslim extremists. "Lots of money comes from the U.A.E.," the Yemeni official said.

*　　*　　*

The killing of al-Harethi represented a dividend in the drive to track down suspected Al Qaeda terrorists who had fled Afghanistan and moved to Saudi Arabia, Yemen, Somalia, and other countries, a goal that had preoccupied American intelligence since the fall of the Taliban. Administration officials praised the Predator attack for its precision and effective use of on-the-spot intelligence. "We've just got to keep the pressure on everywhere we're able to and we've got to deny the sanctuaries," Paul Wolfowitz told CNN. The Hellfire strike, he added, was "a very successful tactical operation."

The operation also marked a dramatic escalation of the American war on terrorism. For more than a generation, state-endorsed assassination has been anathema in the United States. In 1975, after revelations of C.I.A. efforts in the 1960s to kill Fidel Castro and other hostile foreign leaders, a Senate committee led by Frank Church concluded that such plotting "violates moral precepts fundamental to our way of life. . . . We reject absolutely any notion that the United States should justify its actions by the standards of totalitarians. . . . Of course, we must defend our democracy. But in defending it, we must resist undermining the very virtues we are defending." In 1976, President Gerald Ford signed an executive order banning political assassination, and that order remains in force.

In the year after September 11th, however, the targeting and killing of individual Al Qaeda members without juridical process came to be seen within the Bush Administration as justifiable military action in a new kind of war, involving international terrorist organizations and unstable states. Defense Department lawyers concluded that the killing of selected individuals would not be illegal under the Army's Law of War if the targets were "combatant forces of another nation, a guerrilla force, or a terrorist or other organization whose actions pose a threat to the security of the United States."

On July 22, 2002, Secretary of Defense Donald Rumsfeld issued a secret directive ordering Air Force General Charles Holland, the four-star commander of Special Operations, "to develop a plan to find and deal with members of terrorist organizations." He added, "The objective is to capture terrorists for interrogation or, if necessary, to kill them, not simply to arrest them in a law-enforcement exercise." The manhunt would be global in its reach, Rumsfeld wrote, and Holland was to cut through the Pentagon bureaucracy and process deployment orders "in minutes and hours, not days and weeks."

When I asked Rumsfeld's office for comment, in December 2002, after I had obtained the order, I was referred to a press briefing earlier that month in which the defense secretary had been questioned about the Pentagon's policy on the use of the Predator "to assassinate or to kill an Al Qaeda." Rumsfeld initially had responded with a characteristic joke: "I'm working my way over to figuring out how I won't answer that." He then turned serious and said that the policy "is what you all know it to be. There is really no mystery to it. We recruit, organize, train, equip, and deploy young men and women, in uniform, to go out and serve as members of our military. They are not trained to do the word you used"—assassinate—"which I won't even repeat. That is not what they're trained to do. They are trained to serve the country and to contribute to peace and stability in the world."

Nonetheless, many past and present military and intelligence officials expressed alarm at the Pentagon policy about targeting Al Qaeda members even then. Their concerns had less to do with the legality of the program than with its wisdom, its ethics, and, ultimately, its efficacy. Some of the most heated criticism came from within the Special Forces.

Rumsfeld began complaining to his deputies about General Holland's caution soon after September 11th. A few days after the attacks, he asked Holland to compile a list of terrorist targets for immediate retaliation. Holland returned two weeks later with four possible targets—suspected Islamic fundamentalist redoubts in Somalia, Mauritania, the Philippines, and the Triple Frontier, the point where Brazil, Paraguay, and Argentina meet. But the general also told Rumsfeld that an immediate attack wasn't possible, because the military did not have "actionable intelligence" on the proposed targets, according to a defense consultant. The retaliation would have to wait until the war in Afghanistan got under way. The defense secretary was not pleased. In the following months, "actionable intelligence" became a derisive catchphrase among civilian Pentagon officials.

Some senior officers attached to the Joint Chiefs of Staff argued that Rumsfeld's plans would turn the military's most élite forces, the Special Operations Command—which includes the Navy's SEALs and the Army's Delta Force—and the U.S. government's secret undercover team, known as Gray Fox, into hunter-killer teams. These forces train heavily in a wide range of specialties, among them strategic reconnaissance, direct action, unconventional warfare, and psychological operations. (Units of Delta Force and Gray Fox have been deployed in the Gulf region.) Questions of turf were involved. A defense consultant who has maintained close ties to the Special Forces said, "There is concern that emphasis on a target list will turn the Special Operations Forces into a counterterror force and atrophy other attributes."

"They want to turn these guys into assassins," a former high-level intelligence officer told me in an interview at the end of 2002. "They want to go on rumors—not facts—and go for political effect, and that's what the Special Forces command is really afraid of. Rummy is saying that politics is bigger than war, and we need to take guys out for political effect: You have to kill Goebbels to get to Hitler." With regard to Rumsfeld, he added, "The military is saying, 'Who is this guy?' There's a major clash of wills as to what is the future of Special Forces."

A senior Administration official acknowledged that Rumsfeld's plans for Special Operations run "counter to conventional military doctrine." Rumsfeld was at an advantage, the official said, because the senior military leadership suffered from a lack of will. The official noted that Rumsfeld was able to get what he wanted in large measure because he made it a personal issue. "He's the strangest guy I've ever run into," the official said. "He doesn't delegate."

Speaking to journalists in September 2002 about the uses of preëmptive military actions in Iraq and elsewhere, Rumsfeld said, "We all would like perfection; we'd like all the dots connected for us with a ribbon wrapped around it." Americans, he added, "want evidence beyond a reasonable doubt. You want to be able to be certain that you know before anyone's punished." But, he continued, "this isn't punishment. We've got the wrong model in our minds if we're thinking about punishment. We're not. This isn't retaliation or retribution."

In internal Defense Department memos in the year after September 11th, Rumsfeld and the civilian officials close to him had laid out the case for a new approach to the war on terrorism, one that would rely, in part, on the killing of selected individuals. The documents reflected their skepticism toward the generals and admirals who run the Armed Forces. One paper noted, "The worst way to organize for the manhunt . . . is to have it planned in the Pentagon. . . . Our prerequisite of perfection for 'actionable intelligence' has paralyzed us." In another paper Rumsfeld was told, "We 'overplan' for every contingency. . . . This denies us the agility and tactical surprise so necessary for manhunts, snatches, and retribution raids. We must be willing to accept the risks associated with a smaller footprint."

The paper urged the defense secretary to "ensure that the military leadership understands fully the cultural change you seek." The manhunting teams must be kept "small and agile," the paper noted, and "must be able to operate clandestinely, using a full range of official and non-official cover arrangements to travel and to enter countries surreptitiously."

At a press conference in September 2002, one journalist noted the military's growing involvement in police and intelligence activities inside Afghanistan, and asked Rumsfeld whether tracking down Al Qaeda was still the mission. "Well, a manhunt is certainly not what the Armed Forces of the United States are organized, trained, and equipped to do," Rumsfeld answered. "We may have to learn to do that, and we are indeed learning to do it." Paul Wolfowitz, in a discussion of future military operations during an interview with Bill Keller in the *New York Times Magazine* that same month, also noted obliquely that "maybe somewhere along the way we should have a volunteer force that is specifically volunteering for missions other than defending the country." Wolfowitz's idea was characterized by Keller as "the opposite of the Peace Corps, you might say."

The Hellfire attack in Yemen was applauded by many Americans, and also by the media, as progress in the war against terrorism. There were only a few public complaints. Anna Lindh, the Swedish foreign minister, declared that the American military attack, even with Yemeni approval, "is nevertheless a summary execution that violates human rights." She added, "Even terrorists must be treated according to international law. Otherwise, any country can start executing those whom they consider terrorists." Amnesty International also questioned "the deliberate killing of suspects in lieu of arrest, in circumstances in which they did not pose an immediate threat."

However, in conversations at the end of 2002, even American legal experts who were critical of attacks of this kind in pursuit of Al Qaeda did not challenge their legality. "It's not a question of law," Michael Glennon, a professor of international law at Tufts University, said. "It's a matter of policy. Is it wise? Do such attacks increase the possibility of retaliation at home and abroad on the American political and military leadership?" A similar point was made by Philip Heymann, a professor at Harvard Law School. "I don't think Richard Nixon signed the treaty outlawing biological warfare just because he had a deep aversion to biologicals," Heymann told me. "He signed it because it was against U.S. national interests to have a lot of little guys running around with biological agents that could not be deterred by our nuclear arsenal. Assassination is in the same ballpark—it doesn't take much to assassinate a U.S. secretary of state or another Cabinet member." The American goal, he added, should be to outlaw "any weapon that even a small country can use against the big guys." Jeffrey H. Smith, a West Point graduate who served as the C.I.A.'s general counsel during the Clinton Administration, said, "I'm not opposed to shooting people, but it ought to be a last resort. If they're dead, they're not talking to you, and you create more martyrs."

Other military officials I spoke with at the time had similar concerns. "You might be able to pull it off for five or six months," a Pentagon consultant said. "We've created a culture in the Special Forces—twenty- and twenty-one-year-olds who need adult leadership. They're assuming you've got legal authority, and they'll do it"—eagerly eliminate any target assigned to them. Eventually, the intelligence will be bad, he said, and innocent people will be killed. "And then they'll get hung." As for Rumsfeld and his deputies, he said, "These guys will overextend themselves, and they'll self-destruct."

A fatal mistake involving the Predator is known to have taken place at least once before, in Afghanistan. In February 2002, C.I.A. officers and officers attached to the U.S. Central Command watched as a Predator, thousands of feet above ground, captured images of a very tall man being greeted effusively, or so it seemed, by a small group of colleagues. It was quickly agreed that the tall man could be Osama bin Laden, and a request was made through the chain of command to launch a Hellfire. Minutes went by before permission was granted. By then, the men on the ground had disbanded and, shortly afterward, the Predator captured what seemed to be the tall man and two others emerging from a wooded area.

The Hellfire was launched, and devastated the area, killing three people—a terrible scene vividly depicted by the Predator's infrared cameras. Journalists later reported that the victims were three local men who had been scavenging in the woods for scrap metal.

The military's previous experience with assassination programs suggests some of the difficulties involved. In the late 1960s, during the Vietnam War, American Special Forces units worked with the C.I.A. in what became known as the Phoenix Program. The program started small: people believed to be working for the North were culled from South Vietnamese hamlets. In choosing targets for capture or assassination, the Americans relied on information supplied by South Vietnamese Army officers, informers, and village chiefs. By 1970, the program had mushroomed: more than eight thousand suspected Communist sympathizers were assassinated in that year alone. The military command began setting high quotas for targets to be eliminated or neutralized. According to official South Vietnamese statistics, Phoenix claimed nearly forty-one thousand victims between 1968 and 1972; the United States counted more than twenty thousand in the same time span. Subsequent investigations determined that some of the victims had been put on target lists not because of their political beliefs but for personal reasons—to erase a gambling debt, for example, or to resolve a family quarrel.

"The whole thing just kind of slid in one direction," Patrick McGarvey, a C.I.A. agent who had been involved in the Phoenix Program, explained to me in an interview in 1971. "I mean, you can't prove that anybody ever said, 'O.K., we're going to go out and start killing people,' because it just started happening." That year, Congress was told by William E. Colby, the C.I.A. official who ran the program (and later became the director of the C.I.A.), that the early days of the operation had been a "wild and unstable period and a lot of things were done that should not have been done."

*   *   *

A Pentagon adviser who worked closely with the Rumsfeld team vigorously defended its position to me in late 2002, saying, "We have a peacetime military leadership that was Clintonized. And now we're in a war that it doesn't understand. What Rumsfeld wants them to do is to fight it differently, but his way makes most of our senior military leadership's understanding of war fighting irrelevant. He is saying to the military leadership, 'You don't have the answers,' and they don't want to hear that. The argument that Rumsfeld is mean to the chiefs and treats them poorly is, I think, a political operation to make him look like a hip shooter."

Rumsfeld's purpose in authorizing a high-value list of terrorists, the adviser said, was "obviously to go after the command structure of Al Qaeda." He went on, "Capture them? You would if you could. But suppose you had isolated an Al Qaeda group in the Bekaa Valley" —in Lebanon. "It would be hard to capture them." Taking them into custody would probably require ground forces and a major fire-fight; eliminating them, on the other hand, requires only a Hellfire missile. Referring to criticism of Rumsfeld's insistence on targeting individual Al Qaeda members, the adviser said, "I know you've been getting this from the Joint Staff. Some of the snake eaters in Special Forces are against it, too. Of course, I've heard this—'It's not American'—from the military leadership. But it's not because of legality. It's because they don't want to do it." He added, "The idea of not wanting to go after the senior leadership of a paramilitary group that has declared war on you is such a perversion that it's mind-boggling. The problem of a peacetime military is that they cannot conceive of doing what they are paid to do. 'Going after the leadership of Al Qaeda—that's a serious problem.' My God!"

Earlier in 2002, the adviser went on, Rumsfeld had proposed that the Special Operations command be made a "global command" and that it become the dominant agency for all military antiterrorist activities worldwide. Far from seizing the opportunity to be aggressive and "leaning forward," General Holland, the Special Operations commander, "didn't want to do it," the adviser said. He said that civilians in the Defense Department had become convinced that "there are few four-stars leaning forward in the Special Operations command." The adviser added, "We'll have to have a dirty nuke go off to realize how serious this is." What was needed, he said, was a reassessment of all the senior generals and admirals who rose to the top during the Clinton presidency. "We need to find some more fighting generals."

After September 11th, one of Rumsfeld's goals was to give the Pentagon the ability to carry out the kind of clandestine operations that had traditionally been left to the C.I.A. Internal Pentagon memorandums included scathing commentary on the intelligence community. In one, the secretary was urged to keep the Gray Fox unit "out of the hands" of the intelligence community. The paper noted, "Alone, of all organizations within DoD, Gray Fox has the potential, if nurtured, to fight the kind of war the Secretary envisions fighting. . . . Let the intel people get their hooks into Gray Fox and intel will then control what operations can and cannot do."

One recommendation to Rumsfeld called for restructuring Special Operations as a specific agency under the personal command of the defense secretary. The new agency, which would have to be approved by Congress, would take orders only from the defense secretary and thus, the memorandum to Rumsfeld said, overcome internal bureaucratic inertia "to implement the changes you want."

By the end of 2002, some of Rumsfeld's most trusted aides had staged private meetings with past and present military and intelligence officials to discuss expanding the war on terrorism. "There are five hundred guys out there you have to kill," a former C.I.A. official said. "There's no way to sugarcoat it—you just have to kill them. And you can't always be 100 percent sure of the intelligence. Sometimes you have to settle for 95 percent."

The reality remains that action causes reaction, and the November 2002 Predator raid in Yemen was not without consequences. The Yemeni government had planned to delay an announcement of the attack until it could issue a joint statement with Washington. When American officials released the story unilaterally, in time for the midterm elections, the Yemenis were angry and dismayed. Yahya al-Mutawakel, the deputy secretary-general for the ruling General People's Congress Party, complained bitterly that the Administration was far too eager to talk about its success. "This is why it is so difficult to make deals with the United States," al-Mutawakel told the *Christian Science Monitor.* "This is why we are reluctant to work closely with them. They don't consider the internal circumstances in Yemen."

A few weeks later, on November 29, 2002, a powerful explosion shook government buildings in Marib Province, the *Yemen Times* reported, leaving an unmistakable message. "This blast is more than just an explosion," a tribal sheikh told the newspaper. "It must be a message from Al Qaeda saying, 'We are here, and we can strike.' This is serious."

3. Targeting the Insurgency

By December 2003, the Bush Administration had authorized a major escalation of the Special Forces covert war in Iraq. In interviews in November and early December of that year, American officials and former officials said that the main target was the hard-core group of Baathists believed to be behind much of the underground insurgency against the soldiers of the United States and its allies. A new Special Forces group, designated Task Force 121, had been assembled from Army Delta Force members, Navy SEALs, and C.I.A. paramilitary operatives, with many additional personnel ordered to report by January 2004. Its highest priority was the neutralization of the Baathist insurgents, by capture or assassination. The revitalized

Special Forces mission was a policy victory for Rumsfeld, who had struggled for two years to get the military leadership to accept the strategy of what he called manhunts. Rumsfeld had to change much of the Pentagon's leadership to get his way. "Knocking off two regimes allows us to do extraordinary things," a Pentagon adviser told me at the time, referring to Afghanistan and Iraq.

The critical issue, officials agreed, was intelligence. There was much debate about whether targeting a large number of individuals was a practical—or politically effective—way to bring about stability in Iraq, especially given the frequent failure of American forces to obtain consistent and reliable information there. Americans in the field planned to solve that problem by developing a new source of information: they hoped to assemble teams drawn from the upper ranks of the old Iraqi intelligence services and train them to penetrate the insurgency. The idea was for the infiltrators to provide information about individual insurgents for the Americans to act on. A former C.I.A. station chief I spoke to in late November 2003 described the strategy in simple terms: "U.S. shooters and Iraqi intelligence." He added, "There are Iraqis in the intelligence business who have a better idea, and we're tapping into them. We have to resuscitate Iraqi intelligence, holding our nose, and have Delta and agency shooters break down doors and take them"—the insurgents—"out."

A former intelligence official said at the time that getting inside the Baathist leadership could be compared to "fighting your way into a coconut—you bang away and bang away until you find a soft spot, and then you can clean it out." An American who has advised the civilian authority in Baghdad similarly said, "The only way we can win is to go unconventional. We're going to have to play their game. Guerrilla versus guerrilla. Terrorism versus terrorism. We've got to scare the Iraqis into submission."

In Washington, there was widespread agreement on one point: the need for a new American approach to Iraq. There was also uniform criticism of the military's existing response to the growing

American casualty lists. One former Pentagon official who worked extensively with the Special Forces command, and who favors the new military initiative, said, "We've got this large conventional force sitting there and getting their ass shot off, and what we're doing is counterproductive. We're sending mixed signals." The problem with the way the United States has been fighting the Baathist leadership, he said, is "(a) we've got no intelligence, and (b) we're too squeamish to operate in this part of the world."

Referring to the American retaliation against a suspected mortar site, the former official said, "Instead of destroying an empty soccer field, why not impress me by sneaking in a sniper team and killing them while they're setting up a mortar? We do need a more unconventional response, but it's going to be messy."

Inside the Pentagon, it was, by then, understood that simply bringing in or killing Saddam Hussein and his immediate circle—those who appeared in the Bush Administration's famed "deck of cards"—would not stop the insurgency. The new Special Forces operation was aimed instead at the broad middle of the Baathist underground. But many of the officials I spoke to at the time were skeptical of the Administration's plans. Many of them feared that the proposed operation—called "preëmptive manhunting" by one Pentagon adviser—had the potential to turn into another Phoenix Program. The former Special Forces official warned that the problem with head-hunting is that you have to be sure "you're hunting the right heads." Speaking of the now coöperative former Iraqi intelligence officials, he said, "These guys have their own agenda. Will we be doing hits on grudges? When you set up host-nation elements"—units composed of Iraqis, rather than Americans—"it's hard not to have them going off to do what they want to do. You have to keep them on a short leash."

The former official said that the Baathist leadership apparently relies on "face-to-face communications" in planning terrorist attacks. This made the insurgents less vulnerable to the Army's Gray Fox, which has particular expertise in interception and other technical means of intelligence gathering. "These guys are too smart to touch cell phones or radio," the former official said. "It's all going to succeed or fail spectacularly based on human intelligence."

A former C.I.A. official with extensive Middle East experience identified one of the key players on the new American-Iraqi intelligence team at the end of 2003 as Farouq Hijazi, a Saddam loyalist who served for many years as the director of external operations for the Mukhabarat, the Iraqi intelligence service. He had been in custody since late April. The C.I.A. man said that over the previous months Hijazi had "cut a deal," and American officials were "using him to reactivate the old Iraqi intelligence network." He added, "My Iraqi friends say he will honor the deal—but only to the letter, and not to the spirit." He said that although the Mukhabarat was a good security service, capable, in particular, of protecting Saddam Hussein from overthrow or assassination, it was "a lousy intelligence service."

The official went on: "It's not the way we usually play ball, but if you see a couple of your guys get blown away it changes things. We did the American thing—and we've been the nice guy. Now we're going to be the bad guy, and being the bad guy works."

Told of such comments, the Pentagon adviser, who is an expert on unconventional war, expressed dismay. "There are people saying all sorts of wild things about manhunts," he said. "But they aren't at the policy level. It's not a no-holds policy, and it shouldn't be. I'm as tough as anybody, but we're also a democratic society, and we don't fight terror with terror. There will be a lot of close controls—do's and don'ts and rules of engagement." The adviser added, "The problem is that we've not penetrated the bad guys. The Baath Party is run like a cell system. It's like penetrating the Vietcong—we never could do it."

*   *   *

Stephen Cambone, the undersecretary of defense for intelligence, whose star was rising in Rumsfeld's Pentagon in late 2003, was deeply involved in developing the new Special Forces approach. Cambone shared Rumsfeld's views on how to fight terrorism. They both believed that the United States needed to become far more proactive in combatting terrorism, searching for terrorist leaders around the world and eliminating them. And Cambone, like Rumsfeld, had been frustrated by the reluctance of the military leadership to embrace the manhunting mission. Since his confirmation, he had been seeking operational authority over Special Forces. "Rumsfeld's been looking for somebody to have all the answers, and Steve is the guy," a former high-level Pentagon official told me. "He has more direct access to Rummy than anyone else."

One of the key planners of the Special Forces manhunt offensive was Lieutenant General Boykin, Cambone's military assistant. After a meeting with Rumsfeld early last summer—they got along "like two old warriors," the Pentagon consultant said—Boykin postponed his retirement, which had been planned for June, and took the Pentagon job, which brought him a third star. In that post, the Pentagon adviser told me, Boykin became "an important piece" of the planned escalation. In October 2003, the *Los Angeles Times* reported that Boykin, while giving Sunday-morning talks in uniform to church groups, had repeatedly equated the Muslim world with Satan. The previous June, according to the paper, he told a congregation in Oregon that "Satan wants to destroy this nation, he wants to destroy us as a nation, and he wants to destroy us as a Christian army." Boykin praised President Bush as a "man who prays in the Oval Office," and declared that Bush was "not elected" President but "appointed by God." The Muslim world hates America, he said, "because we are a nation of believers."

There were calls in the press and from Congress for Boykin's dismissal, but Rumsfeld made it clear that he wanted to keep his man in the job. Initially, he responded to the *Times* report by praising the general's "outstanding record" and telling journalists that he had neither seen the text of Boykin's statements nor watched the videotape that had been made of one of his presentations. "There are a lot of things that are said by people in the military, or in civilian life, or in the Congress, or in the executive branch that are their views," he said. "We're a free people. And that's the wonderful thing about our country." He added, with regard to the tape, "I just simply can't comment on what he said, because I haven't seen it." Four days later, Rumsfeld said that he had viewed the tape. "It had a lot of very difficult-to-understand words with subtitles which I was not able to verify," he said at a news conference, according to the official transcript. "So I remain inexpert"—the transcript notes that he "chuckles" at that moment—"on precisely what he said." Boykin's comments were referred to the Pentagon's Inspector General's office for review; in August 2004, according to the *Washington Post*, a report, initially promised for April, had yet to be issued.

Boykin had been involved in other controversies as well. He was the Army combat commander in Mogadishu in 1993, when eighteen Americans were slain during the disastrous mission made famous by Mark Bowden's book *Black Hawk Down*. Earlier that year, Boykin, a colonel at the time, led an eight-man Delta Force that was assigned to help a Colombian police unit track down the notorious drug dealer Pablo Escobar. Boykin's team was barred by law from providing any lethal assistance without presidential approval, but there was suspicion in the Pentagon that it was planning to take part in the assassination of Escobar, with the support of American Embassy officials in Colombia. The book *Killing Pablo*, an account, also by Mark Bowden, of the hunt for Escobar, describes how senior officials in the Pentagon's chain of command became convinced that Boykin, with the knowledge of his Special Forces superiors, had exceeded his authority and intended to violate the law. They wanted Boykin's unit pulled out. It wasn't. Escobar was shot dead on the roof of a barrio apartment building in Medellín. The Colombian police were credited with getting their man, but, Bowden wrote, "within the special ops community . . . Pablo's death was regarded as a successful mission for Delta, and legend has it that its operators were in on the kill."

"That's what those guys did," a retired general who monitored Boykin's operations in Colombia told me. "I've seen pictures of Escobar's body that you don't get from a long-range telescope lens. They were taken by guys on the assault team." (Bush Administration officials in the White House, the State Department, and the Pentagon, including General Boykin, did not respond to requests for comment.) Morris Busby, who was the American ambassador to Colombia in 1993 (he is now retired), vigorously defended Boykin. "I think the world of Jerry Boykin, and have the utmost respect for him. I've known him for fifteen years and spent hours and hours with the guy, and never heard him mention religion or God." The retired general also praised Boykin as "one of those guys you'd love to have in a war because he's not afraid to die." But, he added, "when you get to three stars you've got to think through what you're doing." Referring to Boykin and others involved in the Special Forces planning, he added, "These guys are going to get a bunch of guys killed and then give them a bunch of medals."

One step the Pentagon took in the war against the Iraqi insurgency was to seek active and secret help from Israel, the United States' closest ally in the Middle East. According to American and Israeli military and intelligence officials, Israeli commandos and intelligence units have worked closely with their American counterparts at the Special Forces training base at Fort Bragg, North Carolina, and in Israel to help them prepare for operations in Iraq. Israeli commandos were expected to serve as ad hoc advisers—again, in secret—when full-field operations began. (Neither the Pentagon nor Israeli diplomats would comment. "No one wants to talk about this," an Israeli official told me in late 2003. "It's incendiary. Both governments have decided at the highest level that it is in their interests to keep a low profile on U.S.-Israeli coöperation" on Iraq.)

The American-Israeli liaison on Iraq amounted to a tutorial on how to dismantle an insurgency. One former Israeli military-intelligence officer summarized the core lesson this way: "How to do targeted killing, which is very relevant to the success of the war, and what the United States is going to have to do." He told me that the Americans were being urged to emulate the Israeli Army's small commando units, known as the Mistaravim, which operate undercover inside the West Bank and Gaza Strip. "They can approach a house and pounce," the former officer said. In the Israeli view, he added, the Special Forces units must learn "how to maintain a network of informants." Such a network, he said, has made it possible for Israel to penetrate the West Bank and Gaza Strip organizations controlled by groups such as Hamas, and to assassinate or capture potential suicide bombers along with many of the people who recruit and train them. On the other hand, the former officer said, "Israel has, in many ways, been too successful, and has killed or captured so many mid-ranking facilitators on the operational level in the West Bank that Hamas now consists largely of isolated cells that carry out terrorist attacks against Israel on their own." He went on, "There is no central control over many of the suicide bombers. We're trying to tell the Americans that they don't want to eliminate the center. The key is not to have freelancers out there."

Many regional experts, Americans and others, were convinced that the Baathists were still firmly in charge of the insurgency, although they were thought to have little direct connection with Saddam Hussein. An American military analyst who works with the American-led Coalition Provisional Authority in Baghdad told me that by December 2003, he had concluded that "mid-ranking Baathists who were muzzled by the patrimonial nature of Saddam's system have now, with the disappearance of the high-ranking members, risen to control the insurgency." He added that after the American attack and several weeks of confusion, these Baathists had become organized, and were directing and leading operations against Americans. During an interview in Washington in late 2003—a few weeks, as it turned out, before Saddam Hussein's capture, on December 14th—a senior Arab diplomat told me, "We do not believe that the resistance is loyal to Saddam. Yes, the Baathists have reorganized, not for political reasons but because of the terrible decisions made by Jerry Bremer"—the director of the C.P.A. "The Iraqis really want to make you pay the price," the diplomat said. "Killing Saddam will not end it."

Similarly, a Middle Eastern businessman who has advised senior Bush Administration officials told me at the time that the reorganized Baath Party was "extremely active, working underground with permanent internal communications. And without Saddam."

There was disagreement, inevitably, on the extent of Baathist control over the insurgency. The former Israeli military-intelligence officer said, "Most of the firepower comes from the Baathists, and they know where the weapons are kept. But many of the shooters are ethnic and tribal. Iraq is very factionalized now, and within the Sunni community factionalism goes deep." He added, "Unless you settle this, any effort at reconstruction in the center is hopeless."

The American military analyst agreed that the emphasis, even then, on Baathist control overlooked "the nationalist and tribal angle." For example, he said, the anti-coalition forces in Falluja, a major center of opposition, were "driven primarily by the sheikhs and mosques, Islam, clerics, and nationalism." The region, he went on, contains "tens of thousands of unemployed former military officers and enlistees who hang around the coffee shops and restaurants of their relatives; they plot, plan, and give and receive instructions; at night they go out on their missions."

This military analyst, like many officials I spoke to, also raised questions about the military's more conventional tactics—the aggressive program underway at the time, code-named Iron Hammer, of bombings, nighttime raids, and mass arrests aimed at trouble spots in Sunni-dominated central Iraq. The insurgents, he told me, had quickly developed a response. "Their S.O.P."—standard operating procedure—"is to go further out, or even to other towns, so that American retribution does not fall on their locale. Instead, the Americans take it out on the city where the incident happened, and in the process they succeed in making more enemies."

The brazen Iraqi attacks on two separate American convoys in Samarra, on November 30th, provided further evidence of the diversity of the opposition to the occupation. Samarra had been a center of intense anti-Saddam feelings, according to Ahmed S. Hashim, an expert on terrorism who is a professor of strategic studies at the U.S. Naval War College. In an essay published the previous August by the Middle East Institute, Hashim wrote, "Many Samarra natives —who had served with distinction in the Baath Party and the armed forces—were purged or executed during the course of the three decades of rule by Saddam and his cronies from the rival town of Tikrit." Hashim also wrote that "The type of U.S. force structure in Iraq—heavy armored and mechanized units—and the psychological disposition of these forces which have been in Iraq for months is simply not conducive to the successful waging of counterinsurgency warfare."

An adviser to the Special Forces command told me that infighting among the various senior military commands had made it difficult for Special Forces teams on alert to take immediate advantage of time-sensitive intelligence. After enduring repeated criticism from Rumsfeld for his reluctance to authorize commando raids without specific, or "actionable," intelligence, General Holland retired in November 2003. Rumsfeld also made a systematic effort to appoint officers who had worked closely with Special Forces to the top military jobs. A former Special Forces commander, Army General Peter Schoomaker, was brought out of retirement in July and named Army Chief of Staff. Thomas O'Connell, an Army veteran who served in the Phoenix program in Vietnam, and who, in the early 1980s, ran Gray Fox, became the civilian assistant secretary for special operations in the Pentagon. Early in November 2003, the *New York Times* reported the existence of Task Force 121, and said that it was authorized to take action throughout the region, if necessary, in pursuit of Saddam Hussein, Osama bin Laden, and other terrorists. (The task force was then commanded by Air Force Brigadier General Lyle Koenig, an experienced Special Forces helicopter pilot who was replaced in spring 2004 by Rear Admiral William McRaven, who had recently been on the National Security Council staff.) At that point, the former Special Forces official told me, the troops were still "chasing the deck of cards. Their job was to find Saddam, period."

Other Special Forces, in Afghanistan, were busy targeting what is known as the A.Q.S.L., the Al Qaeda senior leadership list. The task force's search for Saddam was, from the beginning, daunting. "The high-profile guys around Saddam were the *murafaqin*, his most loyal companions, who could stand next to him carrying a gun," Scott Ritter, the former United Nations weapons inspector who, from 1994 to 1998, directed a special U.N. unit that eavesdropped on many of Saddam Hussein's private telephone communications, told me in late 2003. "But now he's gone to a different tier—the tribes. He has released the men from his most sensitive units and let them go back to their tribes, and we don't know where they are. The manifests of those units are gone; they've all been destroyed." Ritter added, "Guys like Farouq Hijazi can deliver some of the Baath Party cells, and he knows where some of the intelligence people are. But he can't get us into the tribal hierarchy." The task force, in any event, soon shifted its focus from the hunt for Saddam to the spreading guerrilla war.

There was also a debate going on inside the Administration

about American and Israeli intelligence that suggested that the Shiite-dominated government of Iran might be actively aiding the Sunni-led insurgency in Iraq—"pulling the strings on the puppet," as one former intelligence official put it. Many in the intelligence community were skeptical of this analysis. The Pentagon adviser compared it to "the Chalabi stuff," referring to the discredited prewar intelligence on W.M.D. supplied by Iraqi defectors. But I was told by several officials that winter that the intelligence was considered to be highly reliable by civilians in the Defense Department. A former intelligence official said that one possible response under consideration at the time was for the United States to train and equip an Iraqi force capable of staging cross-border raids. The American goal, he said, would be to "make the cost of supporting the Baathists so dear that the Iranians would back off," adding, "If it begins to look like another Iran-Iraq war, that's another story."

The requirement that U.S. Special Forces units operate in secrecy, a former senior coalition adviser in Baghdad told me, provided an additional incentive for increasing their presence in Iraq. The Special Forces in-country numbers are not generally included in troop totals. Bush and Rumsfeld were insisting that more American troops were not needed, but that position was challenged by many senior military officers in private conversations. "You need more people," the former adviser, a retired admiral, told me. "But you can't add them, because Rummy's taken a position. So you invent a force that won't be counted."

At present, there is no legislation that requires the President to notify Congress before authorizing an overseas Special Forces mission. The Special Forces has been expanded enormously in the Bush Administration. The 2004 Pentagon budget provides more than $6.5 billion for their activities—a 34 percent increase over 2003. An August 2003 congressional study put the number of active and reserve Special Forces troops at forty-seven thousand, and suggested that the appropriate House and Senate committees needed to debate the "proper overall role" of Special Forces in the global war on terrorism. In a conversation at the end of 2003, a former intelligence official depicted the Delta and SEAL teams as "force multipliers"—small units that can do the work of much larger ones and thereby increase the power of the operation as a whole. He also implicitly recognized that such operations would become more and more common; when Special Forces target the Baathists, he said, "it's technically not assassination—it's normal combat operations."

Secrecy and wishful thinking, a Pentagon official told me in the spring of 2004, were defining characteristics of Rumsfeld's Pentagon. "They always want to delay the release of bad news—in the hope that something good will break," he said. The habit of procrastination in the face of bad news led to disconnects between Rumsfeld and the Army staff officers who were assigned to planning for troop requirements in Iraq. In mid-2003, the Pentagon official told me, when it became clear that the Army would have to call up more reserve units to deal with the insurgency, "we had call-up orders that languished for thirty or forty days in the office of the secretary of defense." Rumsfeld's staff always seemed to be waiting for something to turn up—for the problem to take care of itself, without any additional troops. The official explained, "They were hoping that they wouldn't have to make a decision." The delay meant that soldiers in some units about to be deployed had only a few days to prepare wills and deal with other family and financial issues.

The same deliberate indifference to bad news was evident that year, the Pentagon official said, when the Army conducted a series of elaborate war games. Planners would present best-case, moderate-case, and worst-case scenarios, in an effort to assess where the Iraq war was headed and to estimate future troop needs. In every case, the number of troops actually required exceeded the worst-case analysis. Nevertheless, the Joint Chiefs of Staff and civilian officials in the Pentagon continued to insist that future planning be based on the most optimistic scenario. "The optimistic estimate was that at this point in time"—mid-2004—"the U.S. Army would need only a handful of combat brigades in Iraq," the Pentagon official said. "There are nearly twenty now, with the international coalition drying up. They were wildly off the mark." The official added, "From the beginning, the Army community was saying that the projections and estimates were unrealistic." Now, he said, "we're struggling to maintain a hundred and thirty-five thousand troops while allowing soldiers enough time back home."

None of the Bush Administration's machinations with secret operations and secret forces could stop Iraq's steady slide to chaos, as the insurgency grew throughout the first half of 2004. By the end of June, when the United States, working through the Coalition Provisional Authority, formally returned sovereignty—what little there was—to the Iraqis, the dominant mood in Baghdad was pessimism. Many wealthy Iraqis and their families were deserting Baghdad in anticipation of continued, and perhaps heightened, suicide attacks and terror bombings. "We'll see Christians, Shiites, and Sunnis getting out," Michel Samaha, the Lebanese Minister of Information, reported. "What the resistance is doing is targeting the poor people who run the bureaucracy—those who can't afford to pay for private guards. A month ago, friends of mine who are important landowners in Iraq came to Baghdad to do business. The cost of one day's security was about twelve thousand dollars."

Whitley Bruner, a retired intelligence officer who was a senior member of the C.I.A.'s task force on Iraq a decade ago, told me that the new interim government was urgently seeking ways to provide affordable security for second-tier officials—the men and women who make the government work. Earlier that month, two such officials—Kamal Jarrah, an Education Ministry official, and Bassam Salih Kubba, who was serving as deputy foreign minister—were assassinated by unidentified gunmen outside their homes. "It's going to be a hot summer," Bruner said after returning from a trip to Baghdad in June. "A lot of people have decided to get to Lebanon, Jordan, or the Gulf and wait this one out."

VII.

A MOST DANGEROUS FRIEND

1. Gambling on Musharraf

There are a few important things to know about Pakistan. It is a nuclear power that harbors some of the most dedicated and potentially destabilizing anti-American Islamic activists in the world. And its president, General Pervez Musharraf, is considered by the Bush Administration to be an indispensable and loyal ally in the war against terrorism—someone who is willing to take on the mullahs. The reality is that Musharraf, who seized power in a bloodless coup against Pakistan's elected government, in 1999, has been constantly expanding his authority over a population, an army, and an intelligence service that do not trust him or fully support him. He narrowly survived two assassination attempts in December 2003. The gravest danger to Musharraf has come from within; many of his political problems stem from the perception that he is George Bush's man. And so while he supplied tough talk on terrorism for American consumption after September 11th, he said, and did, much less at home.

Musharraf's duplicity was accepted without complaint by Washington: the Administration believed that it had few alternatives. The result is that a short-sighted foreign policy is keeping a near-despot in power and doing little, if anything, to improve the daily lives of the Pakistani people, and thus deal with the conditions that create more terrorists. I've written about Pakistan several times since September 11th, most recently in March 2004, and the one constant about the Musharraf regime has been its inconstancy. South Asia remains on edge.

———

By the end of October 2001, the Bush Administration's hunt for Osama bin Laden and his Al Qaeda network had evolved into a regional crisis that put Pakistan's nuclear arsenal at risk, exacerbated the instability of the government of General Pervez Musharraf, and raised the possibility of a nuclear conflict between Pakistan and India. As the American air campaign in Afghanistan produced civilian casualties, the political pressure on Musharraf intensified—externally from street demonstrations led by fundamentalists in Islamabad, Quetta, Peshawar, and elsewhere, and internally from members of his own military and the influential Inter-Services Intelligence, or I.S.I. These unintended consequences of the President's decision to wage war on the Taliban government in Afghanistan created a serious rift between the American government's intelligence and diplomatic experts on South Asia and the decision makers of the Bush Administration.

A Pakistani diplomat I talked to at the time acknowledged that the situation was "explosive." Much of the concern stemmed from the Reagan Administration's decision to finance many of today's Taliban leaders in their successful war against the Soviet Union's presence in Afghanistan. Pakistan was the main conduit for American support. "At one time, it was a three-way game," the diplomat said. "The C.I.A., the I.S.I., and the mujahideen were creating these Frankensteins"—the Taliban—"and now the C.I.A. has pulled out, but you can't totally destroy the Frankensteins."

The Administration's top officials viewed the threat to Musharraf as dangerous but manageable. "I was worried initially," a senior military planner told me in late 2001. "But Musharraf has done a good job. He's put the hard-liners in a box and locked it." The officer was referring to Musharraf's decision, the same day that the air war began, to force the resignation or reassignment of a group of Army and intelligence officers he considered untrustworthy. "Nobody's going to move against Musharraf unless there's an uprising in the streets," a second Pakistani diplomat told me. "How to prevent the uprising is to stop dropping bombs on civilian targets."

A former Pakistani diplomat I spoke to soon afterward took issue with the Bush Administration's belief that Musharraf had resolved the loyalty issue by replacing top commanders with officers believed to be less ideological. "To remove the top two or three doesn't matter at all," he said. "The philosophy remains." The I.S.I., he added, is "a parallel government of its own. If you go through the officer list, almost all of the I.S.I. regulars would say, of the Taliban, 'They are my boys.'"

Other officials I spoke to at the time suspected Musharraf of seeking to placate the fundamentalists by looking the other way during terrorist attacks, allegedly sponsored by the I.S.I., on Indian targets in the disputed region of Kashmir, which is dominated by India but has a mostly Muslim population, and is a highly emotional issue for fundamentalists in the I.S.I. and the Taliban. (The Taliban and Al Qaeda have declared the elimination of India's presence in Kashmir as a major goal.) A former high-ranking government official, who had direct knowledge of the situation, said, "the Bush Administration is so focussed on the target and the objective that it's lost its peripheral vision. If Musharraf is toppled in a coup, or fears he'll be toppled, or, as a price for not being toppled, gives the I.S.I. permission to ratchet it up in Kashmir, that's very dangerous."

The White House's dilemma was clearly spelled out in a speech given by Senator Joseph R. Biden Jr., a Democrat and, at the time, the chairman of the Senate Foreign Relations Committee, on October 22, 2001. "The President has not been as blunt as I'm going to be," Biden told a meeting of the Council on Foreign Relations. "Pakistan may very well, and Musharraf may, in fact, collapse. It may be gone. . . . If that were the case, we would find ourselves with a whole hell of a lot more forces in the region than we have now."

Referring to the war in Afghanistan, which was then underway, Biden asked rhetorically, "How much longer does the bombing continue? Because we're going to pay an escalating price in the Muslim world. We're going to pay an escalating price in the region. And that in fact is going to make the aftermath of our 'victory' more difficult. . . . I hope to God it ends sooner rather than later." Biden also had these words for the Musharraf regime: "We have to make clear to the Pakistanis that, notwithstanding the fact that we need you very much right now . . . if you are going to continue to foment the terror that does exist in Kashmir, then you are operating against your own near-term interests, because that very viper can turn on you."

Biden came as close as any Democrat had come since September 11th to straightforward criticism of President Bush's war aims. The White House had no specific response, but Speaker of the House Dennis Hastert, a Republican from Illinois, depicted Biden's public skepticism as "completely irresponsible." In a statement, Hastert said that the "American people want us to bring these terrorists to justice. They do not want comments that may bring comfort to our enemies."

At the same time, some of the U.S. government's most experienced South Asia experts had had doubts about Musharraf's ability to maintain control over the military and one very specific concern: who would control Pakistan's nuclear arsenal in the event of a coup. There were also fears that a dissident group of fundamentalist officers might try to seize a warhead.

*   *   *

Pakistan has had the bomb since 1987, when its nuclear laboratories successfully fabricated a warhead. Dr. Abdul Qadeer Khan, who developed Pakistan's uranium enrichment program, is revered today by his countrymen as the father of its nuclear bomb. Khan had spent more than a decade setting up an illicit network in Europe that enabled him to obtain the necessary gas centrifuges to produce the weapons-grade uranium. Khan's program was highly secret, but not to the C.I.A., whose agents provided a stream of accurate reports to the Reagan Administration throughout the 1980s. Pakistan was then the United States' most important ally in the struggle to oust the Soviet Union from Afghanistan, and the White House chose not to act on the information. In 1989, the first Bush Administration had assured Congress that Pakistan did not possess such weapons—although it knew better—in order to gain continued approval for military aid to the country. Nuclear proliferation and a nuclear black market ring were secondary issues. In 1998, Pakistan successfully tested a nuclear device, heralded as the Islamic world's first atomic bomb. Pakistan is now estimated to have dozens of warheads, which can be delivered by intermediate-range missiles and a fleet of F-16 aircraft.

Within two weeks of September 11th, Bush lifted the sanctions that had been imposed on Pakistan because of its nuclear program. In the view of American disarmament experts, the sanctions had in any case failed to deal with one troubling issue: the close ties between some scientists working for the Pakistan Atomic Energy Commission and radical Islamic groups. "There is an awful lot of Al Qaeda sympathy within Pakistan's nuclear program," an intelligence official told me. One American nonproliferation expert said, "If we're incinerated next week, it'll be because of H.E.U."—highly enriched uranium—"that was given to Al Qaeda by Pakistan."

One U.S. intelligence officer expressed particular alarm over the questioning in Pakistan, in October 2001, of two retired Pakistani nuclear scientists, who were reported by authorities to have connections to the Taliban. Both men, Sultan Bashiruddin Mahmood and Chaudry Abdul Majid, had spent their careers at the Pakistan Atomic Energy Commission, working on weapons-related projects. The intelligence officer, who is a specialist in nuclear proliferation in South Asia, depicted this revelation as "the tip of a very serious iceberg," and told me that it showed that pro-Taliban feelings extended beyond the Pakistani Army into the country's supposedly highly disciplined nuclear-weapons laboratories. Pakistan's nuclear researchers are known for their nationalism and their fierce patriotism. If two of the most senior scientists are found to have been involved in unsanctioned dealings with the Taliban, it would suggest that the lure of fundamentalism has, in some cases, overcome state loyalty.

A former high-level State Department official, who maintained close contact with events in Pakistan, told me in October 2001 that he understood that Musharraf had assured the Bush Administration that "only the most reliable military people remain in control of the arsenal, and if there's any real worry he'd disarm them. He does not want the crazies to precipitate a real war." By then, however, the Administration was reviewing and "refreshing" its contingency plans for securing, or possibly "exfiltrating," Pakistan's warheads in the event that Musharraf's government lost control.

An élite undercover unit operating under Pentagon control with C.I.A. assistance—trained to slip into foreign countries and find suspected nuclear weapons, and disarm them if necessary—was exploring plans for an operation inside Pakistan, past and present government officials told me. "They're good," one American said. "If they screw up, they die. They've had good success in proving the negative"—that is, in determining that suspected facilities in third-world countries were not nuclear-related.

The American team was apparently getting help from Israel's most successful special operations unit, the storied Sayeret Matkal, also known as Unit 262, a deep-penetration unit that has been involved in assassinations, the theft of foreign signals-intelligence materials, and the theft and destruction of foreign nuclear weaponry. Members of the Israeli unit arrived in the United States a few days after September 11th, an informed source said, and trained with American Special Forces units at undisclosed locations.

Such operations depend on intelligence, however, and there was disagreement within the Administration about the quality of the C.I.A.'s data. The American intelligence community could not be sure, for example, that it knew the precise whereabouts of every Pakistani warhead—or whether all the warheads that it has found were real. "They've got some dummy locations," an official told me. "You only get one chance, and then you've tried and failed. The cat is out of the bag."

Some senior officials said that they were confident that the intelligence community could do its job, despite the efforts of the Pakistani Army to mask its nuclear arsenal. "We'd be challenged to manage the problem, but there is contingency planning for that possibility," one Bush military adviser told me that October. "We can't exclude the possibility that the Pakistanis could make it harder for us to act on what we know, but that's an operational detail. We're going to have to work harder to get to it quickly. We still have some good access."

The skeptics among intelligence and military officials I spoke to challenged that view. The C.I.A., they noted, provided effective information on the warheads in the late 1980s and early 1990s, when it worked closely with the Pakistani military in Afghanistan. At that time, the United States was a major supplier of arms and military technology to Pakistan. The agency recruited informants inside the Pakistan Atomic Energy Commission, and the National Security Agency found a way to intercept the back-channel communications of Dr. A. Q. Khan. But by the time the war in Afghanistan got underway those assets no longer existed. "We lost our interest in that area, and we do not have the same level of contact or knowledge that we once did," a former high-level C.I.A. officer said. "Today, there is a whole set of information that, when it comes down to it, we don't have. We can't count warheads. We never had the capacity to count," he said. "The idea that you know where the warheads are at any given moment is not right. As the operation approaches and the question 'How certain are you?' is asked, it becomes more difficult. The fact is, we usually know hours later. We never could do it in real time."

Other officials expressed concern about what any team sent to Pakistan could really accomplish without risking significant casualties. "How are you going to conduct a covert commando operation in the middle of the country?" the former high-level State Department official said. "We don't know where this stuff is, and it would take far more than a commando operation to get at it."

A government expert on Pakistan's nuclear capabilities depicted the issue in strategic terms: "The United States has to look at a new doctrine. Our nuclear strategy has to incorporate the fact that we might have a nuclear-armed fundamentalist government in Pakistan. Even if we know where the weapons are now, it doesn't mean we'll know where they are if the fundamentalists take over. And after Pakistan it could be Iran and Iraq. These are countries that support state terrorism."

A senior military officer, after confirming that intense planning for a possible exfiltration of warheads was under way, said that he had been concerned not about a military coup but about a localized insurrection by a clique of I.S.I. officers in the field who had access to a nuclear storage facility. "The Pakistanis have just as much of a vested interest as we do in making sure that that stuff is looked after, because if they"—I.S.I. dissidents—"throw one at India, they're all cooked meat." He was referring to the certainty of Indian nuclear retaliation. Intelligence officials told me they believed that, in case of an imminent threat, the Indian military's special commando unit was preparing to make its own move on the Pakistani warheads.

*　　*　　*

In a CNN television interview with Larry King on October 22, 2001, Musharraf dismissed the American concerns about the integrity of Pakistan's nuclear arsenal, depicting them as the thoughts of those in the West "who don't really understand the reality of Pakistan. . . . We have an excellent command-and-control system which we have evolved, and there is no question of their falling into the hands of any fundamentalists." However, in an interview in 2000 with Jeffrey Goldberg, Musharraf described the arsenal's command-and-control mechanism as consisting of "a geographic separation between the warhead and the missile. . . . In order to arm the missile, the warhead would have to be moved by truck over a certain distance. I don't see any chance of this restraint being broken." He would not say how far apart the warhead and its launching missile were, or who controlled the system on a minute-to-minute basis.

"That's not a command-and-control system," one American intelligence expert subsequently told me. "You always keep the weapons separate." Musharraf's description, he added, was "like the argument the Pakistanis used to use in the late 1980s and early 1990s that they did not have a bomb because they hadn't put the components together." An intelligence expert also suggested that the Musharraf account was not credible. "What happens in a crisis? Are you going to have to drive warheads to the delivery vehicles? And leave you vulnerable to an enemy strike? A real command-and-control system allows you to have them ready to go, but always under the control of the leadership."

Pakistani military officials have approached Pentagon officials several times in the past decade in an unsuccessful attempt to get support for an upgrading of Pakistan's nuclear command-and-control mechanisms. Senior military and proliferation officials in the Clinton Administration told me, however, that they had determined that such assistance was barred by the Treaty on the Nonproliferation of Nuclear Weapons, ratified in 1968, which prohibits declared nuclear states from providing any support or guidance to any emerging nuclear power. One former Pentagon official caustically depicted the Clinton Administration's Pakistani command-and-control debate as being similar to the debate over condoms in high schools and needle exchanges: "If you give out condoms, are you condoning teenage sex? If you give out needles, are you condoning drugs? By helping with command-and-control, are you condoning nuclear weapons?"

One longtime C.I.A. operative who served under cover in South Asia argued that Musharraf was simply telling Washington what it wants to hear. "Why should he tell us the truth?" the operative said. "He's fighting for his life. We sit there dumbly listening to him, and it's wrong."

———

After the American invasion of Afghanistan, there was widespread speculation in the Indian press about Musharraf's political standing: had he bought support, and time, from his antagonists within the I.S.I. by acquiescing to guerrilla excursions inside Kashmir? My interviews with Indian diplomats in this period inevitably turned to the issue of nuclear weapons.

India's nuclear warheads are more numerous, more sophisticated, and more powerful than Pakistan's—it has between sixty and ninety warheads while Pakistan is thought to have between thirty and fifty. (Pakistan is outmatched conventionally, as well; India's Army is twice as large, and its population is more than seven times as large.) A retired C.I.A. officer who served as station chief in South Asia told me that what he found especially disturbing in the ongoing confrontation between the two countries was the "imperfect intelligence" each had as to what the other side's intentions were. "Couple that with the fact that these guys have a propensity to believe the worst of each other, and have nuclear weapons, and you end up saying, 'My God, get me the hell out of here.'"

When I traveled to New Delhi in late 2001, I got a sense of how dangerous the situation was. In one conversation, an Indian diplomat who had worked at the highest levels of his country's government told me that he believed India could begin a war with Pakistan and not face a possible nuclear retaliation. He explained, "When Pakistan went nuclear, we called their bluff." He was referring to a tense moment in 1990, when India moved its army en masse along the Pakistani border. "We found, through intelligence, that there was a lot of bluster." He and others in India concluded that Pakistan was not willing to begin a nuclear confrontation. "We've found there is a lot of strategic space between a low-intensity war waged with Pakistan and the nuclear threshold," the diplomat said. "Therefore, we are utilizing military options without worrying about the nuclear threshold." If that turned out to be a miscalculation and Pakistan initiated the use of nuclear weapons, he said, then India would respond in force. "And Pakistan would cease to exist."

It did turn out to be a miscalculation. The American National Security Agency was monitoring the situation in 1990 when intercepts revealed that Pakistan's leadership had "panicked," as a senior intelligence official put it, at the prospect of a preëmptive Indian strike and had readied its small arsenal of nuclear warheads. The crisis was resolved after American diplomats intervened. Afterward, intelligence analysts concluded that leaders in both nations were willing to run any risk, including that of nuclear war, to avoid political or military defeat in Kashmir. Conditions were no more stable in the following years. A nuclear-threat assessment published in January 2001 by the secretary of defense bleakly concluded, "Given the long-standing hostility between the two countries, even a minor conflict runs the risk of escalating into an exchange of missiles with nuclear warheads."

Kashmir remains an issue that could spark a general war in South Asia. The territory, on the northern border of India, spanning the Himalayas, has been a subject of dispute since 1947, when

Britain's withdrawal from the subcontinent led to the partition of the Raj into India and Pakistan. India and Pakistan have gone to war twice over Kashmir, in 1948 and 1965, each time without a clear resolution. In 1949, a ceasefire brokered by the United Nations placed about two-thirds of Kashmir, whose population was 75 percent Muslim, under the control of India, and gave nominal control of the remaining third to Pakistan. A U.N. resolution called for a plebiscite to allow the people of Kashmir to vote on their political fate, but India has not permitted the election to take place, insisting that Pakistan must first withdraw its troops. Pakistan refused to do so unless India also withdrew. Over the years, India has taken advantage of the impasse by increasing military and political control over its mandated area of Kashmir, infuriating the Muslims there, and Pakistan has responded by sponsoring terrorism in an effort to foment revolution.

The ancestral home of the late prime minister Jawaharlal Nehru, Kashmir has a revered status for Indians, and many believe that their country needs to hold on to the Muslim region in order to maintain its identity as a secular nation. Pakistanis believe that Kashmir, because of the Muslim predominance, should have become part of their nation at Partition. For most Indians and Pakistanis, it is an issue beyond political compromise. The territory is now divided along a carefully drawn line of control, but cross-border incursions—many of them bloody—occur daily.

On October 1, 2001, Islamic terrorists exploded a car bomb near the state legislature building in Srinagar, Kashmir, killing at least thirty-eight people, more than half of them civilians, and wounding scores of others. Two weeks after the car bombing, the Indians responded by shelling military positions across the ceasefire line. In a press conference, the Indian defense minister, George Fernandes, warned, "When it comes to punishing the enemy, we will hold back nothing."

The Indians were already enraged by the Bush Administration's designation of Pakistan as its chief ally in the Afghanistan war. The former State Department official said that Musharraf, eager to find a way to justify the war to the Pakistani public, had sought in talks with U.S. officials to provide Pakistan's support in exchange for an American commitment to endorse the Pakistani position in Kashmir. The senior intelligence analyst confirmed that Indians had been alarmed by the muted private response of the Bush Administration to the October 1st bombing incident in Kashmir. "I've seen tough messages to the Pakistanis—'Keep these guys under control,'" he noted, but that message was not sent this time. He went on, "The I.S.I. is being allowed by Musharraf to develop policies of its own—to run Afghan policy and Kashmir policy. And that's where the danger is, if we continue to push the Indians." Referring to the senior managers of the Bush Administration, the intelligence analyst said, "Americans have underestimated Indian anger."

"Musharraf has two-timed you," a recently retired senior member of India's diplomatic service told me in New Delhi in late 2001. "What have you gained? Have you captured Osama bin Laden?" He said that although India would do nothing to upset the American campaign in Afghanistan, "We will turn the heat on Musharraf. He'll go back to terrorism as long as the heat is off."

Milton Bearden, the former C.I.A. station chief in Pakistan who helped run the Afghan war against the Soviet Union in the late 1980s and worked closely with the I.S.I., scoffed at that characterization. "Musharraf doesn't have time to two-time anybody. He wakes up every morning and has to head out with his bayonet, trying to find the land mines," Bearden said. "What can he do? Does he really have the Army behind him? Yes, but maybe by only 48 to 52 percent."

A senior Pakistani diplomat I spoke to a few months after September 11th depicted India as suffering from "jilted-lover syndrome" —referring to the enormous amount of American attention and financial aid that the Musharraf government was receiving. He added that the critical question for Pakistan, India, and the rest of South Asia is "Will the Americans stay involved for the long haul, or will attention shift to Somalia or Iraq? I don't know."

There was an unsuccessful terrorist attack on October 22, 2001, this time on an Indian airbase in Kashmir. It failed when a group of would-be suicide bombers were killed in a shoot-out, but the event— it was the first time an airbase had been targeted—led India's prime minister, Atal Behari Vajpayee, to reject an offer from Musharraf to hold talks. Musharraf responded by warning darkly that Pakistan was "not a small country."

On December 13th, a suicide squad of five heavily armed Muslim terrorists drove past a barrier at the Indian Parliament, in New Delhi, and rushed the main building. At one point, the terrorists were only a few feet from the steps to the office of India's vice president, Krishan Kant. Nine people were killed in the shoot-out, in addition to the terrorists, and many others were injured. In India, the Parliament assault was regarded as comparable to September 11th. The country's politicians and the press felt that a far greater tragedy had only narrowly been averted. Indian intelligence quickly concluded that the attack had been organized by operatives from two long-standing Kashmiri terrorist organizations that were believed to be heavily supported by the I.S.I.

Brajesh Mishra, India's national security adviser, told me that if the attack on the Parliament had resulted in a more significant number of casualties "there would have been mayhem." India deployed hundreds of thousands of troops along its border with Pakistan, and publicly demanded that Musharraf take steps to cut off Pakistani support for the groups said to be involved. "Nobody in India wants war, but other options are not ruled out," Mishra said.

Bearden believed that the Indian government cynically used the Parliament bombing to rally public support for the conflict with Pakistan. "The Indians are just playing brinkmanship now—moving troops up to the border," he said. "Until September 11th, they thought they'd won this thing—they had Pakistan on the ropes." Because of its nuclear program, he said, "Pakistan was isolated and sanctioned by the United States, with only China left as an ally. Never mind that the only country in South Asia that always did what we asked was Pakistan." Bearden went on: "Musharraf is not going to be a Kemal Atatürk"—the founder of the secular Turkish state—"but as long as he can look over his shoulder and see that Rich Armitage"—the United States deputy secretary of state—"and Don Rumsfeld are with him he might be able to stop the extremism."

"The Indians are much stronger than the Pakistanis," a former high-ranking United States government official said. An invasion of Pakistan would be against India's interests, he said, because it would "force Musharraf's hand": if he responded, it would trigger a wider war; if he failed to respond, it could provoke a coup that would topple him. "Either way, India is worse off." He added, however, that the Indian government and its military and intelligence agencies remained deeply divided over how to proceed in Kashmir. "India could feel sufficiently provoked to preëmpt militarily," he said.

Under prodding from the Bush Administration, Musharraf took some action against his country's fundamentalist terror organizations in late 2001, including freezing some bank accounts. "Musharraf has not done as much as the Indians want," a Bush Administration official who is deeply involved in South Asian issues said. "But he's done more than I'd thought he'd do. He had to do something, because the Indians are so wound up." The official also said, however, that Musharraf could not last in office if he conceded the issue of Kashmir to India, and would not want to do so in any case. "He is not a fundamentalist but a Pakistani nationalist—he genuinely believes that Kashmir 'should be ours.' At the end of the day, Musharraf would come out ahead if he could get rid of the Pakistani and Kashmiri terrorists—if he can survive it. They have eaten the vitals out of Pakistan."

Not everyone in the intelligence community believed that Musharraf could stop the cross-border activity even if he wanted to. "I doubt he is encouraging these attacks in Kashmir," a former official said. "But it's very hard for him to control it. He's not going to alienate the I.S.I.—he's going to need them if and when it comes to stopping a demonstration. He has less control than Arafat has over the terrorists in the West Bank."

An American intelligence official told me that the Musharraf regime had added to the precariousness of the military standoff with India by reducing the amount of time it would take for Pakistan to execute a nuclear strike. By the beginning of 2002, he said, the time it took to get the warheads in the air was cut to just three hours— "and that's too close. Both sides have their nukes in place and ready to roll." The Bush Administration official involved in South Asian issues added, "Both nations need to sit down and work out the red lines"—the points of no return. "They've never done that."

"Nitrogen and glycerine are being shaken up here," the former high-ranking government official said. "The Pakistanis are the small, scared ones. And they might use nuclear weapons as an equalizer. The danger is that the fifty-year dynamic between India and Pakistan is the backdrop for a scenario in which someone could hit a button."

2. The Ultimate Black Market

In June 2002, the C.I.A. delivered a comprehensive analysis of North Korea's nuclear ambitions to President Bush and his top advisers. The document, known as a National Intelligence Estimate, was classified as Top Secret S.C.I. (for "sensitive compartmented information"), and its distribution within the government was tightly restricted. The C.I.A. report made the case that North Korea had been violating international law—and agreements with South Korea and the United States—by secretly obtaining the means to produce weapons-grade uranium.

The document's most politically sensitive information, however, was about Pakistan. Since 1997, the C.I.A. said, Pakistan had been sharing sophisticated technology, warhead-design information, and weapons-testing data with the Pyongyang regime. Pakistan, one of the Bush Administration's important allies in the war against terrorism, was helping North Korea build the bomb.

In 1985, North Korea signed the Nuclear Nonproliferation Treaty, which led to the opening of most of its nuclear sites to international inspection. By the early 1990s, it became evident to American intelligence agencies and international inspectors that the North Koreans were reprocessing more spent fuel than they had declared, and might have separated enough plutonium, a reactor by-product, to fabricate one or two nuclear weapons. The resulting diplomatic crisis was resolved when North Korea's leader, Kim Jong Il, entered into an agreement with the Clinton Administration, in 1994, to stop the nuclear-weapons program in return for economic aid and the construction of two light-water nuclear reactors that, under safeguards, would generate electricity.

Within three years, however, North Korea had begun using a second method to acquire fissile material. This time, instead of using spent fuel, scientists were trying to produce weapons-grade uranium from natural uranium—with Pakistani technology. One American intelligence official, referring to North Korea's plutonium project in the early 1990s, said, "Before, they were sneaking." Now "it's off the wall. We know they can do a lot more and a lot more quickly." The report, he added, "points a clear finger at the Pakistanis. The technical stuff is crystal clear—not hedged and not ambivalent."

Whether North Korea had actually begun to build warheads was not known at the time of the 1994 crisis, however, and, according to the C.I.A. report, was still not known. The report, those who read it said, included separate and contradictory estimates from the C.I.A., the Pentagon, the State Department, and the Department of Energy regarding the number of warheads that North Korea might have been capable of making, and provided no consensus on whether or not the Pyongyang regime was actually producing them.

North Korea is economically isolated; one of its main sources of export income is arms sales, and its most sought-after products are missiles. And one of its customers was Pakistan, which needed the missiles to more effectively deliver the warheads to the interior of its rival, India. In 1997, according to the C.I.A. report, Pakistan began paying for missile systems from North Korea in part by sharing its nuclear-weapons secrets. According to the report, Pakistan sent prototypes of high-speed centrifuge machines to North Korea. And sometime in 2001 North Korean scientists began to enrich uranium in significant quantities. Pakistan also provided data on how to build and test a uranium-triggered nuclear weapon, the C.I.A. report said.

A former senior Pakistani official acknowledged that his government's contacts with North Korea increased dramatically in 1997; the Pakistani economy had foundered, and there was "no more money" to pay for North Korean missile support, so the Pakistani government began paying for missiles by providing "some of the know-how and the specifics." Pakistan helped North Korea conduct a series of "cold tests"—simulated nuclear explosions, using natural uranium—which are necessary to determine whether a nuclear device will detonate properly. Pakistan also gave the North Korean intelligence service advice on "how to fly under the radar," as the former official put it—that is, how to hide nuclear research from American satellites and U.S. and South Korean intelligence agents.

It had taken Pakistan a decade of experimentation, and a substantial financial investment, before it was able to produce reliable centrifuges; with Pakistan's help, the North Koreans had "chopped many years off" the development process, the intelligence official noted. It is not known how many centrifuges are now being operated in North Korea or where the facilities are. (They are assumed to be in underground caves.) The Pakistani centrifuges, the official said, are slim cylinders, roughly six feet in height, that could be shipped "by the hundreds" in cargo planes. But, he added, "all Pakistan would have to do is give the North Koreans the blueprints. They are very sophisticated in their engineering." And with a few thousand centrifuges, he said, "North Korea could have enough fissile material to manufacture two or three warheads a year, with something left over to sell."

Over the years, there have been sporadic reports of North Korea's contacts with Pakistan, most of them concerning missile sales. Much less has been known about their nuclear ties. In the past decade, American intelligence tracked at least thirteen visits to North Korea made by A. Q. Khan, the Pakistani nuclear scientist. Khan was placed under American surveillance because of his clandestine visits to North Korea. (He often travelled in disguise on such trips.) More troubling intelligence came in the late 1990s, when it was learned from sensitive sources that he also made at least one secret visit to an Iranian nuclear facility. American officials believe that he brought no actual materials with him to Iran—just his years of hands-on experience in bomb making. "This guy moves around," one American intelligence official said of Khan. "He's in bad places at bad times."

In October 2002, after news of the Korean uranium program came out, the *New York Times* ran a story suggesting that Pakistan was a possible supplier of centrifuges to North Korea. General Pervez Musharraf, Pakistan's leader, attacked the account as "absolutely baseless," and added, "There is no such thing as collaboration with North Korea in the nuclear area." The White House appeared to accept Musharraf's statement. In November, Secretary of State Colin Powell told reporters he had been assured by Musharraf that Pakistan was not currently engaging in any nuclear transactions with North Korea. "I have made clear to him that any . . . contact between Pakistan and North Korea we believe would be improper, inappropriate, and would have consequences," Powell said. "President Musharraf understands the seriousness of the issue."

An American intelligence official I spoke with called Pakistan's behavior the "worst nightmare" of the international arms-control community: a Third World country becoming an instrument of proliferation. "The West's primary control of nuclear proliferation was based on technology denial and diplomacy," the official said. "Our fear was, first, that a Third World country would develop nuclear weapons indigenously; and, second, that it would then provide the technology to other countries. This is profound. It changes the world." The official said, "The transfer of enrichment technology by Pakistan is a direct outgrowth of the failure of the United States to deal with the Pakistani program when we could have done so. We've lost control."

The C.I.A. report remained unpublicized throughout the summer and early fall of 2002, as the Administration concentrated on laying the groundwork for a war with Iraq. Many officials in the Administration's own arms-control offices were unaware of the report. "It was held very tightly," an official told me. "Compartmentalization is used to protect sensitive sources who can get killed if their information is made known, but it's also used for controlling sensitive information for political reasons."

President Bush's contempt for the North Korean government was well known, and made the White House's failure to publicize the C.I.A. report or act on it all the more puzzling. In his State of the Union address in January of 2002, Bush cited North Korea, along with Iraq and Iran, as part of the "axis of evil." Bob Woodward, in *Bush at War*, his book about the Administration's response to September 11th, recalls an interview at the President's Texas ranch in August: " 'I loathe Kim Jong Il!' Bush shouted, waving his finger in the air. 'I've got a visceral reaction to this guy, because he is starving his people.' " Woodward wrote that the President had become so emotional while speaking about Kim Jong Il that "I thought he might jump up."

The Bush Administration was put on notice about North Korea even before it received the C.I.A. report. In January of 2002, John Bolton, the undersecretary of state for arms control, declared that North Korea had a covert nuclear-weapons program and was in violation of the nonproliferation treaty. That February, the President was urged by three members of Congress to withhold support for the two reactors promised to North Korea, on the ground that the Pyongyang government was said to be operating a secret processing site "for the enrichment of uranium." In May, Bolton again accused North Korea of failing to coöperate with the International Atomic Energy Agency. Nevertheless, on July 5th Condoleezza Rice, who as national security adviser presumably had received the C.I.A. report weeks earlier, made it clear in a letter to the congressmen that the Bush Administration would continue providing North Korea with shipments of heavy fuel oil and nuclear technology for the two promised energy-generating reactors.

The Administration's fitful North Korea policy, with its mixture of anger and seeming complacency, was in many ways a consequence of its unrelenting focus on Iraq. Late in 2002, the White House released a national security strategy paper authorizing the military "to detect and destroy an adversary's WMD assets"—weapons of mass destruction—"before these weapons are used." The document argued that the Armed Forces "must have the capability to defend against WMD-armed adversaries . . . because deterrence may not succeed." Logically, the new strategy should have applied first to North Korea, whose nuclear-weapons program was far more advanced than Iraq's. The Administration's goal, however, was to mobilize public opinion for an invasion of Iraq. One American intelligence official told me at the time, "The Bush doctrine says MAD"—mutual assured destruction—"will not work for these rogue nations, and therefore we have to preëmpt if negotiations don't work. And the Bush people knew that the North Koreans had already reinvigorated their programs and were more dangerous than Iraq. But they didn't tell anyone. They have bankrupted their own policy—thus far—by not doing what their doctrine calls for."

Iraq's military capacity had been vitiated by its defeat in the Gulf War and years of inspections, but North Korea was one of the most militarized nations in the world, with more than 40 percent of its population under arms. Its artillery was especially fearsome: more than ten thousand guns, along with twenty-five hundred rocket launchers capable of launching five hundred thousand shells an hour, were positioned within range of Seoul, the capital of South Korea. The Pentagon estimated that all-out war would result in more than a million military and civilian casualties, including as many as a hundred thousand Americans killed. A Clinton Administration official recalled attending a congressional briefing in the mid-1990s at which Army General Gary Luck, the commander of U.S. forces in Korea, laconically said, "Senator, I could win this one for you—but not right away."

In early October 2002, James A. Kelly, assistant secretary of state for East Asian and Pacific affairs, flew to Pyongyang with a large entourage for a showdown over the uranium-enrichment program. Kelly was authorized to tell the Koreans that the United States had learned about the illicit uranium program, but his careful instructions left him no room to negotiate. His scripted message was blunt: North Korea must stop the program before any negotiations could take place. The C.I.A. report had predicted that North Korea, if confronted with the evidence, would not risk an open break with the 1994 agreement and would do nothing to violate the nonproliferation treaty. "It was dead wrong," an intelligence officer told me. "I hope there are other people in the agency who understand the North Koreans better than the people who wrote this."

"The Koreans were stunned," a Japanese diplomat who spoke to some of the participants told me. "They didn't know that the U.S.

knew what it knew." After an all-night caucus in Pyongyang, Kang Suk Ju, the first vice foreign minister of North Korea, seemed, at first, to confirm the charge when he responded by insisting upon his nation's right to develop nuclear weapons. But what he didn't talk about was whether it actually had any such weapons. Kang Suk Ju also accused the United States, the Japanese diplomat said, of "threatening North Korea's survival." Kang then produced a list of the United States' alleged failures to meet its own obligations under the 1994 agreement, and offered to shut down the enrichment program in return for an American promise not to attack and a commitment to normalize relations. Kelly, constrained by his instructions, could only restate his brief: the North Koreans must act first. The impasse was on.

But, as with the June C.I.A. report, the Administration kept quiet about what had happened in Pyongyang. It did not inform the public until October 16th, five days after Congress voted to authorize military force against Iraq. Even then, according to Administration sources quoted in the *Washington Post*, the Administration went public only after learning that the North Korean reaction—with obvious implications for the debate on Iraq—was being leaked to the press. On the CBS program *Face the Nation* on October 20th, Condoleezza Rice denied that news of the Kelly meeting had been deliberately withheld until after the vote. President Bush, she said, simply hadn't been presented with options until October 15th. "What was surprising to us was not that there was a program," Rice said. "What was surprising to us was that the North Koreans admitted there was a program."

"Did we *want* them to deny it?" a former American intelligence expert on North Korea asked me afterward. He said, "I could never understand what was going on with the North Korea policy." Referring to relations between the intelligence service and the Bush Administration, he said, "We couldn't get people's attention, and, even if we could, they never had a sensible approach. The Administration was deeply, viciously ideological." It was contemptuous not only of the Pyongyang government but of earlier efforts by the Clinton White House to address the problem of nuclear proliferation—a problem that could only get worse if Washington ignored it. The former intelligence official told me, "When it came time to confront North Korea, we had no plan, no contact—nothing to negotiate with. You have to be in constant diplomatic contact, so you can engage and be in the strongest position to solve the problem. But we let it all fall apart."

The result was that in October as in June, the Administration had no option except to deny that there was a crisis. When the first published reports of the Kelly meeting appeared, Rice repeatedly emphasized that North Korea and Iraq were separate cases. "Saddam Hussein is in a category by himself," Rice said on ABC's *Nightline*. One arms-control official told me, "The White House didn't want to deal with a second crisis."

In the following months, the American policy alternated between tough talk in public—vows that the Administration wouldn't be "blackmailed," or even meet with North Korean leaders—and private efforts, through third parties, to open an indirect line of communication with Pyongyang. North Korea, meanwhile, expelled international inspectors, renounced the nonproliferation treaty, and threatened to once again begin reprocessing spent nuclear fuel.

In a speech in June 2002, Robert Gallucci, a diplomat who was put in charge of negotiating the 1994 agreement with Pyongyang, and who is now dean of the School of Foreign Service at Georgetown University, recalled that Bush's first approach to North Korea had been to make it "a poster child" for the Administration's arguments for a missile-defense system. "This was the cutting edge of the threat against which we were planning and shaping our defense," he said. "There was a belief that North Korea was not to be dealt with by negotiation.

"But then September 11th happened, and September 11th

meant that national missile defense could not defend America, because the threat was going to come not from missiles but from a hundred other ways as well," he said. "And so we've come full circle. . . . North Korea and other rogue states who threaten us with weapons of mass destruction threaten not only because they themselves might not be deterrable but because they may transfer this capability to those who can't be deterred or defended against."

In an interview with me in early 2004, Gallucci called A. Q. Khan "the Johnny Appleseed" of the nuclear-arms race. Gallucci, who was a consultant to the C.I.A. on proliferation issues, told me, "Bad as it is with Iran, North Korea, and Libya having nuclear-weapons material, the worst part is that they could transfer it to a non-state group. That's the biggest concern, and the scariest thing about all this—that Pakistan could work with the worst terrorist groups on Earth to build nuclear weapons. There's nothing more important than stopping terrorist groups from getting nuclear weapons. The most dangerous country for the United States now is Pakistan, and second is Iran." Gallucci went on: "We haven't been this vulnerable since the British burned Washington in 1814."

3. Washington's Deal

On February 4, 2004, Dr. A. Q. Khan appeared on Pakistan's state-run television network in Islamabad and confessed that he had been solely responsible for operating an international black market in nuclear-weapons materials. The broadcast came after a series of revelations about the nuclear programs of Iran and Libya, which included evidence that both countries had received nuclear materials from Pakistan. Khan's confession was accepted by a stony-faced Pervez Musharraf, who had dressed for the occasion not in the civilian clothes he often wore as president but in commando fatigues.

The next day, on television again, Musharraf, who claimed to be shocked by Khan's misdeeds, nonetheless pardoned him, citing his service to Pakistan (he called Khan "my hero"). Musharraf told the *New York Times* that he had received a specific accounting of Khan's activities in Iran, North Korea, and Malaysia from the United States only the previous October. "If they knew earlier, they should have told us," he said. "Maybe a lot of things would not have happened."

It was a make-believe performance in a make-believe capital. In interviews soon afterward in Islamabad, a planned city built four decades ago, politicians, diplomats, and nuclear experts dismissed the Khan confession and the Musharraf pardon with expressions of scorn and disbelief. For two decades, journalists and American and European intelligence agencies had linked Khan and the I.S.I., the Pakistani intelligence service, to nuclear-technology transfers, and it was hard to credit the idea that the government Khan served had been oblivious.

"It is state propaganda," Samina Ahmed, the director of the Islamabad office of the International Crisis Group, a nongovernmental organization that studies conflict resolution, told me. "The deal is that Khan doesn't tell what he knows. Everybody is lying. The tragedy of this whole affair is that it doesn't serve anybody's needs." Mushahid Hussain Sayed, who was a member of the Pakistani senate, said with a laugh, "America needed an offering to the gods—blood on the floor. Musharraf told A. Q., 'Bend over for a spanking.'"

A Bush Administration intelligence officer with years of experience in nonproliferation issues told me, "One thing we do know is that this was not a rogue operation. Suppose Edward Teller had suddenly decided to spread nuclear technology and equipment around the world. Do you really think he could do that without the government knowing? How do you get missiles from North Korea to Pakistan? Do you think A. Q. shipped all the centrifuges by Federal Express? The military has to be involved, at high levels." The intelligence officer went on: "We had every opportunity to put a stop to the A. Q. Khan network fifteen years ago. Some of those involved today in the smuggling are the children of those we knew about in the 1980s. It's the second generation now."

In public, the Bush Administration accepted the pardon at face value. Within hours of Musharraf's television appearance, Deputy Secretary of State Richard Armitage praised him as "the right man at the right time." Armitage added that Pakistan had been "very forthright in the last several years with us about proliferation." A White House spokesman said that the Administration valued Musharraf's assurances that "Pakistan was not involved in any of the proliferation activity." A State Department spokesman said that how to deal with Khan was "a matter for Pakistan to decide."

Musharraf had, of course, been an ally in the war on terrorism. According to past and present military and intelligence officials, however, Washington's support for the pardon of Khan was predicated on what Musharraf had agreed to do next: look the other way as the United States hunted for Osama bin Laden in a tribal area of northwest Pakistan dominated by the forbidding Hindu Kush mountain range, where he was believed to be operating. American commanders had been eager for permission to conduct major sweeps in the Hindu Kush for some time, and Musharraf had repeatedly refused them. Now, with Musharraf's agreement, the Administration was able to authorize a major spring offensive involving the movement of thousands of American troops. Musharraf proffered other help as well. A former senior intelligence official said to me, "Musharraf told us, 'We've got guys inside. The people who provide fresh fruits and vegetables and herd the goats'" for bin Laden and his Al Qaeda followers. "It's a quid pro quo: we're going to get our troops inside Pakistan in return for not forcing Musharraf to deal with Khan."

"It's going to be a full-court press," one Pentagon planner told me in early 2004. The plans called for some of the most highly skilled Special Forces units, such as Task Force 121, to be shifted from Iraq to Pakistan. Special Forces personnel around the world were briefed on their new assignments, one military adviser told me, and in some cases were given "warning orders"—the stage before being sent into combat.

A large-scale American military presence in Pakistan could create an uproar in the country and weaken Musharraf's already tenuous hold on power. The operation represents a tremendous gamble for him personally and, by extension, for the Bush Administration—if he fell, his successor might be far less friendly to the United States. One of Musharraf's most vocal critics inside Pakistan is retired Army Lieutenant General Hamid Gul, a fundamentalist Muslim who directed the I.S.I. from 1987 to 1989, at the height of the Afghan war with the Soviets. If American troops start operating from Pakistan, there will be "a rupture in the relationship," Gul told me in early 2004. "Americans think others are slaves to them." Referring to the furor over A. Q. Khan, he added, "We may be in a jam, but we are a very honorable nation. We will not allow the American troops to come here. This will be the breaking point." If Musharraf had made an agreement about letting American troops operate in Pakistan, Gul said, "he's lying to you."

The greatest risk may have been not to Musharraf, or to the stability of South Asia, but to the ability of the international nuclear monitoring institutions to do their work. Many experts fear that, with Khan's help, the world has moved closer to a nuclear tipping point. After his pardon, the former senior intelligence official told me, analysts throughout the American intelligence community were asking, "How could it be that Pakistan's done all these things—developed a second generation of miniaturized and boosted weapons—and yet the investigation has been shorted to ground?" His own assessment was blunt. He told me, "Khan was willing to sell blueprints, centrifuges, and the latest in weaponry. He was the worst nuclear-arms proliferator in the world and he's pardoned—with not a squeak from the White House."

*   *   *

In December 2003, President Bush and Prime Minister Tony Blair
jointly announced that Muammar Qaddafi, the Libyan leader, had
decided to give up his nuclear-weapons program and would permit
inspectors from the I.A.E.A. to enter his country. The surprise announcement, the culmination of nine months of secret talks, was
followed immediately by a six-day inspection by the I.A.E.A., the
first of many inspections, and the public unveiling of the role of yet
another country, Malaysia, in the nuclear black market. Libya had
been able to purchase hundreds of millions of dollars' worth of nuclear parts, including advanced centrifuges designed in Pakistan,
from a firm in Malaysia, with a free-trade zone in Dubai serving as
the main shipping point. It was a new development in an old arms
race: Malaysia, a high-tech nation with no indigenous nuclear ambitions, was retailing sophisticated nuclear gear, based on designs
made available by A. Q. Khan.

The centrifuge materials that the inspectors found in Libya had
not been assembled—in most cases, in fact, the goods were still in their
shipping cases. "I am not impressed by what I've seen," a senior nonproliferation official told me. "It was not a well-developed program—
not a serious research-and-development approach to make use of what
they bought. It was useless. But I was absolutely struck by what the
Libyans were able to buy. What's on the market is absolutely horrendous. It's a Mafia-type business, with corruption and secrecy."

I.A.E.A. inspectors, to their dismay, even found in Libya precise
blueprints for the design and construction of a half-ton nuclear
weapon. "It's a sweet little bomb, put together by engineers who
know how to assemble a weapon," an official in Vienna told me.
"No question it'll work. Just dig a hole and test it. It's too big and
too heavy for a Scud, but it'll go into a family car. It's a terrorist's
dream."

In a speech on February 5, 2004, at Georgetown University,
George Tenet hailed the developments in Libya as an American intelligence coup. Tenet said, "We learned of all this through the pow-

erful combination of technical intelligence, careful and painstaking analytic work, operational daring, and, yes, the classic kind of human intelligence that people have led you to believe we no longer have." But interviews with former C.I.A. officials and with two men who worked closely with Libyan intelligence present a different story.

Qaddafi had been seeking a reconciliation with the West for years, with limited success. Then, a former C.I.A. operations officer told me, Musa Kusa, the longtime head of Libyan intelligence, urged Qaddafi to meet with Western intelligence agencies and open up his weapons arsenal to international inspection. The C.I.A. man quoted Kusa as explaining that, as the war with Iraq drew near, he had warned Qaddafi, "You are nuts if you think you can defeat the United States. Get out of it now. Surrender now and hope they accept your surrender."

One Arab intelligence operative told me that Libyan intelligence, with Qaddafi's approval, then quickly offered to give American and British intelligence details about a centrifuge deal that was already under way. The parts were due to be shipped aboard a German freighter, the *BBC China*. In October, the freighter was seized, and the incident was proclaimed a major intelligence success. But, the operative said, it was "the Libyans who blew up the Pakistanis," and who made the role of Khan's black market known. The Americans, he said, asked "questions about those orders and Libya said it had them." It was, in essence, a sting, and was perceived that way by Musharraf. He was enraged by what he called, in a nationally televised speech last month—delivered in Urdu, and not officially translated by the Pakistani government—the betrayal of Pakistan by his "Muslim brothers." There was little loyalty between seller and buyer. "The Pakistanis took a lot of Libya's money and gave second-grade plans," the Arab intelligence operative said. "It was halfhearted."

The intelligence operative went on, "Qaddafi is very pragmatic and studied the timing. It was the right time. The United States wanted to have a success story, and he banked on that."

* * *

Mohamed ElBaradei, the I.A.E.A.'s director general, told me, in an interview at the organization's headquarters in Vienna in early 2004, that the key nonproliferation issue had become the threat from terrorist groups and other non-state actors. "I have a nightmare that the spread of enriched uranium and nuclear material could result in the operation of a small enrichment facility in a place like northern Afghanistan," he said. "Who knows? It's not hard for a non-state to hide, especially if there is a state in collusion with it. Some of these non-state groups are very sophisticated."

Many of the other diplomats I spoke to in Vienna at the time expressed frustration at the I.A.E.A.'s inability, thanks to Musharraf's pardon, to gain access to Khan. "It's not going to happen," one diplomat said. "We are getting some coöperation from Pakistan, but it's the names we need to know. 'Who got the stuff?' We're interested to know whether other nations that we're supposed to supervise have the stuff." The diplomat told me he believed that the United States was unwilling to publicly state the obvious: that there was no way the Pakistani government didn't know about the transfers. He said, "Of course it looks awful, but Musharraf will be indebted to you."

The I.A.E.A.'s authority to conduct inspections is limited. The nations that have signed the nonproliferation treaty are required to permit systematic I.A.E.A. inspections of their declared nuclear facilities for research and energy production. But there is no mechanism for the inspection of suspected nuclear-weapons sites, and many at the I.A.E.A. believe that the treaty must be modified. "There is a nuclear network of black-market centrifuges and weapons design that the world has yet to discover," a diplomat in Vienna told me. In the past, he said, the I.A.E.A. had worked under the assumption that nations would cheat on the nonproliferation treaty "to produce and sell their own nuclear material." He said, "What we have instead is a black-market network capable of producing usable nuclear materials and nuclear devices that is not limited to any one nation. We have nuclear dealers operating outside our front door, and we have no control over them—no matter how good we are in terms of verification."

There would be no need, in other words, for A. Q. Khan or anyone else in Pakistan to have a direct role in supplying nuclear technology. The most sensitive nuclear equipment would be available to any country—or any person or group, presumably—that had enough cash. "This is a question of survival," the diplomat said, with a caustic smile. He added, "Iraq is laughable in comparison with this issue. The Bush Administration was hunting the shadows instead of the prey."

Another nonproliferation official depicted the challenge facing the I.A.E.A. inspection regime as "a seismic shift—the globalization of the nuclear world." The official said, "We have to move from inspecting declared sites to 'Where does this shit come from?' If we stay focussed on the declared, we miss the nuclear supply matrix." At this point, the international official asked me, in all seriousness, "Why hasn't A. Q. Khan been taken out by Israel or the United States?"

Husain Haani, who was a special assistant to three prime ministers before Musharraf came to power and is a visiting scholar at the Carnegie Endowment for International Peace, noted when we spoke in early 2004, with some pride, that his nation had managed to make the bomb despite American sanctions. But, he told me, Khan and his colleagues had gone wholesale: "Once they had the bomb, they had a shopping list of what to buy and where. A. Q. Khan can bring a plain piece of paper and show me how to get it done—the countries, people, and telephone numbers. 'This is the guy in Russia who can get you small quantities of enriched uranium. You in Malaysia will manufacture the stuff. Here's who will miniaturize the warhead. And then go to North Korea and get the damn missile.'" He added, "This is not a few scientists pocketing money and getting rich. It's a state policy."

Haani depicted Musharraf as truly "on the American side," in terms of resisting Islamic extremism, but, he said, "he doesn't know *how* to be on the American side. The same guys in the I.S.I. who have done this in the last twenty years he expects to be his partners. These are people who've done nothing but covert operations: One, screw India. Two, deceive America. Three, expand Pakistan's influence in the Islamic community. And, four, continue to spread nuclear technology." He paused. "Musharraf is trying to put out the fire with the help of the people who started the fire," he said.

"Much of this has been known for decades to the American intelligence community," Haani added. "Sometimes you know things and don't want to do anything about it. Americans need to know that your government is not only downplaying this but covering it up. You go to bed with our I.S.I. They know how to suck up to you. You let us get away with everything. Why can't you be more honest? There's no harm in telling us the truth—'Look, you're an ally but a very disturbing ally.' You have to nip some of these things in the bud."

In January 2004, Musharraf insisted once again, this time at the World Economic Forum in Davos, Switzerland, that he would not permit American troops to search for Al Qaeda members inside Pakistan. "That is not a possibility at all," he said. "It is a very sensitive issue. There is no room for any foreign elements coming and assisting us. We don't need any assistance."

Nonetheless, a senior Pentagon adviser told me that, as of mid-February, the spring offensive was on. The operation, American officials said, was scheduled to involve the redeployment to South Asia of thousands of American soldiers, including members of Task Force 121. The logistical buildup began in mid-February, as more than a dozen American C-17 cargo planes began daily flights, hauling helicopters, vehicles, and other equipment to military bases in Pakistan. Small teams of American Special Forces units had been stationed in northwestern Pakistan since the beginning of the Afghanistan war in the fall of 2001.

The senior Pentagon adviser, like other military and intelligence officials I talked to at the time, was cautious about the chances of getting what the White House wants—Osama bin Laden. "It's anybody's guess," he said, adding that ops sec—operational security—for the planned offensive was poor. The former senior intelligence official similarly noted that there was concern inside the Joint Special Operations Command, at Fort Bragg, North Carolina, over the reliability of intercepted Al Qaeda telephone calls. "What about deception?" he said. "These guys are not dumb, and once the logistical aircraft begin to appear"—the American C-17s that had been landing at an airbase in Pakistan—"you know something is going on."

"We've got to get Osama bin Laden, and we know where he is," the former senior intelligence official said at the time. Osama bin Laden was "communicating through SIGINT"—talking on satellite telephones and the like—"and his wings have been clipped. He's in his own Alamo in northern Pakistan. It's a natural progress—whittling down alternative locations and then targeting him. This is not, in theory, a 'Let's go and hope' kind of thing. They've seen what they think is him." But the former official added that there were reasons to be cautious about such reports, especially given that bin Laden hadn't been seen for so long.

Two former C.I.A. operatives with firsthand knowledge of the Pakistan-Afghanistan border areas said that the American assault, if it did take place, would confront enormous logistical problems. "It's impenetrable," said Robert Baer, who visited the Hindu Kush area in the early 1990s, before he was assigned to lead the C.I.A.'s anti-Saddam operations in northern Iraq. "There are no roads, and you can't get armor up there. This is where Alexander the Great lost an entire division. The Russians didn't even bother to go up there. Everybody's got a gun. That area is worse than Iraq." Milton Bearden recounted, "I've been all through there. The Pashtun population in that belt has lived there longer than almost any other ethnic group has lived anywhere on Earth." He said, "Our intelligence has got to be better than it's been. Anytime we go into something driven entirely by electoral politics, it doesn't work out."

One American intelligence consultant noted that American forces in Afghanistan had crossed into Pakistan in "hot pursuit" of Al Qaeda suspects in previous operations, with no complaints from the Pakistani leadership. If the American forces struck quickly and decisively against bin Laden from within Pakistan, he added, "Musharraf could say he gave no advance authorization. We can move in with so much force and firepower—with so much shock and awe—that we will be too fast for him." The consultant said, "The question is, how deep into Pakistan can we pursue him?" He added, "Musharraf is in a very tough position."

At home, Musharraf was still in danger over his handling of the nuclear affair. Chaudry Nisar Ali Khan, a former government minister who now heads an opposition party, said, "Pakistani public opinion feels that A. Q. has been made a scapegoat, and international opinion thinks he's a threat. This is a no-win situation for Musharraf. The average man feels that there will be a nuclear rollback, and Pakistan's immediate deterrent will be taken away. It comes down to an absolute disaster for Musharraf." He added, "He's opened up Pandora's box, and he will never be able to manage it."

———

The American task force did come to Pakistan in the spring of 2004, as I wrote, but very secretly—and only after Musharraf staged a puzzling offensive of his own in the Hundu Kush. In mid-March, the Pakistani government announced that hundreds of its troops were engaged in a bitter battle against Al Qaeda forces and other terrorists. Musharraf himself told a CNN interviewer that he was sure "there's a high-value target" in the area, and government aides encouraged speculation that Dr. Ayman al-Zawahiri, bin Laden's most senior deputy, was about to be seized—if not bin Laden himself.

Over the next two weeks, the Pakistani army fought a series of battles against what were said to be hundreds of militants, with heavy casualties on both sides. In the end, no senior Al Qaeda were captured and, despite much speculation in the international press, it wasn't clear who was fighting who, or why. As the *New York Times* put it, "What exactly had happened in the isolated corner of Pakistan where the battle had raged was a riddle" and that "the pivotal question centered on Pakistan's army: Just how hard was it really trying to capture and kill terrorists?" One possibility, of course, was that the always-careful Musharraf was putting up a smokescreen to mask the American Special Forces that were to come. Those commandos, members of Admiral McRaven's Task Force 121, remained on the hunt inside the Pakistani border for bin Laden throughout the spring and summer of 2004, while Musharraf was able to survive political pressure from the Army and the intelligence service. As the months passed, however, and the American presidential elections grew closer, the crucial question remained: where was Osama bin Laden?

VIII.

THE MIDDLE EAST AFTER 9/11

The specter of an American failure in Iraq has created new anxieties and new alliances, and reshaped the politics of the Middle East. Before the war, the neoconservatives in the Bush Administration had convinced themselves—and the President and Vice President—that the road to Middle East democratization and peace ran through Baghdad. Once the regime of Saddam Hussein was cast aside, they argued, democracy would spread among all factions in Iraq and move on to Iran, Syria, Saudi Arabia, and Lebanon. Countries across the region would renounce terrorism and embrace the West. Israelis also welcomed the invasion because the United States, its best ally, was now much more present in the Middle East.

Things did not work out as planned; terrorism, instead of democracy, is now spreading through the region. The stories that follow are about nations with one essential element in common: they present challenges that the Bush Administration, driven by its obsession with Iraq, has been unwilling to address. In Saudi Arabia, a corrupt royal family is implicated in the movement that opposes it; Iran, now the dominant power in the region, is on the verge of becoming a nuclear power as well; and Syria is torn between wanting to work with the West and its self-proclaimed role as a pan-Arab leader. The Israelis also are disaffected, and seeking a risky new partnership with Kurdistan, while Syria, Iran, and Turkey have put aside their regional rivalries to form a new alliance. All of these countries have been directly affected by the chaos in the region, for which the Bush Administration seems to have few answers. The result: heightened tension and heightened danger.

1. Saudi Arabia: Corruption and Compromise

Beginning in 1994 or earlier, the National Security Agency collected electronic intercepts of conversations between members of the Saudi Arabian royal family, which is headed by King Fahd. The intercepts depicted a regime increasingly corrupt, alienated from the country's religious rank and file, and so weakened and frightened that it had brokered its future by channelling hundreds of millions of dollars in what amounted to protection money to fundamentalist groups that wished to overthrow it.

The intercepts demonstrated to analysts that by 1996 Saudi money was supporting Osama bin Laden's Al Qaeda and other extremist groups in Afghanistan, Lebanon, Yemen, and Central Asia and throughout the Persian Gulf region. "Ninety-six is the key year," one American intelligence official told me. "Bin Laden hooked up to all the bad guys—it's like the Grand Alliance." As bin Laden became, more and more, "a lethal force to be dealt with," the Saudi regime, he said, had "gone to the dark side."

In interviews soon after September 11th, current and former intelligence and military officials portrayed the instability of the Saudi regime—and the vulnerability of its oil reserves to terrorist attack—as the most immediate threat to American economic and political interests in the Middle East. The officials also said that the Bush

Administration, like the Clinton Administration, was refusing to confront this reality, even in the aftermath of the terrorist attacks.

The Saudis and the Americans arranged a meeting between Defense Secretary Donald Rumsfeld and King Fahd during a visit by Rumsfeld to Saudi Arabia shortly before the beginning of the air war in Afghanistan, in October 2001, and pictures of the meeting were transmitted around the world. The United States, however, knew that King Fahd had been incapacitated since suffering a severe stroke, in late 1995. A Saudi adviser told me at the time of the visit that the king, with round-the-clock medical treatment, was able to sit in a chair and open his eyes, but was usually unable to recognize even his oldest friends. Fahd was being kept on the throne, the National Security Agency intercepts indicate, because of a bitter family power struggle. Fahd's nominal successor is Crown Prince Abdullah, his half brother, who was to some extent the de facto ruler; he and Prince Sultan, the defense minister, were the people Rumsfeld really came to see. But there was infighting about money: Abdullah had been urging his fellow princes to address the problem of corruption in the kingdom— unsuccessfully, according to the intercepts. "The only reason Fahd's being kept alive is so Abdullah can't become king," a former White House adviser told me.

The American intelligence officials were particularly angered, early on, by the refusal of the Saudis to help the F.B.I. and the C.I.A. run "traces"—that is, name checks and other background information— on the nineteen men, fifteen of them believed to be from Saudi Arabia, who took part in the attacks on the World Trade Center and the Pentagon. "They knew that once we started asking for a few traces the list would grow," one former official said. "It's better to shut it down right away." He pointed out that thousands of disaffected Saudis had joined fundamentalist groups throughout the Middle East. A month after the attacks, a senior intelligence official confirmed the lack of Saudi coöperation and told me, angrily, that the Saudis "have only one constant—and it's keeping themselves in power."

*   *   *

The N.S.A. intercepts revealed the hypocrisy of many in the Saudi royal family, and why the family had become increasingly estranged from the vast majority of its subjects. Over the years, unnerved by the growing strength of the fundamentalist movement, it failed to deal with the underlying issues of severe unemployment and inadequate education, in a country in which half the population is under the age of eighteen. Saudi Arabia's strict interpretation of Islam, known as Wahhabism, and its use of *mutawwa'in*—religious police —to enforce prayer, was rivalled only by the Taliban's. And yet for years the tabloid newspapers have been filled with accounts of the Saudi princes—there are thousands of them—going on drinking binges and partying with prostitutes, while taking billions of dollars from the state budget. The N.S.A. intercepts were more specific. In one call, Prince Nayef, who has served for more than two decades as interior minister, urged a subordinate to withhold from the police evidence of the hiring of prostitutes, presumably by members of the royal family. According to the summary, Nayef said that he didn't want the "client list" released under any circumstances.

The intercepts produced a stream of sometimes humdrum but often riveting intelligence from the telephone calls of several senior members of the royal family, including Abdullah; Nayef; Sultan, whose son Prince Bandar has been the Saudi ambassador to the United States since 1983; and Prince Salman, the governor of Riyadh, Saudi Arabia's capital. There was constant telephoning about King Fahd's health after his stroke, and scrambling to take advantage of the situation. On January 8, 1997, Prince Sultan told Bandar about a flight that he and Salman had shared with the king. Sultan complained that the king "barely spoke to anyone," according to the summary of the intercept, because he was "too medicated." The King, Sultan added, was "a prisoner on the plane."

Sultan's comments became much more significant a few days later, when the N.S.A. intercepted a conversation in which Sultan told Bandar that the king had agreed to a complicated exchange of fighter aircraft with the United States that would bring five F-16s into the Royal Saudi Air Force. Fahd was evidently incapable of making such an agreement, or of preventing anyone from dropping his name in a money-making deal.

In the intercepts, princes talk openly about bilking the state, and even argue about what is an acceptable percentage to take. Other calls indicate that Prince Bandar, while serving as ambassador, was involved in arms deals in London, Yemen, and the Soviet Union that generated millions of dollars in "commissions." In a PBS *Frontline* interview broadcast on October 9, 2001, Bandar, asked about the reports of corruption in the royal family, was almost upbeat in his response. The family had spent nearly $400 billion to develop Saudi Arabia, he said. "If you tell me that building this whole country . . . we misused or got corrupted with fifty billion, I'll tell you, 'Yes.' . . . So what? We did not invent corruption, nor did those dissidents, who are so genius, discover it."

The intercepts made clear, however, that Crown Prince Abdullah was insistent on stemming the corruption. In November of 1996, for example, he complained about the billions of dollars that were being diverted by royal family members from a huge state-financed project to renovate the mosque in Mecca. He urged the princes to get their off-budget expenses under control; such expenses are known as the hiding place for payoff money. (Despite its oil revenues, Saudi Arabia has run a budget deficit in every year but one in the last two decades, and now has a large national debt.) A few months later, according to the intercepts, Abdullah blocked a series of real estate deals by one of the princes, enraging members of the royal family. Abdullah further alarmed the princes by issuing a decree declaring that his sons would not be permitted to go into partnerships with foreign companies working in the kingdom.

Abdullah was viewed by Sultan and other opponents as a leader who could jeopardize the kingdom's most special foreign relationship—someone who is willing to penalize the United States, and its oil and gas companies, because of Washington's support for Israel. In an intercept dated July 13, 1997, Prince Sultan called Bandar in Washington and informed him that he had told Abdullah "not to be so confrontational with the United States."

The Fahd regime was a major financial backer of the Reagan Administration's anti-communist campaign in Latin America and of its successful proxy war in Afghanistan against the Soviet Union. Oil money bought the Saudis enormous political access and leverage in Washington. Working through Prince Bandar, they contributed hundreds of millions of dollars to charities and educational programs in the United States. American construction and oil companies do billions of dollars' worth of business every year with Saudi Arabia, which is the world's largest oil producer. (As of the end of 2000, Halliburton, the Texas-based oil-supply business formerly headed by Vice President Dick Cheney, was operating a number of subsidiaries in Saudi Arabia.)

In the Clinton era, the White House did business as usual with the Saudis, urging them to buy American goods, like Boeing aircraft. The kingdom was seen as an American advocate among the oil-producing nations of the Middle East. The C.I.A. was discouraged from conducting any risky intelligence operations inside the country and, according to one former official, did little recruiting among the Saudi population, which limited the U.S. government's knowledge of the growth of the opposition to the royal family.

In 1994, Mohammed al-Khilewi, the first secretary at the Saudi Mission to the United Nations, defected and sought political asylum in the United States. He brought with him, according to his New York lawyer, Michael J. Wildes, some fourteen thousand internal government documents depicting the Saudi royal family's corruption, human rights abuses, and financial support for terrorists. He claimed to have evidence that the Saudis had given financial and technical support to

Hamas, the extremist Islamic group whose target is Israel. There was a meeting at the lawyer's office with two F.B.I. agents and an assistant U.S. attorney. "We gave them a sampling of the documents and put them on the table," Wildes told me a month after September 11th. "But the agents refused to accept them." He and his client heard nothing further from federal authorities. Al-Khilewi was granted asylum and began living under cover.

The Saudis were also shielded from Washington's foreign policy bureaucracy. A government expert on Saudi affairs told me that Prince Bandar dealt exclusively with the men at the top, and never met with desk officers and the like. "Only a tiny handful of people inside the government are familiar with U.S.-Saudi relations," he explained. "And that is purposeful."

In the aftermath of the terrorist attacks in New York and Washington, the royal family repeatedly insisted that Saudi Arabia had made no contributions to radical Islamic groups. When the Saudis were confronted by press reports that some of the substantial funds that the monarchy routinely gave to Islamic charities may actually have gone to Al Qaeda and other terrorist networks, they denied any knowledge of such transfers. Prince Sultan repeated the mantra in his news conference with Rumsfeld on October 3rd, saying that Saudi Arabia "does not approve by any means and does not agree by any means to the support of terrorism, and there is nobody in the Kingdom of Saudi Arabia who funds such groups."

The intercepts, however, have led many in the intelligence community to conclude otherwise. For example, according to an official with knowledge of their contents, the intercepts show that the Saudi government, working through Prince Salman, contributed millions to charities that, in turn, relayed the money to fundamentalists. "We knew that Salman was supporting all of the causes," the official told me.

On July 31, 1996, the N.S.A. intercepted an encrypted message from Iranian intelligence revealing that Abdullah Nuri, a fundamentalist radical then waging political war inside Tajikistan, had attended a meeting in Iran with Osama bin Laden (described by the Iranians as "the head of the Islamic movement in Saudi Arabia"). At the meeting, the intercept reported, bin Laden asked Nuri "to abandon the civil war against the leadership in Tajikistan and fight the United States." Bin Laden sent a similar message to a leading Egyptian terrorist. By then or soon after, the American intelligence community had more than enough raw intelligence to conclude that both Nuri and bin Laden were receiving money from prominent Saudis.

The Bush Administration chose not to confront the Saudi leadership over its financial support of terror organizations and its refusal initially to help in the investigation. "As far as the Saudi Arabians go, they've been nothing but coöperative," President Bush said at a news conference on September 24, 2001. The following day, the Saudis agreed to formally cut off diplomatic relations with the Taliban leadership in Afghanistan. Eight days later, at a news conference in Saudi Arabia with Prince Sultan, the defense minister, Rumsfeld was asked if he had given the Saudis a list of the September 11th terrorist suspects for processing by their intelligence agencies. Rumsfeld, who had been admired by many in the press for his bluntness, answered evasively: "I am, as I said, not involved with the Federal Bureau of Investigation that is conducting the investigation. . . . I have every reason to believe that that relationship between our two countries is as close—that any information I am sure has been made available to the Kingdom of Saudi Arabia."

The Saudis gave Rumsfeld something in return—permission for U.S. forces to use a command-and-control center, built before the Gulf War, in the pending air war against the Taliban. In the preceding years, the Saudis had also allowed the United States to use forward bases on Saudi soil for special operations, as long as there was no public mention of the arrangements.

The American military action in Afghanistan triggered alarm in the international oil community and among intelligence officials who had been briefed on a C.I.A. study, put together in the mid-1980s, of the vulnerability of the Saudi fields to terrorist attack, which was then still secret. The report was "so sensitive," a former C.I.A. officer told me, "that it was put on typed paper," and not into the agency's computer system, meaning that distribution was limited to a select few. According to someone who saw the report, it concluded that with only a small amount of explosives terrorists could take the oil fields off line for two years.

The concerns, both in the United States and in Saudi Arabia, about the security of the fields became more urgent than ever after September 11th. A former high-level intelligence official depicted the Saudi rulers as nervously "sitting on a keg of dynamite"—that is, the oil reserves. "They're petrified that somebody's going to light the fuse."

"The United States is hostage to the stability of the Saudi system," a prominent Middle Eastern oil man, who did not wish to be cited by name, told me in an interview a few weeks after the attacks. "It's time to start facing the truth. The war was declared by bin Laden, but there are thousands of bin Ladens. They are setting the game—the agenda. It's a new form of war. This fabulous military machine you have is completely useless." The oil man, who has worked closely with the Saudi leadership for three decades, added, "I've talked to these people. I've listened to them. People like me have been deceiving you. We talk about how you don't understand Islam, but it's a vanilla analysis. We try to please you, but we've been aggrieved for years."

The Saudi regime "will explode in time," the oil man said. "It has been playing a delicate game." As for the terrorists responsible for the September 11th attacks, he said, "Now they decide the timing. If they do a similar operation in Saudi Arabia, the price of oil will go up to $100 a barrel." He went on, "This is a complicated issue and it's hard work. You need to understand the subtleties. But there is no one, I can assure you, from George Bush to Colin Powell who can sit with you and give you an analysis of the Islamic world, and they're the decision makers. I'm afraid that this will reach a point where no American will be able to walk the streets in a fundamentalist society."

In the 1980s, in an effort to relieve political pressure on the regime, the Saudi leadership relinquished some of its authority to the *mutawwa'in* and permitted them to have a greater role in day-to-day life. One U.S. government Saudi expert complained in October 2001 that religious leaders had been allowed to take control of the press and the educational system. "Today, two-thirds of the Saudi Ph.D.s are in Islamic studies," a former presidential aide told me. There was little attempt over the years by American diplomats or the White House to moderate the increasingly harsh rhetoric about the United States. "The United States was caught up in private agreements"—with the Saudi princes—"while this shit was spewing in the Saudi press," the former aide said. "That was a huge mistake."

A senior American diplomat who served many years in Saudi Arabia recalled his foreboding upon attending a training exercise at the kingdom's most prestigious military academy, in Riyadh: "It was hot, and I watched the cadets doing drills. The officers were lounging inside a *suradiq*"—a large pavilion—"with cold drinks, calling out orders on loudspeakers. I thought to myself, How many of these young men would follow and die for these officers?" The diplomat said he came away from his most recent tour in Saudi Arabia convinced that "it wouldn't take too much for a group of twenty or thirty fundamentalist enlisted men to take charge. How would the kingdom deal with the shock of something ruthless, small, highly motivated, and of great velocity?"

"The Saudis have been indulged for so many decades," the diplomat went on. "They are so spoiled. They've always had it their way. There's hardly anything we could say that would impede the 'majestic instancy' of their progress. We're their janissaries." He was referring to the captives who became élite troops of the Ottoman Empire.

"The policy dilemma is this," a senior general told me. "How do we help the Saudis make a transition without throwing them over the side?" Referring to young fundamentalists who have been demonstrating in the Saudi streets, he said, "The kids are bigger than the daddy."

2. Syria: A Lost Opportunity

On the night of June 18th, 2003, Task Force 20, an American Special Operations team stationed in Iraq, expanded its operations dozens of miles inside Syria. Military intelligence had observed large numbers of cars and trucks speeding toward the border, and senior officers suspected that the vehicles were carrying fleeing members of the Iraqi leadership. Communications intercepts had indicated that there were more Syrian soldiers congregated along the border than usual, including some officers. The military concluded, according to a senior Administration official, that "something down there was going on." Two days earlier, one of Saddam Hussein's closest aides, Abid Hamid Mahmud, had been captured, and told his interrogators that he and Saddam's two sons had sought refuge in Syria but were turned back. Although the Syrian government denied knowledge of the brothers' whereabouts, the military was now ready to cross the border to stop any future flight attempts. Sometime after midnight, Army helicopters and Bradley Fighting Vehicles attacked two groups of cars heading into Syria, triggering enormous explosions and fireballs that lit up the night sky. A gas station and nearby homes were destroyed. Task Force 20 sped across the border into Syria. Five Syrian guards were injured and flown to Iraq in American helicopters for medical treatment, and several other Syrians were seized, handcuffed, and detained before being released.

Pentagon officials subsequently praised the nighttime mission. "I'm confident we had very good intelligence," Air Force General Richard B. Myers, chairman of the Joint Chiefs of Staff, said at a Pentagon news conference on June 24th. Secretary of Defense Donald Rumsfeld told reporters, "There were reasons, good reasons, to believe that the vehicles that were violating the curfew that existed in that area were doing it for reasons other than normal commerce." Asked if he believed that senior Iraqi leaders had been killed in the raid, Rumsfeld said, "We're trying to find out."

In fact, according to current and former American military and diplomatic officials, the operation was a fiasco in which as many as eighty people—occupants of the cars and trucks as well as civilians living nearby—were killed. The vehicles, it turned out, were being used to smuggle gasoline. The Syrian government said little publicly about the violation of its sovereignty, even when the Pentagon delayed the repatriation of the injured Syrian border guards—reporters were told that the guards had not been fully interrogated—for ten days.

Weeks later, questions about the raid remained: Why had American forces crossed the border? And why had the Syrian response been so muted? An American consultant who had recently returned from Iraq said, "I don't mind so much what we did, but it's the incompetence with which we did it." The next month, two retired veterans of the C.I.A.'s clandestine service, Vincent Cannistraro and Philip Giraldi, who consulted on intelligence issues, noted in a newsletter for their private clients that the attacks had been based on "fragmentary and ambiguous" information and had led to increased tension between Rumsfeld and the C.I.A. director, George Tenet.

Tenet's involvement was significant. American intelligence and State Department officials told me that by early 2002 Syria had emerged as one of the C.I.A.'s most effective intelligence allies in the fight against Al Qaeda, providing an outpouring of information that came to an end only with the invasion of Iraq. Tenet had become one of Syria's champions in the interagency debate over how to deal with its government. His antagonists include civilians in the Pentagon who viewed Syria, despite its intelligence help, as part of the problem. "Tenet has prevented all kinds of action against Syria," one diplomat with knowledge of the interagency discussions told me.

Syria is one of seven nations listed by the State Department as sponsors of terrorism. It has been on the list since 1979, in large part because of its public support for Hezbollah, the radical Islamic party that controls much of southern Lebanon. Hezbollah claimed responsibility for, among other acts, the 1983 bombing of the American Marine barracks in Beirut, which left two hundred and forty-one Marines dead. Syria has also allowed Hamas and Palestinian Islamic Jihad, two groups that have staged numerous suicide bombings inside Israel, to maintain offices in Damascus.

Nevertheless, after September 11th the Syrian leader, Bashar Assad, initiated the delivery of Syrian intelligence to the United States. The Syrians had compiled hundreds of files on Al Qaeda, including dossiers on the men who participated—and others who wanted to participate—in the September 11th attacks. Syria also penetrated Al Qaeda cells throughout the Middle East and in Arab exile communities throughout Europe. That data began flowing to C.I.A. and F.B.I. operatives.

Syria had accumulated much of its information because of Al Qaeda's ties to the Syrian Muslim Brotherhood, Islamic terrorists who have been at war with the secular Syrian government for more than two decades. Many of the September 11th hijackers had operated out of cells in Aachen and Hamburg, where Al Qaeda was working with the Brotherhood. In the late 1990s, Mohammed Atta and other Al Qaeda members, including Mohammed Haydar Zammar, who is believed to have been one of the organization's top recruiters, worked on occasion at a German firm called Tatex Trading. Tatex was infiltrated by Syrian intelligence in the 1980s; one of its shareholders was Mohammed Majed Said, who ran the Syrian intelligence directorate from 1987 to 1994. By mid-2002, Zammar was in Syrian custody.

Within weeks of the September 11th attacks, the F.B.I. and the C.I.A., with Syria's permission, began intelligence-gathering operations in Aleppo, near the Turkish border. Aleppo was the subject of Mohammed Atta's dissertation on urban planning, and he travelled there twice in the mid-1990s. "At every stage in Atta's journey is the Muslim Brotherhood," a former C.I.A. officer who served undercover in Damascus told me. "He went through Spain in touch with the Brotherhood in Hamburg." Robert Baer agreed that the Syrians had more to offer. "The Syrians know that the Saudis were involved in the financing of the Muslim Brotherhood, and they for sure know the names," Baer told me.

Syria also provided the United States with intelligence about future Al Qaeda plans. In one instance, the Syrians learned that Al Qaeda had penetrated the security services of Bahrain and had arranged for a glider loaded with explosives to be flown into a building at the U.S. Navy's 5th Fleet headquarters there. Flynt Leverett, who served on the National Security Council and later became a fellow at the Saban Center at the Brookings Institution, told me that Syria's help "let us thwart an operation that, if carried out, would have killed a lot of Americans."

Syria's efforts to help seemed to confound the Bush Administration, which was fixated on Iraq. According to many officials I spoke to, the Administration was ill prepared to take advantage of the situation and unwilling to reassess its relationship with Assad's government. Leverett told me that "the quality and quantity of information from Syria exceeded the agency's expectations." But, he said, "from the Syrians' perspective they got little in return for it."

For thirty years, Hafez Assad, Bashar Assad's father, ruled Syria through the socialist Baath Party. The journalist Thomas Friedman has described Hafez Assad as looking "like a man who had long ago been stripped of any illusions about human nature." He dealt with his opponents brutally. In 1982, after years of increasingly violent terrorist attacks throughout Syria, Hafez Assad ordered a massive military assault on the Muslim Brotherhood in the northern city of Hama. He saw the group as a threat to his control of Syria, and his forces, showing little mercy, killed at least five thousand people, many of them civilians, in a month-long battle that left the city in ruins. Shortly after the death of his father, in June 2000, Bashar took over the presidency.

Unlike his father, Bashar was routinely depicted in Western newspapers not as ruthless but as unsure, inexperienced, and unable to control a corrupt Old Guard. In June 2003, I visited him at his office in Damascus. Tall, gangly, and seemingly shy and eager to please, Assad was waiting at the door for me. He offset his tentative and somewhat fussy manner with humor. He was frank about his reasons for speaking to me: he wanted to change his image, and the image of his country. "September 11th was like out of a Hollywood movie—beyond anyone's imagination," he said. "But it was not surprising as a concept. We actually experienced innocents being killed on our streets, and we know how it feels." Syria had sent official expressions of sympathy, backed by offers to share intelligence. "We thought Al Qaeda was not different than the Muslim Brotherhood as a state of mind," Assad said.

"For us," Assad said, September 11th "was a good opportunity. The need to coöperate was very self-evident, and it was in our interest. It was also a way to improve relations." Syria hoped to get off the list of state sponsors of terrorism; its case was based in part on the fact, acknowledged by the State Department, that it hadn't been directly implicated in a terrorist act since 1986. On a practical level, removal from the list would make Syria eligible for trade and other economic aid—and arms sales—from which it was barred.

In interviews and public statements, Assad had tried to draw a distinction between international terrorists and those he called part of the "resistance" in Israel and the occupied territories, including young Palestinian suicide bombers. It is a distinction that few in the Bush Administration would endorse. Syria's enmity toward Israel has been unrelenting, as has its criticism of the United States for its support of Israel. In a typical comment, made in late March to *Al Safir*, a Lebanese newspaper, Assad declared, "No one among us trusts Israel; not the Syrians, not any other Arabs. . . . We must be very careful. Treachery and threats have always been Israeli characteristics. Through its existence, Israel always poses a threat."

Assad and his advisers—many of whom are his father's cronies—had hoped that their coöperation in the hunt for Al Qaeda would allow them to improve and redefine their relations with the United States. But there was a major obstacle: Syria's support for Hezbollah. In the fall of 2002, however, General Hassan Khalil, the head of Syria's military intelligence, told Washington that Syria was willing to discuss imposing some restrictions on the military and political activities of Hezbollah. The Syrians wanted a back channel to Washington—that is, a private means of communicating directly with the President and his key aides. The general requested that the C.I.A. be the means of back-channel communication.

The proposal went nowhere. A former State Department official told me that the C.I.A., ecstatic about the high level of coöperation with Syrian intelligence, "didn't want to destroy the 'happy talk' about Al Qaeda by dealing with all the other troubling issues in the back channel." The State Department, he added, did not like the agency's having access to U.S.-Syrian diplomatic correspondence. And the Pentagon, preoccupied with the Iraq war and ideologically hostile to Syria, vehemently opposed a back channel.

Itamar Rabinovich, a former Israeli ambassador to Washington, acknowledged at the time that he was aware of the key Syrian intel-

339 THE MIDDLE EAST AFTER 9/11

ligence role in the war against Al Qaeda, but he made it clear that Israel's distrust of Syria remained acute. Rabinovich wondered aloud whether, given the quality of their sources, the Syrians had had advance information about the September 11th plot—and failed to warn the United States. He said that under the elder Assad the Syrians had been "masters of straddling the line." He added, "Hafez negotiated with us, and he supported Hezbollah. The son is not as adept as the father, who could keep five balls in the air at the same time. Bashar can only handle three—if that. He has good intentions, but he's not in control. He can't deliver."

By early 2003, despite intense American pressure, Bashar Assad had decided that Syria would not support the invasion of Iraq. Coöperation on Al Qaeda was now a secondary issue.

In our interview, Assad said that his opposition to the war was based on principle. "Could the Iraqi people ignore an American occupation because they hated Saddam? The United States doesn't understand the society—not even the simplest analysis." His decision was also driven by internal politics. The United States had demanded, before the war, that Syria monitor and curtail the heavy flow into Iraq of smuggled arms and other military necessities from Syrian entrepreneurs—many with high-level political connections. "The U.S. had satellite photographs of the equipment and information on high-ranking Syrian officials," a foreign diplomat with close ties to Washington said. "Bashar did not cut it off. The United States got furious."

Even Assad's most hopeful supporters told me that it was not clear how much control he had over his own government. Murhaf Jouejati, a Syrian-born political scientist now at Washington's Middle East Institute, told me, "Bashar is trying to reach out to the people, and the people like him, but what stands in the way is the financially corrupt state."

Hafez Assad supported the first Gulf War, and Dennis Ross, who was President Clinton's special envoy to the Middle East, told me in mid-2003 that Bashar Assad had "bet wrong" in refusing to support the United States this time. "He got nervous after the war and sent a series of messages saying he wants peace," Ross said. He added, "Assad has to know that he won't get by on the cheap—he truly must cut off support for Hezbollah, Hamas, and the Islamic Jihad." But, Ross went on, if he did so the United States should reward him "by renewing talks on the Golan Heights"—land Israel occupied in 1967. Ross said that there was no indication that the Administration was pursuing such an approach.

Instead, in late March 2003, Rumsfeld accused Syria of supplying Iraq with night-vision goggles and other military goods. He also suggested that Iraqi weapons of mass destruction might be stashed there. Syria denied the assertions, and members of the intelligence community I spoke to characterized the evidence against Syria as highly questionable. The Syrians were rattled by the threats, in part because many in and close to the Bush Administration have been urging regime change in Damascus for years. In 2000, the Middle East Forum, a conservative Washington think tank, issued a study offering many of the same reasons for taking military action against Syria that were later invoked against Iraq. "The Defense Department pushed for the hard line on Syria," a former State Department official told me. "I think Rummy was at least testing the waters—to see how far he could go—but the White House was not ready."

In Washington, a few months into the Iraq war, there was anger about what many officials saw as the decision of the Bush Administration to choose confrontation with Syria over day-to-day help against Al Qaeda. In a sense, the overriding issue was not American policy toward Syria, but the Bush Administration's unresolved competition between ideology and practicality—and between the drive to go to war in Iraq and the need to fight terrorism. The collapse of the liaison relationship has left many C.I.A. operatives especially frustrated. "The guys are unbelievably pissed that we're blowing this away," a former high-level intelligence official told me. "There was a great channel at Aleppo. The Syrians were a lot more willing to help us, but they"—Rumsfeld and his colleagues—"want to go in there next."

"There is no security relationship now," a Syrian foreign ministry official told me at the time. "It saddens us as much as it saddens you. We could give you information on organizations that we don't think should exist. If we help you on Al Qaeda, we are helping ourselves." He added, almost plaintively, that if Washington had agreed to discuss certain key issues in a back channel, "we'd have given you more. But when you publicly try to humiliate a country it'll become stubborn."

"Up through January of 2003, the coöperation was top-notch," a former State Department official said. "Then we were going to do Iraq, and some people in the Administration got heavy-handed. They wanted Syria to get involved in operational stuff having nothing to do with Al Qaeda and everything to do with Iraq. It was something Washington wanted from the Syrians, and they didn't want to do it."

Differences over Iraq "destroyed the Syrian bet," said Ghassan Salamé, a professor of international relations at Paris University who served, until April 2003 as Lebanon's minister of culture. "They bet that they could somehow find the common ground with America. They bet all on coöperation with America." A Defense Department official who has been involved in Iraq policy told me that the Syrians, despite their differences with Washington, had kept Hezbollah quiet during the war in Iraq. This was, he said, "a signal to us, and we're throwing it away. The Syrians are trying to communicate, and we're not listening."

3. Iran: The Next Nuclear Power?

In late 2001, the Islamic Republic of Iran, depicted by the State Department as one of the world's most active sponsors of state terrorism, appeared to be on the way to becoming one of America's newest—and most surprising—allies in the war against Osama bin Laden and Al Qaeda. And one of America's oldest allies didn't like it. On October 24th, more than two weeks after the American air war in Afghanistan began, Israel sent a government delegation to Washington for official talks. The delegation included Gideon Frank, the director general of the Israeli Atomic Energy Commission, and Major General Uzi Dayan, the head of Israel's National Security Council, and its purpose was to warn the Americans, not for the first time, about new evidence of Iran's efforts to become the world's next nuclear power.

The Israeli message, as a participant summarized it, was characteristically blunt: the Iranian atomic-bomb program was making rapid progress, and something had to be done about it. The warning posed a dilemma for the Bush Administration. Iran, which had long-standing religious and political ties to Afghanistan, had offered to let American search-and-rescue helicopters stage operations from bases on its soil and had relayed sensitive intelligence from Afghanistan to the United States.

Since September 11th, Iran's president, Mohammad Khatami, a reformer who was seeking to improve relations with Washington, had repeatedly criticized bin Laden's interpretation of Islam. The Taliban had assassinated nearly a dozen Iranian diplomats in Mazar-i-Sharif in 1998, two years after they seized power. Iran was eager to protect its political interests—and its borders. The American intelligence community, however, was unsure of the extent of Khatami's independence from Iran's conservative religious leaders. The mullahs remained in control of the country's intelligence services, which financed and worked closely with Hezbollah and other terrorist organizations that operate inside Israel.

Iran's secret push for the bomb was being closely monitored by American intelligence agencies, and American and Israeli officials had met in secret since the mid-1990s to share information on its nuclear program. (Israel has had a nuclear arsenal for decades, although it has never publicly acknowledged this.) Iran had always denied that it was trying to build a bomb. ("I hate this weapon," President Hashemi Rafsanjani, Khatami's predecessor, told *60 Minutes* in 1997.) Nonetheless, many American and Israeli intelligence officials estimated that Iran was only three to five years away from having launchable warheads. The immediate question was whether the country had passed the point of no return—the point where its domestic capability could no longer be derailed by export controls or interdiction of potential suppliers. "They're closer to that point than we should be comfortable about—and the fact that we can't pin it down also makes me uncomfortable," one American intelligence officer told me.

Iran began its pursuit of nuclear weapons in the mid-1970s, when Shah Mohammad Reza Pahlavi was flush with oil money, ambition, and American support. The shah invested an estimated $6 billion in nuclear projects, and Siemens, the West German conglomerate, completed more than half the construction needed for the installation of two reactors at Bushehr, near the Persian Gulf. Thousands of Iranians were abroad, studying physics and related subjects. American intelligence reports indicated that the shah also planned to build a nuclear bomb; a nuclear-weapons design team had been set up, and covert efforts were made to acquire the materials and know-how necessary to produce weapons.

This effort came to an abrupt end in 1979, when the shah was overthrown. Iran was, eventually, taken over by the Provisional Revolutionary Government, headed by Ayatollah Ruhollah Khomeini. In *Going Nuclear*, a 1987 study of the spread of nuclear weapons, the proliferation expert Leonard S. Spector noted presciently that if American policy makers had understood more about the power of Muslim fundamentalism and anti-American sentiment in Iran, they might have acted more aggressively to keep the Shah's nuclear assets out of the new government's hands. Nonetheless, throughout the 1980s there seemed to be little reason for official concern, as Iran and Iraq fought a devastating war that weakened both. Iran's nuclear programs were essentially shut down, and the half-completed buildings at Bushehr were badly damaged in an Iraqi bombing raid.

The war ended in 1988, with Iran's defeat. The ruling mullahs turned once again to West Germany and Siemens, but the German government, under pressure from Washington—"Death to America" was still the Iranian rallying cry—decided to end its nuclear involvement in Iran.

At the time, Iran and the Soviet Union's mutual antagonism to the United States did not translate into a close relationship with each other. After Ayatollah Khomeini's death, in 1989, however, the Iranian religious leadership, in a major geopolitical shift, signed a comprehensive arms and trade agreement with the Soviets that included coöperation on the "peaceful uses of atomic energy." The Yeltsin government agreed to rebuild Iran's bombed-out facilities at Bushehr, and, in 1995, the two countries signed an $800 million contract under which the Russians would help install a powerful reactor there, to be run by a Russian-Iranian team. Since then, a vast complex of buildings has been constructed at the site. Russia also began a training program for Iranian physicists and technicians. Intelligence officials told me in late 2001, however, that Iran's most important nuclear production facilities were not at Bushehr, which is open to international inspection by the International Atomic Energy Agency, but at clandestine sites under military control.

Following the pattern set by Pakistan, Iran established a maze of covert companies to conceal its nuclear program. In the two years prior to September 11th, according to a former senior Pentagon official, intelligence services had observed "extensive digging" in Iran as nuclear engineers rushed to construct hidden production facilities. "We know that they're going deep and clandestine," the former official said. An Israeli official confirmed that the hidden sites were "spread all around the country." The Iranians apparently hoped to minimize the potential damage from what another American intelligence official called "the Israeli version of counterproliferation"—a preëmptive air strike. (In 1981, the Israeli Air Force attacked and destroyed the new Iraqi Osirak reactor a few months before it was scheduled to come on line.) A European diplomat who had undertaken sensitive United Nations assignments in Iran for the past two decades told me, in late 2001, "This is the time to call their bluff. This is a time for the U.S. to really make or break it with Iran."

The initial focus of American and Israeli intelligence was less on Iran's progress in building the bomb than on what Iran might be able to buy ready-made from Russia. After the breakup of the Soviet Union, in 1991, military officers, whose forces were starved for cash, sometimes proved willing to sell off weapons, including missiles, to almost anyone. Some nuclear material was also left behind in the former Soviet Republics, and Iran is believed to have made a serious effort in the early 1990s to buy specialized goods for nuclear weapons from a newly independent Kazakhstan.

Under the Clinton Administration, there were some small successes in the struggle to contain Russian greed and prevent Iran from getting the atomic bomb. With help from the Mossad, the Israeli intelligence agency, U.S. officials isolated a group of private companies in Germany, Ukraine, and the Czech Republic that were willing to sell nuclear technology to questionable customers, and persuaded them to discontinue their Iranian contacts. Other potential trading partners were discouraged from doing business with Iran through diplomatic initiatives, economic sanctions or aid, and political arm twisting. Throughout its second term, however, the Clinton Administration continued to emphasize publicly the threat posed by Saddam Hussein's regime in Iraq—an emphasis that tended to take the pressure off Iran. "It was always a question of priority," a former Pentagon official recalled. "NATO expansion was a more important issue, and there was Bosnia, Kosovo, and Chechnya."

George W. Bush's election, in 2000, led to a suspension of the meetings regarding Iran between the United States and Israeli officials. One former official explained that both sides had been reluctant to continue them. "When Bush took over, it dropped off the White House radar screen," the former official said. "And the Israelis really didn't push it with the new guys. Part of it may have been that the new guys needed time. And part of it may have been the intifada"—the renewed guerrilla war between Israel and the Palestinians. Another official said that the Israelis simply "pulled their punches" in the early days of the Bush presidency.

The Bush Administration's 2002 budget proposal called for dramatically reducing the outgoing Clinton Administration's allocation for programs aimed at safeguarding the Russian nuclear stockpile. One factor was the Bush Administration's determination to persuade Putin to drop the 1972 anti-ballistic-missile treaty and join Washington in constructing a worldwide missile-defense system.

In 2001, according to American officials, Israel assembled evidence showing that at least two Russian export companies had continued illicit shipments to Iran of highly specialized aluminum and steel products that were essential for the assembly and operation of centrifuges. The Israelis brought their concerns to Washington in October 2001. Their contact was now John Bolton, the undersecretary of state for arms control and international security. The Israelis found the Administration preoccupied with Iraq, with the coming war against Osama bin Laden and the Taliban, and with its new-found allies in the war against terrorism.

As of the end of 2001, the American intelligence community, in formal evaluations, listed Iran as posing a more immediate nuclear-proliferation threat than Iraq. "Everyone knows that Iran is the next one to proliferate—to possess a nuclear weapon," an American nuclear-intelligence analyst told me at the time. "Iran has been the number one concern about who's next for the last couple of years at the highest level of the government." He pointed out that, after the Gulf War, the much criticized United Nations inspection program had "shut down Iraq's nuclear program to a large extent." The Iraqis, he went on, "have the knowledge—they could very quickly get back up to speed, but the international community isn't letting them do that. They're not as far along as Iran."

The Bush Administration continued to concentrate on the threat posed by Iraq. "It's more important to deal with Iraq than with Iran, because there's nothing going on in Iraq that's going to get better," a senior Administration strategist told me in late 2001. "In Iran, the people are openly defying the government. There's some hope that Iran will get better. But there's nothing in Iraq that gives you any hope, because Saddam rules so ruthlessly. What will we do if he provides anthrax to four guys in Al Qaeda?" He said, "If Iraq is out of the picture, we will concentrate on Iran in an entirely different way."

Iran's help in the war in Afghanistan, and many of its internal developments—from growing discontent with religious strictures to the increasing participation of women in political life—were encouraging to U.S. officials. But, one American official told me, it was also understood in Washington that Iran would continue to pursue the bomb. "Even if Thomas Jefferson became president, Iran is going to go nuclear," he said.

Some Israeli officials privately acknowledged that the extent of the Bush Administration's resolve in derailing the Iranian effort to build a bomb would be tied to the progress and outcome of the war on terrorism. "It's going to depend on how much success you have with Osama bin Laden," one Israeli official said. "If the terror continues, there is no alternative for the U.S. but to go to Iran for help."

An American four-star general I spoke to at the end of 2001 depicted the issue of priorities in more graphic terms. "We'll tell the

Pakistanis and the Russians to back off their help for Iran's bomb," he said, "but that's Chapter 2, after we put our boy"—bin Laden— "in a body bag."

———

In August of 2002, the National Council of Resistance of Iran, a soon-to-be defunct opposition group, held a press conference in Washington. The National Council had served as the political wing of the People's Mujahideen Khalq, a group that had been on the State Department's list of terrorist organizations since 1997, and it had lobbied in Washington for decades, offering information—not always accurate—about Iran. This time, the National Council came up with something new: it announced that it had evidence showing that Iran had secretly constructed two extensive nuclear-weapons facilities in the desert south of Tehran. The two plants were described with impressive specificity. One, near Natanz, had been depicted by Iranian officials as part of a desert-eradication program. The site, surrounded by barbed wire, was said to include two work areas buried twenty-five feet underground and ringed by concrete walls more than eight feet thick. The second plant, which was said to be producing heavy water for use in making weapons-grade plutonium, was situated in Arak and ostensibly operated as an energy company.

Inspectors from the I.A.E.A. eventually followed up on the National Council's information—and it checked out. A building that I.A.E.A. inspectors were not able to gain full access to on a visit in March 2003 was found on a subsequent trip to contain a centrifuge facility behind a wall made of boxes. Inspectors later determined that some of the centrifuges had been supplied by Pakistan. They also found traces of highly enriched uranium on centrifuge components manufactured in Iran and Pakistan. The I.A.E.A. could not immediately determine whether the uranium originated in Pakistan: the enriched materials could have come from the black market, or from a nuclear proliferator yet to be discovered, or from the Iranians' own production facilities.

In October 2003, the Iranian government, after months of denials and obfuscation—and increasingly productive inspections—formally acknowledged to the I.A.E.A. that it had secretly been producing small quantities of enriched uranium and plutonium, and had been operating a pilot heavy-water reactor program, all potentially in violation of its obligations under the nuclear-nonproliferation treaty. Some of the secret programs, Iran admitted, dated back eighteen years. At first, the country's religious leadership claimed that its scientists had worked on their own, and not with the help of outside suppliers. The ayatollahs later admitted that this was not the case, but refused to say where the help had come from.

On a trip to the Middle East in early 2004, I was told that a number of years earlier the Israeli signals-intelligence agency, known as Unit 8200, had broken a sophisticated Iranian code and begun monitoring communications that included talk between Iran and Pakistan about Iran's burgeoning nuclear-weapons program. The Israeli intelligence community had many covert contacts inside Iran, stemming from the strong ties it had there before the overthrow of the shah; some of these ties still existed. Israeli intelligence also maintained close contact with many Iranian opposition groups, such as the National Council. A connection was made—directly or indirectly—and the Israeli intelligence about Iran's nuclear program reached the National Council. A senior I.A.E.A. official subsequently told me that he knew that the council's information had originated with Israeli intelligence, but he refused to say where he had learned that fact. (An Israeli diplomat in Washington, asked to comment, said, "Why would we work with a Mickey Mouse outlet like the council?")

The Israeli intercepts were shared, in some form, with the U.S. intelligence community, according to the former senior intelligence official, and they showed that high-level officials in Islamabad and Tehran had frequent conversations about the I.A.E.A. investigation and its implications. "The interpretation is the issue here," the former official said. "If you set the buzzwords aside, the substance is that the Iranians were saying, 'We've got to play with the I.A.E.A. We don't want to blow our cover, but we have to show some movement. There's no way we're going against world public opinion—no way. We've got to show that we're coöperating and get the Europeans on our side.'" (At the time, Iran was engaged in negotiations with the European Union on trade and other issues.) It was clear from the intercepts, however, the former intelligence official said, that Iran did not want to give up its nuclear potential. The Pakistani response, he added, was "Don't give away the whole ballgame and we'll look out for you." There was a further message from Pakistan, the former official said: "Look out for your own interests."

In the official's opinion, Pakistan and Iran have survived the crisis: "They both did what they said they'd do, and neither one has been hurt. No one has been damaged. The public story is still that Iran never really got there—which is bullshit." (In June 2004, I.A.E.A. inspectors told me that the huge complex at Natanz, which was said to total nearly eight hundred thousand square feet and was still under construction, would be sheltered in a few months by a roof whose design allows it to be covered with sand. Once the work was completed, the complex would "be blind to satellites, and the Iranians could add additional floors underground," an I.A.E.A. official said.)

A high-level intelligence officer who has access to the secret Iran-Pakistan exchanges told me, when I interviewed him in Tel Aviv, that Israel remained convinced that "the Iranians do not intend to give up the bomb. What Iran did was report to the I.A.E.A. the information that was already out in the open and which they cannot protect. There is much that is not exposed." Israeli intelligence, he added, continued to see digging and other nuclear-related underground activity in Iran.

Iran's leaders continued to insist that their goal was to produce nuclear energy, not nuclear weapons, and, in a public report in November 2003, the I.A.E.A. stopped short of accusing them of building a bomb. Cautiously, it stated, "It is clear that Iran has failed in a number of instances over an extended period of time to meet its obligations . . . with respect to the reporting of nuclear material and its processing and use. . . . To date, there is no evidence that the previously undeclared nuclear material and activities referred to above were related to a nuclear weapons programme."

Privately, however, senior proliferation experts I spoke to later were far less reserved. "I know what they did," one official in Vienna told me, speaking of the Iranians. "They've been lying all the time and they've been cheating all the time." Asked if he thought that Iran already had the bomb, the official said no. Asked if he thought that Iran had enough enriched uranium to make a bomb, he said, "I'm not sure."

4. Israel, Turkey, and the Kurds

In July 2003, Israel, which had been among the most enthusiastic supporters of the war in Iraq, began warning the Administration that the American-led occupation would face a heightened insurgency—a campaign of bombings and assassinations—later that summer. Israeli intelligence assets in Iraq were reporting that the insurgents had the support of Iranian intelligence operatives and other foreign fighters, who were crossing the unprotected border between Iran and Iraq at will. The Israelis urged the United States to seal the nine-hundred-mile-long border, at whatever cost.

The border stayed open, however. "The Administration wasn't ignoring the Israeli intelligence about Iran," Patrick Clawson, who is the deputy director of the Washington Institute for Near East Policy and has close ties to the White House, explained in mid-2004. "There's no question that we took no steps last summer to close the border, but our attitude was that it was more useful for Iraqis to have contacts with ordinary Iranians coming across the border, and thousands were coming across every day—for instance, to make pilgrimages." He added, "The questions we confronted were 'Is the trade-off worth it? Do we want to isolate the Iraqis?' Our answer was that as long as the Iranians were not picking up guns and shooting at us, it was worth the price."

Clawson said, "The Israelis disagreed quite vigorously with us last summer. Their concern was very straightforward—that the Iranians would create social and charity organizations in Iraq and use them to recruit people who would engage in armed attacks against Americans."

A former Administration official who had supported the war completed a discouraging tour of Iraq late that fall. He visited Tel Aviv afterward and found that the Israelis he met with were equally discouraged. As they saw it, their warnings and their advice had been ignored, and the American war against the insurgency was continuing to founder. "I spent hours talking to the senior members of the Israeli political and intelligence community," the former official recalled. "Their concern was 'You're not going to get it right in Iraq, and shouldn't we be planning for the worst-case scenario and how to deal with it?'"

Ehud Barak, the former Israeli prime minister, who supported the Bush Administration's invasion of Iraq, took it upon himself at about the same time to privately warn Vice President Dick Cheney that America had lost in Iraq; according to an American close to Barak, he said that Israel "had learned that there's no way to win an occupation." The only issue, Barak told Cheney, "was choosing the size of your humiliation." Cheney did not respond to Barak's assessment. (Cheney's office declined to comment.)

In a series of interviews in Europe, the Middle East, and the United States in the late spring of 2004, officials told me that by the end of the previous year Israel had concluded that the Bush Administration would not be able to bring stability or democracy to Iraq, and that Israel needed other options. Israel's leadership had come to

THE MIDDLE EAST AFTER 9/11 **353**

believe, as a former Israeli military intelligence officer told me, that in terms of salvaging the situation in Iraq "it doesn't add up. It's over. Not militarily—the United States cannot be defeated militarily in Iraq—but politically." Prime Minister Ariel Sharon's government had decided, I was told, to minimize the damage that the war was causing to Israel's strategic position by expanding its long-standing relationship with Iraq's Kurds and establishing a significant presence on the ground in the semi-autonomous region of Kurdistan. Several officials depicted Sharon's decision, which involves a heavy financial commitment, as a potentially reckless move that could create even more chaos and violence as the insurgency in Iraq continued to grow.

Israeli intelligence and military operatives were, by mid-2004, quietly at work in Kurdistan, providing training for Kurdish commando units and, most important in Israel's view, running covert operations inside Kurdish areas of Iran and Syria. The Israeli operatives include members of the Mossad, Israel's clandestine foreign-intelligence service, who work undercover in Kurdistan as businessmen and, in some cases, do not carry Israeli passports.

Asked to comment before my account of the Israeli presence ran in *The New Yorker*, Mark Regev, the spokesman for the Israeli embassy in Washington, said, "The story is simply untrue and the relevant governments know it's untrue." Kurdish officials declined to comment at the time, as did a spokesman for the State Department.

However, a senior C.I.A. official acknowledged in an interview that the Israelis were indeed operating in Kurdistan. He told me that the Israelis "think they have to be there." Asked whether the Israelis had sought approval from Washington, the official laughed and said, "Do you know anybody who can tell the Israelis what to do? They're always going to do what is in their best interest." The C.I.A. official added that the Israeli presence was widely known in the American intelligence community.

*   *   *

The Israeli decision to seek a bigger foothold in Kurdistan—characterized by the former Israeli intelligence officer as Plan B—raised tensions between Israel and Turkey. It provoked bitter statements from Turkish politicians and, in a major regional shift, a new alliance among Iran, Syria, and Turkey, all of which have significant Kurdish minorities. In early June, *Intel Brief*, a privately circulated intelligence newsletter produced by Vincent Cannistraro, a retired C.I.A. counterterrorism chief, and Philip Giraldi, who served as the C.I.A.'s deputy chief of base in Istanbul in the late 1980s, said:

> Turkish sources confidentially report that the Turks are increasingly concerned by the expanding Israeli presence in Kurdistan and alleged encouragement of Kurdish ambitions to create an independent state. . . . The Turks note that the large Israeli intelligence operations in Northern Iraq incorporate anti-Syrian and anti-Iranian activity, including support to Iranian and Syrian Kurds who are in opposition to their respective governments.

In the years after the first Gulf War, Iraq's Kurds, aided by an internationally enforced no-fly zone and by a U.N. mandate providing them with a share of the country's oil revenues, managed to achieve a large measure of independence in three northern Iraqi provinces. As far as most Kurds are concerned, however, historic "Kurdistan" extends well beyond Iraq's borders, encompassing parts of Iran, Syria, and Turkey. All three countries feared that Kurdistan, despite public pledges to the contrary, would declare its independence from the interim Iraqi government if conditions don't improve after the transfer of sovereignty.

Israeli involvement in Kurdistan was not new. Throughout the 1960s and 1970s, Israel actively supported a Kurdish rebellion against Iraq, as part of its strategic policy of seeking alliances with non-Arabs in the Middle East. In 1975, the Kurds were betrayed by the United States, when Washington went along with a decision by the shah of Iran to stop supporting Kurdish aspirations for autonomy in Iraq. Betrayal and violence became the norm in the next two decades. Inside Iraq, the Kurds were brutally repressed by Saddam Hussein, who used airpower and chemical weapons against them. In 1984, the Kurdistan Workers Party, or P.K.K., initiated a campaign of separatist violence in Turkey that lasted fifteen years; more than thirty thousand people, most of them Kurds, were killed, and the Turkish government ruthlessly crushed the separatists. In the spring of 2004, the P.K.K., now known as the Kongra-Gel, announced that it was ending a five-year unilateral ceasefire and would begin targeting Turkish citizens once again.

In Iraq, there were fears that the Kurds would move to seize the city of Kirkuk, together with the substantial oil reserves in the surrounding region. Kirkuk is dominated by Arab Iraqis, many of whom were relocated there, beginning in the 1970s, as part of Saddam Hussein's campaign to "Arabize" the region, but the Kurds consider Kirkuk and its oil part of their historic homeland. "If Kirkuk is threatened by the Kurds, the Sunni insurgents will move in there, along with the Turkomen, and there will be a bloodbath," an American military expert who is studying Iraq told me. "And, even if the Kurds do take Kirkuk, they can't transport the oil out of the country, since all of the pipelines run through the Sunni-Arab heartland."

The Iraqi Kurdish leadership was furious when, in early June 2004, the United States acceded to a U.N. resolution on the restoration of Iraqi sovereignty that did not affirm the interim constitution that granted the minority Kurds veto power in any permanent constitution. Kurdish leaders immediately warned in a letter to President Bush that they would not participate in a new Shiite-controlled government unless they were assured that their rights were preserved. "The people of Kurdistan will no longer accept second-class citizenship in Iraq," the letter said.

A top German national security official said in an interview soon before the transfer of sovereignty that "an independent Kurdistan with sufficient oil would have enormous consequences for Syria, Iran, and Turkey" and would lead to continuing instability in the Middle East—no matter what the outcome in the rest of Iraq was. There was also a widespread belief, another senior German official said, that some elements inside the Bush Administration—he referred specifically to the faction headed by Paul Wolfowitz—would tolerate an independent Kurdistan. This, the German argued, would be a mistake.

A Kurdish declaration of independence would trigger a Turkish response—and possibly a war—and also derail what has been an important alliance for Israel. Turkey and Israel have become strong diplomatic and economic partners in the past decade. Thousands of Israelis travel to Turkey every year as tourists. Turkish opposition to the Iraq war has strained the relationship; still, Turkey remains oriented toward the West and, despite the victory of an Islamic party in national elections in 2002, relatively secular. It is now vying for acceptance in the European Union. In contrast, Turkey and Syria have been at odds for years, at times coming close to open confrontation, and Turkey and Iran have long been regional rivals. One area of tension between them is the conflict between Turkey's pro-Western stand and Iran's rigid theocracy. But their mutual wariness of the Kurds has transcended these divisions.

A European foreign minister, in a conversation in May 2004, said that the "blowing up" of Israel's alliance with Turkey would be a major setback for the region. He went on: "To avoid chaos, you need the neighbors to work as one common entity." The Israelis, however, viewed the neighborhood, with the exception of Kurdistan, as hostile.

Iraqi Shiite militia leaders like Moqtada al-Sadr, the former American intelligence official said, were seen by the Israeli leadership as "stalking horses" for Iran—owing much of their success in defying the American-led coalition to logistical and communications support and training provided by Iran. The former intelligence official said, "We began to see telltale signs of organizational training last summer. But the White House didn't want to hear it: 'We can't take on another problem right now. We can't afford to push Iran to the point where we've got to have a showdown.' "

In the summer of 2003, according to a document I obtained, the Bush Administration directed the Marines to draft a detailed plan, called Operation Stuart, for the arrest and, if necessary, assassination of Sadr. But the operation was cancelled, the former intelligence official told me, after it became clear that Sadr had been "tipped off" about the plan. Seven months later, after Sadr spent the winter building support for his movement, the American-led coalition shut down his newspaper, provoking a crisis that Sadr survived with his status enhanced, thus insuring that he would play a major, and unwelcome, role in the political and military machinations after the transfer of sovereignty.

The former senior intelligence official told me that Israel's immediate goal after the transfer of sovereignty was "to build up the Kurdish commando units to balance the Shiite militias—especially those which would be hostile to the kind of order in southern Iraq that Israel would like to see." He added, "Of course, if a fanatic Sunni Baathist militia took control—one as hostile to Israel as Saddam Hussein was—Israel would unleash the Kurds on it, too." The Kurdish armed forces, known as the peshmerga, number an estimated seventy-five thousand troops, a total that far exceeds the known Sunni and Shiite militias.

The former Israeli intelligence officer acknowledged that since late 2003 Israel had been training Kurdish commando units to operate in the same manner and with the same effectiveness as Israel's most secretive commando units, the Mistaravim. The initial goal of the Israeli assistance to the Kurds, the former officer said, was to allow them to do what American commando units had been unable to do—penetrate, gather intelligence on, and then kill off the leadership of the Shiite and Sunni insurgencies in Iraq. (I was unable to learn whether any such mission had yet taken place.) "The feeling was that this was a more effective way to get at the insurgency," the former officer said.

The former officer said, "Look, Israel has always supported the Kurds in a Machiavellian way—as balance against Saddam. It's Realpolitik." He added, "By aligning with the Kurds, Israel gains eyes and ears in Iran, Iraq, and Syria. What Israel was doing with the Kurds was not so unacceptable in the Bush Administration." The problem, he said, was that "the growing Kurdish-Israeli relationship began upsetting the Turks no end. Their issue is that the very same Kurdish commandos trained for Iraq could infiltrate and attack in Turkey." In interviews in mid-2004, senior German officials also told me, with alarm, that their intelligence community had evidence that Israel was using its new leverage inside Kurdistan, and within the Kurdish communities in Iran and Syria, for intelligence and operational purposes.

Patrick Clawson, of the Institute for Near East Policy, told me that Iran had to be Israel's overwhelming national security concern. Given that a presence in Kurdistan would give Israel a way to monitor the Iranian nuclear effort, he said, "it would be negligent for the Israelis not to be there." The former American senior intelligence official also said that from the Israelis' perspective their tie to Kurdistan "would be of greater value than their growing alliance with Turkey. 'We love Turkey but got to keep the pressure on Iran.'"

The top German national security official said, however, that he believed that the Bush Administration continually misread Iran. "The Iranians wanted to keep America tied down in Iraq, and to keep it busy there, but they didn't want chaos," he said. A senior European official said, "The Iranians would do something positive in the south of Iraq if they get something positive in return, but Washington won't do it. The Bush Administration won't ask the Iranians for help, and can't ask the Syrians. Who is going to save the United

States?" He added that, at the start of the American invasion of Iraq, several top European officials had told their counterparts in Iran, "You will be the winners in the region."

"The Kurds were the last surviving group close to the United States with any say in Iraq. The only question was how to square it with Turkey," the former Israeli intelligence officer explained. There may be no squaring it with Turkey, however. Over breakfast in Ankara in mid-2004, a senior Turkish official said, "Before the war, Israel was active in Kurdistan, and now it is active again. This is very dangerous for us, and for them, too. We do not want to see Iraq divided, and we will not ignore it." Then, citing a popular Turkish proverb—"We will burn a blanket to kill a flea"—he said, "We have told the Kurds, 'We are not afraid of you, but you should be afraid of us.'" (A Turkish diplomat I spoke to later was more direct: "We tell our Israeli and Kurdish friends that Turkey's good will lies in keeping Iraq together. We will not support alternative solutions.")

Another senior Turkish official explained that his government had "openly shared its worries" about the Israeli military activities inside Kurdistan with the Israeli Foreign Ministry. "They deny the training and the purchase of property and claim it's not official but done by private persons. Obviously, our intelligence community is aware that it was not so."

In a conversation with Middle Eastern diplomats that spring, Turkey's foreign minister, Abdullah Gul, one diplomat told me, described Israeli activities, and the possibility of an independent Kurdistan, as "presenting us with a choice that is not a real choice—between survival and alliance." A third Turkish official told me, "We can tolerate 'Kurdistan' if Iraq is intact, but nobody knows the future—not even the Americans."

"If you end up with a divided Iraq, it will bring more blood, tears, and pain to the Middle East, and you will be blamed," the first senior Turkish official said. "From Mexico to Russia, everybody will claim that the United States had a secret agenda in Iraq: you came there to break up Iraq. If Iraq is divided, America cannot explain this to the world." The official compared the situation to the breakup of Yugoslavia, but added, "In the Balkans, you did not have oil." He said, "The lesson of Yugoslavia is that when you give one country independence everybody will want it." If that happens, he said, "Kirkuk will be the Sarajevo of Iraq. If something happens there, it will be impossible to contain the crisis."

EPILOGUE

In May 2004, at the height of the Abu Ghraib prison abuse scandal, a senior political Republican Party operative was given the reassuring word that Vice President Dick Cheney had taken charge, with his usual directness. The operative learned that Cheney had telephoned Donald Rumsfeld with a simple message: No resignations. We're going to hunker down and tough it out.

Cheney's concern was not national security. This was a political call—a reminder that the White House would seize control of every crisis that could affect the re-election of George Bush. The Abu Ghraib revelations, if left unchecked, could provoke more public doubt about the wisdom of the war in Iraq, and about the sometimes brutal intelligence operations that were used to wage it. The White House and Pentagon also would have to work together to prevent Congress and the press from unraveling an incendiary secret—that undercover members of an intelligence unit that operated in secret in the name of every American had been at Abu Ghraib. The senior leadership in the White House has been aware since January of the mess at Abu

Ghraib, and, more importantly, of the fact that photographs and video-tapes existed, and might someday reach the public. As we have seen, the military chain of command had ignored the possibility of higher-up involvement and moved quickly to prosecute the military police who had committed the acts—"the kids at the end of the food chain," as a former senior intelligence official put it: "We've got some hill-billy kids out of control."

The perception persists that this was Rumsfeld's war, and that it was his assertiveness and his toughness that sometimes led to the bombing of the wrong target or the arrest of innocents. But Cheney's involvement in trying to conceal the import of Abu Ghraib was not unusual; it was a sign of the teamwork at the top. George Bush talked about "smoking them out of their holes" and wanting them "dead or alive," and Rumsfeld was the one who set up the mechanism to get it done. The defense secretary would hold the difficult news confer-ences and take the heat in public, as he did about Abu Ghraib, but the President and Vice President had been in it, and with him, all the way. Rumsfeld handled the dirty work and kept the secrets, but he and the two White House leaders were a team.

There is so much about this presidency that we don't know, and may never learn. Some of the most important questions are not even being asked. How did they do it? How did eight or nine neo-conservatives who believed that a war in Iraq was the answer to in-ternational terrorism get their way? How did they redirect the government and rearrange long-standing American priorities and policies with so much ease? How did they overcome the bureau-cracy, intimidate the press, mislead the Congress, and dominate the military? Is our democracy that fragile? I have tried, in this book, to describe some of the mechanisms used by the White House—the stovepiping of intelligence, the reliance on Ahmad Chalabi, the re-fusal to hear dissenting opinions, the difficulty of getting straight talk about military operations gone bad, and the inability—or unwillingness—of the President and his senior aides to distinguish between Muslims who supported terrorism and those who abhorred it. A complete understanding of these last few years will be a challenge for journalists, political scientists, and historians.

Many of the failings, however, were in plain sight. The Administration's manipulation and distortion of the intelligence about Iraq's ties to Al Qaeda and its national security threat to the United States was anything but a secret in Washington, as the pages of this book make clear. And yet the Republican-led Senate Intelligence Committee, after a year-long investigation, published a report, in July 2004, stating that the critical mistakes were made not in the White House, but at the C.I.A., whose analysts essentially missed the story. There was an astonishing postscript that told much about the disarray in Washington. Three Democrats, John D. Rockefeller IV of West Virginia, the vice chairman of the committee, Carl Levin of Michigan, who is also the ranking Democrat on the Armed Services Committee, and Richard Durbin of Illinois, signed a separate statement disavowing the report's central findings. "Regrettably, the report paints an incomplete picture of what occurred during this period of time," they wrote, noting that the "central issue" of how intelligence was misused by the Administration and the pre-war role of Ahmad Chalabi would be included in a second report—one that was not to be made public until after the presidential election. "As a result," they wrote, "the Committee's phase one report fails to fully explain the environment of intense pressure in which Intelligence Community officials were asked to render judgments on matters relating to Iraq, when policy officials had already forcefully stated their own conclusions in public."

And yet, Rockefeller, Levin, and Durbin put their names on the report, helping to make it appear unanimous and bipartisan. There are, once again, unanswered questions. Why didn't the Democrats take a stronger stand? How much influence did the White House exert on the Republican members of the committee? Why didn't the press go beyond the immediate facts? The inner workings of the committee were in many ways a more important story than its findings.

As of this writing, in August 2004, the Bush Administration continues to wage a war in Iraq by means that ensure that it cannot win. The American investment of billions in high-tech satellites and electronic surveillance, the untold millions paid to informers, and the deployment of the most highly trained Special Forces unit have failed since the early days of the war to produce crucial intelligence about the insurgency—just as all these systems failed to tell us that Saddam Hussein had no weapons of mass destruction. In the spring and summer of 2003, the insurgents operated in small cells of two and three that could not be penetrated. A year later, the cells had become groups of ten to fifteen men, striking at will throughout Baghdad and in the north, and the American intelligence community still could not find and get a fix on the insurgents. Ahmad Chalabi's standing in Washington plummeted as the extent of his manipulations became clear. The White House was forced to install Iyad Allawi, the former enforcer for Saddam Hussein who later became a C.I.A. asset, as the new Iraqi prime minister. The Administration has no strategic plan beyond sustaining the unsustainable Allawi government in power past the presidential elections in November.

Some American military planners had hoped, with the Iraqis now nominally in control, that the overexposed and underprotected Americans in Iraq would be able to limit their offensive operations against suspected insurgent sites and retreat, if the bombings and terror attacks continued, into what some planners in the Joint Chiefs of Staff were calling the "hollow-square concept"—a series of gradual withdrawals that would end at the U.S.-controlled international airport near Baghdad. The American mission would be reduced to protecting its troops, and it would be up to the American-trained Iraqi police and army units to get control of the nation. The American military retreat would be masked, as the reduced American patrols have been since the spring of 2004, by steadily increasing bombing and firepower. By late summer, however, the Bush Administration, which had in earlier crises resisted placing any American soldiers under foreign command, was sending its troops against a Shiite leader at the behest, so commanders said, of Prime Minister Allawi.

But the deepening American quagmire in Iraq will not end until there is a change of leadership in Washington. "If you want to change the situation," a senior European intelligence officer told me in the summer of 2004, "you have to have a vision. And you have to be respected. You are not respected."

The Europeans believe a solution would still be possible if the Bush Administration were prepared to negotiate with Iraq's immediate neighbors, including Syria and Iran. The ideologues in Washington have refused thus far to deal with the world that exists, however, and have yet to agree to a regional meeting. "To avoid chaos," a European foreign minister told me, "you need the neighbors. The positive options are very limited, but we must preserve the territorial integrity of Iraq. An international conference is important to stabilize the situation." One goal is to prevent the Kurds, and any other group that tries, from attempting to seize Iraqi territory and secede, thus triggering more warfare. "The American mindset has changed," the foreign minister said. "There is a different mindset. I don't understand it."

In the other war, in Afghanistan, American soldiers are dying and being wounded in greater numbers—largely hidden from the front page and television news reports. In the summer of 2004, despite the presence of 17,000 U.S. and 6,500 NATO troops, the Taliban controlled ever-increasing tracts in the south and east, and Hamid Karzai, the American-installed president, was still unable to make a public appearance in central Kabul without a phalanx of security, much of it provided by Americans. The much-heralded parliamentary elections have been delayed indefinitely, while the presidential election, so avidly sought by the Bush Administration, was pushed back a month and rescheduled, as of this writing, for October 2004. With or without that election, democracy is not blooming in Afghanistan. European leaders remain fearful of a political collapse in that country, and of the damage this would cause to NATO, which, at the insistence of Washington, has also staked its reputation there.

As he campaigned, in the summer of 2004, George Bush repeatedly reassured audiences that his policies had made America safer. "We've turned the corner," was the refrain in his stump speech. "We're moving America forward by extending freedom and peace around the world." Iraq and Afghanistan, he said, "are now governed by strong leaders. They're on the path to free elections." America, he added, would engage its enemies around the world "so we do not have to face them here at home." The President did not mention the missing weapons of mass destruction, the growing G.I. death toll, the civilian casualties in Afghanistan and Iraq, and the devastation to all aspects of civil life in Iraq. He did not mention the adverse Supreme Court decisions in June of 2004 that challenged the legal basis of his postwar prison system, and told him that foreigners, as well as American citizens, were entitled to due process even in a time of war. And he did not discuss growing alienation and bitterness as Americans, already torn by racial and religious differences, became increasingly politically and economically divided in the past four years.

We have a President who spent months terrorizing the nation with dire warnings about mushroom clouds emanating from Saddam Hussein's arsenal and then could say, as he did in a campaign speech in August of 2004, that it didn't matter. "We may still find weapons,"

Bush said. "We haven't found them yet. . . . Let me just say this to you: knowing what I know today, we still would have gone into Iraq." We have a President who can stand aside as the dogs of war are turned loose on prisoners and then declare, as he did in June 2004, that "America stands against and will not tolerate torture. We will investigate and prosecute all acts of torture and undertake to prevent other cruel and unusual punishment in all territory under our jurisdiction" and that "freedom from torture is an inalienable human right." There are many who believe George Bush is a liar, a President who knowingly and deliberately twists facts for political gain. But lying would indicate an understanding of what is desired, what is possible, and how best to get there. A more plausible explanation is that words have no meaning for this President beyond the immediate moment, and so he believes that his mere utterance of the phrases makes them real. It is a terrifying possibility.

AFTERWORD

At this writing, it's been nearly a year since I published a series of articles in *The New Yorker* outlining the abuses at Abu Ghraib. There have been at least ten official military investigations since then—none of which has challenged the official Bush Administration line that there was no high-level policy condoning or overlooking such abuse. The buck always stops with the handful of enlisted Army Reservists from the 372nd Military Police Company whose images fill the iconic Abu Ghraib photographs, with their inappropriate smiles and sadistic posing of the prisoners.

It's a dreary pattern. A military report is released and, within a few days, a high-level general or admiral appears before the Senate Armed Services Committee—such appearances apparently mark the extent of the Committee's promised "investigation" of Abu Ghraib—and reveals, under questioning, that he had no mandate to investigate the responsibility, if any, of higher-ups such as President George W. Bush and Secretary of Defense Donald Rumsfeld. The reports and the subsequent Senate proceedings are sometimes criticized on editorial pages and by skeptical reports in America's major daily newspapers (which have done a far better job in their coverage of Abu Ghraib than in their reporting on the build up to the Iraqi war). There are calls for a truly independent investigation by the Senate or House, or for a commission modeled on the one that looked into the September 11th attacks, but no such inquiry is authorized. Then, as weeks and months pass with no official action, the issue withers away, until the next set of revelations revives it.

There is much more to be learned. Public interest groups such as Human Rights Watch and the American Civil Liberties Union continue to churn out report after report, based on responses to their Freedom of Information Act requests, demonstrating that systematic military abuse of American prisoners in Iraq, Afghanistan, and at Guantánamo, Cuba, is widespread and tolerated. There is a separate stream of horrific accounts of violent mistreatment and torture from former prisoners who were released from Guantánamo after the U.S. Supreme Court ruled, in the summer of 2004, that they had a right to some semblance of due process. Many Guantánamo detainees have simply been returned to their home countries, after years of confinement, without ever being charged, though hundreds remain behind.

Thus, we are confronted with a gap between what we read and hear about what is really going on from prisoners and human rights groups and what the official inquiries tell us—just as there is a contrast between the daily reality of what we see happening in Iraq and what President George W. Bush and his allies tell us. We have a President who, as I wrote at the end of *Chain of Command*, assures us that there is no American policy condoning or abetting torture when, as we can see with our eyes, the opposite is true.

What do I know? A few things stand out. I know of the continuing practice—going on as this is being written—of American operatives seizing suspected terrorists and taking them, without any meaningful legal review, to interrogation centers in Southeast Asia and elsewhere. The operatives, acting under orders from senior officials in the Pentagon, work in secrecy, with false identity papers, and avoid contact with American diplomats or Central Intelligence Agency operatives on duty in North Africa. Senior officers in the military chain of command, including members of the Joint Chiefs of Staff, are also not always informed, to their anger and dismay. I know of the young Special Forces officer whose highly trained subordinates—six or seven of them—were confronted with charges of prisoner abuse and torture at a secret hearing after one of them e-mailed explicit photographs back home. The officer testified that, yes, his men had done what the photographs depicted, but they—and everybody in the Command—understood that such treatment was condoned by higher-ups.

What else do I know? I know that the decision was made inside the Pentagon in the first weeks of the Afghanistan war—which seemed "won" by December 2001—to indefinitely detain the scores of prisoners who were accumulating daily at American staging posts throughout the country. At the time, according to a memo, in my possession, addressed to Secretary Rumsfeld, there were "800-900 Pakistani boys 13-15 years of age in custody." This was listed under the heading "Public Affairs/Diplomatic/Congressional Issues." I could not learn if all of the young boys had been released, or are still being held somewhere, in Guantánamo—some juveniles are known to have been there—or another detention site about which we have yet to learn. (A Pentagon spokesman, when asked for comment, said that he had no information to substantiate the number in the document, and that there were currently about a hundred juveniles being held in Iraq and Afghanistan; he did not address detainees held elsewhere. He said that they received some special care but added, "Age is not a determining factor in detention. . . . As with all detainees, their release is contingent upon the determination that they are not a threat and are of no further intelligence value. Unfortunately, we have found that . . . age does not necessarily diminish threat potential.") The Pentagon document stated that all detainees should be held as long as necessary, without reference to why they were detained—for example, whether they were directly involved in anti-American activities or not. The document further states that military authorities needed to "establish criteria of what we need to know before making the decision to hold further or release a detainee to his home country." It took a Supreme Court decision more than two years later to compel the Bush Administration to establish the criteria.

The ten official inquiries into Abu Ghraib are asking the wrong questions, at least in terms of fixing the ultimate responsibility for the treatment of prisoners. The legal and moral issue is not high-level knowledge of the specific events in the photographs—of course the President and his senior advisers did not know of the particular acts of insanity repeatedly taking place on the night shift at the prison. The question that never gets adequately asked or answered, though, is this: What did the President do *after* being told about Abu Ghraib? It is here that chronology becomes very important.

The U.S.-led coalition forces swept to seemingly immediate success in the March 2003 invasion of Iraq, and by early April Baghdad had been taken, without significant opposition. America rejoiced in the television images of a statue of Saddam Hussein being hauled down. Rumsfeld depicted the resistance as composed largely of "dead-enders" who would soon be destroyed. Over the next few months, however, the resistance—still being led, as we now know, in large measure by the Baathists and Iraqi military leaders against whom we went to war—grew in scope, persistence, and skill. In August 2003, the resistance (or the insurgency, as the American officials and media came to call it) became more aggressive. The United Nations' mission in Baghdad was destroyed by a car bomb, and the Jordanian Embassy, site of some of America's most sensitive intelligence activities, was successfully targeted. So were oil and water pipelines. At this point there was a decision to get tough with the thousands of prisoners in Iraq, many of whom had been seized in random raids or at roadside checkpoints. Major General Geoffrey D. Miller, an Army artillery officer who, as commander at Guantánamo, had gotten tough with the prisoners there, visited Baghdad to tutor the troops—to "Gitmoize" the Iraqi system. Miller's recommendation was an abrupt departure from Army doctrine. The military police units guarding the prison were no longer to focus strictly on providing a safe, secure, and humane environment, as called for in Army regulations, but instead become, according to the Taguba report, "actively engaged in setting the conditions for successful exploitation of the internees." The soldiers got the message.

By the beginning of October 2003, the reservists on the night shift at Abu Ghraib had begun their abuse of prisoners and casually began taking photographs of what they were doing. The reservists were aware that some of America's elite Special Forces units were also at work at the prison. As I wrote in Part I of this book, those highly trained military men had been authorized by the Pentagon's senior leadership to act far outside the normal boundaries, the normal rules of engagement. There was no secret about the interrogation practices used at Abu Ghraib throughout that fall and early winter, and few objections. In fact, representatives of one of the Pentagon's private contractor firms at Abu Ghraib, who were involved in prisoner interrogation, were told that Condoleezza Rice, who was then the President's national-security adviser, had praised their efforts. It's not clear why she would do so—there was no evidence and none today that the American intelligence community has been able to accumulate any significant intelligence about the operations and procedures of the resistance, who continue today to strike American soldiers and Iraqis. The night shift's activities at Abu Ghraib came to an end on January 13, 2004, when Specialist Joseph M. Darby, one of the 372nd reservists on duty at Abu

Ghraib, provided Army police authorities with a disk full of explicit images. By then, these horrors had been taking place for nearly four months.

Three days later the Army began an investigation, and said so publicly in a bland five-sentence statement that hid more than it conveyed. Secretary Rumsfeld later explained that he was told of the inquiry—and, most importantly, of the photographs—at that time. He relayed what he knew to the President, he said, within days. Rumsfeld also stated that neither he nor the President had bothered to look at any of the photographs at the time, and that he did not do so until shortly after they were made public by *The New Yorker* and CBS's *60 Minutes II*, in late April. But, as I was later told, some members of the top echelon in the Pentagon realized from the beginning of the inquiry that they had a huge problem, and facts of the pending scandal were tightly restricted.

In March, before the pictures came out, General Miller was transferred from Guantánamo and put in charge of the Army's prison system in Iraq, with no public fanfare. And several members of the 372nd Military Police company were sent home that month, earlier than scheduled. The Army, meanwhile, was continuing its quiet inquiry and preparing to bring charges against some of the men and women seen in the photographs.

It's what was not done at that point that is significant. There is no evidence that President Bush, upon learning of the devastating conduct at Abu Ghraib, asked any hard questions of Donald Rumsfeld and his own aides in the White House. How did this go on for so many months without being reported or stopped by senior officers at the prison? What controls exist to monitor such abuses? How widespread are such actions? Why did the reservists involved believe that they could take photographs of their activity with impunity? There was no evidence that they had taken any significant steps upon learning in mid-January of the Abu Ghraib abuses to review and modify the military's policy toward prisoners. I was told by a high-level former intelligence official that within days of the first reports the judicial system was programmed to begin prosecuting the enlisted men and women in the photographs—the bad apples of Abu Ghraib—and to go no further up the chain of command.

In late April, after the CBS and *The New Yorker* reports, there was a series of news conferences and press briefings in Washington and Baghdad that emphasized the White House's dismay over the conduct of a few misguided soldiers at Abu Ghraib, as well as the President's repeated opposition to torture. Miller was introduced anew to the American press corps in Baghdad and it was explained that the general had been assigned to clean up the prison system and instill respect for the Geneva Conventions. At the time the Administration was still presenting Guantánamo as a model of the decent handling of dangerous suspects in the war on terror—even though, as this book makes clear, there were already complaints within the White House and from the F.B.I. about the mistreatment of prisoners at Guantánamo. Miller, after all, had been sent earlier to increase the pressure—to find some way of helping the military command cope with the continuing (and growing) resistance. There is no evidence that Miller's reassignment to Iraq prompted any immediate shake-ups inside the Army command in Iraq, or a renewed determination to root out those military men and women who were abusing prisoners.

Despite Abu Ghraib and Guantánamo—not to mention Iraq and the failure of intelligence—and the various roles they played in what went wrong, Secretary of Defense Rumsfeld kept his job; Condoleezza Rice was promoted to secretary of state; Alberto Gonzales, who commissioned the memos justifying torture, became attorney general; Deputy Secretary of Defense Paul Wolfowitz was nominated to the presidency of the World Bank; and Stephen Cambone, the under-secretary of defense for intelligence and one of those most directly involved in the policies regarding prisoners, was still one of Rumsfeld's closest confidants. President Bush, asked about accountability, told the *Washington Post* shortly before his second inauguration that the American people had supplied all the accountability needed by reelecting him. As of this writing, only seven enlisted men and women have been charged or pled guilty to offenses stemming from Abu Ghraib.

In late April of 2005, the Army's inspector general announced that an internal investigation had absolved four out of five senior officers with authority over prison operations in Iraq—three generals and a colonel—of responsibility for any aspects of the wrongdoing at Abu Ghraib. (It recommended only a reprimand for the fifth, Brigadier General Janis Karpinski.) The investigation concluded that there was no substantiated evidence that the top commanders, including Lietenant General Ricardo S. Sanchez, who ran the Iraqi war in that period, had failed in not preventing or stopping the abuses.

Such action, or inaction, has a special significance for me. In my years of reporting, I have come to know the human costs of such events—and to believe that the soldiers who participate in even the most brutal of war crimes can become victims as well.

In the fall of 1969, it was a series of my reports, as a freelance journalist in Washington, that unraveled the story of the My Lai massacre in South Vietnam. Some five hundred Vietnamese civilians—women, children, and old men—were murdered on March 16, 1968, in cold blood, by a task force of American soldiers. The daylong slaughter was observed and known to dozens of officers within hours, but the Army's most extensive investigation and criminal prosecution focused on a lieutenant named William L. Calley, Jr. He—and not, for example, Samuel Koster, the major general who flew over My Lai in a helicopter that day—became the focal point for public attention and public disparagement.

While researching the story—even after the first article appeared, the national press didn't begin to follow up for weeks, leaving me alone with the story—I learned that a young soldier named Paul Meadlo had been among those GIs who repeatedly fired bullets, at Calley's direction, into a ditch full of civilians. Moments later, a very young boy, perhaps two years old and bloodied, who miraculously survived the onslaught—maybe his mother had somehow tucked him under her body—crawled out of the ditch, crying, and began running away. As I wrote in *My Lai 4*, "Someone hollered, 'There's a kid.' There was a long pause. Then Calley ran back, grabbed the child, threw him back in the ditch, and shot him." Shortly afterward, Paul Meadlo stepped on a land mine and lost one of his feet. When I spoke to his fellow soldiers, eighteen months later, they told me that as Meadlo was being medevacked out of the combat zone, he repeatedly screamed to Calley that God had punished him and that God would punish Calley, too.

I went looking for Meadlo and learned that he had returned to his mother's farm in New Goshen, Indiana. I called from wherever I was—somewhere on the West Coast—and talked briefly to his mother, who made no promises. I told her I was coming nonetheless, and we left it at that. The farm was hardscrabble, with chicken coops and frame buildings that reminded me of the rural scenes painted by Norman Rockwell that filled the covers of the weekly *Saturday Evening Post* of my childhood. Mrs. Meadlo walked out to meet me as I drove up in my rental car. She was about fifty years old, but, with her weathered skin and slight stature, seemed two decades older. I asked to see her son, and she told me he was inside, waiting for me. She told me that when he came home, "He looked like he had just been whipped. He was so nervous he couldn't even hold a cup in his hand. He couldn't even eat." And then she said, with a look I wish those who send young men and women off to war could see, "I gave them a good boy and they made him a murderer."

Thirty-five years later, amidst my frenetic reporting for *The New Yorker* on Abu Ghraib, I was telephoned by a middle-aged woman who said she had something about the prison abuse she wanted to share with me. I flew the next day to meet her over lunch in a restaurant somewhere in the Northeast. She told me that a family member, a young woman, was among those members of the 320th Military Police Battalion, to which the 372nd was attached, who had returned to the United States in March. She came back a different person—distraught, angry, and wanting nothing to do with her immediate family. She moved to a nearby city and lived alone. Her family was confused and frightened, of course, but could not imagine what had gone wrong or how to deal with it. The barrage of news stories about Abu Ghraib seemed relevant, but the young soldier would not discuss it. At some point afterward, the older woman told me, she remembered that she had given the reservist a portable computer with a DVD player to take to Iraq—the soldiers enjoyed watching movies when not on duty. She decided to begin using the computer again herself, and did what people do when they get a computer someone else has been using: routinely opened, inspected, and then erased files. (In her telling, the exploration of the computer had nothing to do with the news from Abu Ghraib, or the young woman's distress.) There was a file marked Iraq that, when opened, poured out an extensive series of digitalized images, in timed sequence, depicting a naked Iraqi prisoner, hands behind his head, flinching in fear before two snarling dogs. The sequence ended with the prisoner on the ground, bleeding profusely from a wound that was apparently inflicted by one of the dogs. One of the images was published in *The New Yorker* and, subsequently, all over the world.

The war, the older woman told me, was not the war for democracy and freedom that she thought her young family member had been sent to Iraq to fight. She could no longer support the war, and that, she said, was why she wanted me to publish the photos. Others must know, she said. There was one other thing she wanted to share with me: Since returning from Iraq, the young woman had been getting tattoos all over her body—large black tattoos. She seemed intent on changing her skin.

Seymour M. Hersh,
Washington, D.C.,
April 2005

ACKNOWLEDGMENTS

No outsider can understand the degree to which reporting and writing at *The New Yorker* is a collaborative process. Since September 11th, I have been bathed in support, indulgence, and rigorous editing and fact checking by my editors, colleagues, and friends at the magazine as we worked up to and beyond the deadlines. David Remnick, the magazine's editor, always put fairness and accuracy before speed; even the very good story could wait if it wasn't the best it could be. Dorothy Wickenden, the executive editor, and Pam McCarthy, the deputy editor, had an open-door policy in terms of support and willingness to listen. Jacob Lewis, the managing editor, and Kate Julian made the trains run on time. John Bennet and, later, Amy Davidson, my primary editors, shared my sometimes overwrought sense of immediacy and importance—but in far more restrained ways. Lauren Porcaro of the editorial staff got everything done when it needed to be done. Perri Dorset, director of public relations, is a professional with superb judgment. Ed Klaris, the magazine's general counsel, remained his usual unflappable self throughout. Natasha Lunn and Kilian Schalk took good care of the important photographs from Abu Ghraib. Ann Goldstein and her copy department colleagues worked heroic hours tending to antecedents and all that, and made every deadline. Risa Leibowitz and Francine Schore, of the editorial business department, got me money, plane tickets, and plenty of encouragement. *The New Yorker*'s much celebrated fact checkers, led by Peter Canby, were dedicated and discreet, as expected, in dealing with very sensitive sources to verify very sensitive information. I especially thank Anne Stringfield, Dan Kaufman, Marina Harss, Andy Young, Gita Daneshjoo, Boris Fishman, Allison Hoffman, Nana Asfour, and Raffi Khatchadourian. My journalistic colleagues at the magazine were unfailingly generous and helpful in sharing information and making my job easier.

The new reporting and published articles in this book were carefully melded together by *The New Yorker*'s Amy Davidson, whose sense of narrative and flow I trust and respect. Dan Kaufman was, as usual, calm and unflinching in his fact checking of the new information in the book. Gil Shochat, my faithful researcher, repeatedly went beyond my requests in pulling together timelines and summaries of key events. David Hirshey of HarperCollins waited patiently for years for this book, and provided invaluable guidance throughout. Thanks also to John Jusino of HarperCollins. Esther Newberg of ICM, my longtime agent—and longtime friend—can put a deal together like no one in the business. My attorney, Michael Nussbaum, continues to keep me out of trouble.

Those most responsible for this book—the past and present government, intelligence, and military officials who have provided me with an alternative history since September 11th—cannot be named, for obvious reasons. There is honor in their anonymity.

This book, and all of my work, would not be without the support and guidance of Elizabeth, my wife of forty years. She is the love of my life.

Seymour M. Hersh
Washington, D.C.

INDEX

Abd, Hayder Sabbar, 38
Abdullah, Crown Prince of Saudi Arabia, 325, 327–28
Abizaid, John, 41, 42, 57
Abrams, Elliott, 6
Abu Ghraib, 361–62
  civilians incarcerated in, 40
  Coalition repurposing of, 21
  covert operations at, 361–62
  dogs used at, 35–36
  escapes from, 39
  as failure of leadership, 40, 46
  hard site at, 24
  under Saddam Hussein, 20–21
  military intelligence teams at, 27, 29–30, 31–32, 61
  overcrowding at, 39
  prisoner deaths at, 24, 44–45
  private contractors at, 32–33, 44
Abu Ghraib, abuses at, 20–72
  C.I.A. and, 45
  comparisons to Guantánamo, 11
  effects of, 65
  investigations into, 25–30, 66–67, 361–62
  photographs of, 22–26, 34–35, 41, 43–44

rape in, 43–44
SAP's role in, 46–48, 59–65
sexual, 23–24, 38–39, 71
Taguba's report on, 22, 26–27, 28, 29–34, 37, 39–41, 44, 46
"actionable intelligence," 266, 267, 282
Addington, David, 6, 10
Aden-Abyan Islamic Army, 262–63
Afghanistan, 5, 18, 37, 48, 62, 73, 324
  Al Qaeda in, 105, 145
  attacks on aid workers in, 147, 153
  authority of warlords in, 145, 151–53, 157–60
  developmental aid needed in, 145, 146, 147
  drug trade in, 151, 154–56, 160–61
  elections in, 156–57, 160
  humanitarian aid in, 152–53
  instability in post-Taliban, 143, 145–48, 152–54, 158–61
  lack of infrastructure in, 152
  military death toll in, 366
  military role of police and intelligence in, 268
  power struggle of tribal clans in, 143

Syrian coöperation with, 334–41
tactical adjustments needed in, 84
use of I.S.I. in Afghanistan of, 131
see also intelligence community
chain of command, 41
Chalabi, Ahmad, 163–65, 168, 180,
 183, 256, 362, 363, 364
 criminal charges against, 164, 165
 "End Game" plan of, 163–67
 lack of State Department support
  for, 165, 170
 military critics of insurrection plans
  of, 174
 and Office of Special Plans, 208
 questions on integrity of, 211,
  215–16
 revised insurrection plans of,
  171–74
 unpopularity of, 179
 see also Iraqi National Congress
Chechnya, 104
chemical weapons, *see* biological and
 chemical weapons
Cheney, Dick, 6, 97, 144, 179,
 187–88, 328, 352
 and Abu Ghraib scandal, 361–62
 C.I.A.'s struggle with, 227, 236, 239
 on defector intelligence, 212, 215
 on *Meet the Press*, 207, 247
 on Niger/Iraq connection, 206–7,
  227, 230, 247
 Tenet defended by, 84
Chiradio, Robert, 89
Christian Peacemaker Teams, 35
Church Committee hearings, 264
Clark, Wesley, 134, 139–40, 142
Clarke, Richard A., 146–47, 151
Clarke, Victoria, 15
Clarridge, Duane "Dewey," 78, 172
Clawson, Patrick, 351–52
Clinton, Bill, 79, 166
 hawks' open letter on Iraq to,
  165–66, 167–68, 169
Clinton, Hillary, 64
Clinton Administration:

intelligence vetting by, 228
Iraq policy of, 163–66, 226
nuclear proliferation policy and,
 295, 303, 310, 345–46
Saudi regime and, 325
Clover, Charles, 141
coalition building, 187
Coalition Provisional Authority
 (C.P.A.), 58, 280, 286
Colby, William, 270
Cold War, 77, 82, 87, 208
Cole, USS, 262
Collins, Joseph, 147, 150, 155
Colombia, 278–79
command-and-control systems,
 295–96
Congress, U.S.:
 FISA's reach expanded by, 115
 war on Iraq resolution of, 203, 204
 see also Senate, U.S.
"Copper Green," 46
Cropsey, Joseph, 221
Czech Republic, 345

Darby, Joseph M., 25
Davis, Javal, 23, 24, 30
Dayan, Uzi, 342
defectors, as intelligence source, 211,
 213–16, 218, 224
Defense Department, U.S., 16, 37–38,
 71
 Abu Ghraib abuse and, 42, 63, 66,
  68–70
 Afghan intelligence of, 123
 Afghanistan presented as success by,
  141–42, 146, 179
 civilian leadership at, 84, 137–38,
  167–68, 169–70, 208, 249–53,
  261, 266, 272, 284–85, 335
 civilian vs. military leadership in,
  137–38, 173, 182–83, 208,
  249–53, 271–72
 exposure of Abu Ghraib conditions
  and, 63
 Iraqi insurgency and, 57, 168

Insights,
Interviews
& More...

Meet **Seymour M. Hersh**

Matt Dellinger

SEYMOUR M. HERSH was born in Chicago in 1937, the son of Eastern European immigrants, and graduated in 1958 from the University of Chicago. After dropping out of law school, he began his newspaper career as a police reporter for the City News Bureau of Chicago. He served in the Army and worked for a suburban newspaper and then for UPI and AP until late 1967, when he joined the presidential campaign of Eugene J. McCarthy as press secretary and speech writer. In 1969, as a freelance reporter, he uncovered a massacre carried out by American soldiers at the Vietnamese village of My Lai. This reporting earned him the Pulitzer Prize. Hersh joined the *New York Times* in 1972, working in Washington and New York. At the *Times,* he reported extensively on the bombing of Cambodia, domestic spying, and the C.I.A.'s efforts against Chile's Salvador Allende, among other topics. He left the paper in 1979, returning twice on special assignment to the *Times'* Washington bureau. Hersh first wrote for *The New Yorker* in 1971 and has been a regular contributor to the magazine since 1993. In 2004, Hersh helped to expose the Abu Ghraib prison scandal in a series of pieces in *The New Yorker.*

Hersh has published eight books, most recently *Chain of Command: The Road from 9/11 to Abu Ghraib,* which was based on his reporting for *The New Yorker.* His earlier books include *The Price of Power: Kissinger in the Nixon White House,* which won the 1983 National Book Critics Circle Award and the *Los Angeles Times* award for biography; *The Samson Option,* a study of American foreign policy and the Israeli nuclear bomb program; and *The Dark Side of Camelot,* on the Kennedy Administration.

Hersh's journalism and publishing honors include, in addition to the Pulitzer, more than a dozen prizes for investigative reporting. In 2004, Hersh won a National Magazine Award for public interest for three of his pieces, "Lunch with the Chairman," "Selective Intelligence," and "The Stovepipe." Early in 2005, he was awarded the National Press Foundation's W. M. Kiplinger Distinguished Contributions to Journalism award, an Overseas Press Club award, and received ▶

Meet Seymour M. Hersh *(continued)*

his fifth George W. Polk Award, making him that award's most honored laureate.

Seymour Hersh is married with three children and lives in Washington, D.C. ⌒

A Discussion with
Seymour M. Hersh

Did you know right away that the Abu Ghraib story would be so important?

When I saw the photographs, I knew. A few weeks earlier, I'd heard that 60 Minutes II at CBS had a very important story about prison abuse, but knew little more than that. When the CBS story did not appear, I decided to pursue it. I've been around Washington a long time and learned the name of someone who was connected, and then did the usual stuff journalists do. I made some telephone calls, took a plane ride, rented a car, and drove to meet someone at a hotel, where I got my first look at the Abu Ghraib photographs. It was a pretty high threshold. There had been many reports, for years, from human rights groups and others, about problems in the military prison system in Iraq, Afghanistan, and Cuba. But once I saw the Abu Ghraib photographs—and the internal report by Army Major General Antonio Taguba— I realized this was different. This was one story that was not going to go away, and it was going to be big.

Has justice been done in the prison abuse case?

No. It's complicated, because I think that the young soldiers who have pled guilty and are going through the legal process right now ▶

> ❝ But once I saw the Abu Ghraib photographs I realized this was different. This was one story that was not going to go away, and it was going to be big. ❞

A Discussion *(continued)*

did bad things, and they should be punished for them. But I think that what they were doing was certainly condoned by their superior officers, and God knows how many people saw them do these things. They weren't alone in the system. There were a lot of people around, a lot of complaints about the abuse, and for a long time nobody did a thing about it. And I also do believe that if we had a serious investigation, which seems increasingly unlikely, that we would find that from the very top on down—and this is some of what my book is about—knowledge of wrongdoing to prisoners existed at the very highest place in the government, and in the White House.

You use a lot of unnamed sources. How do readers know that someone who won't attach his or her name to a story is telling the truth?

Very complicated issue. Of course, I work for The New Yorker; *some of this material appeared first there, and all of the new material was edited and fact-checked by the people at the magazine.* The New Yorker *has this amazingly complicated system, which is that if I use an unnamed source that source has to be known to the editors, and the source almost always discusses with the fact-checker what he's told me. It makes for a lot of difficulties, because the people talking to me have to have enough confidence and faith in me to know that if I tell them somebody else is*

> 66 *The New Yorker* has this amazingly complicated system, which is that if I use an unnamed source that source has to be known to the editors. 99

going to be talking to them, this person will protect them as much as I would.

Basically, what I have been doing since 9/11 is writing what you could call an alternative history of the war, and it's based on information that has been provided to me by people deeply involved in sophisticated intelligence and military issues, and individuals with whom I have a longstanding trust relationship. I have been doing stories for The New Yorker *that have stood the test of time; they have been accurate. The things I have done for this book were done with the same care, and the same kind of checking was involved. And so it's not just a question of trusting me, it's a question of saying to the American government, is this true or not? And the sad truth is that some horrible things, which I described, did happen.*

How do you manage to get officials to reveal to you what is essentially classified information?

Because this is a very frustrated world we live in, in Washington, right now. Let me tell you something about our soldiers. Our military men really care; the officers believe in the notion of in loco parentis. *In other words, they believe that if you—Mom and Dad— give them their boy, their eighteen- or nineteen-year-old boy, to go to fight in war, that the officers are* in loco parentis—*they are the mother and father; they are protecting this child on your behalf. And they can't do* ▶

7

A Discussion *(continued)*

it now. Our soldiers are fighting in desert temperatures against an insurgency that won't go away, about which we have no good intelligence, in a war that nobody believes in very much. The soldiers are, to their credit, not rebelling. They're doing a good job. We can be very proud of our soldiers, and proud of the officers. And so, yes, I wish some of these people talking to me would speak publicly. They don't because of a lot of reasons—career, etc., etc. So I've become a channel. I've been reporting on military affairs since my stories on the My Lai massacre in 1969. I don't dislike the military, and they know it. I think there's a virtue in the American military, which is simply this: They don't look at me and say, "He's a lefty or righty, a hawk or a dove, or a conservative or a liberal." They ask, "Is this a guy who is going to work this story that I tell him, and do everything he can to find out whether it's true or not, and find out more than I tell him? Is he going to protect me all the way? And is he going to get it out in a way that improves things?" And over the years, I've done that. So people talk to me, and they keep on talking to me.

A lot of people high up in the military chain of command, high up in the intelligence community—for this book, people who work in very sensitive jobs, in the White House, for this president—have talked to me simply because there's wrongdoing going on. Though I don't know whether telling it solves it. In this book I write about the disappointing results of the Senate Armed Services Committee's investigation into the Abu Ghraib scandal, and it hasn't gotten much better. But my function is to tell the story in the most accurate way I can, to protect the people who tell it to me, and to take a fragment of a story that somebody gives me and doing the reporting work to make it more complete, which usually also makes it more complicated, more interesting, and to make it deeper. That's what I do. Getting back to the question of unnamed sources, you can't separate this story, or this book, from forty years of work.

What has been your proudest journalistic moment?

Well, you know, I'll tell you something about America that's very unusual, and very remarkable. My parents were immigrants. They came from the old country. Neither one went to college. They didn't finish high school. My mother came from Poland, was a house cleaner. My father was a small-businessman in Chicago. I went to public schools—my father died young, of cancer—and, after graduating from high school, to junior college; the University of Illinois had a branch at Navy Pier. Some professor got me to the University of Chicago, where I went to school. Never paid a cent for education. I got out of college and went to work. I started being a reporter. I wasn't editor of The Harvard Crimson. *I wasn't editor of the* Yale Daily ▶

A Discussion (*continued*)

News. *I hadn't been the editor of the campus newspaper, but I got into journalism, and eleven years after graduating from college, I wrote a story on the My Lai massacre: I'm sticking two fingers into the eye of Richard Nixon, president, and I'm coming from nowhere and doing it, and I'm getting awards, glory—the Pulitzer Prize—in how many countries could you do this? How many countries are there where you could come and be judged by what you do, and by the truth of what you do? So in this country there is this incredible strength. My Lai, in a way, demonstrated to me that this is something worth doing, and I stay optimistic. I think Abu Ghraib is one of those stories like My Lai that's much more significant than mere words or the incident. Just as murdering innocent people in a ditch in Vietnam was not American, subjecting the people in jail, many of them innocents, to that kind of torture is not American. I think that value system—no matter how the politicians gloss it over, no matter how they say it's just done by a few people—makes those incidents much more important. Abu Ghraib has become, like My Lai, sort of a definition of a government gone wrong. And the government can try, the Bush Administration can try and shove it off and push it away, but it really may be the defining way we look at this Administration, in another twenty years: as the people who put us in this war in which we did these kind of heinous acts. So My Lai, Abu Ghraib—these are really wonderful moments*

66 I'm sticking two fingers into the eye of Richard Nixon, president, and I'm coming from nowhere and doing it, and I'm getting awards, glory—the Pulitzer Prize—in how many countries could you do this? 99

for a journalist, as awful as these stories are. And also, the American public doesn't respond, in this case, by attacking the messenger. I've not been attacked as the messenger for this story. There are some stories that transcend that. People appreciate the value of the story because we have to know these things. So that's a long answer to a short question.

What did you think of the practice of embedding journalists in combat units?

I thought it was very clever. This is an Administration for which it's not a question of "Our obligation is to get the story to the press." Their way of looking at it is "How do we handle the press? How do we get what we want out of the press?" When journalists are embedded—first of all, your life depends on the soldiers. They've taken care of you. It's not the best way to cover a war, because it only tells you one small, as they say in the movie business, point of view. You only see the point of view of the solider; you don't see the point of view of the people being shot—not necessarily the enemy but also the innocents. And so, it's a very narrow aperture. I don't fault the journalists for it. The only problem was that there was nothing to compensate for it. Our problem with reporting on the war, in the beginning, is that we really did not get enough of a sense of the civilian casualties. ▶

66 This is an Administration for which it's not a question of 'Our obligation is to get the story to the press.' Their way of looking at it is 'How do we handle the press? How do we get what we want out of the press?' 99

A Discussion *(continued)*

Is the absence of weapons of mass destruction in Iraq still an important story?

Yes, because that's what did it. If President Bush had said, "We're going to go to war because Saddam's a bad guy," we would have said, "Yeah, well, we know it. He's been a bad guy since 1991. What's he doing to us? What's the threat?" George Bush needed—and his Administration needed—a threat, and they manufactured a threat—I don't think there's any question of that. Saddam Hussein was not, we know now—the Senate Intelligence Committee, the 9/11 Commission have all made it clear—connected to Al Qaeda's operations, and it turns out that the whole case was a house of cards. Without the mushroom cloud analogy they used—that we didn't want the smoking gun on W.M.D.s to take "the form of a mushroom cloud"— without that kind of talk for over a year, you could not have persuaded the public, let alone the Congress, that it was important to go to war. It's the worst kind of revisionism that President Bush is doing right now, as I describe in the epilogue of this book, explaining that it's still justified—that's taking us for rubes, and we're not rubes. The American people's understanding was that we went to war to stop somebody who had chemical and biological weapons, and was on the verge of having a nuclear bomb that could threaten us, and that wasn't true. I do think that will come back to haunt him. ❧

Interview adapted from Harper Audio's Chain of Command: The Road from 9/11 to Abu Ghraib

Have You Read?
More by
Seymour M. Hersh

THE DARK SIDE OF CAMELOT

SEYMOUR M. HERSH shows us a John F. Kennedy we have never seen before, a man insulated from the normal consequences of behavior long before he entered the White House. His father, Joe, set the pattern with arrogance and cunning that have never been fully appreciated: Kennedys could do exactly what they wanted and could evade any charge brought against them. Kennedys wrote their own moral code. And Kennedys trusted only Kennedys. Jack appointed his brother Bobby to be keeper of the secrets—the family debt to organized crime, the real state of Jack's health, the sources of his election victories, the plots to murder foreign leaders, and the president's intentions in Vietnam. The brothers prided themselves on another trait inherited from their father—a voracious appetite for women—and indulged it with a daily abandon deeply disturbing to the Secret Service agents who witnessed it. These men speak for the first time about their amazement at what they saw and the powerlessness they felt to protect the leader of their country. ▶

Have You Read? *(continued)*

"Hersh is an old-style muckraker. The fact that he's found more muck in this particular Augean stable than most people want to acknowledge is hardly his fault."

—Gore Vidal,
The New Yorker

The Web Detective

www.newyorker.com

www.unhchr.ch/html/menu3/b/91.htm
*for more information on the
Geneva Conventions*

news.findlaw.com/hdocs/docs/iraq/
tagubarpt.html
*for more information on the
Taguba Report*

www.9-11commission.gov/

www.hrw.org/reports/2004/usa0604/
*for more information about the Human
Rights Watch work on Abu Ghraib*

www.aclu.org/
*for more information on the American Civil
Liberties Union*

www.uniraq.org/
*for more information on the United Nations'
Assistance Mission for Iraq*

www.icrc.org/
*for more information about the International
Committee of the Red Cross*

www.msf.org/
*for more information about Médecins sans
Frontières (Doctors without Borders)*

The Web Detective *(continued)*

www.amnesty.org
*for more information about
Amnesty International*

www.army.mil
*for more information about the
United States Army*

www.centcom.mil
*for more information about the
United States Central Command*

Don't miss the next
book by your favorite
author. Sign up now for
AuthorTracker by visiting
www.AuthorTracker.com.